# THE DRAGON

# THE
# DRAGON
# FEAR AND POWER

M A R T I N   A R N O L D

REAKTION BOOKS

*Dedicated to the memory of my brother, David.*
*A dragon-slayer, if ever there was one.*

Published by
REAKTION BOOKS LTD
Unit 32, Waterside
44–48 Wharf Road
London N1 7UX, UK
www.reaktionbooks.co.uk

First published 2018

Printed and bound in China by 1010 Printing International Ltd

A catalogue record for this book is available from the British Library

ISBN 978 1 78023 897 5

# Contents

A green dragon in the Northern Lights. Photo by Arnar Bergur
Guðjónsson.

# Introduction:
# The Origin of Dragons

We are ignorant of the meaning of the dragon in the same way
we are ignorant of the meaning of the universe, but there is
something in the dragon's image that fits man's imagination,
and this accounts for the dragon's appearance in different places
and periods.

JORGE LUIS BORGES[1]

I F ASKED WHAT a dragon is, most would reply along these lines:
it has four legs and wings, is armoured with scales, hoards gold,
breathes fire or spurts venom (or both), can talk, is wise but
cruel, and has a fondness for eating female virgins, typically ones that are
scantily clad. While it is not difficult to see that such identikit notions of
dragons are chiefly derived from a combination of those depicted in J.R.R.
Tolkien's Middle-earth fantasies and the celebrated myth of St George and
the Dragon, these two depictions are by no means definitive. Indeed, dragons
as depicted across world myth and legend are so varied in their behaviours
and appearances, let alone their cultural significances, that any attempt to
provide any all-purpose description of them is simply not possible. The chief
aim of this book, then, as a cultural history, is to examine those key ideas
about dragons that have since gone on to influence our continuing fascination with them, wittingly or not. Although, as Jorge Luis Borges remarks,
we are as ignorant of their meaning as we are of the meaning of the universe,
it may nevertheless be possible to try and understand what it is about dragons
that seems to have necessitated our imagining them.

Dragons in their various guises are a global phenomenon, a fact that
is in itself a puzzle. How did this come about? For a start, it cannot be a

consequence, at least not in all instances, of cultural contact, the obvious reason being that global awareness of other cultures is a relatively modern occurrence. Thus, for example, that dragons in both Native American and Chinese mythologies were thought of as divinities, monstrous or otherwise, cannot be explained by any cultural contact. Of course, the idea of the dragon could be regarded as having originated in fears of actual living creatures. The crocodiles of India and Egypt and the Komodo dragons of Indonesia serve as good examples of this. This, however, still does not explain fully why dragon myths are present in regions where no such creatures exist. A more persuasive possibility is the one-time global existence of dinosaurs.

Although the existence of our immediate *Homo sapiens* ancestors and the existence of dinosaurs is separated by over 60 million years, it is nonetheless true that those primitive mammals from which humans evolved were the contemporaries of dinosaurs. Given this, the cosmologist Carl Sagan has argued that memories of dinosaurs, and prehistoric predators generally, are hardwired into our brains and that dragons are a realization of our genetically determined memories.[2] While Sagan's theories are, he freely admits, speculations, one cannot wholly discount them. Put simply, Sagan is examining what otherwise might be termed 'the will to survive', and this, we can safely say, is a given.

Yet even if Sagan's ideas can never fully be proved, one thing that is irrefutable is the global legacy of dinosaurs: their skeletons. For our early ancestors, the discovery of the bones of such formidably large creatures would have needed explaining. Mentally reconstructing them as the most fearsome beings imaginable was only to be expected. That the global dragon came about in this way is perfectly possible. This being the case, then the differences between dragons in one region and those in another can be seen to be a result of the development of different cultural norms and values. That which became a cultural standard in Japan was never likely to have become one in Scandinavia.

But it is also possible that we really do not need dinosaurs to account for our dragon myths. Following a similar line of reasoning as Sagan in respect of the evolutionary principles underlying human survival, but thereafter looking at our survival instincts from an anthropologist's point of view, is David E. Jones. The proposition here is what Jones refers to as 'the raptor/snake/cat primate-predator complex'.[3] Set together, the winged raptor, the venomous snake and the sharp-clawed cat amount to all that humans most fear in the animal world, the composite expression of which is the dragon. While Jones's ideas are, in the main, fascinating and persuasive, his tendency to view all dragons as derived from this complex is perhaps stretching a point. Two obvious objections would be that not all dragons breathe fire, a feature, thinks Jones, that is derived from the cat's hot breath; nor do all dragons have the raptor's ability to fly. But as for the snake, that this creature is formative in many ideas about dragons is certain, for the evolution of the dragon in the human mind often began with the snake: Python was the first guardian at Delphi, believed to be the centre of the earth; the Asian *nāga* originates in the king cobra; the Eden serpent goes on to become the Great Red Dragon of Hell; and so on.

All told, the dragon's origins cannot be satisfactorily explained in every detail, although there can be little doubt that the fear of predators is fundamental. What can be explained, however, is why there are often striking similarities between dragons-versus-heroes dramas in cultures that are geographically remote from each other. In order to understand how this came to be requires a consideration of events that go back a mere few thousand years. Arguably the most compelling examples of this are the curious resemblances between such dramas in the broader mythological structures in which they are enacted in Celtic, Graeco-Roman, early Germanic, Persian and Indian/Vedic mythologies.

Since the late eighteenth century, linguists have pondered the significance of the etymological relationship between certain words across what later became known as the Indo-European group of languages; in effect, those languages in which the mythological structures noted above are articulated. This Indo-European group, it has been surmised, must therefore have had a common origin in a Proto-Indo-European people, who during the Bronze Age migrated east and south from Europe. Exceptionally advanced technologically, most significantly their ability to forge metal weaponry and to gain mastery over horses, which were used to pull their chariots into battle, meant that by the late Bronze Age, these peoples had conquered regions from the Mediterranean through Persia to the Indian subcontinent. As a consequence, both their language and their beliefs became embedded throughout this Indo-European group.[4]

Exactly who these people were cannot be said with absolute certainty, but one twentieth-century archaeologist, Marija Gimbutas (1921–1994), put forward the Kurgan hypothesis, a theory that eclipsed the one-time Aryan hypothesis as previously propounded by German scholars and subsequently taken up by the Nazis as a justification for military invasions. Evidence for Gimbutas's theory rests on the excavation of burial mounds, kurgans, across the Indo-European regions, which were clearly the work of the same peoples and the oldest of which were to be found in the Black Sea areas of the Caucasus and the west Urals. It is, then, here that the Proto-Indo-Europeans are believed to have originated.

Analysts of the mythological systems of the Indo-European group have identified certain fundamental similarities in their structures. Central to this is what is known as the trifunctional hypothesis, a theory that was first put forward by the French philologist Georges Dumézil (1898–1986). According to Dumézil's analysis, Indo-European myths reflect indigenous social hierarchies.[5] The highest of the three social functions Dumézil identifies is that performed by rulers or sovereigns, those who command both the priesthood and the law and who are often seen to have magical powers. This function is reflected in the highest gods of the myths; for example, the Indian god Vishnu (or his predecessor Varuna), the Norse god Odin (early Germanic Woden) and the Greek god Zeus (Roman Jupiter/Jove). The middle function is occupied by the warrior figure, who is variously personified in the myths as, for example, the Indian Indra, the Norse Thor and the Greek Heracles (Roman Hercules). Occupying the lowest function are the fertility gods, who are often represented by twins accompanied by a goddess; thus, the Indian horsemen the Ashvins and the female deity Saravati, the Greek Castor and Pollux (the Roman Gemini) and their sister Helen, and the Norse Frey, his twin sister Freyja and their father Njord, the early Germanic equivalent of whom is the goddess Nerthus.

Although as one critic has remarked, 'there are as many differences between Thor and Indra as there are between Iceland and India,' and it could just as readily have been pointed out that the same is also true of the Midgard Serpent and Vritra,[6] such obvious similarities cannot be mere coincidence. Indeed, these dramas also have parallels in the ancient Greek myth of Zeus' battle with Typhon, in the Hittite myth of Baal versus Yam, and in numerous Celtic myths and legends in which heroes (sometimes not admirable ones) tackle dragons in lochs and glens.

It is to this Indo-European group that this book will pay closest attention, for much of our modern notion of the dragon was formulated here, both from the original myths and from subsequent folktales that were derived from them. Close attention will also be paid to that most evil of dragons which originated in serpent form in the Garden of Eden and went on to become the apocalyptic Satan-dragon, as told of in the New Testament's Book of Revelation. This dragon was most often synonymous with paganism, that is to say any beliefs that were non-Christian, and was therefore regarded as the chief enemy of the early Church and the prime target of Christian saints, such as St George.

Yet while the dragon is a global phenomenon, it cannot be said that it has impacted significantly on popular culture in all its forms, as it is clear that dragons in some mythologies have largely tended to remain insular. Notable examples of these are the feathered serpent deity Quetzalcoatl, originally of Mayan and later of Aztec mythology; the two Native American shamans in the forms of the water serpent Kitchi-at'husis and the giant horned snail Weewilmekq, who did battle in Boyden Lake in Washington County, Maine; the flesh-eating dragon-bird Piasa of Illinois; the dreaded creatures known as the Taniwha of Maori legend; and from Aboriginal Australian myths, the monstrous Bunyip and the primordial Dreamtime god, the Rainbow Serpent.[7] Fascinating as these creatures most certainly are, for the purposes of this book, they must remain in their caves and their watery lairs.

As for draconic origins, one last question remains – and it is no small one. Although we can to a large extent understand how the idea of the dragon developed out of survival fears which subsequently cross-pollinated, both as a result of migrations and more stable intercultural contacts, what is more difficult to understand is the significance of the dragon in the human psyche. One way of approaching this question is offered by the theoretics of structural anthropology, most notably in the work of Claude Lévi-Strauss (1908–2009).[8]

Fundamental to Lévi-Strauss's structuralist approach is that the human mind can be understood as being comprised of two opposing forces: Culture and Nature. Culture is that controlled space in which humans establish themselves in relative safety, rear their offspring, cooperate with their neighbours, build and defend their homes and cultivate those food-stuffs best suited to prolonging life. Culture, then, is a product of the human determination to survive under the best possible circumstances. But Nature is all that militates against this and is, in this respect, all that cannot be controlled.

No matter how deep the foundations of Culture, when Nature is unleashed in its most violent form it can reduce everything that humans value to ash and rubble or, as is the case in Asian and East Asian mythologies, cause drought, famine and floods. The Culture/Nature opposition, simply put, is that between life and death, and it is not hard to see how the dragon in its ferocious form can be understood as an embodiment of Nature. Thus, for example, in early Germanic, Celtic and Christian mythologies, the dragon-slayer, as the embodiment of Culture, can be understood as humanity's most strenuous effort to combat Nature's untameable vicissitudes, whereas in Asia and East Asia, the dragon must be appeased and, to try to ensure that it does not use its powers to wreak havoc, revered.

So much is straightforward. But the problem is that humans are of both Culture *and* Nature, and this is one of life's paradoxes, perhaps the greatest of all. One the one hand, human survival depends on cooperation and collective self-interest; on the other, humans are untamed and seething with antisocial impulses that need to be restrained, for when they are not, chaos ensues. More than this, the determination to survive will always be concluded by the inevitability of death. In this sense, dragon blood courses through us all. And no matter whether the dragon is combatted or worshipped, the Culture/Nature drama is played out, to greater and lesser degrees, in the human psyche throughout our existence. If all this is accepted as perfectly reasonable, then the idea of the dragon is not only the projection of our fears of Nature's power but of our deepest fears of ourselves. The dragon is both the dread of our doom and the dread of the part we all play in precipitating it.

*one*

# Dragons in Greek and Roman Mythology

In the mid-third century BC, some ten years into the First Punic War (264–241 BC) between Rome and Carthage, the general Marcus Atilius Regulus and his Roman legions had crossed the Mediterranean to North Africa. Less than one hundred miles from launching their assault on Carthage, they arrived at the Bagrada river, where they were confronted by a huge dragon rearing up from the muddy reed beds. Unable to see any immediate way of repelling it, Regulus ordered his men to seek out an alternative crossing.

Further up-river, with the dragon now nowhere in sight, Regulus' men started to ford across. But before they reached the opposite bank, the water all around them started violently churning. Then suddenly the dragon's gigantic head surfaced, snatched up a man in its jaws and dragged him below the surface. Many others met the same fate and those who had attacked the dragon with their javelins were crushed beneath its coiled tail. But dire though this situation was, this was a siege army equipped with state-of-the-art weaponry. Regulus duly ordered their massive catapults, their ballistae, to be trained on the dragon, so showering a barrage of large boulders down on it until it was eventually battered to death. No crossing could now be made at this place owing to the deadly poisons leaking from the dragon's body.

While variants of this tale are to be found in a number of Roman sources, it was clearly regarded as historical truth, for the original account of it, long since lost, was said to have been set down in an official military communique by Regulus himself. Furthermore, it is widely stated that the dragon's skin, some 36 m (120 ft) in length, was displayed on Rome's Capitoline Hill for the next one hundred years. If this is to be believed, just what kind of creature this was is a complete mystery.[1]

Depiction of the *draco* on the walls of the Temple of Hadrian from the 2nd century AD.

The Bagrada river dragon was not the only one to have been presented as factual in early Roman sources.[2] Suggestive of this is that, from the second century AD until the fall of the Roman Empire in the fifth century, the Roman cavalry clearly regarded the power of the dragon as something worth emulating. So it was that a silver-jawed dragon with a wind-inflated, multicoloured silk body was emblazoned on the lances of the so-named *draconarius* legions and flourished aloft both before battle and in their cavalry games, the *hippika gymnasia*.[3]

Roman mythological beliefs were, of course, very much derived from those of the ancient Greeks, where the thin line between myth and history had, in the fourth century BC, prompted Plato to warn parents that they should not allow their children to be exposed to stories recounted by ancient historians and mythographers, for they 'not only tell lies but bad lies'.[4] As is quite apparent, however, Plato's warning did little to prevent tales of the Greek gods and of heroes, such as Heracles, from becoming a defining feature of the culture of the classical world.

## The nature of Greek mythology

The early literary sources for Greek mythology are numerous and range from the eighth century BC through to Roman poets and historians of the early centuries AD, thus spanning some one thousand years. Given the complex evolution of these myths, there are numerous differences in the various sources concerning the details and significances attached to characters and events. Broadly speaking, the myths can be considered as belonging to four overlapping phases: first, myths of origin (otherwise known as theogonies); second, stories telling of interactions between gods and mortals; third, the Heroic Age, where the narratives are more preoccupied with human rather than divine actions; and fourth, the Trojan War and its aftermath.[5]

As to the nature of Greek mythology, some of this can be understood from its origins in beliefs that all things – human, animal, plant and other natural phenomena – have a spiritual essence. Emerging from this are notions of higher beings that vie for control, so prompting mythic explanations for why it is that mortal life is so precarious. This development may well have been the result of the absorption of ideas necessary for social expansion, which inevitably involved belligerence from or towards neighbouring peoples.

One of the most striking aspects of Greek mythology is that there is no doctrine of the end of things, no eschatology. Unlike in Christian beliefs, where a central tenet is that there will be a final apocalypse or Judgement Day, Greek mythology focuses exclusively on the development of civilization and the gradual overcoming of impediments to social progress. It is therefore the case that troublesome monsters like dragons are increasingly less prominent in successive phases of the mythology, until by the time of Homer's 'histories' of the Trojan War, it is human heroics and divine interventions that dominate, with far fewer distractions in monstrous form.

In order to examine the most noteworthy dragon episodes in Greek mythology, this chapter will draw chiefly on two mythographers from opposite ends of the chronology of sources: the poetry of Hesiod (*fl. c.* 750–650 BC) in his *Theogony* and *Works and Days*; and Pseudo-Apollodorus' prose *Bibliotheca* (second century AD).[6] These and other accounts of the mythology may be regarded as cautionary tales, in other words, advice on how mortals might best conduct themselves in a dangerous world presided over by often unsympathetic gods.

Creatures of extraordinary ability and appearance, mortal and immortal, are, then, central features of the early stages of Greek mythology. As the gods can be just as destructive, self-interested and morally questionable as the monsters, it is not possible to classify the gods and monstrous 'otherness' in terms of oppositions between good and evil; rather, the actions of the Greek gods more reflect the social complexities, competitive individualisms and survival struggles of the human world. There is, therefore, no force for good other than victory over adversaries and the resultant benefits this might bring.

Yet even victories do not always bring benefits, for they can sometimes be the making of a tyrant and, as a consequence, of social oppression. The monsters can often be regarded as epitomizing these social and political negatives, and as far as human beings are concerned, so can the gods. Something of the *nature* of the gods and the monsters is revealed in their origins and the subsequent Titanomachia, the intergenerational, Oedipal conflict between the Titan and Olympian gods.[7]

## Origins: Titans and Olympians

The earth, known as Gaia, originated from Chaos, the great void where neither time nor substance exists. It is from Gaia that Uranus (Sky) emerges asexually, and it is from the incestuous fertilization of Gaia by Uranus that the twelve Titan gods are born, along with two races of giants: the three one-eyed Cyclopes and the three Hekatonkheires, each of which has fifty heads and a hundred hands. Fearing the strength of these creatures, Uranus has them cast into the dungeon of Tartarus, a deep abyss, where they are guarded by the female dragon Campe.[8] But Gaia is most displeased by what Uranus has done and persuades their cleverest and most ruthless son, the sickle-bearing Cronus, perhaps signifying the dawn of Time, to castrate his father.[9]

Worried that, in the future, his children might do the same to him, Cronus now feels obliged to devour them the minute they are born, a practice that his wife, Rhea, understandably abhors. In order to save her last-born son from this fate, Rhea wraps a stone in swaddling clothes and tricks Cronus into swallowing it. The child she saves and has raised in secret on Crete is Zeus. Once fully grown, Zeus visits his mother incognito and feeds his father an emetic, which results in him vomiting up all his previous children. Zeus and his rescued siblings now declare war on Cronus and the other Titans, but it is only once Zeus has freed the Cyclopes and the Hekatonkheires and brought them into his service that the Titans are overthrown. Their punishment is to be hurled into Tartarus, but not before Zeus has castrated Cronus, just as Cronus had always feared.

It is in this way that the Olympian gods, with Zeus as their chief on Mount Olympus, supplanted the Titans. Yet the presence of the offspring of the primordial gods and the Titans remains, mostly in monstrous form, and it is Zeus' task to eliminate them. Many of these creatures are dragons, both male (*drakōn*) and female (*drakaina*), and both serpentine, often in the form of a sea monster (*kētos*), and reptilian.

While the Titans and their offspring are generally viewed as enemies of the Olympians, one particularly sharp-witted Titan, Prometheus ('Forethought'), was neither initially their enemy nor ever one of mankind. Foreseeing the overthrow of the Titans, Prometheus had chosen not to challenge the Olympians and had therefore escaped punishment. Representing both scientific invention and cunning, it was Prometheus who fashioned man from clay during the time of Cronus and was from then onwards man's patron. From the outset, man had had the means to live in good health and comfort and, crucially, to make fire, but Zeus, who is antagonistic to Prometheus' creation, largely because Prometheus has tricked him into allowing man to make less costly sacrifices to him, deprives them of this essential survival aid. But Prometheus, proud and protective of his creation, steals back fire for man, and for this Zeus punishes him by nailing him to a rock, where each day his liver, believed to be the seat of the emotions, is pecked out by an eagle, only to grow back after nightfall.

Yet Zeus is still not satisfied and now arranges for his smith, Hephaestus, to create the most beautiful woman ever to live. This is Pandora ('Allgift'), and Zeus' intention is for her to bring about the misery of man for all time: says Hesiod, 'from her is descended the female sex, a great affliction to mortals as they dwell with their husbands – no fit partners for accursed Poverty, but only for Plenty.'[10] Among the gifts that the gods add to Hephaestus' creation, Hermes, the patron of thieves, contributes 'fashioned lies and wily pretences and a knavish nature by deep-thundering Zeus's design'.

Pandora is then sent to Prometheus' somewhat dull-witted brother, Epimetheus ('Afterthought'), who, fearing Zeus' anger should he do otherwise,

Giorgio Vasari, *The Mutilation of Uranus by Cronus*, 1560.

Heinrich Friedrich Füger, *Prometheus Brings Fire*, 1817.

receives her, despite Prometheus' warning that he should never accept gifts from Zeus 'lest some affliction befalls mortals'. Accordingly, such is Pandora's 'bitch's mind and knavish nature' that when she comes across a certain jar that Prometheus had instructed Epimetheus never to open, she takes off its lid, so releasing all the ills that have plagued mankind ever since.[11] Zeus' vengeance on Prometheus and his human protégés is in this way fulfilled, for as Hesiod reports, the only thing that remains in the jar is Hope.[12]

The obvious irony as regards Prometheus' role in Greek mythology is that, as both the patron of mankind and a trickster of the Olympians, he is ultimately responsible for bringing mankind into conflict with the gods, the result being mortal suffering. Prometheus' Titan origins, once exposed as being no less dangerous to the Olympians than that of the Titan monsters, bring about not only his punishment but that of his creation. As for Pandora, she sets both a standard and a justification for the misogyny that we will see throughout the mythology.

There is, then, a great deal of ambivalence in mankind's relationships with the gods, some of whom are favourable to humans, some of whom are not, often depending on whether their mortal inferiors show sufficient deference, especially when they are unwittingly caught up as mere pawns in Olympian dramas. Yet when it comes to the monsters, there is nothing to be gained for humans by their presence. It is, then, in both Zeus' and mankind's interests that the world be rid of them, particularly, as far as Zeus is concerned, those of Titan origin.

## Echidna and Typhon

The most prolific breeders of monsters, many of which are dragons, are the Titans Echidna and Typhon, known respectively as 'the mother and father of all monsters'. Hesiod's description of Echidna tells of her dragon-like features:

> the wondrous Echidna stern of heart, who is half nymph with fair cheeks and curling lashes, and half a monstrous serpent, terrible and huge, glinting and ravening, down in the hidden depths of the numinous earth . . . immortal nymph and ageless for all time.[13]

Equally dragon-like is Apollodorus' description of Typhon:

> part man, part beast, and in both size and strength he surpassed all the other children of Ge [Gaia]. Down to his thighs he was human in form . . . Below his thighs, he had massive coils of vipers, which, when they were fully extended, reached right up to his head and emitted violent hisses. He had wings all over his body, and filthy hair springing from his head and cheeks floated around him in the wind, and fire flashed from his eyes.[14]

While Zeus is content to leave Echidna and her offspring as a test for future heroes, most notably Heracles, Typhon's destructive powers, which can cause typhoons, tidal waves and volcanic eruptions, oblige him to take action, especially once Typhon directs his powers against the Olympians.

In his first encounter with Typhon, Zeus pelts him with thunderbolts, but when this fails to deter the Titan, Zeus strikes him with an adamantine – that is to say, unbreakable – sickle, so forcing him to flee. With Typhon now severely wounded, Zeus gives chase and attacks him hand-to-hand, the outcome being that Typhon seizes the sickle and cuts Zeus' tendons from his hands and feet. The incapacitated Zeus is then carried through the sea and placed in a cave, where the part-woman, part-dragon Delphyne is left to guard him.[15] It is only through the stealthy intrusion of two other Olympians, who reinsert Zeus' tendons, that Zeus can make his escape.

Once recovered, Zeus descends in his chariot from the heavens and launches a second thunderbolt attack, now forcing Typhon to take refuge on a mountain. It is here that the Fates lend Zeus a hand by tricking Typhon into eating debilitating fruits, most probably of an alcoholic nature.[16] Nonetheless, this does not prevent Typhon from retaliating by hurling entire mountains at Zeus, who succeeds in parrying them with his thunderbolts and causing further injury to Typhon, whose blood gushes into the mountain. When Typhon takes flight again, Zeus raises Mount Etna from Sicily and smashes it down on him. It is beneath this now volcanic mountain that Typhon remains for all time, occasionally issuing forth eruptions of molten rock.

While the Titanomachia and its aftermath tells of the precarious evolution of society against the background of the struggles between rival forces for domination, the dragon-woman Echidna and, as regards feminine wiles, Pandora, clearly represent a male fear of a continuing threat to the patriarchy by female power.[17] The obvious opposite to this perceived menace is that young female who has no power whatsoever. Typically, in such cases, her father has been obliged to make her completely vulnerable to a predatory dragon from which she is then rescued by a hero, to whom, by prior agreement with her father, she is subsequently married off.

Making a good high-status marriage is an advantage for any prospective hero, but the helplessness of the essentially virginal, sacrificial woman compared to the self-willed and powerful male is what really underpins these dramas. The hero's male rival is, in effect, the dragon, whose serpentine appearance is suggestive of male sexual domination. The key difference between the dragon and the hero is whether the female's suitor has her father's approval, which, of course, the dragon never does. The as it were 'arranged marriage' involves a test followed by a reward: rescue the daughter, as the father demands, and she will then be transferred away from his authority and into that of her future husband. The best-known and most influential tale of this kind is that of Perseus and Andromeda.

## Perseus and Andromeda

Perseus is the grandson of Acrisios, king of Argos, whose daughter, Danae, is impregnated by Zeus. Acrisios had long been disappointed by his inability to produce a male heir but when he seeks advice from the Oracle, he is told that Danae will soon give birth to a son, who will kill him. Determined to avoid this fate, Acrisios imprisons the still virginal Danae in an underground bronze chamber.[18] But this is not sufficient to deter the lustful Zeus, who transforms himself into a shower of gold and pours through the chamber's roof onto Danae's lap, so impregnating her. When Acrisios learns that Danae has given birth to a son, he refuses to believe that Zeus is the father and has Danae and the child placed in a wooden chest and cast out to sea. Fortunately, a fisherman named Dictys rescues them near the island of Seriphos and thereafter acts as a father to Perseus until he is fully grown.

Perseus' mother is now courted by Polydectes, the king of the island and brother of Dictys. But Polydectes, a paranoid tyrant, believes that Perseus is an impediment to his courtship and tricks him into agreeing to bring him the head of Medusa, the most fearsome of the three Gorgon sisters, whose one glance causes the immediate petrifaction of anyone who beholds her and whose hair is a mass of writhing snakes. Assisted by the goddess Athene and the god Hermes, Perseus gathers together the necessary equipment for his task: a magical wallet in which to put Medusa's head, Zeus' adamantine sickle, a mirror-bright shield, a cap that would render him invisible and Hermes' winged sandals. Arriving at the cave where the Gorgons are sleeping, Perseus looks only at Medusa's reflection in his shield and manages to decapitate her and escape unharmed with her head in the wallet, despite the pursuit of the other two Gorgons.

It is on his journey home through Ethiopia that he comes across the young maiden Andromeda, bound and exposed as prey for a sea dragon. Andromeda's predicament has resulted from her mother's boast that her daughter is more beautiful than the Nereids, the sea nymphs. For this insult, the Olympian sea god Poseidon has acted on behalf of the Nereids to cause floods and sent a dragon to ravage the realm of Andromeda's father,

Paolo Veronese, *Perseus and Andromeda*, 1578.

Cepheus. Poseidon's wrath, Cepheus is advised by an oracle, will be quelled only once Andromeda is offered in sacrifice. Perseus, who is immediately smitten by Andromeda, tells Cepheus that he will kill the monster in return for his daughter as his bride. All is agreed and Perseus, stationed beside Andromeda, awaits the coming of the monster.

Soon it emerges offshore, heading directly for them. Perseus, still wearing his winged sandals, soars into the air and swoops down, sword in hand, to deliver the creature a mighty blow. As it now rages at him, jaws snapping, Perseus delivers further sword thrusts to its back and ribs but is perturbed when the creature's blood saturates his wings. Changing tactic, he now braces himself against a large rock jutting out of the sea and, when the creature again attacks, he drives his sword repeatedly through its flanks, so finally killing it.[19] Andromeda is now set free and all rejoice, except, that is, for Andromeda's previous suitor and his supporters, who conspire to do away with Perseus. But Perseus, aware of their plotting, gives them just a fleeting glimpse of Medusa's head, immediately turning them to stone.

Once back on Seriphos, Perseus discovers that his mother has been forced to take sanctuary from the violence of Polydectes. Perseus goes before the king and his followers and, revealing Medusa's head before them, turns them too to stone. Perseus' foster-father, Dictys, succeeds his iniquitous brother and the way is now clear for Perseus' marriage to Andromeda to go ahead. Perseus returns his magical aids to those from whom he loaned them and gives the Gorgon's head to Athene.[20] Perseus and Andromeda eventually become royal rulers, but of Tiryns, not of Argos, a circumstance that arises when Perseus feels obliged to trade kingships after he accidentally kills his grandfather, Acrisios, with a badly aimed discus during a sporting tournament. The prophecy that had originally forced both the newborn Perseus and his mother into perilous exile is in this way fulfilled.

As would seem to be apparent in the myths recounted thus far, dragons and monsters generally might well be classified as belonging to two distinct types: those of the Titan old order, and those that act in service to the Olympians. This distinction, however, is not as clear as it might at first appear. In the case now to be considered, that of Heracles, certain of the dragons he is obliged to confront are of Titan origin but are nevertheless in service to Heracles' lifelong enemy Hera, the wife of Zeus.[21] As is the case throughout the mythology, the Olympian gods and goddesses are not bound by old enmities or, for that matter, allegiances. Whatever serves their purpose, whether it be political or personal, is open to use. For both gods and humans, ruthlessness was seen not only as an essential trait but as a virtue.

## The life and labours of Heracles

The Theban warrior Heracles, known as Hercules to the Romans, is without doubt the greatest figure of the Heroic Age. Since monster-slaying is the defining characteristic of the life of Heracles, his encounters with dragons cannot fully be understood outside his wider accomplishments and, indeed, his failings. It is the manner of the begetting of Heracles that in many ways determines that he will later will be forced to undertake his famous twelve labours, for he is conceived as a consequence of a divine intervention while his mother, Alcmene, is awaiting the return of her warrior husband-to-be, Amphitryon. It is significant that both Amphitryon and Alcmene are grand-children of differing lines of descent from the royal house of Perseus.

Amphitryon had been urged by Alcmene to avenge the killing of her eight brothers by pirates. Only on this condition will Alcmene consent to share a bed with Amphitryon. Having raised an army and succeeded in achieving what Alcmene has asked of him, Amphitryon is now but a day's journey away from home and the consummation of his marriage. But Zeus has other plans. Aware that this is the last night that Alcmene will spend alone, and ever on the lookout for a suitable mortal female with whom to perpetuate his line, Zeus seizes his opportunity by contriving to delay Amphitryon's arrival and then assuming his appearance.

So disguised, Zeus goes directly to Alcmene and tells her that he has completed his mission of vengeance, whereupon, true to her word, Alcmene welcomes him into her bed. That this single night is made the length of three is all due to the manipulation of the sun and the moon and the induce-ment of a deep sleep for all mankind by Zeus' servants. When Amphitryon himself returns, Alcmene is, to say the least, surprised to find herself yet again abed with her husband, who is equally surprised by his wife's tired-ness and lack of appreciation. When Amphitryon later learns what Zeus has done, he never again couples with Alcmene for fear of arousing the god's wrath.

Yet Zeus is not allowed to get away with his infidelity, as, nine months later, his own daughter tricks him into boasting in front Hera of his impreg-nation of Alcmene, and further declaring that the child, due to be born that very day, will become king of the noble House of Perseus. Zeus also some-what tactlessly adds that the child will be known as Heracles, the 'Glory of Hera'. Outraged by her humiliation, Hera now obliges Zeus to swear that only the first male child of Perseus' descent to be born before nightfall will inherit Perseus' kingdom. As Hera knows perfectly well, there is another male child of Perseus' lineage also about to be born and she is determined that her husband's bastard will not precede it.

Hera now hastens to the bedside of the pregnant Queen Nicippe, whose husband is of the required ancestry, and succeeds in bringing for-ward her contractions. She then goes and squats cross-legged at Alcmene's bedchamber door, her clothes tied in knots and her fingers entwined, so blocking Alcmene's womb.[22] Thanks to Hera's machinations, Queen Nicippe gives birth to Eurystheus just one hour before Alcmene delivers

Heracles and, unexpectedly the following day, his half-twin Iphicles, the son of Amphitryon.[23] The rivalry between Eurystheus and Heracles is set to be lifelong, as is Hera's hostility towards Heracles.

Although Hera has managed to deprive Heracles of his birthright, for under the circumstances he is both a great-grandson and a brother of Perseus, as a son of Zeus he has almost supernatural gifts, especially in terms of strength and physique. It is also revealed that Zeus had deliberately chosen to impregnate Alcmene in order that their child should become the protector of gods and humans against the malevolent creatures of the old order. Despite Hera's contrivances, it does not mean that Zeus' plans for his son are unattainable, although it does mean that matters will not now be quite so straightforward.

Alcmene's first act after the birth of Heracles is to try to appease Hera by abandoning the child outside the city walls of Thebes with no protection or sustenance. Zeus once again intervenes by persuading his daughter Athene to take Hera for a stroll towards the exact spot where Heracles has been left to die.[24] Shocked by both the baby's size and its perilous circumstances, Athene tells Hera that she has it in her power to nurture the child, for Hera has breast milk. At first oblivious of the baby's identity, Hera clutches Heracles to her bared breast, whereupon he draws on her with such force that a jet of milk is fired into the sky, so creating the Milky Way. In pain, Hera casts Heracles aside, now realizing who the baby actually is and that with Zeus as his father and herself as his surrogate mother, however briefly, she has made him immortal. Just as predicted by Zeus, the Glory of Hera will be exalted. While Hera angrily reflects on what she has now brought about, Athene delivers Alcmene's baby back to her, urging her to take good care of him.

Notwithstanding, or perhaps even because of, her immortalization of Heracles, Hera remains set on his undoing, although as matters go, the outcomes of her anger are almost always unintended. On one occasion, while Heracles is still a babe in arms, Hera sends two fiery-eyed, venom-dripping dragon-serpents into his and his twin's bedchamber. Roused by the screams of Heracles' brother, Amphitryon rushes in only to find the fearless Heracles with a dragon-serpent in each hand, strangling them. To prevent any further threats of this kind to their children, Amphitryon and Alcmene burn the creatures in accordance with ancient ritual, fumigate their home and sacrifice a wild boar to Zeus.

As Heracles grows up on his stepfather's cattle stead, he learns to master the arts of the warrior to an unprecedented degree and becomes

Jacopo Tintoretto, *The Origin of the Milky Way*, c. 1575.

highly accomplished in many disciplines, both physical and intellectual. Yet he is ever given to extreme violence and on more than one occasion metes out deadly punishment to those who are foolish enough to attack him. Growing in stature and ambition, Heracles also overcomes a troublesome lion that has been stealing cattle from the neighbourhood. Having beaten the creature to death with his club, Heracles dons its pelt as a cape and fashions its gaping-mouthed head into what will become his trademark helmet.[25] As Heracles' monster-killings mount up, he also becomes known for carrying a shield with a dragon emblazoned on it.

Heracles' fame spreads rapidly when, as young man, he takes to warfare and repeatedly vanquishes the enemies of Thebes and its allies, often with much cruelty. It is on one of Heracles' campaigns that Amphitryon, who too has fallen under his stepson's spell, is fatally wounded. This only increases Heracles' determination to rid the world of his family's enemies. Rewards follow, both financial and sexual, and after one particular victory, Heracles is invited to impregnate a grateful king's fifty virgin daughters, all of whom deliver him children, while another victory leads to him being married to Princess Megara, daughter of King Creon of Thebes, with whom he has three children.

As might be expected, Hera does not share in the otherwise universal wonder regarding Heracles' abilities. Her response to his increasing renown is to cast a spell of madness over him, during which he slaughters six of his sons and three of his nephews.[26] After a period of despairing, self-imposed exile for his murderous actions, Heracles is advised by the Oracle of Delphi to accept twelve years of enslavement to his age-old rival Eurystheus, who, as Hera intended, is now a king over Perseus' royal patrimony at Tiryns. Reluctant to serve a man whom he considers his inferior, Heracles nevertheless does as advised, for he knows that it will be a justified penance and the only way he can recover his immortal fame.

It is through this course of events that Heracles comes to perform his labours, three of which involve him overcoming dragons and one of which involves the abduction of a dragon. The obvious irony is that Hera's success in bringing shame and ruination to Heracles is perfectly in line with what Zeus had always intended for his son, for it will be through the imposition of the labours that the Olympians will at last be free of many of the monsters of old. However, although Eurystheus initially demands that Heracles perform ten labours, as it turns out he is forced to perform twelve, for Eurystheus has it in his power to discount any labour that is not completed by Heracles unaided and without reward.

## The second labour of Heracles: The Lernaean Hydra

As an offspring of Typhon and Echidna, the Lernaean Hydra is one of the most fearsome dragons of all. This vast creature with nine venomous snake-heads, one of which is believed to be immortal,[27] has reached its maturity in the swamps of Lerna near the east coast of the Peloponnese, where it is accustomed to devouring cattle and terrorizing the populace. The Hydra bears a particular grudge against Heracles, as it has been specially trained by Hera to be a threat to him.

Under instruction from Eurystheus, Heracles heads for the swamps in a chariot driven by his nephew Iolaus and, guided by the ever-helpful

Athene, soon locates the Hydra's lair by a spring in the surrounding hills. Careful to shield himself from the Hydra's deadly venom, Heracles forces it into the open by firing flaming arrows into its lair. As the Hydra emerges, Heracles grasps it firmly but finds himself quickly disadvantaged as it twines itself about one of his legs. Undaunted, Heracles begins striking off the Hydra's heads with his club, but to no avail, as two heads grow back for each one he severs. To make matters worse, a giant crab emerges from the Hydra's lair and attacks his foot.

Freeing himself enough to stamp the crab to death, Heracles now calls out to Iolaus to set fire to the nearby woods and bring burning brands to cauterize the Hydra's head stumps and prevent them from growing back. This tactic is effective and once Heracles has finally managed to sever all the Hydra's heads, he now takes the still-hissing immortal head, part of which is gold, and buries it under a large slab of rock. Heracles then slices open the Hydra's body, disembowels it and dips his arrows into its gall, making them fatal even from the slightest scratch. Yet despite victory in this labour, Eurystheus will not count it, for Heracles had been forced to call for help from Iolaus.[28] Worse still, although the Hydra may have been overcome in life, there is in its death a legacy which, years hence, will have dire consequences for Heracles.

## The tenth labour of Heracles: Geryon

For his tenth labour, Heracles must journey far to the west of the Mediterranean Sea to an island known as Erytheia, where the monstrous warrior Geryon, a grandson of Medusa, grazes his remarkably beautiful red cattle. Geryon's appearance has been variously described in the sources for this myth but a composite of these would be that he has three heads with three bodies joined at the waist, scales and coils, a spiked tail and wings. As his servant Geryon keeps the herdsman Eurytion and, as a ferocious defender of his cattle, the two-headed dog Orthos, which, too, is an offspring of Typhon and Echidna.

Heracles' task is to bring Geryon's cattle to Eurystheus. It is an arduous and hazardous outgoing journey across sun-baked deserts, during which the overheated Heracles aims his arrows at the sun god Helios and is, to his astonishment, rewarded by the god for his audacity with a magical golden cup, which Heracles then uses as a sailing vessel to cross the seas. On arriving at Erytheia, Heracles is immediately attacked by Orthos, whom he clubs to death, whereupon he is attacked by Eurytion, to whom he does likewise. He now rounds up the cattle but as he tries to herd them away is waylaid by the heavily armoured Geryon, in response to which Heracles fires one of the arrows that he had dipped in the Hydra's gall, lodging it in one of Geryon's foreheads, so killing him outright.

The return journey is no easier than the outgoing one, largely owing to Hera, who intervenes to disperse the cattle by sending a gadfly to panic them. It takes Heracles a year to recover only a majority of the herd, as some of them have gone irretrievably wild. Still not content, Hera now sends a flood, forcing Heracles to damn a great river before he and the herd can complete their journey. This time, Eurystheus is satisfied with Heracles' efforts and, doubtless to Heracles' dismay, promptly sacrifices the herd to Hera.[29]

## The eleventh labour of Heracles: Ladon

At the marriage of Zeus and Hera, Hera had received a tree of golden apples from Gaia, which so delighted her that she had it planted out in her beloved Garden of the Hesperides on Mount Atlas in North Africa. Guarding the tree are three nymphs, but Hera comes to suspect the nymphs of pilfering the apples and so brings the many-headed, multi-voiced, unsleeping dragon Ladon to the garden and has it coil itself round the apple tree. For his eleventh labour, Heracles is commanded to bring some of the apples to Eurystheus, which considering their sacred nature, the ownership of Hera and the presence of Ladon is one of his most challenging tasks, not least because, here again, the dragon is one of the brood of Typhon and Echidna.[30]

Unsure as to the exact location of Mount Atlas, Heracles' search takes him through Libya, Egypt and Arabia, where in each region he is forced into accepting single combat with belligerent rulers, all of whom he kills. Heracles finally heads west and reaches Mount Atlas at what Hesiod calls 'the ends of the earth', but still does not know the exact location of the golden apples.[31] In order to find them, Heracles goes to the sea god Nereus and, taking him in a mighty grip, forces him to reveal the garden's secret entrance. Evidently wishing to appease Heracles, Nereus also warns him not to attempt to pluck the apples himself.[32] Heracles now makes his way towards the garden, where he comes across the disgraced Titan god Atlas, whose punishment for challenging the authority of Zeus has been to hold up the sky.[33]

Heracles now offers Atlas a deal: if Atlas were to fetch the apples for him, he would in the meantime take over his strenuous role. Although Atlas is desperate to take a break, he is petrified of Ladon, so Heracles is obliged

HERCVLEA LERNÆ STERNIT [...] [...]RA MANV

*opposite*: Antonio Pollaiolo, *Heracles and the Hydra*, c. 1475.

Lucas Cranach the Elder (1472–1553), *Hercules and the Lernaean Hydra*
(from the *Labours of Hercules*).

Frederick, Lord Leighton, *The Garden of the Hesperides*, 1892.

to deal with this particular problem before they can come to an arrangement. He goes to the wall surrounding the garden and, using nothing but his own keen senses, calculates exactly where Ladon is and fires an arrow over the wall, killing the dragon in an instant. He now returns to Atlas and takes over from him, so allowing Atlas to enter the garden and steal three apples. But Atlas does not want his job back and declares that he will take the apples to Eurystheus himself, promising to return in just a few months. Under the circumstances, this is a *fait accompli* for Heracles, so he cunningly asks Atlas if he will just hold up the sky for a few minutes while he makes a cushion for his head. Atlas, who is not the cleverest of beings, does as is asked, whereupon Heracles scoops up the apples and makes his escape. Heracles then returns to Eurystheus' palace and presents him with the apples, but they are immediately given back to him, for it is considered sacrilege for them to be anywhere but in Hera's garden. It falls to Athene to return them to their rightful place.[34]

## The twelfth labour of Heracles: Cerberus

For his final labour, Heracles must seek out yet another creature spawned by Typhon and Echidna, and bring it unharmed to Eurystheus. This is Cerberus, the guardian of the mouth of Hades, the dread abode of the dead. Cerberus is a beast with three dog-heads, a dragon's tail and a pelt of seething snake heads. Heracles travels to Laconia in the southeastern Peloponnese, where the entrance to Hades is known to be. When he arrives, all the dead souls flee from him, except the Gorgon Medusa, against whom he draws his sword, but he is reassured by Hermes, who had been imprisoned there for trying to gain Persephone as his bride, that she is now no more than a harmless phantom.

As he draws nearer to the gates, many desperate prisoners stretch out their arms to him, hoping to be raised from the dead. Heracles, pitying their plight, kills one of the cattle of Hades for them to quench their thirst by drinking its blood but is first forced to wrestle with the herdsman, whose ribs he crushes before being begged to desist by Persephone. Now he asks Pluto, the god of the underworld, for Cerberus and is told that he can take the beast but that he must not use any of his weapons to subdue it. Heracles finds Cerberus chained to a great gate and, protected from its dragon tail by his lion-skin cape, succeeds in breaking its will by placing it in a stranglehold. Heracles then part carries and part drags the chained Cerberus all the way back to Eurystheus. But the haughty Eurystheus insults Heracles by offering him no more than a slave's portion of food for his trouble, whereupon Heracles, having now completed his labours and so a free man, kills three of Eurystheus' sons. He then returns Cerberus to Hades.

## Hesione and the sea serpent of Troy

Having left the service of Eurystheus, Heracles yet again embarks on a life of warfare. Ever triumphant, there are also murderous frenzies, random violations of women and another period of enslavement for his misdeeds,

Peter Paul Rubens, *Hercules and Cerberus*, 1636.

although on this occasion his female master takes a far more sympathetic view of him than did Eurystheus. But there are also moments of chivalric self-lessness, one of which is Heracles' rescue of the maiden Hesione from a great sea serpent. Given the successive phases of the myths, the tale of Hesione and the sea serpent of Troy might at first be considered a later variant of the Perseus and Andromeda myth. Yet, given that Heracles' encounter with the sea serpent of Troy was first told in Homer's *Iliad* (*c.* eighth century BC) and that the Perseus and Andromeda version cannot be traced back further than the fifth century BC, it may well be that matters are the other way round.[35]

Coming to land near the city of Troy, Heracles happens across the bejewelled but otherwise naked Hesione tied to a rock. Hesione has been left as a sacrifice to the sea serpent by her own father, Laomedon, king of Troy. It transpires that Laomedon had cheated the gods Apollo and Poseidon of the payment agreed for their fortification of Troy. By way of punishment, Apollo sends a great plague and Poseidon dispatches his sea serpent to bring floods to the land and to devour the populace. Advised by an oracle that only the sacrifice of a young female virgin to Poseidon's monster will relieve his subjects of these perils, Laomedon stakes out his daughter as the sacrificial victim. Appalled by what has taken place, Heracles promptly sets Hesione free and then goes to the city and offers to kill the serpent in return for the two white mares that Laomedon had received from Zeus as compensation for the god's rape of his son. Laomedon willingly accepts Heracles' terms.

Heracles now tells the Trojans to build a high wall to prevent the serpent from attacking him as it rises from the sea. Sure enough, the serpent comes to the wall open-mouthed, whereupon Heracles, disguised as Hesione, leaps fully armed down its throat. It takes him three days of hacking away inside the serpent's belly before he kills it and emerges victorious or, as some theorists would suggest, reborn, and in Heracles' case appropriately bald due to the serpent's acidic digestive fluids.[36] Foolishly, Laomedon now reneges on their agreement, upon which Heracles raises an army, attacks Troy and kills him and all his sons, except for Priam, who would go on to succeed his father as king of Troy. As for Hesione, unlike in the myth of Perseus and Andromeda, she is not married off to her rescuer but is instead given as a bride to Heracles' companion, Telamon.

## The death of Heracles

Heracles is journeying home with his second wife, Deianeira, when they come to a river in full spate. Standing close by is the centaur Nessus, who tells Heracles that he is the appointed ferryman of the gods and for a small fee will carry Deianeira safely over the river while Heracles swims across. Heracles agrees and, after hurling his club and bow over to the opposite riverbank, dives in. But Nessus does not follow, and with Deianeira mounted on his back he sets off in the opposite direction, throws her to the ground and attempts to rape her. Heracles quickly reaches the other side and, gathering up his bow, fires at Nessus one of the arrows that he had dipped in the Hydra's gall. With his dying words, Nessus tells Deianeira that if she ever wants to ensure that Heracles is never again unfaithful to her, as he so often has been, she should mix Nessus' semen and blood with olive oil and secretly smear the mixture onto one of Heracles' tunics. Not suspecting the centaur of having a vengeful motive and oblivious of the fact that the centaur's blood is now contaminated by the Hydra's venom, Deianeira concocts the mixture in a jar without Heracles knowing.

Years pass, and Heracles, far from home, wishes to make a sacrifice to Zeus for aiding him in the sacking of the city of Oechalia, where Heracles had killed the entire royal family, except for Iole, the beautiful young daughter of the king. Heracles has Iole sent home to Deianeira, who is immediately suspicious of her husband's intentions. Meanwhile, having not taken with him the finery needed to perform a sacred rite, Heracles dispatches a messenger to Deianeira telling her to send him his best shirt and cloak. Fearful that Heracles may on this occasion be planning to abandon her forever in favour of Iole, Deianeira decides that the time is now right to use Nessus' 'love potion'.

Deianeira sets about weaving a new shirt, which on completion she rubs down with a piece of woollen cloth soaked in the mixture. She also tells the messenger that the shirt must not be exposed to daylight until Heracles is about to put it on. After the messenger has quickly departed by chariot, Deianeira casts the woollen cloth into the courtyard, where, touched by sunlight, it catches fire and causes the surrounding flagstones to bubble with red foam. Now realizing what she has done and knowing that it is too late to alter matters, Deianeira swears that if she has caused her husband's death, she will also cause her own.

Meanwhile, Heracles readies himself for the ritual by putting on his new shirt and setting a fire in front of the sacrificial altar. As the heat begins to warm his clothes, he suddenly cries out in pain, for the Hydra's poison has seeped into his skin and is melting it. Tearing his shirt from his back, his flesh comes loose with it and his exposed bones begin to sizzle in his boiling blood. In agony, Heracles hurls himself into a nearby stream, which only causes him even greater pain. Raging around the countryside like a madman, Heracles comes across the messenger he sent to Deianeira and, suspecting him of treachery, hurls him out to sea, where he turns to stone. Heracles now cries out to be carried to Mount Oeta, not far from his home in Trachis, and it is here that he learns that Deianeira has hanged herself and was innocent of any ill intent towards him. He is finally taken to the top of the mountain, where at his own request he is burned alive on a pyre. Heracles' lifelong combat with monstrous beings and Hera's deadly machinations have finally taken their toll.

In tribute to his son, Zeus rains down thunderbolts; as for Hera's persecution of Heracles, this is no longer of any importance and she willingly consents to Zeus' demand that Heracles be transported to Mount Olympus to take his place alongside the gods. Furthermore, Hera even agrees to play the role of Heracles' mother in a ritual of rebirth, after which she behaves towards him as any good mother would. Heracles is then betrothed to Hera's daughter, Hebe, by whom he has twin sons, gods of youth and sport. The life of Heracles, as without question the most renowned hero of the classical world, was commemorated in widespread cultic practices in both Greece and Rome, as well in the Olympic Games, which were initially held in his honour.

## The meaning of Heracles

Our understanding of Heracles should, in one important sense, be based on his ability to enter regions such as Hades, which was not possible for lesser mortals.[37] Indeed, Heracles cannot be understood in common mortal terms. Like his forebear Perseus, Heracles is a progeny of Zeus, yet unlike Perseus, Heracles is fated to be persecuted throughout his life by Zeus' aggrieved wife, Hera, and it is Hera's curse that brings upon him the fit of madness during which he kills his sons and nephews.

Hera, however, cannot be blamed for all of Heracles' violations, and it is tempting to interpret his moments of madness as a consequence of his occupying that hazardous and uncertain space between mortality and divinity. In this respect, the life of Heracles is one that, by its very nature, lacks any clear definition. On the one hand, he must seek immortality at all costs; on the other, he cannot escape his flawed humanity. As such, the life struggle of Heracles is one in which his identity is always in question, for he neither has the immortal independence of a god nor is he subject to, or indeed the beneficiary of, the social constraints and values of human society. The region that Heracles occupies is in effect one addled by both self-doubt and the wildest of ambitions. In this respect, Heracles and the hinterland are a hyperbolization of life's uncertainties, our fears, our failings and our own labours in pursuit of, if not glory exactly, then at the very least, betterment.

This being the case, while from any moral perspective Heracles could be regarded as little less than a sociopath, albeit one who sometimes regrets his wrongdoings, his determination to achieve immortal fame would have been regarded as deeply admirable, not least because this involved him helping rid the world of the monsters. Yet the manner of his death, which comes about largely as a result of his wife's wholly justified jealousy, suggests that, by *any* standard, it was his conspicuous imperfections that were his actual undoing.

David Vinckboons, *Hercules, Deianeira and the Centaur Nessus*, 1612.

Heracles, then, is a highly complex figure. Through his monster killings he epitomizes that which was required for this early society to prosper; yet as a murderer of innocents and a serial rapist – in this last respect, like father like son – he is as much an agent of chaos as the monsters he overcomes.

However much we might seek to contextualize and so excuse Heracles' crimes as having been perpetrated within an amoral, violent and primitive society, the positive and negative views of him cannot easily be reconciled. In the final analysis, from the ancient Greek point of view, the legend of Heracles is one in which the ultimate virtue of the hero is deemed to be the ruthless pursuit of personal glory, an ambition which once achieved signified immortality. And if that means that the hero is also something of a monster, then so be it.[38]

## Cadmus and the Dragon of Ares

While dragons are often there to hinder progress and threaten life, they can sometimes take an unintentionally constructive role in foundation or charter myths. One example of this concerns the founding of the city of Thebes and the slaying of the Dragon of Ares by Cadmus, who in some sources is said to have assisted Zeus in the slaying of Typhon. Having consulted the Oracle at Delphi, Cadmus is told to follow a cow and to found a city wherever it takes its rest. This he sets out to do, and when the cow stops wandering he sends off some of his men to get water from the nearby spring of Ares, which unbeknown to Cadmus is guarded by a dragon. While the monopolization of a water source by this monster is problematic enough, this particular spring is also said to take the form of a virgin naiad whose purity is being preserved for Ares, the god of war.[39] Given its divinely ordained duties, the dragon kills many of Cadmus' men.[40]

Cadmus now goes in person to confront the dragon and, taking up a great rock, batters it to death. On advice from Athene, Cadmus then extracts its teeth and sows them into the ground. Immediately, an army of bronze-clad men rises up, the Spartoi or 'Sown Men', who set about killing each other until only five are left standing.[41] Despite Cadmus being forced to serve Ares for a lengthy and exhausting period for killing his dragon, he goes on to build Thebes with the assistance of the remaining Spartoi and is rewarded by Zeus with the hand of Harmonia, a daughter of Ares and Aphrodite. Although Cadmus and his wife are themselves destined to become dragons, a direct result of Cadmus expressing his resentment for the punishment he receives for killing the Dragon of Ares, they retain the patronage of Zeus, who sends them to a peaceful afterlife in the Elysian Fields.

## Lamia

As is clear from the myth of Echidna, the female dragon was considered to be at least as deadly as the male. Yet while Echidna is a signifier of female malevolence, tales told of the dragon-woman Lamia express the perceived dangers of the transgressive female. Indeed, this myth is in many ways quite extraordinary, particularly as regards the fascination it has exercised over painters and poets through to modern times.

Said in certain early sources to be of Libyan origin, Lamia, whose character would seem to be based on the Mesopotamian child-killing goddess Lamashtu, is forcefully seduced by Zeus, who, just as in the myth of his siring of Heracles, is found out by Hera. Hera then becomes Lamia's sworn enemy and lays on her a curse, the consequence being that all her children are stillborn. So distressed is Lamia that she grows insanely jealous of other mothers and takes to stealing and killing their children.[42]

As this myth has developed over time, Lamia has come to be represented as a woman above the waist and a serpentine dragon below whose predisposition it is not only to kill children but to eat them. Worse still for Lamia is Hera's additional curse which prevents her from closing her eyes, so rendering her unable to shut out the sight of her dead infants. According to some sources, Zeus then does what he can to ameliorate his wife's curse and grants Lamia the ability to take out her eyes, which, it is said, also conferred on her prophetic powers; however, other sources say that Hera has Lamia's eyes ripped out and thrown into the mountains, after which Lamia forlornly lives out her solitary and dangerously beast-like life in filth and disarray.

Beyond this, folktales told of a whole species of dragon-women known as the Lamiai. These vampiric creatures were said to beguile young men by hiding, in their case, their dragon-shaped upper bodies behind sand dunes but exposing their tails, which took the form of naked young women. Having thus excited the attention of their victims, they would wheel round, grab hold of them with their scaly fingers and drink their blood.[43]

While tales of the Lamiai quite clearly had their origin in men's fear of unchecked female sexuality, the myth of Lamia is not so readily explicable. Raped by Zeus and driven insane by Hera's curse, Lamia would at first seem to be an innocent victim. Yet the power of the myth lies not so much in Lamia's tragic misfortunes but more in her actions as a child-killer. In order to understand what this might indicate, some help can be gained from Sigmund Freud's psychoanalytical theories. Although Freud's views on female psychology, particularly as regards female sexuality, are now notorious for their apparent endorsement of patriarchal values, it is for this very reason that they can be read as descriptions of traditional male perceptions of women as a threat to their authority.

If we take as a starting point the age-old male view that the primary function of women is to bear and nurture their children, then the Lamia myth can be seen as a complete contravention of this assumption. For Freud, male anxieties concerning aberrant female behaviour are wholly justified and are rooted in that which he terms 'penis envy'. This jealousy of male sexuality is effectively a jealousy of male authority and has two consequences: first, that women prefer to give birth to male children, so gaining penis surrogacy and, therefore, power over men; and second, that women remain morally underdeveloped, by which Freud would appear to mean that they are liable to fail to recognize and accept their inferiority to men. The result, concludes Freud, is that, unlike male sexuality, female sexuality 'is veiled in impenetrable darkness, partly in consequence of cultural stunting and partly on account of the conventional reticence and dishonesty of women'.[44]

Whether or not one reads Freud's theories of female psychosexuality as literal or as abstractions, they deliver an excellent account of patriarchal paranoia, albeit that this is wholly unintended. What we have in the Lamia myth, then, is a projection of male fears about what the opposite of the subservient, dutiful female would be; that is to say, that woman who might be termed the 'anti-mother'. From the patriarchy's point of view, this is in no way contradicted or undermined by the myth's account of Lamia's rape and the curse that is then put on her, for Zeus, as the ultimate male authority, is beyond reproach, and as for Hera's curse, the likely thinking here is that only another woman would do such a thing. In effect, the power of the Lamia myth rests on a self-justifying patriarchal narrative that we will see reflected time and again in other tales of dragon-women.

SUCH IS THE COMPLEXITY of Greek mythology that, apart from the typically prejudicial gender distinctions, generalizations about the overall significance of the dragon episodes are best resisted, for as already remarked, dragons are just one form of monstrosity among many.[45] Moreover, it is not always possible to comprehend fully why dragons may attack someone, except, it would seem, out of sheer spite. One example of this would be the killing of Laocoön, a Trojan priest of Poseidon (Lat. Neptune), and his sons by two dragons. No two sources agree precisely on why this comes about. Virgil says that Laocoön was punished by the gods for warning the Trojans about 'Greeks bearing gifts', in other words, the Trojan Horse, while other sources say that he was punished for copulating in front of a sacred shrine.[46] Rationalizations of Laocoön's death like these, however, appear to be little other than that, and it is quite likely that Laocoön's grisly end originally had no specific motive; rather, it simply happened. This randomness would appear to be part of the way of things, the underlying message being that not everything in life is predictable or explicable.

Greek mythology depicts a violent and uncertain world, where the gods are projections of human greed, strife, anxiety, desire and occasional triumph, and where humans look to the skies to appease, accommodate or enlist the gods through cultic ritual invocations of much-needed order. Dragons, whether associated with the nether regions and so with death, as guardians of sacred property such as water sources, as the symbolic representation of human injustices, or as threats to the patriarchy, are all aspects of an 'order versus disorder' opposition, one in which the Greeks appear to have accepted death as 'a natural and irreversible law'.[47] This being the case, any attempt to differentiate morally, or even behaviourally, between gods, heroes, monsters and humans would be a fine point, one that risks missing the underlying realpolitik needs of a nascent civilization.

*two*

# Dragons in the Bible and Saints' Lives

WITHOUT DOUBT THE most potent idea of a dragon ever conceived is that of the Great Red Dragon of Hell, in other words, Satan, as depicted in the New Testament's Book of Revelation. As Christianity, in its various forms, would go on to become the largest established faith in the world, the influence of the Satan dragon on ideas of saintliness, such as St George; on artists, such as William Blake; and in literature, for instance J.R.R. Tolkien's evil dragon Glaurung, is unequalled anywhere else in dragon lore. Revelation's Satan dragon has, of course, its origins in the Old Testament Book of Genesis as the Eden serpent that brought about mankind's ruination. The key elements of this myth are worth recalling in some detail, not only because it is here that the concept of absolute evil originated but because it is in mankind's Fall at Eden that the basis of those gender values that became the bedrock of male authority over women throughout the Judaeo-Christian world were first framed.

## Dragons in the Old Testament

At the outset, God has created Adam 'to dress and to keep' (2:15) the Garden of Eden and to have dominion over all living things.[1] At the centre of Eden, God has placed two sacred trees: the tree of life and the tree of the knowledge of good and evil. While Adam is permitted to eat freely of the fruit of any other tree in Eden, God specifically warns him not to eat from the tree of knowledge, 'for in the day thou eatest thereof thou shalt surely die' (2:17). God then decides that Adam should have 'an help meet' for his responsibilities and therefore creates Eve from one of Adam's ribs: 'And they were both naked, the man and his wife, and were not ashamed' (2:25).

All should be well, indeed perfect, except that God has also created a serpent 'more subtil than any beast of the field' (3:1). This cunning creature comes to Eve and contradicts God by telling her that were she to eat from the tree of knowledge, 'Ye shall not surely die'; rather, as God knows perfectly well, says the serpent, 'your eyes shall be opened, and ye shall be as gods, knowing good and evil' (3:4–5).[2] Tempted, Eve eats the taboo fruit and persuades Adam to do likewise. Immediately, both Adam and Eve are embarrassed by their nakedness and make aprons for themselves from fig leaves. God is most displeased and calls them to account. While Adam blames Eve, Eve blames the serpent, but God is uninterested in finger-pointing. He curses the serpent, which, he proclaims, 'upon thy belly shalt thou go, and dust shalt thou eat all the days of thy life' (3:14). Moreover, says God, 'I will put enmity between thy seed and her [Eve's] seed; it shalt bruise thy head, and thou shalt bruise his heel' (3:15). Turning to Eve, God tells her that her sorrows will be multiplied: she will give birth in pain and her husband will rule over her.

God now turns to Adam and tells him that his future will also be harrowing: his brief life arduous; his ground overrun with thorns and thistles; and his diet little more than the hard-won produce of the soil, 'for out of it wast thou taken: for dust thou *art*, and unto dust shalt thou return' (3:18). Significantly, God's reasoning is as follows:

> Behold, the man is become as one of us, to know good and evil, and now, lest he put forth his hand, and take also of the tree of life, and eat, and live for ever:
>
> Therefore the LORD God sent him forth from the garden of Eden, to till the ground from whence he was taken.

'Eve and the Snake of Eden', 14th-century fresco in the Church of San Michele al Pozzo Bianco, Bergamo, Italy.

> So he drove out the man; and placed at the east of the garden of Eden Cherubims, and a flaming sword which turned every way, to keep the way of the tree of life. (3:22–4)

Certain of the fundamental religious principles and social values of Judaeo-Christian beliefs are thus established. Mortality is a consequence of disobedience to God; women, as represented by the inconstant Eve, are subservient to men; and God is determined that man shall never become like him, for while mankind may have gained godlike knowledge of good and evil, immortality will forever be denied. Accordingly, patriarchal domination, a life that will be nasty, brutish and short, and God's zealous protection of his unique power are all immutable truths.

But what of the serpent, the accursed enemy of accursed mankind? It was probably inevitable that both Jewish and, subsequently, Christian proselytizers and theologians would come to identify the serpent as Satan, the embodiment of chaos and the origin of all things evil. Suggesting this identification, at least in part, was the myth about Adam's first wife, the unbiddable Lilith. For early biblical exegetists, Lilith accounted for why at Genesis 1:28 it says that 'God created man in his own image . . . male and female he created them', that is, before he creates Eve from Adam's rib at Genesis 2:22. Necessarily punctilious although this explanation was deemed to be, the actual origins of Lilith had little to do with Judaism.

The earliest traces of the story of mankind's Fall at Eden are to be found in the Mesopotamian epic of Gilgamesh, which dates back to at least the eighteenth century BC, thus pre-dating the composition of the Torah, the first five books of the Hebrew Bible, also known in Greek translation as the Pentateuch, the 'Five Scrolls'. There are two serpents that would appear to have influenced the idea of the serpent in Genesis: one concerns Lilith, the other concerns the epic's hero, Gilgamesh. A Sumerian version of the epic of Gilgamesh depicts Lilith as a tree-dwelling, screeching demon goddess living in a sacred grove who travels to earth with her alter-ego serpent coiled about her. It takes Gilgamesh to kill the serpent and drive away Lilith, the 'maid of desolation'.[3]

This Lilith episode is just part of Gilgamesh's lifelong search for the secret of eternal life, a prize that ultimately eludes him, for he fails the basic test of being able to stay awake for seven days. By way of compensation, a sympathetic immortal tells him that he may at least regain his youth by retrieving and eating a spiny plant from the bottom of the sea. Gilgamesh succeeds in retrieving the plant, but on his arduous journey home he needs

The Burney Relief, 'Queen of the Night', is a Babylonian sculpture dated to 1800 BC. Whether or not this is Lilith/ Lilitu is debated.

to take a rest. As he sleeps, a serpent approaches and steals the plant out of his hand, eats it and then sheds its skin as it departs, a clear sign, so it was believed, that it had regained its youth. Just like the rest of mankind, there will be no rejuvenation for Gilgamesh and he is doomed to die.[4] What we have then in the Gilgamesh epic are the basic elements of the Eden drama: an evil serpent in a sacred grove and a serpent that guarantees mortality.

Although tales of Lilith as a dreadful demon, sometimes identified as a dragon-serpent, are to be found in numerous Near and Middle Eastern mythologies, the idea of her as a presence in the Garden of Eden comes from Jewish scriptural commentaries and folklore dating back to the third century BC.[5] These were eventually set down in the seventh- to tenth-century AD *Alphabet of Ben Sira*.[6] Broadly speaking, in this source, Lilith refuses to submit to Adam's authority and leaves the Garden of Eden to settle near the Red Sea, where she gives birth to a hundred demonic children every day. According to Ben Sira's hardline patriarchy, Lilith epitomizes the worst kind of woman: sexually dominant, a law unto herself, and so an example

Hugo van der Goes, *Temptation*, 1470. The figure on the right is Satan.

set to women that, if followed, poses a threat to all men. It is from Lilith's Gilgamesh associations and the subsequent non-canonical Hebraic misogyny that she becomes increasingly associated with the Eden serpent and so with Satan. This development is widely reflected in medieval art, where a dragon-like Lilith is shown either in company with Adam and Eve or, more specifically, depicted as a feminized Eden serpent encouraging the hapless Eve to pick fruit from the tree of knowledge.

Other than Lilith, the canonical Hebrew Bible, the Tanakh, uses three main terms for identifying the presence, actions or symbolic significance of what can broadly be understood to be types of dragon.[7] First, there is *nachash*, a serpent that may embody evil power or may alternatively be a symbol of fertility and healing. This term is used in respect of the serpent at Eden and originally meant 'whispering' or 'hissing', meanings that can be considered metaphorically appropriate as regards the serpent's insidious temptations of Eve. Second, there is *tanniyn*, most often meaning a dragon, either on land or sea. Third, there is *saraph*, the 'shining one', which is sometimes just a venomous serpent of the desert, and sometimes more specifically a fire dragon/serpent whose venom enflames the skin of those attacked by it, and on one occasion, a brass serpent with healing powers. In the King James Version of the Old Testament, a translation made between 1604 and 1611, these terms are, generally speaking, translated precisely.[8] While there are clearly conceptual overlaps between *nachash*, *tanniyn* and *saraph* in Hebrew, the importance of them in the Old Testament lies in their association with either good or evil.

With only a few exceptions, albeit important ones, serpents, often in dragon form, were commonly depicted as destructive in pre-biblical mythologies. For example, there is the primordial Egyptian dragon-god Apep (also known as Apophis), a creature of chaos and darkness that rises from the Nile to attack the life-giving sun god Ra as he travels through the night on his solar barge. Similarly, in Babylonian mythology, the essence of chaos is the female spirit Tiamat, a scaly, serpentine creature that spawns a host of dragon-serpents and whose nemesis is the god Marduk, the god of order, the patron of mankind and, in some versions of the myth, Tiamat's son.[9]

Elsewhere in the ancient Near East, preserved in thousands of tablets from the Bronze Age Canaanite trading centre of Ugarit, is the Hittite Baal Cycle, part of which tells of the tyrannical dragon-like sea god Yam challenging, at first successfully, the storm and fertility god Baal for the right to rule over all the gods. In the ultimate confrontation between Yam and Baal, the latter wins through the use of his magical thunderbolts, although differing versions of the myth leave it unclear as to whether or not Yam is killed.[10] Interestingly, Baal's next challenge comes from Mot, the god of death. Although Baal is killed by Mot, he is resurrected, thus, suggest some biblical commentators, prefiguring the death and resurrection of Christ.[11]

The major exception to these fearsome depictions of dragons is another primordial serpent-dragon (in some instances, two serpents), also found in Egyptian sources, the earliest of which dates from the fourteenth century BC. In this case, it is the serpent-dragon Ouroboros, a vast reptilian being that encircles the world and chews on its own tail. Contrary to the Eden and the Gilgamesh serpents, Ouroboros signifies eternal recurrence, a life–death cycle that leads finally to immortality.[12] Possibly associated with Ouroboros is the Egyptian serpent-god Mehen, which coils itself protectively around Ra during his perilous night-time journeys.[13]

It is almost certainly no coincidence that this same dichotomy between positive and negative ideas about serpents and dragons is to be found in the Old Testament, where on the one hand, they can denote divine power, and on the other, mortal danger. Dragons (*tanniyn*) are frequently invoked by the prophets or in the Psalms when the Jewish people are either oppressed by their enemies or have strayed from the path of righteousness. In the main, these draconic invocations are purely rhetorical and typically negative, for example: the wine of sinners of Sodom and Gomorrah 'is the poison of dragons' (Deuteronomy 32:33); part of God's punishment of the unrighteous at the Second Coming will be 'an habitation of dragons' (Isaiah 34:13); and, says the prophet Micah, at the downfall of Samaria and Jerusalem,

Marduk slaying Tiamat, reproduced from a wall panel in the palace of Ashur-nasiripal II, 885–860 BC.

'I will make a wailing like the dragons' (Micah 1:8). Notably, such mentions of dragons are sometimes juxtaposed with an equally negative reference to 'screech owls', which in Hebraic are signified by the name Lilith.

Contrary to all this are the two positive depictions of the dragon-serpent that are told of in connection with Moses. The first of these episodes takes place in Exodus (7:7–17), during the time when Moses is seeking to persuade Pharaoh to allow him to lead his oppressed people out of Egypt. God instructs Moses that when Pharaoh tells him to perform a miracle, his older brother, the prophet Aaron, should cast down his rod before Pharaoh, whereupon it will become a serpent. When this comes about, Pharaoh summons his wise men and sorcerers and has them throw down their rods in response, all of which likewise become serpents. But even when Aaron's serpent swallows them all, Pharaoh remains unmoved. God now tells Moses to go to the banks of the river Nile and when Pharaoh arrives to throw down Aaron's serpent rod, after which Aaron should raise the rod over all of Egypt's water sources and water stores, the outcome being that the Nile is turned to blood and all of Egypt's water contaminated.[14]

Persian manuscript illustration of Moses and Aaron with a serpent.

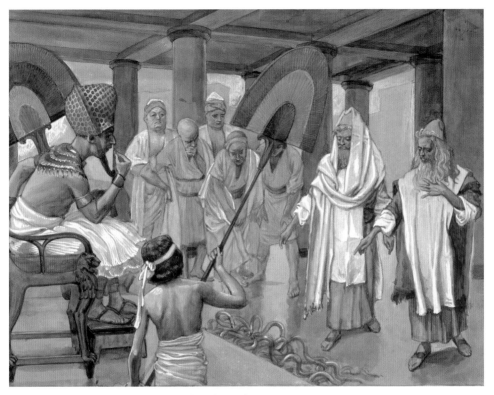

James Tissot, *The Rod of Aaron Devours the Other Rods*, c. 1896–1902.

The second episode is recounted in the Book of Numbers, when Moses, now in search of the Promised Land, is forced to lead the Jewish people along a barren, circuitous route past the borders of their enemies, where there are infestations of deadly snakes. Many are bitten. God now intervenes and tells Moses to make 'a fiery serpent' (*saraph*), simply meaning one made of brass, and to mount it on a pole, and 'it came to pass, that if a serpent had bitten any man, when he beheld the serpent of brass, he lived' (Numbers 21:9).[15] The destruction of this brass serpent is said to have taken place centuries later, when the reforming King Hezekiah sought to destroy any objects that the Israelis, his subjects, had taken to idolizing (2 Kings 18:1–4).

Aside from those metaphorically negative expressions and positive manifestations of God's patronage of the Jews during their wanderings in the wilderness, there is just one other dragon-like creature in the canonical Old Testament that plays a meaningful role. This is the sea monster Leviathan.[16]

Leviathan is described in most detail in the Book of Job, where 34 verses are dedicated to it. As in the book's preceding chapters, God is attempting to rally the forlorn Job by offering him some perspective on his life and limitations. In the course of God's psychotherapy, he asks Job whether he thinks he can in any way have dominion over Leviathan or even agree terms with it. God goes on to describe Leviathan's physical power:

Who can open the doors of his face? his teeth *are* terrible round about.
His scales *are his* pride, shut up together *as with* a close seal.
One is so near to another, that no air can come between them.
They are joined one to another, they stick together, that they cannot be sundered.
By his neesings a light doth shine,[17] and his eyes *are* like the eyelids of the morning.
Out of his mouth go burning lamps, *and* sparks of fire leap out.
Out of his nostrils goeth smoke, as *out* of a seething pot or caldron.
His breath kindleth coals, and a flame goeth out of his mouth.
In his neck remaineth strength, and sorrow is turned into joy before him.
The flakes of his flesh are joined together: they are firm in themselves; they cannot be moved.
His heart is as firm as a stone; yea, as hard as a piece of the nether *millstone*.
When he raiseth up himself, the mighty are afraid: by reason of breakings they purify themselves. (Job 41:14–25)

Besides being a vast, scaly, fire-breathing dragon of the deep, Leviathan is invulnerable to weapons and utterly fearless: 'Upon earth there is not his like, who is made without fear' (Job 41:33).

There are, however, no specific myths about Leviathan, and we are left with a further four tantalizing references.[18] In Psalm 74:14, God is said to 'break the heads of leviathan in pieces' and 'gavest him *to be* meat to the people inhabiting the wilderness', and in Psalm 104:26, Leviathan is mentioned as an example of the marvels of God's Creation. Yet, in Isaiah, it is foretold that God will destroy Leviathan: 'In that day the LORD with his sore and great and strong sword shall punish leviathan the piercing serpent, even leviathan that crooked serpent; and he shall slay the dragon that *is* in the sea.' (Isaiah 27:1) The reference here to 'that day' is to God's ultimate judgement at the end of all time. In the Book of Amos, however, there is what

James Tissot, *Water into Blood*, c. 1896–1902.

Gustave Doré, *Destruction of Leviathan*, 1865.

appears to be another apocalyptic reference to Leviathan in which the sea monster is an instrument of God's power. Amos reports God as saying that even if his enemies are in hiding 'at the bottom of the sea', he will 'command the serpent and he shall bite them' (Amos 9:3). All said, then, the Old Testament references we have for Leviathan do not entirely add up.

The reason for these apparent contradictions may be due to differing sources for, and ideas about, Leviathan. In the description in Job, where God seems almost to relish his creation of the sea monster, and in God's employment of Leviathan in Amos, these may well be derived from the Egyptian myth of the counterbalancing forces of Apep and Ra, both of which could be regarded as being embodied in the power of God. As for the references to Leviathan in Psalms and Isaiah, they would appear to reflect, or perhaps be near the start of, a tradition in which Leviathan is demonized. This conundrum appears to have troubled compilers of the Jewish *Midrash*, an authoritative explanation of Old Testament mysteries, for here it is said that there were two Leviathans, one male and one female, but that God slew the female to prevent them breeding.[19] This belief in a demonic Leviathan had become established in the Middle Ages, by which time Leviathan was regarded as the mouth of Hell through which the damned would pass on Judgement Day.[20]

Illuminated medieval manuscript showing Daniel feeding the dragon while King Cyrus looks on.

Beyond these examples of Old Testament dragons, one other curiosity remains: the apocryphal story of Bel and the Dragon. Although not present in the Tanakh, this second-century BC Aramaic tale was appended to the Book of Daniel in the Greek Septuagint and was initially included in the King James Version.[21] The story tells of the Babylonian monarch Cyrus worshipping idols, which the prophet Daniel, a guest of Cyrus, exposes as misguided. The first idol is a brass and clay statue named Bel, a name meaning 'lord' or 'master', for which the king, believing it to be a god, leaves food and fine wine on a nightly basis, all of which has gone come the morning. When Daniel proves that it is Cyrus's hungry priests and their families who are sneaking in during the night to devour the offerings, Bel is destroyed, as, incidentally, are the priests.[22]

The somewhat embarrassed king now challenges Daniel to prove that his dragon-god, a living creature, is also a fake. Daniel's response is to make cakes of pitch, fat and hair and feed them to the dragon, whereupon it explodes as a result of the cakes being ignited by the dragon's own fire. Although this story of Daniel's conversion of King Cyrus could be regarded as a rather less fortunate example of the intermingling of Greek and Hebrew cultures, Daniel's dragon-slaying technique nonetheless caught the imagination of those writing saints' lives and subsequently became a familiar method of dragon-slaying in European folktales.[23]

While the Bel and the Dragon tale had its own, somewhat unique influence on the dramatics of future dragon-slaying tales, the Old Testament accounts of the dragons cast before Moses by the Pharaoh and of Leviathan would go on to be developed as key expressions of the draconic threats posed to saints (see, for example, the lives of St Thomas and St Philip, below). Not unlike the literary evolution of the Eden serpent into the Great Red Dragon of Hell in the Book of Revelation, these Old Testament dragons similarly became regarded as evil extremities, often as aspects of the Satan dragon. It is, then, to Revelation that we now turn in order to see how the Eden serpent went on to become a highly theatricalized personification of ultimate evil in dragon form.

## Dragons in the New Testament

As time passed and the powerful Judaic schism of Christianity identified the long-awaited Jewish Messiah as Jesus of Nazareth, commentaries on the opposition between good and evil became increasingly extreme. One explanation for this is the persecution of Christians that began in AD 64

'The Woman and the Dragon', from the *Beatus d'Osma*, a Spanish illuminated manuscript of the late 11th century.

under the reign of the Roman emperor Nero and lasted, with certain periods of religious toleration, until Emperor Constantine's legal recognition of Christianity in his Edict of Milan of AD 313. It was in the late first century, during a period of particularly severe persecution as ordered by Emperor Domitian (r. AD 81–96), that Revelation was composed; indeed, scholars have long seen Revelation as a symbolic narration of the suffering of early Christians.[24]

The Book of Revelation is a visionary's account of the Apocalypse, God's Last Judgement.[25] Revelation Chapter 1 tells of the author receiving the momentous truth of Jesus Christ's testimony directly from God. After this there follows a central structure which involves five sections: 1. The messages to the seven Asian churches (2–3); 2. The opening of a scroll with seven seals (5–8:5); 3. The sounding of seven trumpets by seven angels (8–11); 4. The seven spiritual beings (12–15:6); 5. The divine judgements that are made as seven vials are poured onto the earth (16). The concluding part of Revelation tells of God vanquishing all evil, the creation of a new heaven and a new earth, and Christ's promise that his Second Coming is about to take

'Adoration of the Beast and the Dragon', from the *Beatus Escorial*, a Spanish illuminated manuscript of the late 10th century.

place (17–21).[26] It is in section 4 that the dragon, 'that old serpent, called the Devil and Satan' (12:9), makes his first appearance.

A woman who is on the very brink of giving birth to a male child appears in heaven 'clothed in the sun', with the moon under her feet and a crown of stars (12:1). Next appears 'a great red dragon, having seven heads and ten horns, and seven crowns upon his heads' (12:3).[27] This dragon stands before the woman ready to devour the child as soon as it is born. But the dragon is confounded, for when the woman gives birth, God takes her child up to his throne until it is time for him 'to rule all nations with a rod of iron' (12:5). Meanwhile, the woman flees to the wilderness, where God has prepared for her to be fed and kept safe.

Now a great war breaks out in heaven between, on God's side, the Archangel Michael and his angels, and opposing God, the Red Dragon and his angels. The outcome is that Michael triumphs and the Red Dragon and all his rebel army are cast down to earth (12:7–9). Immediately, the dragon goes in pursuit of the woman, but to no avail, as she is now endowed with wings. In fury, the dragon disgorges a great flood, but again the woman is protected when the earth helpfully swallows up the waters. The dragon then turns its wrath on the faithful, who are described as the 'remnant of her seed' (12:14).

In the vision following this, a leopard-like beast with seven heads emblazoned with the word 'blasphemy' emerges from the sea and is endowed with power and authority by the dragon, who also heals one of the beast's mortally injured heads. Awed by and fearful of the dragon's power, humans begin to worship both him and the beast of blasphemy, so creating a satanic cult that lasts for the three and a half years allotted by God. As the beast sets to blaspheming all that is holy, waging war on the saints and corrupting mankind, a second beast, just as powerful as the first, comes up out of the

Nicholas Bataille, *Three Spirits Like Frogs Come from the Dragon's Mouth*, 1373–87.

59

Prayer-book painting of Hell by the Limbourg Brothers, 1412–16.

earth. This beast, with 'two horns like a lamb', speaks 'as a dragon' (13:11), the sure sign of 'a false prophet' (20:10), so giving rise to the worship of the beast of blasphemy and various other idolatrous practices. This second beast is also known by 'the number of his name . . . Six hundred threescore *and* six' (13:17–18), a figure which is also inscribed on the right hand or forehead of all those converted to evil ways. Together, these disciples of Satan cause mayhem.

Revelation then describes the emptying out of the seven vials of God's vengeance on those who took to worshipping these diabolical creatures. At the emptying of the sixth vial, the visionary sees 'unclean spirits' coming out of the mouths of the dragon and the two beasts (16:13), after which follows the final great battle of Armageddon, during which the two beasts are seized and thrown alive into a lake of fire and brimstone (19:20). God then sends an angel with the keys to a bottomless pit: 'And he laid hold on the dragon, which is the Devil and Satan, and bound him a thousand years' (20:2). As only to be expected, once 'loosed a little season' (20:3) from his prison, the dragon sets about corrupting mankind much as before. Now God acts without compromise and the dragon is cast into the same burning lake as the two beasts, where he will suffer torment for all eternity (20:10). It is into this same place – in effect, Hell – that those who transgress in life shall also be cast: 'the fearful, and unbelieving, and the abominable, and murderers, and whoremongers, and sorcerers, and idolaters, and all liars, shall have their part in the lake' (21:18).

Further insight into the nature of Satan in dragon form is offered in the apocryphal Questions (Gospel) of Bartholomew. This text sought to shed light on the more opaque matters of early Christian metaphysics by having Bartholomew interrogate Jesus.[28] In the fourth chapter of the Questions, Bartholomew asks Jesus to reveal 'the adversary of men' (IV:7), meaning the Satan dragon of Revelation, known here as Beliar (the 'Wicked One'). Despite Jesus' warning that the very sight of this monster would cause Bartholomew, the Apostles and Mary to fall down dead, all still urge him to do as Bartholomew asks:

> and the earth shook, and Beliar came up, being held by 660 angels and bound with fiery chains. And the length of him was 1,600 cubits and his breadth 40 cubits, and his face was like a lightning of fire and his eyes full of darkness. And out of his nostrils came a stinking smoke; and his mouth was as the gulf of a precipice, and just one of his wings was fourscore cubits. (IV:12)[29]

When all drop dead as predicted, Jesus breathes life back into them, after which he tells Bartholomew to tread on Beliar's neck, so that 'he will tell thee his work, what it is, and how he deceiveth men' (IV:15).

After much understandable prevarication, Bartholomew pins down Beliar in the manner prescribed and demands that he 'hide nothing' (IV:26). Beliar tells him that he was created as the first of God's angels, the most powerful of them, and goes on to enumerate the hierarchical functions of all the other angels, including those nameless angels that now persecute him in Hades. Then Beliar describes how he and, later, six hundred lesser angels were cast out of heaven for refusing to obey the instruction of Archangel Michael, God's second creation, to worship Adam, 'because he was the image of God' (IV:53). It was owing to God's punishment of him that Beliar vengefully brought about the Fall of Mankind in Eden. This, explains Beliar, was only made possible when Eve became vulnerable to his temptations after drinking from a great spring that was contaminated with his sweat. It is in this way that Bartholomew comes to understand that Jesus is, in all respects, the opposite of Beliar. As a consequence of this epiphany, Bartholomew receives Jesus' blessings for him to act as a minister to the faithful.

The Gospel of Bartholomew provides a unique early insight into the psychology of Satan/Beliar. Here, rather than just motiveless evil, Satan's behaviour towards God is seen as that of a resentful eldest son in an Oedipal rebellion. At the outset, Satan, whose original name Satanael meant 'messenger of God' (IV:25), is busily obeying his father's commands, little knowing that his latest mission, to collect clods and water 'from the four corners of the world' (IV:53), is for God to crown his Creation with Adam.

So when Michael, whom Satan considers his inferior, tells him that it is God's will that he must also serve and honour Adam, the jealous Satan thinks this a paternal step too far. The son thus challenges the father's authority, which leads to him being cast out of heaven, the family home. It then follows that everything that happens on earth for all time is a result of the son striving obsessively to wreck the works of his father, beginning with the Fall at Eden. In the continuing battle, mankind's future prospects depend entirely on whether it uses its God-given free will correctly and judges that, in the final analysis, God will triumph. According to Christian thinking, God's triumph is guaranteed when he recreates himself as his own son and descends to earth to redeem fallen mankind. After this, Satan's days are numbered.

Returning to Revelation, what we are told is the whole history of this family drama, from Creation to Judgement via Eden and Nazareth, except that in this account the method used is allegorical. Exactly how this allegorical code can be cracked has long been questioned. The woman clothed in the sun, for example, could signify Mary, with her male offspring being Jesus, or she could signify the early Church, with the child connoting the faithful. But the Satan dragon is clear enough. This is the greatest monster ever to be imagined, a cosmic evil in service to nobody but itself. Regarding the two beasts, these are aspects of the dragon's destructive grand plan:

blasphemy and false prophecy. It is unlikely to be mere coincidence that the fire-and-brimstone comeuppance of these three aspects of evil is strongly reminiscent of Zeus' punishment of the Titan Typhon, for Revelation does not only draw on scriptural tradition but on classical and Near and Middle Eastern mythologies from the earliest times.

The impact of Revelation's Satan dragon, most obviously on Western culture, cannot be overestimated. This, unsurprisingly, is most apparent in numerous saints' lives, as set down from the earliest of Christian times and on into the Middle Ages. The following examples provide some insight into the huge number of saints' lives that tell of those who, when confronted by a satanic dragon, courageously obeyed God's will and as a result not only were personally saved from eternal damnation but, by example, brought about the conversion, and so the salvation, of many others.

## Saints and dragons

Certainly the most celebrated dragon-slayer of all time is St George. Just as is the case in England, George is revered as the patron saint of cities and countries across the world; for example, in Aragon, Catalonia, Georgia,

Albrecht Altdorfer, *St George Slaying the Dragon*, 16th century.
Raphael, *St George and the Dragon*, c. 1506.

Lithuania, Ethiopia, Bulgaria, Palestine, Portugal, Brazil, Canada, Romania, Germany, Greece, Malta, Moscow, Istanbul, Genoa and Venice. He has traditionally been venerated by soldiers, farmers, archers and horse-riders and has been seen as a guardian of lepers, plague victims and those suffering from syphilis. For many Muslims, most notably those in the Palestinian regions, George is associated with the holy man and martyr Al-Khidr, who is believed to have been both a spiritual guide to Moses and a dragon-slayer.[30] Besides this, thousands of churches – 365 in Georgia alone – are named after George, as well as numerous hospitals and charitable institutions. Exactly how this all came about is in itself quite remarkable, particularly as regards the curious history of how George became best known as a dragon-slayer.

Although firm historical evidence is not available, George is thought to have been a third-century AD Christian of noble Turkish or Palestinian birth who, when both his parents had died, enlisted, as his father had, in the Roman army. Having risen to the high rank of military *tribunus*, and therefore a member of the imperial guard, George was suddenly faced with Emperor Diocletian's edict commanding that all Christian soldiers should renounce their faith or be arrested. George's highly vocal refusal to obey initially led Diocletian to attempt to reason with him, but George was adamant and Diocletian felt he had no other choice than to order George's grisly martyrdom. Witnessing this was Empress Alexandra of Rome, who, admiring George's courage and unshakable faith, immediately converted to Christianity, so causing Diocletian to order that she should meet the same fate as George.[31]

While a sixth-century Byzantine hagiographer describes, in excruciating detail, St George's torture and death on 23 April (Pharmouthi in the Coptic calendar) at the hands of the Persian king Dadianus, who is identified as both 'a dragon of the abyss' and simply 'a dragon', no proof is forthcoming as to whether this early association between George and a dragon went on to be mythologized in later accounts of George as a dragon-slayer.[32] Far more likely, it was owing to Crusaders returning home from the Holy Land, perhaps as early as the late eleventh century, that the dragon fight was added to George's life, much in the manner of those increasingly popular tales of chivalric heroics. Although there can be little doubt that the inspiration behind this particular mythologizing were the widely familiar ancient Greek myths of Heracles' rescue of Hesione and Perseus' rescue of Andromeda,[33] dragon-slaying had long been feature of those saints' lives which testify to God's power over all things satanic, commonly presented in dragon form, and to the ability of his chosen ones, his saints, to triumph over evil.

Master ɪ.ᴀ.ᴍ. of Zwolle, *St George Fighting the Dragon*, 15th century.

The earliest written account of George's dragon-slaying is given in the twelfth-century Greek *Miracula Sancti Georgii*.[34] This, however, remained relatively obscure, and, as is so often the case with saints' lives, the standard and most influential account of George's dragon-slaying is that included in Jacobus de Voragine's hugely popular mid-thirteenth-century collection of saints' lives, the *Golden Legend* (*Legenda aurea*).[35]

It is while George is on his travels as a tribune that he arrives near the city of Silena in Libya. Here there is a large swamp, where a fearsome dragon lives. Despite repeated attempts by both armies and lone heroes, no one has been able to kill it. Worse still is the dragon's habit of approaching the city walls and belching out its fumes, so fatally poisoning many of the inhabitants. At first, the townsfolk try to appease the dragon by leaving it two sheep each day, but when the sheep run short, they make up the deficiency by leaving their children, for which grim necessity they form a lottery. It eventually falls to the king of Silena to sacrifice his daughter, and despite his promising great wealth to his subjects should they agree to spare her, they will have none of it. With no other option remaining, the king bids a tearful farewell to the girl and sends her to the swamp to meet her doom. It is at this point that George appears on the scene.

At first, the girl urges George to depart in haste, but when he learns from her what her predicament is, he insists on standing by her 'in the name

Paolo Uccello, *St George and the Dragon*, c. 1470.

Bernat Martorell,
*St George Killing the
Dragon*, 1434–5.

of Christ'. As the dragon approaches, George raises his spear and delivers
it a severe injury, causing it to collapse. George now tells the girl quickly to
throw her belt around the dragon's neck, the upshot being that it follows her
around 'like the tamest dog'. As she now leads the dragon towards the city, the
townsfolk scatter in fear, whereupon George declares that, providing they all
accept baptism from him, he will kill the creature. All eagerly and sincerely
accept his terms and the dragon is duly slain. The king, now also a convert,
builds a church in honour of the Virgin Mary, from which healing waters
gush. Declining any reward for his deed and having instructed the king in
the right-minded Christian way to rule over his subjects, George departs.

Jacobus then goes on to tell of George's martyrdom, in which the villain
of the piece is Diocletian's prefect Dacian. Yet unlike in earlier accounts,

'Britain Needs You At Once', Parliamentary Recruiting Committee poster, 1915.

George's persecutor gets his divinely ordained comeuppance, for as Jacobus explains, 'while he [Dacian] was on his way back to his palace from the place of execution, fire fell from above and consumed him and his attendants.'

From what can only be called the folklore of George's martyrdom to a myth that achieved near global celebrity, the St George and the Dragon tale would seem to have set a standard for religiously inspired selflessness. As such, St George transcended both political and religious divides. So much is apparent in the English Cross of St George, a red cross on a white background, which was the only saint's flag to survive Henry VIII's purge of Catholic paraphernalia during the English Reformation of the sixteenth century. As St Patrick is for Irish Catholics, St George is for English Protestants, although as one recruiting poster from the First World War suggests, the English are often notoriously unable (some might say disinclined) to differentiate between England and Britain.

In England, as in many other countries, the story of St George became deeply embedded in popular culture.[36] One seventeenth-century broadside ballad, called 'New Ballad of St George and the Dragon', lionizes George as the greatest of heroes and, significantly, if not a little ironically given George's likely Palestinian origins, a hero who was particularly 'for England':

> Read old Stories and there you shall see,
> How St George, St George, he made the Dragon flee;
> St George he was for England, St Denis was for France,
> *Sing, Hony soit qui maly pence.*[37]

George was and continues to be fêted at many English festivals, pageants and parades, some of which date back to pagan times, where George is associated with the passing of the seasons, and there are two folktales that tell of George coming to the aid of local people by slaying a dragon. One of these is set in Brinsop in Herefordshire, where the local church is dedicated to St George, while the other is the tale of George fighting a dragon near the village of Uffington on the Berkshire Downs,[38] and in this case, the subsequent impact of the Uffington dragon on fantasy fiction would prove to be quite extraordinary.

In 1898, the then Berkshire resident Kenneth Grahame, later the author of *The Wind in the Willows*, loosely based his children's short story 'The Reluctant Dragon' on this self-same folktale, so delivering the first literary fantasy that imagined a child befriending a harmless dragon, one that St George declines to slay. Given Grahame's hugely influential precedent, it could well be argued that we have the myth of St George and the dragon to thank for the likes of Julia Donaldson's Zog and Cressida Cowell's Toothless.[39]

While the account of St George's dragon-slaying has a beguiling simplicity, the dragon encounters in many other saints' lives, many of which could be regarded as models for the St George myth, are more complicated, sometimes bewilderingly so. However, like the St George myth, the abiding feature is the dragon's apocalyptic association, a direct consequence of the Revelation's allegorization of traditional biblical lore.

In the influential second-century Christian work *The Shepherd of Hermas*, the shepherd has a vision of a sea monster-dragon as he is walking through the countryside. This vast multicoloured creature, which is heading straight towards him, at first terrifies him, but when God tells him to keep faith and have courage, he braces himself and carries on, whereupon the beast does no more than poke out its tongue out at him. Having gone safely by, the shepherd now meets an angelic female figure who explains to him that the dragon's colours variously represent the sinfulness and eventual doom of the world, those who will be saved and those who will not, and Christ's promise of eternal life.

A similar faith-inspired disregard for a threatening dragon, in this case modelled on Jacob's Ladder as described in Genesis 28:10–19, is given in the early third-century *Passion of St Perpetua*. Here, the imprisoned Perpetua dreams of climbing a ladder to heaven on which is fixed an array of sharp blades and under which is a dragon. Armed only with her religious convictions, Perpetua uses the dragon's head as her first rung, a probable reference to the curse God laid on the serpent at Eden, and proceeds unharmed to ascend into heaven.

A yet more exacting lesson given to a dragon is to be found in the apocryphal *Acts of Thomas*, also set down in the third century. The apostle is in India when he comes across the dead body of young man by the wayside. Sensing that this may well be a trap, Thomas is unsurprised when a huge male dragon emerges and, without further ado, somewhat bizarrely tells him that he has bitten and fatally poisoned the youth because he, the dragon, has fallen in love with the young woman whom the youth was courting. When Thomas demands to know from whom the dragon is descended, the dragon boasts that he is the son of the Eden serpent and kin to Leviathan, who, he says, encircles the world and chews on its own tail.[40] Thomas now condemns the dragon and commands him to revive the youth by sucking the venom out of his body. After some protest, the dragon does as he is told, resulting in the youth coming back to life and the dragon, now inflated with air and venom, exploding.[41]

By the fourth century, accounts of dragons had become deeply associated with pagan opposition to Christian evangelizers. Among the most colourful of these tales are those told about St Philip the Apostle, who in company with his virginal sister Mariamne and the apostle Bartholomew is directed by Jesus to convert the inhabitants of Asia Minor, beginning in what is present-day Turkey.[42] To this end, they head down the 'Road of Snakes' to Ophiorhyme, the 'City of Snakes', where the idol Echidna, 'the mother of all snakes', is worshipped by the populace.[43] In order to protect her, Jesus tells Mariamne to disguise her womanhood lest the snake-dragons attempt to corrupt her, as had been the case with Eve.

Not long into their journey, they enter a wilderness of dragon-women, where they encounter a leopard which, having humbled itself before them, brings forward a young goat that it has rescued from the dragons' terrain. As both the leopard and the goat can speak and believe themselves to be Christian humans, they are permitted to join Philip's mission as guides to Ophiorhyme. Some days later, the sky darkens ominously and the travellers are attacked by a vast fire-bellied dragon attended by a host of its snake offspring. Refusing to take flight, Philip leads his company in prayer and immediately the dragon and all the snakes are struck by lightning and pulverized.

Nevertheless, their troubles with dragons are far from over, for soon they are met by fifty demons who, at Philip's command to them to reveal their true form, emerge from the roadside as huge snakes followed by another great fiery dragon. These creatures, descendants of Satan and kin to the snakes that the Pharaoh raised against Moses, acknowledge themselves to be powerless in the face of the messianic power invested in Philip and offer to build a sacred city as a shrine to 'the crucified one', as long as they are then allowed to flee to a place where they will no longer be of trouble. Philip accepts these terms and the city is built and very soon populated by thousands of Christian converts.

The missionaries now arrive at Ophiorhyme, where the 'snake people' devotees of Echidna initially perceive them to be of their own kind, despite Philip having earlier brought about the death of the two dragons guarding the city gates. Having established themselves at a healer's deserted clinic, Philip, Mariamne and Bartholomew set about performing charitable deeds, healing the sick, converting the populace and destroying the snakes, but soon encounter fierce resistance from the more powerful residents and the priesthood of Echidna. In due course, they are arrested and forced to

Detail of Filippino Lippi, *St Philip Driving the Dragon from the Temple of Hieropolis*, *c*. 1487–1502, in Strozzi Chapel, Santa Maria Novella, Florence.

endure torture and humiliation, which they bear with great dignity. With the intervention of St John the Apostle and the manifestation of Jesus, Mariamne and Bartholomew are set free, but Philip is crucified upside down. Outraged by the barbarism of his persecutors, Philip sets a curse on Echidna, causing an abyss to open up and swallow her along with thousands of her followers. Philip then breathes his last and ascends to heaven.

Outlandish and sometimes perplexing as this particular saint's life often is, there is nonetheless some historical basis to it. In actuality, Ophiorhyme is the ancient ruined city of Hierapolis, adjacent to the modern-day Turkish city of Pamukkale. As more reliable histories inform us and as archaeological evidence confirms, it was here that reverence for Philip became a powerful cult after his martyrdom, and here too where Mariamne founded an outpost of the austere sect of Encratite nuns and lived out her life in peace. As for Philip's trials and tribulations with dragons, this metaphorization of his missions was evidently widespread. This can be seen in the late fourth-century *Historia certaminis apostolici* (History of the Apostolical Contest), a collection of apocryphal writings said to have been compiled by Abdias, reputedly the first bishop of Babylon, who was believed to be one of Christ's 72 disciples mentioned collectively in the Gospel of Luke (10:1–20).

In Abdias's compilation, Philip is recorded as having preached for some twenty years across Asia Minor. As might be expected, Philip meets much opposition, and on one occasion he is arrested and taken before a temple statue of the Roman god Mars, from which a ferocious dragon emerges and begins attacking Philip's captors. Along with the physically injured, many more people are made gravely ill by the dragon's pestilential breath. Taking command of the situation, Philip advises those present to tear down the statue and raise in its stead a holy cross. This they do, whereupon Philip commands the dragon to leave the temple and seek out an abode where it can do no harm to humans. The very minute this happens, the sick and injured are restored to full health and repent their pagan folly and, almost certainly to Philip's consternation, take to worshipping him instead.

A not dissimilar story to Philip's expulsion of the temple dragon is that told in several versions of the life of St Sylvester, who historically became pope at Rome in AD 314, thus under the protection of Constantine the Great, the first Roman emperor to embrace Christianity. Sylvester's story, as given in the *Acts of Sylvester*, tells of a dragon that lived in a pit on the Tarpeian rock in Rome. It is the practice of those who are described as 'profane virgins' and 'mages' (sorcerers) to descend the pit's many stairs, 'as if to Hell', to make sacrifices and offer food to the beast. One day, the dragon ascends the stairs and although it is not actually coming out of the pit, its breath alone is sufficient to cause the deaths of many. Urged by pagans to prove God's power by containing the dragon, Sylvester at first declines to agree to such a test of faith, but after a vision in which St Peter instructs him how this might be done, he does as the pagans had urged him. Undeterred by the pagans' attempts to frighten him, he succeeds in chaining the gates at the bottom of the steps, so incarcerating the dragon for all time, and as a consequence, in baptizing all the dragon's previous servants.[44]

As these early saints' lives show, the killing, expelling or taming of dragons and venomous snakes most commonly acts as a demonstration of the power of prayer and of God's authority over all things. Tales of this kind abound in early Christian narratives, some of whose saintly protagonists are historical figures, others pure fiction.[45] The following examples of saints overcoming dragons are typical: imprisoned and tortured for refusing to forsake God, St Margaret (Marina) of Antioch is swallowed by a dragon, but when she makes the sign of the cross, the dragon explodes and she re-emerges unharmed, thereafter to be revered as the patron saint of child-birth;[46] St Hilarion commands a ravaging dragon to settle on a pyre which he then sets alight; the saintly Ammon the Hermit tames two dragons and has them guard his hermitage from thieves and causes another dragon to burst apart when he prays to God; St Donatus employs the unusual tactic of spitting into a dragon's mouth and so killing it; the exiled St Victoria expels a dragon from a nearby town by praying before it and, in so doing, achieves the conversion of the town's obstinate pagans; St Andrew lays a divinely inspired fatal curse on a dragon that has killed a young boy, whom the saint then revives; and similarly, it is prayer that rescues St Caluppan and causes the expulsion of two dragons from his sanctuary when he is otherwise paralysed with fear.

Without exception, the power of God's chosen ones over dragons refer, often explicitly in the narratives, to God's struggles against, and ultimate triumph over, Satan, ranging from the Fall at Eden to the birth of Christ. Although these plot structures are inevitably formulaic there is also much inventiveness and, in some instances, symbolic subtlety. One further example of this is the story of the death and burial of a noble woman whose life had many moral shortcomings and whose place of interment is violated by a dragon and her body devoured by it. Only as a result of the prayers of St Marcellus does the dragon beg for forgiveness and depart from the place, never to be seen again. Here, the dragon is not simply satanic but can be interpreted more specifically as a symbol of the sins of the woman, just as its eventual penitence and departure can be interpreted as God's forgiveness of her.

Many of these saints' lives continued to be seen as important exemplars into the Middle Ages, largely owing to the *Golden Legend*. As Christianity spread throughout Europe, new conversions generated new saints' lives, often containing ancient hagiographic motifs such as the banishment or elimination of dragons and/or snakes. In some instances, these stories, like that of St George, went on to become deeply associated with ideas of national identity.

For Ireland, it is the fifth-century life of the Romano-British 'Apostle of Ireland' St Patrick that testifies to the snake-free purity of that country's lands and the fidelity of its peoples. That Ireland is a country without snakes was remarked upon by the Venerable Bede in AD 731. Although Bede does not credit this to St Patrick, he does perceive in it something bordering on the supernatural:

There are no reptiles and no snake can exist there; for although often brought over from Britain, as soon as the ship nears land, they breathe the scents of its air, and die. In fact, almost everything in this isle confers immunity to poison, and I have seen that folk suffering from snake-bite have drunk water in which scrapings from the leaves of books from Ireland had been steeped, this remedy checked the spreading poison and reduced the swelling.[47]

Yet it was not until the late twelfth century that Gerald of Wales gave Patrick partial credit for a snake-free Ireland, and not until Jocelin of Furness's early thirteenth-century *Life of Patrick* that Patrick, with the assistance of an angel, is said to have gathered all the snakes together on high promontory in County Mayo and 'cast down the whole pestilential host [to be] swallowed up by the ocean'.

Tales of Patrick's expulsion of the snakes, or more specifically dragons, persisted in Irish folklore, which tell of his battles against the she-dragon demons Caoranach and Corra, although the many variants of Patrick's supposed battles against dragons do not always agree that he killed them but instead suggest he limited their activities to particular lochs (loughs).[48]

St Margaret of Antioch in an illuminated manuscript, c. 1440.

Nevertheless, that which conferred Europe-wide renown of Patrick's accomplishment was its inclusion, albeit briefly, in the *Golden Legend*, where, like Bede, it is also said that 'even the woods and bark from the trees in that region effectively counteract poison.'[49] That it is now known that post-glacial Ireland never had any snakes is perhaps beside the point, for as Ireland's patron saint, Patrick had ensured that a serpentine plague was expunged in the process of converting a pagan people. As in traditional saints' lives, serpents are the evil manifestation of all manner of non-Christian practices, and in this sense, pre-conversion Ireland was overrun with abhorrent beings.

IN THE OLD AND NEW Testaments, as in saints' lives, the ever-increasing tendency to polarize good and evil conferred on dragons the role of the monstrously incarnate Satan. This, as has been pointed out throughout this chapter, is all a direct consequence of the massive influence of the Book of Revelation's Great Red Satan dragon. As a consequence, retrospective interpretations were placed on the meaning of the serpent at Eden, a myth, as we have seen, that has its origins in non-Jewish sources. Unlike in Graeco-Roman mythology, where dragons are ambivalently associated with the acts of the gods and with challenges to mankind, dragons in the New Testament amount to all that stands in the way of the urgent need to convert all mankind to Christian beliefs, a conversion imperative that is not present in Judaism.

Dragons as evil, then, are an obnoxious presence in whatever form they take and must therefore be confronted, typically by invoking God's supreme power in order to overmaster them. As a consequence, dragons came to mean anything that is not unflinchingly Christian, including any form of human weakness. As we have also seen, according to the gender prejudices of both Judaism and Christianity, it is women's sexuality that both epitomizes and encourages human weakness, and therefore must either be restrained or altogether curtailed. With such ideas becoming entrenched in Christian culture, alongside the similar prejudices of classical mythology that were carried with it in the conversion process, it was inevitable that the dragon-woman would become a staple of folklore and legend throughout Christendom.

# three

# The Germanic Dragon, Part 1: Old Norse Mythology and Old English Literature

The dragon must be in the barrow,
aged, proud in treasure.

S O I T I S said in the Old English wisdom poem 'Gnomic Verses.'[1] Although explicitly Christian in its overarching philosophy, many of this poem's blunt, seemingly resigned statements concerning the nature of things will have dated back to pagan times. It is as if to say, 'the dragon and its ways are a fact; always have been, always will be.' Certainly, as the previous chapter indicated, dragons were as much an obsession for Germanic Christians as they were, or had been, for Germanic pagans. Even when dragons were not wreaking havoc, the belief that simply the sight of them was an omen of disaster was widespread. When, for instance, the Vikings made their first attack on England at the North Sea island monastery on Lindisfarne in AD 793, the *Anglo-Saxon Chronicle* entry for that date laments the event in apocalyptic language:

> This year dire forewarnings came over the land of the Northumbrians and miserably terrified the people. There were great whirlwinds and lightning, and fiery dragons were seen flying in the air. A great famine followed and a little after that, in the same year, the ravaging of heathen men lamentably destroyed God's church at Lindisfarne through robbery and slaughter.[2]

It might well be said that the invocation of dragons to explain misfortune was something of a cliché. Nonetheless, dragons in the more extensive sources to be found in early Germanic literature are often functioning in a more complex way to signify deep social anxieties. In this and the following chapter, dragon tales from Anglo-Saxon England and medieval Scandinavia and Germany will be considered against the fraught backgrounds that gave rise to them as a dire threat to human security and, in some cases, the cosmic order.[3]

## Dragons in the Icelandic Eddas

Our oldest sources for the myths and legends of Germanic paganism are contained in what is known as the *Poetic Edda*, an extraordinary collection of poems that was written down in Iceland during the thirteenth century and had long been part of an oral culture.[4] Nevertheless, the *Poetic Edda* is only a partial account of pagan beliefs, for a good deal of material not preserved in it was well known to medieval Iceland's greatest man of letters, Snorri Sturluson (1179–1241). Careful to avoid offending Church doctrine, Snorri systematized the old lore as a handbook for aspiring poets, so providing an explanation for the epithetical terminology of traditional verse forms. For example, Snorri notes that kennings (figurative, often metaphorical, devices) for a sword include 'adder of battle', 'mighty war-snake' and 'worm of the slain', a clear indication that Nordic warriors saw the power of dragon-like creatures as something worth emulating in battle.[5] Snorri's invaluable *Prose Edda* was completed around AD 1220.

According to the strictly mythological aspects of both the *Poetic Edda* and the *Prose Edda*, there are two dragons in particular that the gods, and therefore humanity, should dread.[6] These are the flying reptilian dragon Nídhögg, whose name means 'the one striking full of hatred', and the vast marine snake the Midgard or World Serpent, also known as Jörmungand (Mighty Snake). Their location in the mythological scheme of things is not without significance.

The Norse cosmos is envisioned as having three tiers housing nine worlds, the homes to gods, dwarfs, elves, giants and humans. In the top tier is Asgard, the citadel of the gods, and Valhalla, the 'Hall of the Slain', where Odin, the chief of the gods, gathers his great army of fallen human heroes in preparation for the final great battle of Ragnarök. In the middle tier is Midgard (Middle-earth), where both humanity and the chief enemies of the gods, the giants, dwell. Surrounding Midgard is a great ocean and it is here that the Midgard Serpent coils itself round Midgard's entire circumference, biting on its own tail. In the lowest tier is Hel, the frozen realm of those who have died of illness or old age, or, in some accounts of it in both the *Poetic Edda* and *Prose Edda*, a place more like the Christian Hell, where those who have in some way transgressed in life are punished. Presiding over Hel is the goddess of the same name, and stalking that region of Hel known as Náströnd (Strand of the Dead) is Nídhögg.

At the centre of the Norse cosmos is Yggdrasil, the World Tree or, literally, 'Odin's Horse', a great life force whose roots are gnawed and damaged by Nídhögg. While Nídhögg's origins are unknown, the Midgard Serpent, the great wolf Fenrir and the goddess Hel are the children of the initially mischievous but ultimately malicious god Loki. Together, they are known as 'Loki's monstrous brood' and, along with Nídhögg, no creatures in the whole of Norse mythology are more dangerous than they.[7] These beings are the nearest we get to a pagan articulation of evil, of horror in both the worlds of the living and the dead.

While no myths are told specifically about Nídhögg, its formidable power and morbid appetite are described in two Eddic poems: *Grímnismál* (Sayings of Grímnir) and *Völuspá* (Prophecy of the Seeress). *Grímnismál* tells how Odin, deceptively calling himself Grímnir (the 'hooded' or 'hidden one') has a brutal encounter with his wife's protégé, one Geirröd. In the course of what in effect is the prolonged torture of Odin, much knowledge is imparted by him about the Norse cosmos and its inhabitants, including details of the damage Nídhögg and a host of venomous serpents inflict on Yggdrasil:

> More snakes
> lie under the ash of Yggdrasil
> than any fool can guess.
> Goin and Moin,
> they are the sons of Grafvitnir,
> Grabak and Grafvollud,
> Ofnir and Svafnir.
> Think I that they shall always
> rend the branches of the tree.[8]

> Yggdrasil's ash
> endures great pain
> more than anyone can know.
> A hart gnaws it from above,
> it rots at the sides,
> and Nídhögg cuts it from below.[9]

Schematization of the Norse cosmos showing the Midgard Serpent encircling Middle-earth and Níðhögg at the roots of Yggdrasil.

While Yggdrasil represents the vital energies of life, Nídhögg represents all that threatens them.

In *Völuspá* it is the limitations of Odin's knowledge and the uncertainties that lie ahead that force him to summon a female visionary from the underworld in order to enlighten him. Speaking of herself in the third person, the Seeress (*völva*) tells him of the entire span of the mythology, past, present and future. Her description of Nídhögg's abode in Hel is particularly gruesome:

> A hall sees she standing
> far out from the sun,
> on the Strand of the Dead.
> Northwards face the doors,
> poison drips in
> through the smoke vents.
> That hall is made from
> serpents' spines.
>
> Sees she there wading
> in murky streams
> perjurers
> and murderers
> and those who corrupted
> other men's wives.
> There Nídhögg sucks
> the corpses of the dead . . .[10]

The Seeress's second mention of Nídhögg is just as disturbing, perhaps even more so. In the final few verses of her prophecy, she clearly states that Ragnarök is not the end of all things, for the world is reborn and certain gods either survive the cataclysm or are returned to life from Hel. In this new world, all is green pastures, good cheer and pleasure: a utopia. But in the very last verse, just before the Seeress sinks back into the underworld, she makes this enigmatic statement:

> Then comes the shadowy dragon flying,
> the gleaming serpent rises up
> from Dark of the Moon Hills.
> In his pinions, Nídhögg carries,

as he flies over the vale,
dead bodies.
Now must she sink.[11]

The meaning of what the Seeress says here can be interpreted in two ways. On the one hand, the arrival of Nídhögg could be taking place in real time, in the moment that the Seeress is speaking, and so the appearance of the dragon portends the start of Ragnarök. If this is the case, then the rebirth of the gods is a sign of hope for the future. On the other hand, it could be understood to mean that Nídhögg also inhabits the reborn world after Ragnarök. If this is what is meant, Creation to Ragnarök is a cyclical process, one that continues to repeat a doom-laden future; in other words, no matter how often the world is reborn, chaos will always ensue, for that is the ultimate fate of all living things.

Nídhögg is the most disquieting representation of a dragon in the old Germanic world. This creature is motiveless in its behaviour: there is no gold hoard to protect and no terrified virgin to imprison such as we see elsewhere in the early Germanic legendary material. All Nídhögg does is inflict tortures on the dead, seek to wreck the essence of life and, above all, bring about that which all societies fear most: disorder. Perhaps understandably, there is no dragon-slaying hero that can combat so great a power of darkness as is embodied in Nídhögg.

The Midgard Serpent does, at least, have an equally fearsome heroic enemy. This is the warrior god Thor, the bane of all the monstrous beings at large in Midgard. The first of Thor's three encounters with the serpent occurs when he is tricked by the giant Útgarda-Loki into performing a series of apparently simple feats, one of which is that he should lift a cat above his head.[12] As with all the trials he has to undergo in this particular myth, Thor

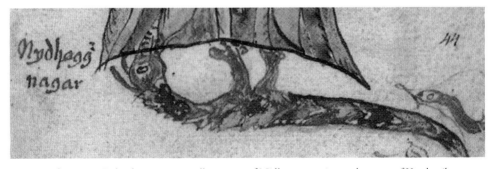

Seventeenth-century Icelandic manuscript illustration of Nídhögg gnawing at the roots of Yggdrasil.

Johann Heinrich Fuseli/Füssli, *Thor Battles the Midgard Serpent*, 1790.

fails, managing only to raise one of the cat's paws off the ground. Owing to the giant's magical deceptions, what Thor does not realize is that he is in fact trying to lift the Midgard Serpent.

The subsequent realization that he has been humiliated causes Thor to seek vengeance to restore his reputation.[13] He sets off across Midgard to the ocean-side home of the giant Hymir and demands to be taken along on a

Friedrich William Heine, *The Battle of the Doomed Gods*, 1882, showing Thor and the Midgard Serpent, Odin and the wolf Fenrir, and Frey and the flaming giant Surt at Ragnarok.

fishing expedition. Needful of bait, Thor rips off the head of a large ox. Forced by Thor to sail further and further out to sea, Hymir becomes anxious. Thor now casts his baited line and succeeds in hooking the Midgard Serpent, which he drags to the surface and brays with his great hammer, Mjölnir. Panicking, Hymir cuts Thor's line, so setting the god's catch free. Infuriated by Hymir's cowardice, Thor punches him overboard and strides ashore. While other Old Norse sources suggest that Thor killed the Midgard Serpent in this encounter, if we view the mythology as a time-bound sequence, this is clearly not so.[14]

Thor's final encounter with the Midgard Serpent is on the great battlefield of Ragnarök. Unable to save his father, Odin, from the jaws of the wolf Fenrir, Thor advances on the Midgard Serpent and succeeds in striking it dead, but, having staggered back nine paces, he succumbs to its poison.[15] As is said in *Völuspa*:

> Then comes the famous
> child of Jörd [Thor],
> Odin's son steps forward,
> the protector of Earth
> strikes the serpent in fury,
> all must abandon their homes.

Nine steps takes
Fiorgyn's child [Thor],
with difficulty,
back from the serpent
beyond derision.[16]

Rather like Yggdrasil and Níðhögg, Thor and the Midgard Serpent denote a binary opposition between life's positives and negatives.

The mutual destruction of gods and monsters is, of course, the dramatic culmination of Ragnarök, but even so, the killing of the hero by his dragon adversary is rare in Germanic legends.[17] The one major instance of this happening is told in the Old English poem *Beowulf*, and here it is not impossible that the idea of the famed hero's disastrous last battle with a dragon is, in essence, modelled on the myth of Thor and the Midgard Serpent.

## Beowulf and the monsters

It is the sixth century and the kingdom of the Geats, an area that is now southwestern Sweden, has enjoyed peace and prosperity for fifty years under the rule of King Beowulf. But unknown to the king, trouble of the worst kind is brewing. A badly treated slave, a person of no account, has fled the cruelty of his princely owner and sought refuge in a remote clifftop mound overlooking the sea. Unwittingly, he has entered an ancient barrow, where once the sole survivor of a race of warriors had concealed all his tribe's great wealth and awaited his own miserable ending. Not long after, an airborne, 15-metre, fire-breathing reptilian dragon happened across the barrow and has remained there for three hundred years, zealously guarding the treasure hoard as its own.

It is this scene that the desperate slave has, to his horror, chanced upon. About to be attacked, he grabs the nearest of object of value, a bejewelled golden cup, and flees for his life. Once back at his master's home, he is quickly reinstated in return for his booty. Meanwhile, having discovered its loss and but a single human footprint, the dragon is consumed with fury and bent on vengeance on whosoever it can find. Come nightfall, the dragon soars from its lair and sets about reducing the land of the Geats to ashes. Nothing is spared in the nightly conflagrations: farms, fortresses and even King Beowulf's resplendent throne room are engulfed in flame.

Beowulf is not a man given to despondency but this turn of events shocks and confuses him, even to the point of his wondering whether he had somehow offended 'the Almighty'. Yet knowing, as he always has, that inaction is not an option, he plans his counterattack. He will not raise an army but, protected by his newly forged iron shield, will instead lead a select company of eleven warriors clad in iron mail. Now informed of the source of the dragon's grievance, Beowulf obliges the reluctant slave to lead them to the barrow, where, single-handed and heedless of danger, he intends to confront the despoiler of his realm.

Stationing his men at a safe distance and advancing to the cliff face, where a boiling stream gushes from beneath the barrow, Beowulf cries out a challenge. As the dragon emerges spewing fire, Beowulf quickly comes to realize that his sword, Nægling, a trusted heirloom, appears to have little impact on the scaly beast. Witnessing their king's dire straits, all but one of his men desert him. His name is Wiglaf, Beowulf's distant cousin, as yet untested in battle. Shoulder to shoulder, Beowulf and Wiglaf attack the dragon, but when Wiglaf's limewood shield is incinerated by the dragon's fire, he is forced to take shelter behind Beowulf's shield. Nevertheless, with the dragon momentarily distracted, Beowulf manages to strike it in the head, shattering his sword and receiving in return a severe bite to the neck. Now Wiglaf makes his own attack and succeeds in rending the dragon's underbelly, staunching its fire and allowing Beowulf to deliver a killer knife thrust to its ribs.

Yet Beowulf's victory comes at great personal cost, for he is mortally wounded by the venomous bite. In his dying speech, he confers the succession on Wiglaf, is consoled by the sight of the treasure that his people will now receive and asks that his ashes be interred on a headland overlooking the sea. Under Wiglaf's command, the dragon's body is heaved into the sea and the deserters are dispossessed and exiled. But Beowulf is deluded and his hopes for the future of the Geats prove false, for the treasure is now revealed to be cursed and consequently of no benefit to his people. Much of it is destroyed on Beowulf's funeral pyre and what remains is buried forever in Beowulf's newly built headland barrow. As is now foreseen, with Beowulf gone, the future for the Geats is bleak, for ancient tribal grievances, held in suspension during Beowulf's long reign, will rapidly resume.

This, then, is a broad summary of the main action of the last thousand lines of *Beowulf*, almost one-third of the entire poem. But it is far from a full account of what is said in these lines, for the majority of them are taken up with recollections of what happened in tribal wars of the past, of bloody battles and generational feuds, of dire warnings from experience and ancestral memories, and of dread forebodings for the future. Like the rest of the poem, the tone is one of regretful sadness, of a haunting sense of loss. Yet, throughout all this doom and gloom is a celebration of those who acted honourably and showed courage, endurance and unwavering loyalty to their kinfolk and their allies, no matter how great the risk to their own lives. Among such heroes, Beowulf is exemplary.

*Beowulf* exists in just one manuscript, dated approximately to the year AD 1000. Although the date of its actual composition has been a subject of fierce scholarly debate since the poem was first translated over two centuries ago, on balance, the mid-eighth century looks to be the likeliest. The chief question concerning the poem's origins is this: how did it come about that a poem set in fifth- and sixth-century heathen Scandinavia was composed in Christianized Anglo-Saxon England? About this, we can only speculate. First, it has to be borne in mind that the Anglo-Saxons were a North Germanic people who conquered and settled in England at a time roughly contemporary with the events recorded in the poem. Second, even if the legend of Beowulf was not imported directly by the Anglo-Saxon invaders, trade links with the pagan north continued. It is quite possible that the legend arrived on English shores that way.

Irrespective of these questions, old traditions that tell of life's harshness and the proper way to conduct oneself die hard. A legend of *Beowulf's* magnitude would not easily have been forgotten, no matter what its underlying ideology. That said, Christian influence on the poem is undeniable. References to the Bible are plentiful, although there is no mention of Christ. Similarly, the values and beliefs of pre-Christian heroic society are present throughout, although there is no mention of the pagan gods: Woden (ON Odin), Thunor (ON Thor) and company.[18] The best we can say is that a tale of pagan wars and heroics was overlaid with Christian sensibilities and that, once set in the hands of an Anglo-Saxon poet of genius, it is this combination of pagan and Christian ideals that lends to the poem its uniqueness of expression.

The historical veracity of the poem is similarly complex. We know from other sources that many characters in the poem, particularly those of high rank, were actual historical figures. The conspicuous exception is Beowulf himself, and it is notable that the poem makes no mention of him having any siblings and is explicit in stating that he has no children. With the death of Beowulf and later of Wiglaf, their line, from a tribe known as the Wægmundings, is extinguished. So, the character of Beowulf is a fiction, an idea. For us to understand what he represents, and in turn what his fatal encounter with a dragon might mean, we must take into account what the poem tells us of his deeds.

Beowulf's primary and unique role in the poem is that of monster-killer. As a young man, he travels with his warrior band from Geatland (most probably Götaland) to Denmark, where Heorot, the Dane's magnificent palace, has been under attack for twelve years by the rabid troll-like creature Grendel. We are told that Grendel is descended from the biblical character Cain, who after perpetrating the world's first fratricide is condemned by God to a life in exile. Many have been killed during Grendel's murderous night-time forays, and the ageing Danish king, Hrothgar, is at a loss as to what he can do to prevent more mayhem.

Little is known of Beowulf at the time of his arrival at Heorot, except that his father had once enjoyed Hrothgar's protection and that, as a debt of honour, Beowulf feels duty-bound to help the king. He is given a mixed reception, with one of Hrothgar's chief advisers publicly casting doubt on Beowulf's claims of already having performed great feats. Our first acquaintance with Beowulf is, therefore, not unlike that of the 'unpromising hero' of folktale, that youthful figure thought of as unremarkable by all who know him but who goes on to confound expectations and accomplish great feats. Despite the criticism of Beowulf, which he confidently and effectively rebuts, King Hrothgar welcomes him. Beowulf now declares that he will fight Grendel single-handed and unarmed.

That night, Beowulf and his men await the intruder in Heorot's great hall. Sure enough, Grendel arrives, smashes open the door, grabs the nearest man and sets about eating him. He then reaches for Beowulf but is staggered to discover himself caught in a mighty grip. As Grendel attempts to escape, Beowulf, unflinching, rips the creature's arm from its socket, so forcing it to rage back into the night and die. Beowulf hangs Grendel's arm high on the hall's wall as testament to his victory. Much feasting ensues, during which, as tribute to Beowulf's great deed, one of the king's thanes improvises a poem about a legendary dragon-slayer, named here as Sigemund.[19] But that is not the end of Denmark's problems, for now Grendel's demonic mother comes in search of vengeance. She descends with fury on the mead hall and, just like her son, grabs the nearest man. As the warriors draw their swords, she takes flight still carrying her victim, this time one of King Hrothgar's most trusted advisers.

Beowulf and his men ready themselves for pursuit. They track the monster to her fenland lair, which lies beneath a deep lake roiling with serpents and 'sea-dragons' (*sædracan*; l. 1426), one of which Beowulf kills with an arrow. Nearby they find the severed head of Hrothgar's abducted adviser. Beowulf now dons his armour and, bearing a precious sword loaned to him by the very Dane who had previously cast aspersions on him, plunges into the lake, swims down and eventually discovers the monster in her cave. As they grapple, he is drawn deeper and deeper into the cave, where he is further attacked by the serpents. His attempt to settle matters with his borrowed sword proves futile, but he then eyes a huge ancient sword nearby, seizes it and decapitates his demented adversary. Then, noticing the dead body of Grendel, he decapitates that too. The bloodstained sword, which, it transpires, is of giant origin, begins to melt, leaving only its ornate hilt. Clutching this and Grendel's head, Beowulf swims back to his comrades. The suffering of the Danes, at least as far as monsters are concerned, is over.

What, then, does all this tell us about the significance of the dragon in the poem? While Beowulf's monster-slayings are clearly central to the message of the poem, the sociopolitical context in which they are enacted is inseparable from this message. The poet's chief aim is to provide a critique of, or perhaps a mournful elegy on, the fractious, fragmented and chauvinistic nature of heroic society, from which we learn that little of what is achieved in terms of wealth and well-being will last. There will be treachery and usurpations, attempts to create peace will fail and war will be ubiquitous. Like all societies at all times, heroic society really required three things in order to prosper: social harmony, the resolution of disputes and, in order to ensure loyalty in times of strife, reward, or as the poet puts it, the 'distribution of rings'.

Taking Beowulf's monstrous foes one at a time, we can see that that they represent the antitheses of these essentials. Grendel is the very opposite of social harmony. He is a loner who loathes hearing the joyous sounds of those feasting in the mead hall. While society, by definition, requires consideration of others, Grendel has none and actively seeks the obliteration of those for whom social bonds are paramount. Concerning Grendel's mother, she can be regarded as the epitome of the feud mentality, although it should also be noted that in taking vengeance for her kin, she does only what the men do, who are then renowned as heroes. As scholars in recent decades have observed, what we see in the depiction of Grendel's mother is as much a result of patriarchal hypocrisy as it is a critique of the politics of feud.[20] As regards the meaning of the dragon, a creature that murders for gold and hoards it only for its own sake, it is the misuse of power, the failure to distribute rings, that it symbolizes; in short, the dragon is a monstrous embodiment of greed.

In heroic society, greed, along with the vanity that typically accompanies it, was considered to be the root of all evil, and the *Beowulf* poet is explicit in saying as much. One notable condemnation of cupidity is contained in King Hrothgar's 'sermon', delivered shortly after Beowulf has returned from the killing of Grendel's mother. Warning Beowulf of the hazards and temptations of great power, something for which he is surely destined, he refers to the demise of the once noble and courageous Heremod, an ancient Danish king. Hrothgar tells how, ultimately, King Heremod 'brought no pleasure to the Danes . . . he murdered his companions . . . abandoned the joys of men . . . grew bloodthirsty, never did he give the Danes rings for the sake of glory . . . Joyless, he lived to suffer for his wrongdoings.'[21] One person's ruthless self-interest can be the ruination not only of all those over whom they have power but of themselves. This surely applies just as much to the dragon, whose miserly satisfaction depends entirely on squatting on its treasure trove and who, when disturbed, wreaks havoc. That Beowulf and the dragon, selflessness and selfishness, respectively, cancel each other out is characteristic of the poem's pessimism or, one might think, realism.

This contrast between heroism and catastrophe is made throughout the poem. It is what critics have referred to as 'ironic juxtaposition';[22] that is to say, when something praiseworthy or hopeful is described it is immediately overshadowed by a description of something contemptible or disastrous. One telling example also involves reference to the notorious King Heremod. This occurs when Hrothgar's thane pays poetic homage to Sigemund the dragon-slayer as part of the celebrations following on from Beowulf's killing of Grendel.

Sigemund, we are told, gained great wealth and fame from overcoming a dragon, but then, with scarcely a breath drawn, the poet turns to King Heremod's tyranny, eventual overthrow and the ensuing turmoil for his people. Beowulf, says the poet, 'became cherished by his friends, by all mankind', whereas 'crime took hold' of Heremod.[23] Not only does this juxtaposition of the heroic restoration of order and the tyrannous descent into chaos foreshadow Beowulf's unprofitable and fatal encounter with a dragon, but it foreshadows the imminent attack of Grendel's mother. As J.R.R. Tolkien remarks, 'Disaster is foreboded. Defeat is the Theme.'[24] The dragon is the ultimate guarantee of that.

## Monsters and wonders

Three other texts in which dragons figure, all of which would appear to have been well known in Anglo-Saxon times, are also worthy of consideration. Perhaps significantly, two of these – *The Wonders of the East* and *The Letter of Alexander to Aristotle*, both of which were translated into Old English from Latin sources – are collected in the same manuscript source as *Beowulf*. The third text, which self-evidently draws upon the other two but for which no Old English translation now exists (if it ever did), is the bestiary *Liber monstrorum* (Book of Monsters).[25] As this has been dated to the seventh or early eighth century, it is not impossible that the *Beowulf* poet, quite clearly a learned man, was influenced by it and also by the other two texts, particularly in respect of his representations of Grendel, Grendel's mother and the dragon. Moreover, the *Liber*'s early mention of Hygelac, the Geatish king and uncle of Beowulf who is described as one of the 'monsters of amazing size' whose 'bones are preserved on an island in the Rhine and . . . are shown as a wonder to travellers from afar', has provoked much scholarly debate as to the relationship between the *Liber* and *Beowulf*.[26] While no firm conclusions are ever likely to be reached about such intertextualities, it is nonetheless discernible that Anglo-Saxon literary culture was not entirely undiscriminating when it came to reports of exotic monsters.

The *Liber monstrorum* consists of some 120 short paragraphs split into three sections, all of which include accounts of dragon-like creatures but the last of which is entirely devoted to serpents of various kinds.[27] Two things can be said as far as the author is concerned. One is that he was deeply familiar with Graeco-Roman myths and legends. The other is that he is a rather unwilling informant, one who is deeply sceptical about many of his sources, most notably those which he considers to be of pagan origin and which he is inclined to dismiss as 'shaggy and scaly tales'. Nevertheless, despite his reservations as a Christian, the author proceeds as he would appear to have been instructed by his superior.

In the first and second parts of the *Liber*, we are told of 'a certain monster in Arcadia called Cacus', a cave-dwelling creature that 'spews flames from his chest' and is given to grabbing bulls by the tail and dragging them into his lair. Also noted are those dragon creatures tackled by Hercules/Heracles, for instance, the Lernaean Hydra and Cerberus, as well as a creature with fifty heads which vomits fire from all its mouths and is armed with fifty shields and swords.[28] The final section on serpents also recounts a number of tales involving Hercules, some of which are either garbled or strange elaborations, most probably owing to the vagaries of oral transmission. One such case is the Styx dragon, 'the greatest snake in the whole world', which is said to encircle what is presumably Hades. Yet the author cannot sometimes resist passing judgement on his sources, as he does regarding the tale of Cleopatra being pursued by 'twin snakes with monsters and clouds barking from the sky'. About this, says the author, 'just as a lie has created monsters and ethereal snakes on this queen's back, so too do the lying fables of poets wilfully fake very many things for themselves which do not occur'. Seemingly wearied by his labours, the author ends his report as follows:

> Now amongst these serpents . . . some true things are found, and some lacking all truth. There are also still very many snakes of serpentine kind, like Dispades, Reguli, Haemorroides, Spegali, Natrices, concerning which I have now found nothing remarkable or worthy of notice.

Turning to *The Wonders of the East*, which comprises just 37 short paragraphs, little is said there concerning dragons and serpents that is not repeated in the *Liber*. The difference, however, is that the author of *Wonders*, on the surface of things, appears to be wholly ingenuous as regards the monstrous beings he describes, in that there is not a word of doubt expressed anywhere. Nevertheless, the very last paragraph somewhat cryptically tells of the brothers Iamnes and Mambres. These characters are known to have figured in a lost or deliberately obscured apocryphal text from the Book of Exodus as the sorcerers who challenged Moses when he petitioned the Egyptian pharaoh to free the Israelites. Here the author of *Wonders* tells of Mambres being warned by the now deceased Iamnes that God has punished him for his idolatry, his error of judgement, and that he now resides in Hell, 'where there is the great heat of eternal punishment'. In all likelihood, what the author is cautioning us about is our own ingenuousness, our own errors of judgement, when it comes to believing what others, including himself, have reported.

The *Liber* also summarizes many of the accounts of monstrous or otherwise unknown creatures that are related in *The Letter of Alexander to Aristotle*, itself dating from the fourth century BC. The most extravagant of these accounts concerning dragon-like serpents is worth repeating at a little greater length. The *Letter* tells of Alexander the Great's journey of conquest to India, during which he and his men had a great number of unpleasant, often deadly encounters with 'serpents and wild beasts'. One of these occurred just after a number of men had been trampled to death by what would appear to be hippopotamuses, referred to by Alexander as 'water-monsters'. Determined to press on, Alexander rallies his army and goes in search of fresh water. After an arduous journey, they arrive at a lake and pitch camp, light fires and, just before nightfall, set out two thousand golden lanterns, which they believe will help protect them. Not so, for as darkness falls scorpions invade the campsite, followed by 'horned serpents' red, black and white, whereupon 'the whole country resounded with the hissing of the serpents, and we had no little terror of them', says Alexander.

But this is only the start, for as the horned serpents depart, two- and three-headed, scaly, poison-breathed serpents with three-pronged tongues and 'the size of columns . . . some even bigger' come slithering down on their backs from the nearby hillsides, clearly intent on drinking from the lake and heedless of anything in their way. Thirty men of Alexander's army and twenty of his personal retainers are killed in the ensuing chaos. Come daylight, after more attacks from a riot of wild animals later that same night, Alexander orders all his guides, presumably native Indians, to be disciplined for leading them into this perilous territory, just as has previously been his wont on this expedition. By way of punishment on this occasion, they are bound, their legs broken and their hands cut off, 'so that they might be devoured that night by the serpents on their way to the water'. In this respect, at least, one might readily conclude that Alexander was no less of a horror than the monsters that so troubled his invading army.

Nevertheless, the *Letter* was clearly viewed as evidence of the admirable life and deeds of Alexander, a judgement of him that would go on to become part of an establishment doctrine. Reflecting this was the medieval Church's inclusion of Alexander as one of the highly esteemed Nine Worthies, a group that consisted of three Christian, three Jewish and three pagan heroes.[29] It is, then, perhaps a little ironic given Alexander's report on the dragons he encountered in India that in the numerous medieval versions of the *Alexander Romance*, an almost hagiographic biography which was first set down in Greek in the third century AD, Alexander is said to have been sired by a dragon.

This came about when the exiled Egyptian king Nectanebus II, an accomplished magician and astrologer, prophesied to Alexander's mother, Olympias, wife of King Philip II of Macedon, that she will be visited and impregnated by the ancient Egyptian god Amun and will conceive a son. The deceitful Nectanebus then assumes the appearance of a dragon and goes to Olympias to make good his 'prophecy': 'he reared himself up and placed his chin upon her hand, then he flipped his whole body into her lap and kissed her with his forked tongue.'[30]

King Philip, meanwhile, has a dream in which it is foretold that his illegitimate son will grow up to be a conqueror; convinced of Alexander's great destiny, he raises the child as his own. Relations between Alexander and Nectanebus, however, are not so positive and when the still youthful Alexander

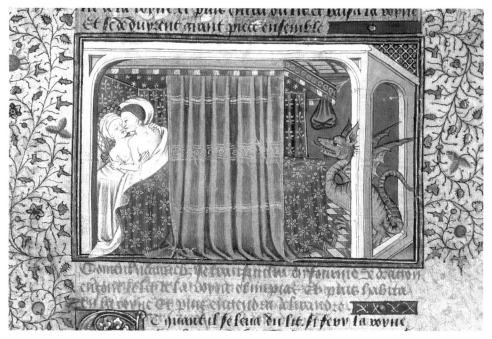

Fifteenth-century illustration of 'A Dragon in the Bedroom: The Conception of Alexander the Great'.

ends up killing Nectanebus by pushing him into a ditch, Nectanebus reveals with his dying words that it is he who is Alexander's real father. Even so, Alexander is unperturbed by his patricide and subsequently presents himself as one of divine descent, irrespective.

While the early Germanic dragon would fade from cultural memory until texts such as *Beowulf* were recovered many centuries later, set together, *The Letter of Alexander to Aristotle* and the *Alexander Romance* would go on to form the basis of an ideal, epitomized by Alexander the Great, about human behaviour that would be endorsed and promoted by secular and religious authorities alike.[31]

WHAT, THEN, CAN be learned from Anglo-Saxon and Old Norse poetry and related texts about attitudes towards dragons? That which is most clear is that the dragons are not always specific in their targeting of humankind; rather, their threat is towards all who have the misfortune to encounter them. Just like the dragon in *Beowulf*, they are universal terrors, which – Alexander the Great's megalomania excepted – are the precise opposite of anything positive, of anything that might enhance or prolong life. While the author of the *Liber monstrorum* took a dim view of all that could not be endorsed by Christian beliefs, some dragon tales could be accommodated as part of God's Creation; in other words, as demonic forces that are best avoided or, if not, confronted, even in the knowledge of the certain death of those who dared to do so. Just as did Beowulf.

Níðhögg apart, which in any case is the doom of all who cross its path, the bitter outcomes for the heroes in their battles with the Midgard Serpent and the nameless dragon in *Beowulf* amount to tragedies, not just for the heroes but for all whom they seek to protect.[32] It does not matter whether the guiding principles are drawn from pagan or Christian beliefs, the message, in the final analysis, is that all earthly triumphs come to nought. When Thor, the supreme warrior hero, steps forward to combat the Midgard Serpent, he does so, we can assume, in the knowledge that this is a battle he cannot win. This final act functions as an example to all to meet their end undaunted, uncompromised by fear or doubt. Despite all, Thor acts in faith.

The same may be said of Beowulf. Here, the poet looks back to a time different from that of his own, to a Heroic Age, and recognizes that the tribulations, uncertainties and inevitable outcomes that his remote pagan ancestors endured are universals throughout all time. In creating the character of Beowulf, he presented a model of stoicism and determination, a figure who is resolute despite the huge odds stacked against him.[33] As heroes, Thor and Beowulf are abstractions of the will to survive. As dragons, the Midgard Serpent and the dragon that proves to be Beowulf's nemesis are abstractions of all that militates against survival. In whatever way we might seek to locate the temporal meaning of these dragons, for instance, in *Beowulf* as greed, their ultimate meaning is death itself. In this regard, Níðhögg is the quintessence.

Arthur Rackham, *Sigurd Slaying Fafnir*, 1911.

*four*

# The Germanic Dragon, Part 2: Sagas of Ancient Times

IN TERMS OF literary output, Iceland was the most productive country in medieval Europe. Hundreds of Icelandic sagas were set down from the twelfth to the fifteenth century, many of which were of substantial length. Among their various subjects are the lives of saints, biographies of mainland Scandinavian kings, realist-style novels about the early settlers, free translations of Greek and Roman epics, and fantastical accounts of the lives and deeds of heroes of the pre-settlement age. Although dragons feature in a number of these saga genres, it is in the last group, the sagas of ancient times (*fornaldarsögur*), that we find dragons in their most potent form.[1]

Without doubt the most interesting and influential of the sagas of ancient times is the thirteenth-century *Völsunga saga* (Saga of the Völsungs), which, like *Beowulf*, features a greedy dragon, cursed gold and superhuman heroics.[2] This saga found its inspiration in old Germanic tales concerning Sigurd the Völsung, or Siegfried as he is otherwise known, and would become the chief inspiration behind Richard Wagner's late nineteenth-century four-opera sequence *Der Ring des Nibelungen*, known collectively as the *Ring Cycle*. Wagner's achievement was lauded by him as his *Gesamt-kunstwerk*, his total artwork, one which Adolf Hitler would perversely endorse as an expression of Nazi ideology.[3] On a somewhat less contentious note, the Völsung legend, alongside that of the hero Beowulf, was also an inspiration for what have proved to be the most influential fantasy fictions of modern times: J.R.R. Tolkien's Middle-earth novels, *The Hobbit* (1937) and *The Lord of the Rings* (1954–5). It is therefore to this saga and its relatives that this chapter will pay closest attention, followed by an examination of other sagas in which dragons assume their typically threatening role.[4]

## Cursed gold and the *Saga of the Völsungs*

The dragon episode in the *Saga of the Völsungs* begins with Odin, Loki and the rather enigmatic god Hœnir exploring the world outside Asgard. They arrive at the waterfall Andvari's Fall, where they see an exceptionally large otter eating a freshly caught salmon. Loki hurls a stone at the otter, killing it outright. The gods then gather up both otter and salmon and go on their way until they come to a farm, where they seek lodgings for the night. The head of the household is Hreidmar, who has three sons and is skilled in magic. The gods show Hreidmar their catch, cheerfully announcing that they have ample provisions for an evening meal. When Hreidmar sees the otter, he summons his sons, Fáfnir and Regin, and tells them that their brother Otter has been killed and that the culprits stand before them. The gods are promptly seized and bound.

By way of recompense, the gods now offer Hreidmar as much wealth as he could want. Hreidmar skins the otter and says that they will need both to fill and cover the skin with gold. Odin sends off Loki to meet Hreidmar's demands. Loki goes straight to the sea goddess Rán and borrows her great fishing net. He then returns to Andvari's Fall, where he casts the net and draws up a pike, which he knows to be the dwarf Andvari in disguise. Also aware of Andvari's particular skills, Loki escorts the dwarf to his cave, where he demands a great ransom in return for his captive's freedom: Andvari must give over all his gold. As the gold is being brought out, Loki notices the dwarf attempting to conceal a gold ring under his arm. Loki demands this too but Andvari pleads with the god to let him keep it, for this is the magic ring Andvari's Gift (*Andvaranaut*) that can create more gold. Unsurprisingly, Loki refuses.

Now stripped of all he owns, Andvari lays a curse on the ring, saying that whosoever comes to own the gold will be doomed. Loki thanks the dwarf for what he regards as helpful information, takes the ring anyway and returns to Hreidmar's farm, where Odin, dazzled by the sight of Andvari's Gift, decides to keep it for himself. The otter's skin is now stuffed with the gold and the gods set about covering it with what remains, just as Hreidmar had demanded. But when they declare the job done, Hreidmar is not satisfied, for one whisker of the otter is still visible. Odin has no choice but to cover it with Andvari's Gift. Set free and about to depart, Loki passes on the ring's deadly curse to Hreidmar.

With the gods now departed, Fáfnir and Regin demand their share of the gold from their father, but when he declines to give them anything, they kill him. Regin then expects to go half shares with his elder brother. But Fáfnir puts on his father's 'helm of terror' (*aegishjálmr*), a magical helmet or mask or perhaps even a rune-like symbol that causes visual deceptions, and without further ado drives Regin from the house, empty-handed. Fáfnir now takes the gold to a nearby heath and constructs a lair where he can guard his fortune. In the passing of time, Fáfnir turns into a dragon.

## Sigurd, Regin and Fáfnir

Regin now finds employment as a smith at a royal household, where he is required to take on the fosterage of a stable boy called Sigurd, an impressive and promising youth. Regin teaches Sigurd many things and soon learns that Sigurd's father was the legendary Völsung king Sigmund, who had been killed in battle by a royal love rival when Sigurd was yet unborn. Regin also learns that the Völsung wealth is in safe keeping with Sigurd's mother, Hjördís, who has remarried and is under the protection of a number of kings still loyal to the Völsungs. Knowing all this, Regin taunts Sigurd about his lack of personal wealth and, conspicuously, a horse. This latter deficiency is soon rectified when Odin intervenes to help Sigurd gain possession of the horse Grani, a descendant of Odin's own extraordinary horse, the eight-legged Sleipnir.

As Sigurd gets older, he increasingly sees avenging the death of his father as his fundamental duty, but Regin has other ideas. Rightly equipped, thinks Regin, Sigurd is just the one who could overcome his transmogrified brother and so provide him personally with the wealth to which he feels he is entitled. It is to this end that he tells Sigurd of the origin of the gold and just where Fáfnir can be found. That he omits to mention his part in the murder of his father is a fair illustration of Regin's deceptive nature.

Persuaded that he should tackle Fáfnir after he has fulfilled his familial duty, Sigurd has Regin forge him a sword, but when Sigurd tests it by striking the anvil, it breaks. The same thing happens when Regin tries a second time. Sigurd now journeys to visit his mother and asks for Gram, his father's smashed sword. His mother is pleased to give him the sword fragments and is convinced that her son will go on to win great renown. Sigurd then passes the sword pieces to Regin and demands that Gram be reforged. Having done so, when Sigurd now strikes the anvil with Gram, it is the anvil that breaks. Sigurd then rides off to raise a great army and succeeds in avenging his father. On his return, he sets out with Regin to confront Fáfnir.

When Sigurd and Regin arrive on the heath where Fáfnir is ensconced, they find a track along which Fáfnir is accustomed to crawl to take a drink of water. On this evidence, Fáfnir is quite clearly a much larger creature than Regin had previously implied. Before running for safety, Regin advises Sigurd to dig a ditch, sit in it and stab the dragon in its heart as it crawls overhead. Sigurd starts to do as much but is interrupted by a bearded old man who tells him it would be better to dig several ditches, so as to contain the torrent of dragon's blood that would surely ensue and, presumably, to prevent Sigurd from drowning in it. The old man, who then departs, is Odin. Sigurd does as advised and soon, amid a terrifying din, the dragon comes crawling along, blowing poison before him. Yet Sigurd is unafraid, and as the dragon passes overhead he plunges Gram up to the hilt into the beast's chest and, blood-soaked, leaps out of the ditch.

Realizing that he has been delivered a death-blow, Fáfnir enquires who it is that has done this to him. As recounted in both the *Saga of the Völsungs* and the Eddic poem *Fáfnismál* (The Lay of Fáfnir),[5] at first, Sigurd dissimulates, for to reveal his true identity could, even still, put him at a disadvantage. But Fáfnir is not fooled, and when he rejects Sigurd's reply as a lie, Sigurd declares his name and lineage. Fáfnir then asks who it was that put him up to such a thing when all others fear his 'helm of terror', in response to which Sigurd simply boasts of his own judgement and courage. While Fáfnir derides Sigurd, he is nonetheless content to supply wise answers to Sigurd's questions about the three female agencies of Fate, the Norns, and the coming of Ragnarök, a clear sign that Fáfnir has access to knowledge that is denied to mere humans. More than this, Fáfnir reveals that he knows that it was Regin who urged Sigurd to kill him and tells Sigurd that Regin will not hesitate to kill him also. Finally, Fáfnir advises Sigurd to depart in haste while he still can. Undaunted, Sigurd declares that he will first gather up the gold from Fáfnir's lair. With his dying words, Fáfnir tells Sigurd of the gold's curse, but Sigurd is undeterred and, having damned Fáfnir to Hel, simply asserts that no man lives forever.

With Fáfnir now dead, Regin emerges from his hiding place to congratulate Sigurd but, somewhat strangely, expresses guilt over his own part in the killing of his brother. This, however, is little more than a means of distracting Sigurd, who has criticized him for his cowardice, and a justification for what he is now about to do to Sigurd. Regin then sets about drinking the dragon's blood, for legend states that to do so will make him invulnerable, and demands that Sigurd cut out and roast its heart for him to eat. This, he says, will be Sigurd's atonement for the slaying.

Sigurd dutifully does what Regin asks, but when he tastes the heart to see whether it is properly cooked, he discovers that he can now understand the speech of birds. It is from the birds that he learns that it would be unwise to leave Regin alive, for just as Fáfnir foresaw, Regin is planning Sigurd's death. So warned, Sigurd draws Gram and slices off Regin's head. With the gold saddled onto the powerful Grani and the 'helm of terror' now in his possession, Sigurd rides away to what turns out to be an even more perilous encounter.[6] Just as the birds had suggested to him, he seeks out a sleeping 'battle maiden', the Valkyrie Brynhild, who was once in service to Odin. It is in this way that Sigurd meets the love of his life and, ultimately, his doom. The curse on Andvari's Gift and, as later becomes apparent, the gold generally will yet again be fulfilled.

## History and legend

Seventeen of the 35 poems in the *Poetic Edda* either touch on matters concerning the Völsung legends or are wholly devoted to them, and it is highly likely that there have been other poems that have not survived. Based on sources we know of and some that we do not, Snorri Sturluson's *Prose Edda* includes a compelling and detailed summary of the Völsung legends. The first part of this is presented as an explanation for why a kenning for 'gold' is 'otter payment'.[7] Besides these sources and the *Saga of the Völsungs* itself, several tales of German origin feature versions of the Sigurd legend, two of which do so extensively.[8]

The most detailed account is provided in the Middle High German epic poem the *Nibelungenlied* (Song of the Nibelungs).[9] Delivered in the grand chivalric style that was typical of medieval Romance tales, the hero, here named as Siegfried, also becomes tragically embroiled with characters that can be identified with those in the Icelandic sources.[10] Yet only brief mention is made of the hero's dragon-slaying. The dramatic importance of this episode in this poem is that, having killed the beast, Siegfried, as is the case with Regin in the *Saga of the Völsungs*, bathes in its blood so that his skin will become impervious to weaponry. The problem is that a fallen leaf has prevented the dragon's blood from touching one small spot on Siegfried's back. Once Siegfried's enemies learn of his 'Achilles heel', his death soon follows. In some senses, Siegfried, covered in scaly skin, possessing super-human powers, great wealth and vulnerable in just one spot, is as much like Fáfnir as he is Sigurd.[11]

In the other source, the thirteenth-century *Thidrek's Saga* (Þiðreks *Saga af Bern*), some aspects of the Sigurd legend are recounted that broadly follow the same trajectory as the *Song of the Nibelungs*.[12] Also written in high style, this saga is perhaps a translation of an earlier Low German tale or perhaps a Norwegian compilation based on numerous German sources. Here, the atmospherics, like those in the *Song of the Nibelungs*, are essentially Christian, and there are also key differences from the Icelandic sources in the telling; for example, it is Regin who is the dragon (or maybe just in disguise as one) that the foundling Sigurd must kill. Either way, this dragon is no Fáfnir, for Sigurd kills it easily by bashing it over the head with a stick, after which he bathes in its blood and then eats it. Having done so, Sigurd, like Siegfried in the *Song of the Nibelungs*, gains scaly skin and, like Sigurd in the *Saga of the Völsungs*, the ability to understand birdsong.

In actuality, the Sigurd legend as told in *Thidrek's Saga* is secondary to the saga's main focus. This is on the life of Dietrich von Bern, the Thidrek of the saga's title, whose adventures would appear to have originated in legends concerning Theodoric the Great, an Ostrogoth king who established a kingdom in Italy in the late fifth and sixth centuries. Thidrek kills two dragons during his career. The first is in company with another hero when they rescue a man from a flying dragon's maw. The second is when he is captured by a dragon that has killed a local king. In this episode, Thidrek's captivity is not long-lasting, for not unlike Beowulf in the fight against Grendel's mother, Thidrek is fortunate enough to find a sword in the dragon's lair with which he kills both it and its progeny. One consequence of this second dragon-slaying is that Thidrek marries the king's widow, so becoming a king himself. That Thidrek is able to breathe fire on one occasion again suggests a blurring of lines between the hero's powers and that of his dragon adversaries.

By contrast, the pithy *Saga of the Völsungs*, although steeped in pagan mythology, is set in a world that is rather more commonplace than that of the courtly refinements of the *Song of the Nibelungs* and *Thidrek's Saga*. These stylistic differences indicate something of the complexity of the processes involved in the differing Scandinavian and German strands of the legend's evolution in pagan and, later, Christian Europe. Nevertheless, there are real historical contexts for all these sources dating back to the European migration period during the fourth and fifth centuries AD and to the territorial strife that continued into the sixth century. This was a turbulent time when the northern borders of the Roman Empire collapsed under pressure from German tribes streaming southward and westward. During the same period, nomadic Eurasian warriors, under the leadership of Attila the Hun, displaced the Ostrogothic tribes from their Black Sea empire and surged westward into the same regions as the Germans in search of plunder and conquest.[13]

Much of the setting for the Sigurd/Siegfried legend is German-occupied fifth-century Burgundy (not to be confused with modern-day Burgundy in France), which places it precisely at the point where tribal conflicts would have been most great, that is to say, on the northwestern banks of the Rhine. While actual historical figures can be identified, such as Attila the Hun, or Etzel as he is called in the *Song of the Nibelungs* and Atli in the *Saga of the Völsungs*, chronological and geographical anomalies prevent us from reading the legends with any historical precision. Nonetheless, among a number of suggestions, one tempting possibility for a prototype Sigurd/Siegfried is the sixth-century Merovingian king Sigebert (r. AD 561–75), whose territories included the Kingdom of Burgundy. Sigebert had a wife named Brunhilda, and he himself had a troublesome family, which led to his murder, over which Brunhilda is said to have taken bloody revenge. Although this is not quite how it is in medieval Icelandic sources, it is tantalizingly close in terms of names and family conflicts.[14]

## The roles of Odin and the Rhinegold

While the legend's historicity is a tangled web of possibilities, one question about which answers can be framed concerns the dragon and the cursed gold episode as it is fully recounted in the *Saga of the Völsungs*. Before doing so, we first need to examine Odin's role in both the saga and the wider mythology, as here is the essence of the saga's tragedy.

It will be remembered that it was Odin who helped Sigurd to obtain his horse Grani and that when Sigurd is digging a ditch in the track leading to Fáfnir's waterhole, Odin again makes an appearance and gives him advice. Yet these are not the only interventions in the saga by Odin, for Odin is present from the saga's outset when he guides the outlaw Sigi, who is said to be his own son, out of the land towards great wealth and power. Shortly before Sigi is overthrown and killed in an insurrection, he has a son, Rerir, who also becomes pre-eminently powerful. Rerir's problem, however, is that he and his wife cannot conceive an heir. In order to do so, they pray to Odin's wife, Frigg, to help them. In answer, Frigg has Odin send a 'wish maiden' with an apple of fertility, which leads to Rerir's wife falling pregnant. But Rerir becomes ill and dies before his child is born, and after a six-year pregnancy his wife insists that the child be cut from her, knowing that this will cause her death. The child, Völsung, is the male heir his parents had long wanted. Once grown up and thanks to more divine interventions, Völsung marries the self-same wish maiden that Odin had sent to help Rerir and his wife. The line duly proliferates.

At the centre of King Völsung's great hall is the huge tree Barnstokkr (Barnstock). One day, a one-eyed stranger turns up and thrusts a great sword up to the hilt into it, declaring that whosoever can draw it out will never receive a finer gift from him. This, again, is Odin, and the sword is Gram, the weapon that Sigurd will later have reforged in order to avenge his father and afterwards overcome Fáfnir. Reminiscent of the way in which King Arthur obtained Excalibur, the only person capable of drawing Gram is Völsung's eldest son, Sigmund, Sigurd's father.

Not long after, Völsung dies in a battle against a king who has married his daughter and is jealous of Sigmund's retrieval of Gram. It takes many trials and tribulations before Sigmund can reclaim his birthright, but having done so, he eventually marries the princess Hjördís, his first marriage having been calamitous. Hjördís soon conceives, but before she gives birth to Sigurd, Sigmund is ambushed and killed. The decisive moment in Sigmund's last stand is when a spear-wielding one-eyed stranger enters the fray and appears to side with the opposition. When Sigmund attempts to disarm him, Gram is smashed to pieces. With his dying words, Sigmund tells his wife that this stranger was Odin, for he, Sigmund, is no longer of any earthly use to the god.

It is noticeable that many of Sigurd's ancestors come to a typically bloody end not long after their wives have either conceived or just given birth. The exception is Völsung, but in his case, his death follows shortly after Odin has ensured that his son, Sigmund, has drawn Gram out of Barnstokkr. Odin's interventions clearly involve ensuring that the Völsung line continues, and as concerns this objective, it would appear that Odin is set on what might be called a programme of genetic engineering in order to produce the ultimate warrior. The culmination of Odin's interventions in five generations of Völsungs is in the birth of Sigurd, and in this, his personal mission would at first appear to have been fulfilled.

Odin has many talents, ranging from his deep wisdom to his mastery of poetry, but all these are in service to a much grander purpose: the gathering together of that great army of human heroes in Valhalla that he needs as part of his preparations for Ragnarök. But the victory Odin strives for at Ragnarök does not come about, for, as noted in the previous chapter, this ultimate battle results in mutual destruction, including Odin's own death. The Völsung genetic engineering programme, then, is part of Odin's great plan. But Odin's success in this project is debatable, not least when the ultimate fate of Sigurd is taken into account.

As alluded to earlier, after Sigurd has killed Fáfnir and seized the cursed gold, he sets out to find the Valkyrie Brynhild, whom he finds sleeping deeply and bound tight in armour. It is the function of Valkyries to follow Odin's bidding in ensuring that the great warriors he wants for Ragnarök are slain in battle and then transported to Valhalla. But in this particular duty Brynhild has betrayed her master by, contrary to his instructions, allowing one particular warrior to triumph in battle rather than be killed. As punishment, Odin curses her, pricks her with a 'sleeping thorn' and casts her out of Valhalla.

If this were not bad enough, not long after Sigurd meets her and cuts her free from her armour, he gives her Andvari's Gift as a love token. She is thus doubly cursed, and, as we already know, Sigurd's possession of Fáfnir's gold will eventually precipitate his doom, which for him is to be murdered in his bed. This comes about at the bidding of the lovelorn and embittered Brynhild, for Sigurd was tricked into drinking an 'ale of forgetfulness' by the mother of the woman he then marries, Princess Gudrún. As testimony to his love for Gudrún, Sigurd gives her some of Fáfnir's heart to eat, so making her 'much grimmer and wiser than before'.[15] These newfound qualities will quickly become essential, one major reason being that Sigurd retrieves Andvari's Gift from Brynhild and gives it to Gudrún, after which she too is cursed.

It is widely said elsewhere in Old Norse sources that, in order for a warrior to get to Valhalla, he must die in battle, preferably with sword in hand, just as it came about with Sigurd's father, Sigmund. Although the *Saga of the Völsungs* tells how Sigurd, before dying in the arms of Gudrún, manages to hurl his sword at his murderous assailant and kill him, nowhere in any source does it state that he then gets to Valhalla.[16] Given this somewhat ignominious death of the ultimate warrior, the only afterlife Sigurd can know is in Hel, that frozen underworld from which escape is impossible. Supporting this probability are two poems in the *Poetic Edda*, 'Helreið Brynhildar' (Brynhild's Ride to Hel) and the 'Guðrúnarhvöt' (The Whetting of Gudrún), both of which may have been composed in Iceland based on earlier oral traditions.[17]

In 'Brynhild's Ride to Hel', Brynhild, now dead, reflects on the tragedy of her life and expresses her determination to travel to Hel to be reunited with Sigurd. In 'The Whetting of Gudrun', it is Sigurd's wife, Gudrún, who reflects on her many personal tragedies and recalls that Sigurd, whose future had been foretold to him, had promised to visit her from Hel after his death. It is also said in the *Saga of the Völsungs* that Brynhild's last living act is to order the killing of Sigurd's three-year-old son by Gudrún.[18] This being so, there is no male heir to continue the Völsung line, in which case a major consequence of Sigurd's death is to bring about the exhaustion of Odin's investment, seemingly without any future return on it. It is also notable that the ultimate fate of the gold in the saga is to be submerged forever in the river Rhine where it runs through old Burgundy, that very place in early European history where for centuries warring tribes had striven for supremacy.

It is, then, tempting to interpret the cursed gold as a symbol of the Rhine itself, for folk memories of ancient times, like those recorded in the *Saga of the Völsungs*, recalled that no one could ultimately take possession of, and keep, those western lands through which it flowed. Indeed, in the saga it is only owing to Gudrún's brothers' heroic refusal to give in to their captor's, King Atli's, torture that it is in the Rhine that the gold ends up with no living person knowing exactly where. The underlying principle here would seem to be that just as it is concerning the doom of the gods, so it is for the doom of mankind.

It is with regard to this ubiquitous ill fate that the figure of Fáfnir can be understood. Just like the dragon in *Beowulf*, Fáfnir is the dark side of humanity's struggle to survive, when self-interest takes priority over tribal loyalty and collective survival. This will always be so, for dragon tendencies are part of humanity's very nature. Moreover, when romantic psycho-dramas are added to the equation, no amount of intervention by Odin can change things. That Odin has limitations is central to the saga's message,

Detail of the Ramsund Stone showing Sigurd impaling Fáfnir.

Drawing of the Ramsund Stone.

inasmuch as those he seeks to manipulate are ultimately unbiddable. 'Gæð a wyrd swa hio scel!', 'Fate goes always as it will!',[19] as Beowulf says: cursed gold and the heedless greed for it are signifiers of this inevitability.

The sources the author drew on and crafted into saga form had evidently become common European literary currency in the ninth and tenth centuries, owing largely to the Vikings, who carried their stories with them aboard their dragon-prowed longships during their impressively expansive travels. Testimony to Viking enthusiasm for the Sigurd and Fáfnir tale is to be found on church staves, baptismal fonts and rune stones, both in their homelands and elsewhere where they made their presence felt. The Church's tolerance of this pagan iconography was simply to do with the fact that dragons, according to Christian lights, were associated with Satan, while dragon-slayers were associated either with saints or with heroes who have divine sanction.[20]

One of the most remarkable of these depictions is the Swedish Ramsund stone, which is dated to the year 1030. Carved on this flat rock is Sigurd roasting Fáfnir's heart, the birds that warn him of his accomplice's duplicity, Grani tethered to a tree, and the headless Regin. All these images are encircled by a great serpent impaled from below on Sigurd's sword. Perhaps identifying with the tragic nature of the legend, the creator of this carving left this commemoration in runic script on Fáfnir's body: 'Sigrid, Alrik's mother, Orm's daughter, made this bridge for the soul of Holmgeir, father of Sigrod, her husband.'[21]

## Gold-Thórir

The corrupting power of gold that can turn its owner into a dragon, as it did to Fáfnir, is told of in a number of Icelandic sagas. One example in which the dragon motif is central to the plot is the *Gull-Þóris saga*, the *Saga of Gold-Thórir* (also known as *Þorskfirðinga saga*).[22] The saga's main character, the Icelander Thórir, later known as Gold-Thórir, has journeyed with his nine blood brothers to Norway, where they are scraping a living fishing for cod. One evening, Thórir sees a strange fire glowing on a nearby mountainside. Enquiring as to what this might be, he is told that it is a cairn fire and that guarding it is the troll Agnarr, whose treasure is stored beneath the cairn. Despite dire warnings to keep well away, Thórir and his companion, Ketilbjörn, decide to break into the cairn and take the treasure. To their way of thinking, the risk involved would be worth it if they could then give up their dull lives as fishermen.

Their adventure does not start well, for as they scale the mountain, a great tempest throws them back down the slope. Unable even to stand and wearied by their efforts, they eventually fall asleep. Thórir dreams that Agnarr comes to him and, having chastised him for his intended robbery, reveals that he is Thórir's uncle. Given this family tie, Agnarr offers to help Thórir, providing he seeks out a different treasure hoard. Should Thórir agree to this, Agnarr will equip him with fine weaponry, a fire-proof tunic and gloves with healing powers. After some argument over Agnarr's own treasure, they finally come to an agreement, whereupon Agnarr tells Thórir the tale of the treasure he is now to seek out:

> There was a Viking named Valr, who owned much gold; he carried the treasure into a certain cave in the north, near Dumbshaf, and laid himself down on it and [so did] his sons with him, and all of them turned into flying dragons. They have helmets on their heads, and swords under their wing-pits.[23]

Agnarr then gives Thórir a goblet of potion, telling him that he should take two draughts from it and Ketilbjörn just one, but that under no circumstance should they drink more than this. Thórir now awakes to find Agnarr's gifts beside him, including the potion; however, having drunk from it as instructed, Thórir then drains the goblet. Once more, sleep falls upon them and Agnarr again appears in Thórir's dreams. After telling Thórir that he will come to regret having taken a third draught of the potion, Agnarr advises him how best he might overcome Valr and his sons.

Thórir and his companions now journey to Valr's cave, which lies deep in a mountain across a great ravine. At first, only Thórir is prepared to make the hazardous crossing of the ravine but eventually his determination persuades several of the others to join him. On successfully reaching the cave they find themselves in pitch darkness and unable to proceed any further. Thórir calls upon Agnarr to aid them, at which point a powerful shaft of light reveals the cave's depths, from which they can now hear the hissing of dragons. As they approach the dragons' lair, the light shaft hits the dragons, knocking them out. Seizing the moment, Thórir and his men launch their attack, stabbing all the dragons under their wings. But when Thórir seizes a great helmet from the largest of these comatose beasts, it awakens, grabs one of his men in its teeth and, followed by the other dragons, flies out of the cave, spouting fire. While those outside the cave are being attacked by the dragons, Thórir and company gather up the treasure hoard and manage safely to transport it and themselves back across the ravine. Then, having healed the wounded survivors with Agnarr's gloves, they set off home with their booty, most of which Thórir keeps for himself, an act of selfishness that does not find favour with all of his accomplices.

Back in the Þorskafjörðr district of northwest Iceland and now a man of phenomenal wealth, Thórir goes on to establish himself as a powerful landowner and, through various treacherous and typically murderous means, acquires even greater wealth. Yet Thórir is not content, and his greed, malice and petty-minded dealings with his neighbours leads to much conflict and to him being widely feared and considered dishonourable. Thórir's vindictiveness, we can assume, has come about partly owing to his drinking too much of Agnarr's potion, and partly owing to the socially divisive effect of the gold. In the end, when one of Thórir's sons dies in battle, he mysteriously disappears, after which there are reports of a dragon seen flying down the mountains towards a certain waterfall, which later comes to be known as Gullfoss (Golden Falls). Those in the locality conclude that this is the transformed Thórir and that somewhere beneath the falls he lies in miserly solitude on his treasure hoard.[24]

While the *Saga of Gold-Thórir* is not explicit in saying that the gold taken from Valr's cave carried a curse, the message would nevertheless seem to be that great wealth can be the cause of great damage. For those who come to possess such material power, this damage is not only presented in terms of moral failings but in terms of the manifestation of these failings in dragon form. Indeed, this saga is quite unusual in two senses: first, in that dragons frame the narrative, so establishing a contrast between the fantastical and the familiar; and second, in its focus on the disturbing personality changes of its central character.[25]

Unlike Fáfnir, about whom we know nothing before he gained the gold except that he killed his father to get it, Thórir is at first presented as a natural leader who is 'in all accomplishments . . . far ahead of his contemporaries in age'.[26] Although the effect of the gold on Thórir is noticed by his companions, even before he gets his hands on it – 'They found that Þórir [Thórir] was altogether a different person from what he had been' – his transmogrification takes a lifetime.[27] So it is that the story of Thórir's life is played out against a backdrop of those real-life community disputes that are so familiar in sagas where matters of a supernatural nature have little, if any, bearing on the plot. In this respect, the *Saga of Gold-Thórir* could well be read as commentary on what was famously summed up by Lord Acton as 'Power tends to corrupt, and absolute power corrupts absolutely.'

The saga's dragon episodes have also been compared in structural terms to the monster fights in *Beowulf*. Known as the 'Bear's Son' folktale structure, this is most apparent in respect of Beowulf's descent into the lake to fight Grendel's mother, the manner of him doing so being not unlike Thórir's descent in Valr's cave.[28] Yet while Beowulf, who lives and dies uncorrupted and incorruptible, is quite clearly no Thórir, the poem's rather strange account of that sole survivor, whose last act is to hide his tribe's treasure on the heath, does suggest a possible analogy with Thórir. In this case, it is tempting to think that the arrival of the dragon shortly after the death of this sole survivor is none other than himself, now transformed.[29] However, the key difference here lies in the gradual degeneration of Thórir's once admirable character back in Iceland, where 'He became unpleasant and difficult to deal with, all the more so the older he grew.'[30]

Thórir's negative impact on those who are forced to have dealings with him, and so the community at large, are in effect the whole point of the saga's plot after the Valr's cave episode. As an incipient dragon, Thórir bears all the hallmarks of one long before he disappears and is then said to have metamorphosed. The dragons in the *Saga of Gold-Thórir*, then, are not only symbols of the avaricious and powerful, such as the tyrannical King Heremod in *Beowulf*, but, in the personage of the draconic Thórir, of the dystopia that follows in their wake.[31]

## Ragnar Lodbrók and the lindworm

The thirteenth-century *Ragnars saga Loðbrókar* (Saga of Ragnar Lodbrók) appears to have been written as a sequel to the *Saga of the Völsungs*, quite possibly by the same author.[32] In this saga, the hero, Ragnar, takes as his third and last wife the orphan Aslaug, also known as 'Kráka' (Crow), who in the *Saga of the Völsungs* is the child born to Brynhild from her brief affair with Sigurd. It is not, however, in relation to his marriage to Aslaug that Ragnar assumes the role of dragon-slayer but to that of his second wife, Thora, the daughter of a Swedish earl.

Not far from his royal residence, Thora's father has built an enclosed bower for his beloved daughter. It is the earl's custom to send daily a present to Thora. One day, he sends her a little snake, which she places in a chest with a lining of gold for it to lie on. Soon, the snake begins to grow and take the form of a lindworm, a two-legged dragon-snake, and at the same time, the gold mysteriously begins to increase. Eventually, the dragon has grown so large that the chest cannot contain it, and in the passage of time it cannot even be contained in the bower and must lie outside, encircling it. Only the servant who feeds it an ox for every meal dares go near the creature. Deeply perturbed by the danger his daughter is now in, the earl promises the hand of Thora and all the dragon's gold to anyone who can kill it. No one is eager to attempt such a thing.

It is summer and the young Ragnar and his Viking crewmates set anchor in a creek not far from the bower. It is Ragnar's practice to customize his own clothes, which include a cape boiled in pitch and shaggy trousers. As a consequence, Ragnar is ultimately given the nickname Lodbrók, meaning 'hairy breeches'. Thus attired, Ragnar comes ashore alone before dawn, rolls his pitch cape in the sand and walks to where the lindworm lies coiled. He strikes the beast twice with his spear and succeeds in delivering it a death blow, but as he turns to depart, a jet of the lindworm's blood strikes him between the shoulders; thanks to his protective clothing, however, Ragnar is unscathed. Woken by the din of the lindworm's shrieks, Thora hastens to the bower door, hails Ragnar and asks who he is. Ragnar replies with a rather cryptic verse in which he boasts of his dragon-slaying, and goes on his way without further comment. Come daylight, all are amazed to find the lindworm dead with the point of Ragnar's spear still embedded in its flesh. It is no easy task to dispose of its body.

The earl, puzzled as to who it was that had performed a deed that no other dared take on, compels all his subjects to attend a great assembly, a *thing*, in an attempt to get to the truth of the matter. The day of the *thing* arrives and Ragnar shows up in company with his crewmates. When the earl calls for anyone who might be able to prove ownership of the spearhead to step forward, Ragnar proudly does so with the spear's shaft in his hand. The gold and the hand of the grateful Thora are now given to him. Sadly for Ragnar, after a few years of happy marriage, Thora dies and he, grief-stricken, resumes his Viking life.

The manner of Ragnar's eventual death is darkly ironic, for he is captured in Northumbria in northern England and thrown swordless into the King of York's snake pit. Stoical to the end and confident that he will be taken up to Valhalla, Ragnar shows no pain and, according to the twelfth-century poem 'Krákumál' (The Death Song of Ragnar Lodbrók), he boasts of his many deeds, including his slaying of the lindworm, which he refers to with the kennings 'ground-wolf', 'heather-eel' and 'earth-coil'.

> We hewed with our swords.
> It was so long ago,

Hugo Hamilton, *The Death of Ragnar Lodbrok*, 1830, etching.

when we went to Gautland
for the killing of the ground-wolf.
There we won fair Thora,
after which, when I had laid
that heather-eel down,
people called me Lodbrók,
for I slew the earth-coil
with inlaid bright steel.[33]

The epitome of Viking manly fortitude, Ragnar's dying words are 'Laughing shall I die.' It is Ragnar's nonetheless humiliating end, says the saga, that prompts Ragnar's four sons by Aslaug to invade England and establish their kingdom at York.[34] Here legend merges into history, for three of the Viking leaders mentioned in contemporary or near-contemporary historical sources as the conquerors of York in AD 866 bore the same names as Ragnar's sons in the saga, although this would have been well known to a saga fabulist of the thirteenth century. As for all else told of the life and times of Ragnar in his saga, it is matter of continuing debate as to whether it has any bearing on historical truth.[35]

The most obvious and immediate inspiration for Ragnar's obviously fictional dragon-slaying are older written versions that appear in various other Scandinavian sources. For example, in the late twelfth- to early thirteenth-century *Gesta Danorum* (History of the Danes) composed by the Christian cleric Saxo Grammaticus, two tales are told that parallel the saga's account of events leading to Ragnar and Thora's betrothal. In one, the hero, Alf, also drapes himself in protective clothing before going on successfully to contend with two giant snakes that were originally given to the young Alvid by her overprotective father.[36] In the other, it is the hero, known here as Regner, who kills a bear and a hound in order to win the hand of the maiden Lathgertha.[37] But this marriage does not last, and Regner goes in pursuit of Thora, whom he wins in exactly the same way as is told in the saga, except that in Saxo's account he must first kill two great snakes, just as is described in the tale of Alf and Alvid.[38]

Yet it may not have been only Saxo's tales that prompted the saga author to introduce a dragon. One Icelandic folktale, 'The Water-snake of Lagarfljót', which was first recorded in 1345 but is almost certainly far older, tells how a girl with an increasingly large and threatening dragon-snake manages to cast both it and the gold-lined box she keeps it in into a deep river, where it is said to remain to this day.[39] Nor can we discount the possibility that Greek myths had migrated north, particularly in this case that of Perseus and Andromeda, for this myth has a plot structure in common with the Germanic tales, not least in what may be termed the dragon–girl–slayer 'love triangle'.

## Frothi and Bödvar Bjarki

In the tale of Frothi (Fródi), which is also contained in Saxo's *Gesta Danorum*, it is not an amorous motive but, quite explicitly, an economic one that drives the hero to seek out a dragon in its lair.[40] Frothi has inherited his father's kingdom but is alarmed to discover that his father's numerous wars have depleted the royal coffers to such an extent that he cannot now afford to pay his soldiers. The kingdom is therefore dangerously exposed. One day, Frothi is fascinated to hear an approaching fellow countryman singing a song about a local dragon, seemingly for Frothi's personal benefit. It is in this way that Frothi learns that the dragon lives on a nearby island and guards a vast treasure. But, says the songster, it is huge, with coiled serpentine features, scaly skin, spiked fangs and a triple tongue that projects deadly acidic venom. Even so, he goes on, there is a way of dealing with it, for at the lower reaches of its belly there is a soft spot and it is here that any attack should be directed. In preparation for an encounter with this dragon, a man would need to stretch bull-hide over his shield and cover himself with oxhide. Frothi, who does not need telling twice, prepares just as advised and goes off alone to confront it.

The dragon is returning from its waterhole when Frothi makes his first attack, but at first his sword proves inadequate. His second attack with javelins is no more successful, but when he then aims his sword at the dragon's belly, he hits the mark. Despite the dragon's attempt to bite him, both he and his shield remain unharmed. After the dragon 'gasps away its life and poison at the same time', Frothi gathers up the treasure and returns to his main task of equipping his army for war, an undertaking that now has no financial impediment.

The similarities between Frothi's heroics and Sigurd's slaying of Fáfnir are striking and are doubtless the result of hundreds of years of legends mingling and giving rise to new variants. The same is true, if not more so, of the dragon-slaying episode involving the bear-begotten warrior Bödvar Bjarki, as told in the early thirteenth-century Icelandic *Hrólfs saga kraka* (Saga of Hrólf the Pole-ladder).[41] This saga focuses on the life of the legendary sixth-century Danish king Hrólf Kraki (Kraki meaning 'pole-ladder'), whose rule is perhaps the most celebrated of any in early Germanic literature and who in *Beowulf* is named as a nephew of King Hrothgar. It is also possible that Bödvar Bjarki is himself a version of Beowulf, whose name can translated as 'Bee-wolf' or 'Bee-hunter', a kenning for 'bear'. Yet unlike in the *Beowulf* poem and the *Saga of the Völsungs*, the monster-slaying here contributes little to the story's main action other than to exemplify Bödvar's courage and ursine strength.

It is midwinter, and the king's men have become uncharacteristically gloomy. The newly arrived Bödvar asks one of them, Hott, a man with a reputation for timidity, why this is so. Hott explains that for two winters a terrible winged dragon has laid waste to the land and devoured their cattle stock. Under direct order from King Hrólf, no man is allowed to risk his life confronting this monster. But Bödvar thinks otherwise, and that night he forces the terrified Hott to go with him to seek out the ravager. They soon find it, and while Hott is paralysed with fear, Bödvar steps forward, only to discover that he is, at first, unable draw his sword. When he is finally able to free it from its scabbard, it takes but one mighty lunge to kill the dragon. Bödvar now picks up the quaking Hott and carries him to see the creature's dead body. Not only this, but Bödvar makes Hott swallow two mouthfuls of the dragon blood and eat some of its heart. He then challenges Hott to a fight and is pleased to see that Hott has become as courageous as any. They now prop up the dragon to make it appear that it still lives and return home.

The following day, King Hrólf asks if there is any news of the dragon's whereabouts. A watchman reconnoitres and reports that it is alive and heading right for them. The king's men arm themselves and go to head it off, but when the king places himself before it he can see no movement. Hott then volunteers to strike it dead, as long as the king lends him his prized sword. Astonished at Hott's changed manner, the king readily consents. Hott walks up to the dragon and swipes it with the sword, whereupon it falls over. Hott is renamed Hilt in honour of his newfound daring.

Apart from the saga's *Beowulf* connections, including that of a dragon that ravages the land, this dragon-slaying digression is most obviously similar to the Sigurd and Fáfnir fight in the *Saga of the Völsungs*. Indeed, Bödvar and Hott as Sigurd and Regin looks very like a parody of the killing of Fáfnir, one that concludes with an absurd happy ending whereby a one-time coward proves his mettle by striking down an already dead dragon. On this occasion, any significance that could be ascribed to the dragon-slaying may amount to little more than that the saga's author, who was quite clearly drawing on long-established dragon-slaying tradition, chose to have a bit of fun with it.

ONE IMMEDIATE POINT about dragons in early Germanic sources is their diversity of appearances and abilities. We have them as serpentine or reptilian, crawling or flying, fire breathing and/or venom projecting, and talking eloquently or roaring dumbly. They also have a diverse range of primary functions: guarding treasure hoards, which the hero then acquires to his advantage or, as with Sigurd, Beowulf and Gold-Thórir, to the disadvantage of both themselves and others; imprisoning virgin girls, whom the hero then sets free and, just as importantly, proves both his manhood and entitlement to her; and, in the case of Bödvar and Hott, a dragon that serves no other purpose than to entertain. In identifying the roles and functions of a dragon, we also identify those of the hero, inasmuch as dragons are most clearly the social threats that a great champion must seek to overcome.

This said, some Old Northern dragons transcend the merely social and act as commentaries on the very nature of being. While commentaries like these may not be celebrations of great prospects for the future, they teach a lesson. It is when human life is at its most abject or perilous that some individuals show whether they can maintain some dignity and resolve. Those who do are heroes, and the legends that remember their deeds confer on them immortality. As one Eddic poem says, 'that which will never die is the good reputation one wins to oneself.'[42] This issue of reputation is in fact central to our understanding of the early Germanic hero and is worth further consideration.

The most obvious feature of a reputation culture, or what might otherwise be called a shame culture, is the distinction between this and a guilt culture. In the former, typically a non-literate society, what matters most is how others judge you; in the latter, typically a literate society, what commonly matters most is the judgement of an all-powerful being, for example, the Judaeo-Christian God. As the neuropsychologist A. R. Luria reported after interviewing non-literate peoples in Central Asia in the 1930s, when he asked them 'How would you describe yourself?' a typical answer was, 'Ask others; they can tell you about me.'[43] To put it simply, in a reputation culture, who you are is no more and no less than what others think of you. For heroes such as Beowulf, then, there could be no turning back, no avoiding the monsters, for as Wiglaf says after Beowulf's death, 'Deað bið sella earla gehwylcum þonne edwitlif!' (Death is better to any earl than a disgraced life!).[44]

Nevertheless, the social positives of a reputation culture are deeply intertwined with troubling negatives. It has been widely noted that the Germanic dragon often appears to have a lot in common with the undead

(Old Norse *draugr*). This association has been identified in terms of harrowing behaviours, arcane wisdom and remote barrows, typically located either in chthonic regions or 'set on [a] high headland looking out to sea . . . a favourite spot in particular for the graves of those who are thought likely to be restless after death'.[45] Likewise, as concerns dragon-slayers, there is sometimes what has been seen as a 'life to death and back again' cycle.[46]

This cycle is particularly evident in Sigurd's overcoming of Fáfnir, when, having stabbed Fáfnir from below, he is drenched in dragon blood, much like a newborn child emerging from its mother's womb. After this, the as it were 'reborn' Sigurd assumes the dragon's power, most obviously, in a negative sense, in his taking of the cursed gold. Further reinforcing this idea, to some extent at least, is that Fáfnir's 'helm of terror' and the helmets worn by the dragons that Gold-Thórir tackles in Valr's cave could be understood as a form of nihilistic weaponry. For those challenged with this weaponry, there is not only a fear of death but, more than this, 'a terror of non-Being – of dissolution or of remaining trapped in the liminal, dragonish place on the threshold of identity'.[47] That Sigurd and Gold-Thórir are both prepared to confront this prospective sense of nothingness and thereafter take with them the dragon headgear, is a measure of their ability, either for good or ill, to tread that line between the living and the dead. One implication of this theory is that combat with a dragon is performed outside any conventional understanding of time and space.

No matter which way we look at it, the association of dragons with death is fundamental, and, one might add, obvious, for death and destruction are their meat and drink. The Germanic dragon is a code which, when unravelled, is a statement about life's iniquities and fragilities and, by association, about what personal qualities are required to combat these problems, even if these qualities achieve little more than to set an example to others.

The battle of the Red and White Dragons with the hooded Merlin explaining their significance to King Vortigern: 15th-century miniature from a manuscript of the St Albans Chronicle.

*five*

# Dragons in Bestiaries and Celtic Mythology

B Y THE TIME of the European Middle Ages, Christian and classical ideas about dragons had more or less coalesced to create a dragon tradition, an evolution of ideas about their forms and meanings that were set down in numerous bestiaries comprising scholarly commentaries on exotic creatures.[1] As the hugely influential, anonymous twelfth-century bestiary *The Book of Beasts* shows, the medieval Christian view of dragons was typically moralizing and didactic.[2] Based on the equally moralizing *Physiologus*, a bestiary set down in Greek at some point between the second and fourth centuries AD, and its many successors down through the ages, *The Book of Beasts* contains some 150 entries. As this is almost three times as many as in *Physiologus*, it is a fair indication of the continuing and growing enthusiasm for nature's wonders.[3]

Noting the entry in *Physiologus*, *The Book of Beasts* contrasts the 'Dragon' with the 'Panther', for whom the dragon is 'the only animal which it considers as an enemy'. The panther, we are told, symbolizes 'Our Lord Jesus Christ', who after being crucified descended to Hell, 'there binding the Great Dragon', in other words, Satan. Thus, when the panther emits the 'sweet smell' of its 'belch', the dragon 'flees into the caves of the earth, being smitten with fear', where it 'remains motionless, as if dead'. Similarly, a small elephant, referred to as 'a very Insignificant Elephant', is uniquely capable of raising up much larger elephants that have been trapped by hunters, for this creature is immune to all evil. Like the panther, the 'Insignificant Elephant' denotes Christ, as well as, in its case, the Good Samaritan, whose selfless actions in coming to the aid of an injured man in dangerous territory are described by Christ as exemplifying the virtue of loving one's neighbour. This, says the bestiary's author, is comparable to Adam and Eve's redemption from the subversion of the Eden dragon-snake by Christ's resurrection.[4]

Focussing specifically on Draco the Dragon, 'the biggest . . . of all living things on earth' and which is 'bred in Ethiopia and India, in places where there is perpetual heat', we are told that its strength lies in its tail rather than in its teeth and that 'it inflicts injury by blows rather than by stinging', so making it 'harmless as regards poison'. Drawing on the same theological conventions as the previous entries, Draco the Dragon is here again equated with Satan, who 'is said to have a crest or crown because he is the King of Pride', stating that anybody who is 'ensnared by the toils of crime he dies, and no doubt he goes to Hell'.[5]

Much more in a similar vein is told in respect of several other entries that concern dragons or other creatures traditionally associated with them, such as crocodiles, whales and the mythic basilisk, all of which carry demonic and/or fatal consequences. However, the entry for 'Viper', a creature typically associated with dragons in the Bible, is particularly curious. Unborn vipers, it is said, gnaw through their mother's side and 'burst out to her destruction'. Moreover, the male viper 'puts his head into the female's mouth and spits semen into it', whereupon the female 'bites off his head when he tries to take it out again', the net result being that both parents perish in one way or the other during the reproductive process.

Explaining all this with some perplexity is an analogy with 'the habits of married couples'. The husband, we are told, 'may be uncouth, disorderly, slippery and tipsy' but all the same the wife does not shun him when he demands coitus, as apparently she should, but instead '*She* embraces the slipperiness of the serpent'. This, concludes the author, is like 'the lady-snake who bites off his head' and is the same wickedness as that exhibited by Eve when she tempted Adam with the fruit of the tree of knowledge. Actions such as these by the female are a justification for the man to 'take the leadership, for fear that he should once again be ruined by feminine whims'. There then follows a lengthy sermon about female deceptions and the dangers they pose to male decency. While exactly how these conclusions were reached from the behaviour of vipers is, to say the least, baffling, it nonetheless reflects the insecurities of the patriarchy and a prejudicial view of women that dates back to the Book of Genesis and in all likelihood to subsequent rabbinical commentaries that judged Adam's first wife to have been the demonic dragon-woman Lilith.[6]

The most obvious feature of the medieval bestiary is its establishment orthodoxy. In these, the dragon was considered not only as a threat to mankind but as an allegory for all the evils in the world, as perceived from a Christian perspective. The dragon, it was implied, is the embodiment of

Bern Physiologus, *Dragon and Panther*, 9th century.

everything contrary to divine law and therefore a real and present danger to all that gives stability to human society.

## Celtic dragons: Irish

While dogmatic Christian conclusions about dragons, like those found in bestiaries, clearly established their identities and significances, medieval high culture representations of them were also influenced by indigenous traditions, notably Celtic myth and legend. The two main strands of this mythology are those found in the Gaelic languages, chiefly in Irish and Scottish sources, and those found in the Brittonic languages, chiefly in Welsh and Cornish sources.

In addition to those analogues to Celtic mythology that are apparent in the Indo-European group (see Introduction), it is also the case that much later mythological influences were absorbed. As the Celtic homelands during the La Tène period (*c.* 500–100 BC) were spread wide across Western and Eastern Europe and on into Asia Minor, there can be no doubt that neighbouring mythologies left their imprint. These cultural assimilations would not only be from Graeco-Roman mythology but from Middle Eastern mythologies, thus long before the arrival of Christianity in Ireland in the latter half of the fifth century. One possible example of this is the Celtic belief that some dragons acted as guardians between this world and the fairy otherworld, usually at a sacred grove or a loch. This idea may well have been derived from the ancient Egyptian reverence for the river Nile crocodile god, Sobek. Nevertheless, while the cross-pollination of mythologies was, as we have already seen, bound to happen, such is the complexity of the pre-literate history of the Celts that identifying the origins of their myths is more a matter of suppositions based more on similarities than absolute certainty.

The Celtic dragon, then, is the oldest in Western Europe, mythological traces of which date back to the Iron Age. Preserved in verse and prose in Old and Middle Irish manuscripts from the eighth to the seventeenth century, a sequence of four main cycles has been identified: the Mythological Cycle, the Ulster Cycle, the Fenian Cycle and the Historical Cycle, all of which, to greater or lesser degrees, were further infused with Graeco-Roman lore and, of course, with Christian values and beliefs by their post-conversion redactors. Besides these influences, the active presence of Vikings in Ireland from the ninth century to the eleventh century clearly had an impact on indigenous ideas about dragons, one that is particularly conspicuous in Celtic art.[7]

The Mythological Cycle tells of the coming of a supernatural people known as the Túatha Dé Danann (People of the Goddess Danu), who were led by Nuada Airgetlám, Nuada of the Silver Arm, and were initially seen as the beneficent gods. Having overcome the inhabitants of Ireland, the Fir Bolg, meaning warriors swollen with battle fury, their chief enemies were the demonic Fomorians, the gods of chaos led by Balor Birugderc, Balor of the Evil Eye. After a series of battles, resulting in the deaths of both Nuada and Balor, the Túatha Dé Danann eventually triumphed, only to be overcome by the invading Milesians, the original Celts or Gaels, and driven into an underground otherworld where they became known as the *sidh*, a fairy people.[8]

The Ulster Cycle, set in northeast Ireland in the first century AD, recounts the heroic deeds of Conachar (aka Conchobar) mac Nessa, king of Ulster, and the renowned warrior Cú Chulainn. Similarly, the Fenian Cycle, which is set in the provinces of Munster and Leinster in the third century AD, is also concerned with human heroics, principally those of Fionn mac Cumhaill and his warrior band, the Fianna.[9] This cycle, one that sets its heroes' adventures in both the human and the spirit worlds, is where we find most mention of dragons, commonly referred to as *péists*. Lastly, the Historical Cycle consists of verse tributes by court poets to their kings, ranging from the wholly legendary kings of the fifth century through to the historical High King of Ireland Brian Boru (r. 1002–14).

## Fionn mac Cumhaill

Despite scientific conclusions that there never were serpents of any kind in post-glacial Ireland, thus rendering medieval accounts of St Patrick's expulsion of them in the fifth century as hagiographic aggrandisement, myths and legends that refer to dragons, mostly metaphorically or as depicted on ornamentation but occasionally as actualities, are plentiful.[10] In the seventeenth-century poem 'The Chase of Sliabh Teuim' in *Duanaire Finn* (Book of the Lays of Finn), set down by the soldier and scribe Aodh Ó Dochartaigh, Caílte mac Rónáin, the nephew of Fionn mac Cumhaill, tells of Fionn's numerous killings of dragons.

After a long day's hunting, Fionn and the Fianna arrive at Loch Cuan, where a monster calling itself Height of Battle, with a head bigger than a hill, eye hollows large enough to fit a hundred heroes and a tail longer than eight men, demands to be fed. When Fionn questions the monster about its origin, it tells him that it is the son of the Greek dragon Crouch of the Rock and that it has come to Ireland from Greece with the sole purpose of combatting Fionn and the Fianna. When Fionn orders his men to attack the dragon, many are slain, either by the showers of spines it emits or by being swallowed alive, this latter fate soon becoming Fionn's. Yet Fionn hacks his way out of the dragon's belly, liberates many of his men and mortally injures the beast.[11]

Caílte then goes on to recount, or rather list, dragon-like monster slayings by Fionn and his army at Loch Neagh, Loch Cuilleann, Benn Edair, Glen Dorcha, Erne Fell, Loch Eiach, Ath Cliath, Loch Lein, Loch Righ, Glenarm, Loch Sileann, Loch Foyle, the River Shannon, Loch Eamhuir, Glen Inne, Loch Meilge, Loch Cera, Loch Mask, Loch Laeghaire, Loch Lurgan and the River Bann, not to mention Fionn's killings of numerous giants, spectres, wild men and phantoms. As Caílte reports, 'there was not a reptile in Ireland's glens but he took by the force of his blows.'[12]

The extent to which Aodh Ó Dochartaigh's poem was inspired by seventeenth-century Irish Catholic resistance to English-imposed Protestantism, as much as it was by mythological traditions, may well have been significant. But even so, its mythological credentials are validated in the

Fenian Cycle's twelfth-century *Acallam na Senórach* (Colloquy with the Ancients), which supports the belief that Fionn mac Cumhaill and the Fianna were once responsible for ridding Ireland of serpents of every kind – except one, that is. As concerns this particular exception, Caílte is once again the chief reporter of Fionn's exploits.

Having survived into considerable, if not improbable, old age, Caílte and Fionn's son, Ossian, are being questioned by Eochaid Lethderg, king of Leinster, in the presence of St Patrick, from whom they have all received blessings. The king asks Caílte why it was that, having rid Ireland of so many monsters, Fionn and the Fianna had not killed the notorious dragon of the Glen of Ros Enaigh. Caílte explains that 'their reason was that the creature is the fourth part of Mesgegra's brain, which the earth swallowed there and converted into a monstrous worm.' Caílte then adds that this particular dragon, which had killed a hundred of the Fianna as well as their much valued hunting hounds, is not fated to die until the coming of the *Tailchenn*; in other words, Christianity as preached by St Patrick, a disciple of which would one day bind it until Judgement Day.[13]

## Mesgegra's brain

In order to understand what Caílte is alluding to in his mention of 'Mesgegra's brain', we must turn to the Ulster Cycle, much of which concerns the feuding Irish kingdoms in and around the first century AD, in this particular case, that of the long-standing enmity between the kingdom of Ulster and those of Leinster and Connacht. In the episode known as 'The Siege at Howth', the young Ulster warrior Conall Cernach challenges Mesgegra, at that time the ageing king of Leinster, to a sword fight and succeeds in decapitating him. As was a custom among triumphant warriors, Conall extracts Mesgegra's brain, which he then calcifies and rolls into a ball and later places on a shelf as an enviable trophy. The brainless head is left to the keeping of Mesgegra's grieving wife.[14] Despite all, it is prophesied that Mesgegra will yet have his revenge.

Later in the cycle, in 'The Tragical Death of King Conachar',[15] Cet mac Mágach, a Connacht warrior who was known for his mischief, craftily steals the brain from two of Conall's court jesters and takes to carrying it in his belt with the intention of one day using it to kill some illustrious opponent, preferably one of the Ulster champions. His chance comes when he rustles cattle from the Ulstermen and is then pursued by them and their king, Conachar mac Nessa. An army of fellow Connacht-men quickly comes to Cet's aid, and a battle ensues. Conachar, who is well known for his good looks, soon withdraws from the battle and presents himself before a large group of admiring womenfolk, unaware that Cet has concealed himself among them. With Conachar now a clear target, Cet takes out his slingshot and fires Mesgegra's brain at him, so lodging it inextricably in his skull.

Conachar survives, albeit relatively incapacitated, for another seven years, whereupon, in what is quite clearly a Christian interpolation,[16] a druid tells him that Jesus Christ has been crucified that very day. Enraged by this news, Conachar takes to hacking with his sword at a woody grove in Feara Rois, a place close to the Glen of Ros Enaigh, at which point Mesgegra's brain breaks out from his skull, so killing him. Mesgegra has in this way taken his revenge on the Ulstermen.

Although the story of how 'a fourth part of Mesgegra's brain' ended up in ferocious dragon form in the Glen of Ros Enaigh, as told by Caílte, is lost, the refusal of Fionn and the Fianna to challenge it would seem to indicate their unwillingness to interfere in an ancestral blood feud. The tale of Mesgegra's brain suggests that dragons acted not only as guardians at the gates of a world beyond but as epitomizations of human discord.

## Fergus mac Léti

Discord is also at the heart of the myth of Fergus mac Léti, who is said to have been an early Ulster king, although precisely when is not known.[17] Having ruthlessly overcome and seized land and property from his tenants, Fergus goes on a trip to the sea coast, where he falls asleep. As he sleeps, sprites known as *luchorpáin*, or leprechauns – the first known mention of these renowned 'little people' – steal away his sword and carry him into the sea. But when Fergus's feet touch water, he awakes, seizes three of the leprechauns and demands that they grant him certain wishes in return for their freedom. To this they agree, and Fergus is given the superhuman power to swim under seas, pools and lakes without ever having to surface to take breath. Yet there is one exception, state the leprechauns, which is that his newfound power will not include his ability to swim under Loch Rudhraighe, which lies on his own territory (identified as Dundrum Inner Bay, County Down). Inevitably, in the passage of time, this is precisely what Fergus does, and as a consequence he encounters a vast dragon-serpent, the Muirdris, that swells up and contracts like a bellows. So terrifying is this creature that, before he escapes to dry land, Fergus's mouth swivels round to the back of his head, a deformity about which Fergus is uniquely oblivious.

Fergus's disfigurement is permanent and his druids debate whether their king's defect should allow him to remain king. In the end, they decide to do all they can to conceal Fergus's face, both from himself and from his subjects. It is therefore agreed that only a very limited number of trusted nobles and servants may attend the king and that his palace should be stripped of all mirrors. For seven years this stratagem works, until one day Fergus's female slave, Dorn, fails to wash his face correctly and he whips her. Dorn, who was originally the noblewoman mother of one of Fergus's subjugated tenants, now sets about ridiculing his disfigurement and fetches a mirror. Appalled, Fergus slices her in two with his sword and immediately sets off for Loch Rudhraighe to seek vengeance on the Muirdris. For a day and a night they battle, until Fergus finally succeeds in hacking off the Muirdris's head, with which he then swims to the shore. As he emerges from the loch, with his face now restored to normal, he raises the severed head aloft and declares, 'I am the survivor!', whereupon he drops down dead from exhaustion. For a month, Loch Rudhraighe is stained red with the dragon's blood.

The myth of Fergus mac Léti is evidently about the excessive ambitions of its hero and the subsequent consequences for him, but, as scholars have observed, there is also an underlying legal context that explores the limits of the rights of those in authority.[18] In this respect, the interventions of the leprechauns, Fergus's disfigurement and his final fatal encounter with the Muirdris function as otherworldly judgements on him for his illtreatment of his tenants. The continuing popularity of this particular myth would nonetheless seem to have transcended legal intricacies and is rested more on the downfall of the hero for his acts of ruthlessness and his excessive pride, the latter of which is ironized in his disfigurement. As for this tale's cultural legacy, it was perhaps the intervention of the leprechauns that, in the eighteenth century, attracted Jonathan Swift, whose tale of Lemuel Gulliver in Lilliput (*Gulliver's Travels*, 1726) is believed to have been inspired by a copy of the Fergus myth that came into his possession.

## 'The Death of Fraoch'

The transmission of Irish myths down through the centuries, from oral tradition to early manuscripts to folktale renderings, led to considerable variation in their tellings. A notable example of this is the tale of Fraoch (also known as Fraích and Fráech), who, with varying degrees of significance, is in all accounts said to have fought a dragon. Dating from the eighth century and preserved in four manuscripts in the eleventh-century *Yellow Book of Lecan*, Fraoch, a remarkably handsome young man, is originally said to have successfully overcome the monster during his courtship of the royal maiden Findabair. Thereafter, he goes on to have numerous adventures, until he meets his end, still relatively young, in the famous myth of the *Táin Bó Cúailnge* (The Cattle Raid of Cooley).[19]

Yet the story of his wooing of Findabair and the dragon episode clearly struck a popular chord, as can be seen in a traditional Gaelic folktale set on the Isle of Mull in western Scotland. Recorded in the sixteenth-century *Book of the Dean of Lismore*, it is in this tale, known as 'The Death of Fraoch', that the dragon is Fraoch's undoing. The following account draws on the *Yellow Book of Lecan* for the first part of the myth, which concerns Fraoch's difficulties with the parents of Findabair, after which the Scottish folktale version of his fate is recounted.[20]

Fraoch's father is Idad of Connacht, about whom little is known, and his mother is Bofind of the fairy people, the *sidh*, so suggesting that Fraoch has access to and qualities from the Celtic otherworld. While still quite young, Fraoch is given twelve supernatural white cows by his mother. For eight years he tends to the cows, until one day Princess Findabair comes to his attention and he is immediately infatuated. Encouraged by her interest in him and despite being of lower social standing than she, Fraoch decides to visit her parents, Queen Medb and King Ailill, to ask for her hand in marriage. Before doing so, he goes to see his mother, who gives him fifty fabulously attired mounted warriors, along with hunting hounds, buglers, harpists, jesters and many other knightly extravagances.

Arriving at the royal castle, a large crowd gathers to view Fraoch and his retinue, the like of which no one has seen before. For over two weeks, Fraoch and company are given lavish hospitality, in return for which they entertain their hosts with their hunting exploits and the ravishing beauty of their harpist's music, which, incidentally, causes several people to die from sheer sorrow on hearing it, seemingly without recrimination from the king and queen. Then one morning Fraoch follows Findabair to a nearby loch where she is accustomed to bathe, and asks her to come away with him. Knowing that her parents would never agree to such a match, Findabair indicates that she may indeed be prepared to elope.

So encouraged, Fraoch now asks King Ailill to grant him his daughter, but the bride price demanded, which includes his supernatural cows, is far beyond anything Fraoch could raise, and, somewhat dismayed, he says as much. Ailill now suspects that Fraoch might take Findabair away anyway, something that would not only dishonour him but would provoke the other kings of Ireland to attack him for his weakness. For the king, the only solution is to have Fraoch killed.

Yet Ailill still has Fraoch's attention, and he requests that Fraoch bring the poorly Queen Medb some rowan berries, which were believed to have healing properties, from an island tree on a nearby loch. While assuring Fraoch that the disturbingly black waters of the loch can cause him no harm, what Ailill fails to disclose is that this particular tree is guarded by a green dragon. Fraoch does as he is asked and, seeing the dragon curled up by the tree, manages to steal past it and gather a handful of berries.[21] Yet for Queen Medb this is not enough, for, she says, what she also needs is a branch from the tree. Despite him now knowing the dangers, Fraoch clearly understands that his reputation hangs in the balance and he sets off. By this time, however, Findabair has realized what her parents are intending and she follows Fraoch with a sword concealed about her.

Fraoch once again believes he has eluded the dragon, and, doubtless keen to avoid a third journey, he uproots the entire rowan tree.[22] But he is mistaken, for as he swims back to shore, the dragon follows him, attacks and bites off his arm. Horrified by what she has seen, Findabair plunges into the water in the hope of passing her sword to her beloved. Now Ailill emerges from his nearby hiding place and hurls a five-pointed spear at Fraoch, which he catches and hurls back, narrowly missing the king. Having given the sword to Fraoch, who then decapitates the dragon, Findabair swims back. Yet when Fraoch reaches the shore, the dragon's head in hand, it is clear to Findabair that he is dying and she faints. When she awakes, Fraoch's lifeless blood-stained hand is cradled in hers, whereupon she declares, 'Though now but food for birds-of-prey, thy renown on earth is traced.'[23] Findabair then dies of grief.

It was in this way that the often confusing tale in the *Yellow Book of Lecan* was reformulated to give the hero a romantically tragic ending, all owing to his determination to win Findabair, while at the same time preserving his reputation as a fearless warrior. Although the dragon in the earlier accounts of Fraoch's life is simply an obstacle that the hero must and does overcome, it is not difficult to see that the dragon, as it figures in the folklore version, is the symbolic expression of the murderous determination of his prospective partner's parents to prevent his match with their daughter.

## Celtic dragons: Merlin and the Red Dragon of Wales

The extent to which Irish myths and legends influenced mainstream medieval Romance is difficult to assess, not least because it was set down in Gaelic and therefore tended to remain an insular literary culture until well into the Middle Ages.[24] It is nevertheless quite clear that notions of a heroic ideal and the threatening presence of dragons featured in all the Celtic regions from the earliest times. That dragons played a key role in Welsh myths is, then, only to be expected. And in this case there can be no doubt about the huge, even formative, influence that Celtic dragons had on Romance literature, chiefly as a result of Geoffrey of Monmouth's *Historia regum Britanniae* (The History of the Kings of Britain). Writing in Latin around 1136, Geoffrey brought literary accounts of Celtic myth and legend to the attention of non-Gaelic speakers for the first time.

Spanning over two thousand years, from the Trojan War to the Anglo-Saxon settlement of Britain, and based on a number of early sources,

Celtic Red Dragon medieval woodcut.

Geoffrey's history has little factual merit.[25] Nonetheless, as a pseudo-history its impact on that body of indigenous legends 'The Matter of Britain', particularly as it concerns the life and times of King Arthur, was without rival. It is in this context that we find that figure who went on to become Arthur's chief adviser, the prophet and wizard Merlin, and it is from the young Merlin that we hear most about dragons and their symbolic meanings in the wars between the British, meaning here the Celtic Britons, and the Saxons.

It is the mid-fifth century and Vortigern, king of the Britons, is under threat from two invading armies. From the east are the Saxons led by Horsa and Hengist, who have already laid waste to much of his kingdom, while from the north are the persistently troublesome Picts. Unable to fight effectively on both fronts, Vortigern grants the Saxons land to the east of his kingdom on the condition that they help him overcome the Picts. Aware of the dangers of this arrangement, Vortigern now sets his masons the task of building an unassailable fortress on Mount Snowdon, but, for reasons unfathomable to the king, the earthworks are repeatedly shattered by tremors. On seeking the advice of his wizards, Vortigern is told that he must find a fatherless boy, kill him and sprinkle his blood on the fortress, so making it impregnable.

Envoys are dispatched throughout the kingdom to search for such a youth, at first with little success, but on visiting Carmarthen they come across two young boys, one taunting the other for never having had a father. The latter child, they discover, is Merlin, who, as it turns out, is the son of a mysterious male figure who had visited and impregnated his mother in her dreams and has not been heard of since.[26] Merlin is thus seized and taken to Vortigern. Learning that he is about to be put to death and the reasons for it, Merlin tells the king that the wizards have lied and that beneath the fortress's foundations there lies a pool of water and that beneath this pool are two large caves. It is the inhabitants of these caves, says Merlin, that are causing the tremors. Amazed by Merlin's knowledge, Vortigern orders the pool drained, whereupon the caves are revealed, and from them two fire-breathing dragons emerge – one white, one red – which immediately set about fighting each other. At first the White Dragon has the upper hand and forces the Red Dragon to the edge of the pool, but then the Red Dragon retaliates, forcing the White Dragon back.

Asked by the king what all this means, Merlin enters into a trance and delivers his prophecy.[27] The Red Dragon, he says, is the Christian British, while the White Dragon is the pagan Saxons, those to whom the king has offered land.[28] The Red Dragon shall be overcome by the White Dragon, all its caverns occupied, the country's mountains levelled, its streams overflowing with blood and the Christian faith all but destroyed. But the Red Dragon shall recover its strength and, for a while, the White Dragon will be subdued and 'the buildings in its little garden torn down'. This, though, is a short-lived recovery, for the Red Dragon 'will revert to its true habits and struggle to tear itself to pieces'. The White Dragon will then invite the daughter of the German Worm to Britain and the land will be 'planted with strange seed'.

So matters will remain for the next 450 years, until 'vengeance for its treason' shall fall upon the German Worm and 'the White Dragon shall be rooted up from our little gardens and what is then left of its progeny shall be decimated.' Yet this is not the end of the turmoil, for more dragons shall follow. Among these will be a great serpent that shall devour all those that pass by, and a worm, whose breath is fire, which shall consume the trees and corrupt the women. Then a great giant shall rise up against it and, in turn, be challenged by the Dragon of Worcester, which is defeated, mounted and eventually stabbed with a poison sword by the giant, so dying in the coils of its own tail. And so the mayhem continues.

Although its precise meanings are often somewhat obscure, the prophecy of Merlin allegorizes Britain's history, starting with the rule of Vortigern and the succession of Uther Pendragon, so named after he saw a comet in the shape of a dragon while marching to war.[29] Thereafter, Merlin's prophecy moves to Uther's son, Arthur, whose might and brilliance would temporarily bring some measure of peace and stability, despite his ultimately destructive familial relations. It then proceeds right on through to Geoffrey of Monmouth's own time. Replete with a chaos of dragons and numerous other monstrous beings, the underlying message would appear to be that what lies in store for the British are centuries of disarray, during which the country will be conquered time and again. Despite repeated attempts to defend the realm, the fate of the British is sealed and their land ultimately reduced to no more than the territories of Wales and Cornwall. This, as Merlin suggests by stating that that 'true habit' of the Red Dragon is 'to tear itself to pieces', is due to the failure of the Celts to unite against their adversaries.

Unlike in Ireland, where dragon tales would appear to be a combination of memories of myths brought with the Celts from their original homelands and of Christian notions of ultimate evil, the Welsh dragon would seem to have a rather more curious history. The idea of the Red Dragon may well have first been inspired by the Roman *draconarius* cavalry standards and their domination of the British for over 350 years, starting in the first century AD. The idea of the White Dragon, conversely, indicates the

Christian abhorrence of Germanic paganism. This view would have become entrenched during the fourth and early fifth centuries, a turbulent time when the Roman Empire approved Christianity; the empire collapsed, forcing withdrawal from Britain; and the Anglo-Saxons seized the opportunity to attack the now vulnerable British Celts. Merlin's diametric opposition of the Red Dragon and the White Dragon is in fact unique in dragon lore, and, given that the Red Dragon features to this day on the Welsh flag as the key symbol of national pride, might be considered a little ironic in the light of Merlin's view of it as a creature given to self-destructive tendencies.

ALTHOUGH THE MYTHS and legends involving Celtic dragons are the oldest in Western Europe, the problem in identifying their original significances is in many ways problematic. The chief difficulty lies in the fact that, unlike, for example, in Greek mythology, where the myths were recorded centuries before the arrival of Christianity, Celtic mythology was only set down after the conversion; in some cases, long after. The result of this major cultural shift is that the original myths are overlaid with value judgements that were introduced by their Christian redactors and, in oral traditions, by Christian ideas generally. Nevertheless, it is possible to see certain defining characteristics, or what may be termed 'trace myths', in Celtic dragon tales.

As was noted at the outset of this chapter, one common feature of the Gaelic or Irish dragon is its association with water sources, most

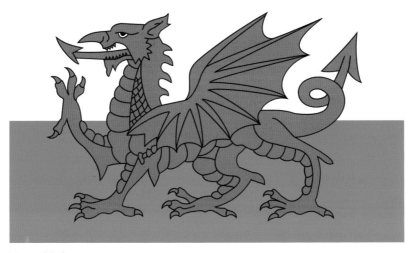

The Welsh flag.

obviously lochs. Here the dragon typically functions as a fierce guardian of its territory, a place that is clearly between the human world and that of the fairy people. In effect, the Gaelic dragon resides in a marginal region, one which humans enter at their peril, for direct access to fairyland was something denied, unless, as is the case with Fraoch, being of fairy descent allowed such access. Yet even in Fraoch's case, just as it is in Fergus mac Léti's, any attempt to intrude into this place or to overcome and so remove the dragon obstacle has dire consequences. It may well be, as has been widely observed, that the Gaelic dragon in the original myths was not so much a demonic threat, like the Mesgegra's brain dragon, but more one associated with the supernatural power of the otherworld and therefore a creature whose energies once merited reverence and respect.

As time passed, however, and Christian ideas of evil, such as are expressed in dragon-form in bestiaries and, of course, the Book of Revelation, the Gaelic dragon became increasingly seen as a threat to civilization. This would account for Fionn mac Cumhaill's lifelong mission to rid the country of dragons, not unlike in the famous myth of Patrick purging Ireland of serpents of all kinds. And it may also account for why dragons came to be seen as an epitomization of human discord.

The Brittonic or Welsh dragon, as described in Geoffrey of Monmouth's account of Merlin's doom-laden prophecies, is a markedly different creature, for here its allegorical function is to articulate both the tribal identity of the ancient Britons, in the form of the Red Dragon, and all that threatens it, in the form of the White Dragon. Beyond noting this, the main significance of Geoffrey's pseudo-history is as a forerunner of the Arthurian literature phenomenon. Nevertheless, this move from myth to literature led not only to dragons being portrayed as little more than passing, somewhat caricatured, monstrosities for the knight-hero to overcome but, over time, to ideas about them to become exhausted. Excepting in folktales, the power of the medieval dragon, much inspired by its Celtic forebears, rested largely on its function as an aggrandizer of its slayer.[30] In short, our vision of the original Celtic dragon is not only one fogged by, as it were, its Christianization, but one that, as a consequence, would soon run out of steam.

In the following chapter, we turn to a draconic mythology that is never likely to run out of steam. This is the Asian dragon, most notably the Chinese dragon, a creature whose influence on modern depictions of dragons is indisputable.

Duanwu Festival dragon boat.

## six

# Asian and East Asian Dragons

NOWHERE IN THE world is the dragon more deeply embedded in the culture than in China. Long regarded as a symbol of dynastic power and authority, and therefore as a creature that all should respect and seek to emulate, the Chinese reverence for dragons dates back over thousands of years, as is apparent in centuries-old art, ornamentation, architecture and literature. Nor is this simply a matter of much-prized antiquity, for the Chinese dragon's potency remains central to the country's sense of identity to this day: children are schooled in the ways of the dragon; scarcely is there a community without a dragon dance troupe; the annual Dragon Boat Festival (Duanwu Festival) is celebrated nationwide; and the dragon is one of the auspicious twelve signs of the Chinese zodiac.

In its oldest form, the Chinese dragon, the *long* (or *lung*), is typically considered to be wise and benevolent. Yet this is not to say that the dragon is in any way tamed and harmless, for if disrespected, it can also be the cause of floods, typhoons and all manner of natural catastrophes. This destructive side of the Chinese dragon is given even greater emphasis in legends and folktales, and in these accounts certain Chinese dragons are not so dissimilar to, for example, the ancient Greek Titan god Typhon or the fire-spewing beast in *Beowulf*.[1] Complicating our understanding of the Chinese dragon is the country's great territorial and ethnic diversity, the inevitable consequence being that Chinese culture cannot, in all respects, be said to be uniform. Moreover, with the eastward spread of Buddhism into China during the first and second centuries AD, there came tales of the Indian *nāga* dragon. As the influence of the *nāga* on ideas about the *long* was significant, it is to India that we shall first turn.

## The Indian *nāga* dragon

Originating in fears of the deadly king cobra with its characteristic hooded head, myths of the Indian dragon were first recorded in the sacred Hindu hymns of the *Rig Veda*, a text probably composed between 1500 and 1200 BC. It is here that the battle between the warrior god Indra and the serpent-dragon Vritra is told.[2] As a personification of drought, Vritra threatens all life and it is Indra's sole purpose to rid the world of this monster. Having drunk vast quantities of the ritual stimulant Soma, Indra takes three strides forward and attacks Vritra with his lightning-bolt emitting weapon, Vajra. Retaliating, Vritra strikes Indra with his coiled tail, so smashing his upper and lower jaws. But Indra is undeterred and, having raised Vritra aloft, hurls him down, killing him outright, after which Indra turns Vajra on Vritra's mother, Danu, killing her also. It was in this way that the waters of the world were liberated.

In the later Sanskrit *Purana* accounts of the Indra/Vritra myths, which date from approximately the fourth century AD, Vritra is said to have swallowed Indra, only then being forced to vomit him back up when he is confronted by all the other gods. Fearful of Vritra's power, the chief of the gods, Vishnu, now tells Indra that he must no longer attack Vritra with weapons made of metal, wood or stone, nor with anything wet or dry, and neither during day nor night. But Indra has no intention of abandoning his

Vishnu and Lakshimi on Shesha Nāga, *c.* 1870.

mission. Having patiently bided his time, he eventually sees Vritra by the sea shore at twilight, it therefore being neither day nor night. Vishnu, too, recognizes the opportunity and comes to Indra's aid by entering the foam of the waves, which was considered neither wet nor dry, and in this way allowing Indra to shape-shift into foam and to attack and strangle the unwary Vritra. Vritra's dead body now explodes, releasing much-needed water to flood across the parched land, and the heavens to open and rain to fall.

Vritra belongs that class of dragons known as the *nāga* (f. *nāgini*), a creature often described as bearing a pearl.[3] Four classes of *nāga* have been identified: heavenly *nāgas* that support the palaces of the gods; divine *nāgas* that, if appropriately revered, control the skies to the benefit of crop growers; earthly *nāgas* that control ground waters; and hidden *nāgas* which guard treasures in remote caves and abandoned palaces, both on land and deep underwater. While *nāgas* were sometimes considered helpful to humans and gods, the *Mahabharata*, an epic Hindu text believed to date back to the eighth or ninth century BC, describes them as 'snakes . . . of virulent poison, great prowess and excess of strength, and ever bent on biting other creatures.'[4]

This negative view of the *nāga* should nevertheless be tempered somewhat by an understanding of the *nāga's* susceptibilities to life's miseries and misfortunes. The following quote from a third-century AD Buddhist text, in which a servant's master explains to him just how much better his lot in life is compared to that of the *nāga*, despite its palatial comforts, makes precisely this point:

> 'The Nāga', said he, 'has to endure three kinds of sufferings: his delicious food turns into toads as soon as he takes it in his mouth; his beautiful women, as well as he himself, change into serpents when he tries to embrace them; on his back he has scales lying in the reverse direction, and when sand and pebbles enter between them, he suffers pains which pierce his heart. Therefore do not envy him.'[5]

That *nāgas* are, in certain respects, just like humans in both their sorrows and their joys is apparent throughout the myths.

As told in the *Mahabharata*, the chief enemy of the *nāgas* is Garuda, a gold- and green-feathered eagle with red wings, four human arms, the face of a man and a body large enough to eclipse the sun.[6] Garuda was hatched from an egg given to his mother, Vinata, by her husband, the god Kashyapa, which she kept safe for five hundred years. But Kashyapa has twelve other wives, one of whom is Kadru, the mother of all *nāgas*. It is

Bridge of two *nāga* kings to the Elephant Temple Thep Wittayakhom Vihara, Wittayakom, Wat Baan Rai, Korat, Thailand.

with Kadru that Vinata makes the reckless bet that the seven-headed divine horse Uchchaihshravas is pure white, whereas Kadru believes it to have a black tail. The price the loser will have to pay is to become a slave to the winner. It so comes about that, on discovering that the horse is wholly white, the conniving Kadru orders her thousand *nāga* sons to twist themselves around its tail to make it appear black, a task they only agree to perform after their mother curses them and threatens to have them all killed. As a result of this deception, not only is Vinata enslaved but so too is Garuda, an indignity that he will not tolerate, neither for own sake nor for his mother's.

When Garuda asks the *nāgas* what they would want in return for his mother's freedom, he is told that they will only accept the magical potion Amrita that would grant them immortality. Garuda steals this potion from the gods but, once his mother is freed from servitude, cunningly ensures that it is spilled, thus denying the *nāgas* eternal life. From here on, the vengeful Garuda becomes the bane of all *nāgas*, which he is often prone to devour, a practice which the gods at first endorse.

Yet on one occasion, Garuda's *nāga*-eating compulsion brings about his humiliation. This is when the *nāga* Sumukha, a most handsome youth when in human form, wishes to get married to the daughter of Indra's charioteer but cannot do so because Garuda has sworn to eat him in a month's time. When Garuda learns that Vishnu and Indra intend to give Sumukha a dose of the immortality potion, so obviating Garuda's threat to eat him, he challenges their authority, boasting that he is so powerful that he can bear the weight of the world on his back. In reply, Vishnu demands that Garuda prove his strength by bearing just his weight. But when Vishnu places his hands on Garuda's shoulders, the weight is unbearable and he breaks down in tears. Now realizing that he taken a step too far, Garuda humbles himself before the gods and apologises to Sumukha. The potion is then given to Sumukha and the marriage goes ahead as previously intended.

A similarly sympathetic tale of a *nāga*, this time one with cosmic significance, is that told of the many-headed Prince Shesha, who lives in the universal ocean and is regarded by all as a wise and compassionate creature. But Shesha's *nāga* brothers are not so benign and take pleasure in inflicting pain on all other beings, a sadism that includes torturing their sisters. When Shesha, appalled and shamed by his brothers' wickedness, penitently takes to inflicting comparable pain on himself, the creator-god, Brahma, respecting Shesha's self-discipline but pitying his suffering, grants Shesha's request to preserve his mind from harm. In return, Brahma gives Shesha the responsibility of using his formidable strength to rest the earth's foundation on his hooded heads and bring stability to the still volatile firmament. It is in this

Nadalal Bose, *Garuda*, 1913.

Ida Made Tlaga, *Garuda*,
19th century.

cosmic role that Shesha is also identified as Ananta, the immortal ruler of
all dragons on whose back rides the all-powerful Vishnu.

Life-supporting cosmic significance is also ascribed to the vast *nāga*
Vasuki, whose function is to churn all those substances, sometimes referred
to as 'cosmic milk', that form the essence of life. Other *nāgas*, like the *nāga*
king Takshaka and the hermit *nāga* Paravataksha, have rather more terres-
trially dramatic myths associated with them. In Takshaka's case, he is driven
from his palace by his human enemies, enacts murderous vengeance on
those who brought about his exile and, in desperation, takes to highway
robbery. When captured and about to be executed, a young Brahmin sage
speaks up in Takshaka's defence, the outcome being that Takshaka is released
and allowed to live in peace alongside his one-time human enemies.

The myth of the half-human, half-snake, hidden *nāga*, Paravataksha,
introduces him as the possessor of a great sword once owned by the gods, a
weapon that grants him the power to cause earthquakes. Yet Paravataksha
has no such destructive intention and lives peaceably in his palace behind a
concealed water-filled cave, which is visible only at sunset and to which the
entrance is, even then, marked only by the presence of two swans. Trouble

comes to Paravataksha in the form of a wicked sorcerer who has learned of the sword's existence and is determined to take possession of it. But to do so, the gurus say, requires him to have the assistance of a troop of heroes. Having grown old, and despairing that this will never come to pass, the sorcerer is eventually fortunate enough to encounter a king and his warrior band who agree to assist him.

Noting the spot where the swans have settled, the sorcerer stations himself nearby and chants a charm with the intention of debilitating Paravataksha, while the king and his men ready themselves for attack. Suddenly, the ground begins to quake, whereupon a dazzlingly beautiful woman appears and fixes her gaze on the now dumbstruck sorcerer. As the woman disappears, Paravataksha emerges and, brandishing his sword, strikes the sorcerer dead. Turning then to the warriors, the *nāga* first blinds them with the fire burning in his eyes, then deafens them with his thunderous curse. So stricken, the king and his warriors chaotically flee for their lives, leaving Paravataksha to resume his agreeably solitary existence.[7]

Encounters with *nāgas*, in this next case a cunningly seductive *nāgini*, could also result in marital infidelity. Somewhat ironically, the royal, semi-divine hero Arjuna has gone on a year-long pilgrimage in order to atone for violating the terms of his marriage. On his arrival at the Ganges, he decides to bathe, but as he enters deep water, a current seizes him and drags him down. Even so, he has no sense of drowning and he quickly comes to realize that he is in the grip of a powerful dragon-woman. Arriving at her underwater palace, she reveals herself to be Ulupi, the daughter of a *nāga* king. She also reveals that she is in love with Arjuna and wants him as her own. But Arjuna declines her proposal, explaining that, as a pilgrim, he has taken a vow of celibacy. Cleverly, Ulupi argues that this vow only applies to his wife. Seemingly easily persuaded, Arjuna spends one night with the *nāgini*, who later bears him a son. In due course, in order to free Arjuna from a curse that has been put on him, Ulupi is responsible for planning his death at the hands of his son, but, having wrought Arjuna's end, Ulupi then uses her pearl to bring him back to life. As for Arjuna's infidelity, whether or not his wife discovered his betrayal of her is left unsaid, most likely because her role in the myth was deemed irrelevant.[8]

In these early myths, *nāgas* can be both life-affirming and life-denying, often depending on how they are treated. With the advent of Buddhism in India sometime between the fourth and the sixth century BC, the *nāga*, whether congenial or uncongenial, comes to be viewed as a creature from which lessons can be learned about how better to deal with and understand

Statue of the Buddha sheltered by the *nāga* Mucalinda, Wat Mai Complex, Luang Prabang, Laos, Indochina.

life's mysteries and, as a result, move closer to achieving enlightenment. One such myth is recorded in the *Mahavagga*, as written down in the ancient Pāli language in the first century BC but believed to have been composed shortly after the Buddha's death. This tells how, as the Buddha sat meditating beneath the Bodhi tree, a great storm began to brew up. Seeing the approach of this tempest and aware that the Buddha was so deep in thought that he was oblivious of the looming danger, the *nāga* king Mucalinda coils himself round the Buddha seven times and spreads his great hooded head over him. The storm rages for seven days, after which Mucalinda uncoils himself, assumes human form and raises his hands respectfully before the Buddha.[9]

But the Buddha's encounters with *nāgas* were not always quite so positive. Also in the *Mahavagga*, it is said that the Buddha visited a monastery at Uruvelā (near Benares), where he asked for a night's lodgings in the sacred firehouse. When warned that this place is occupied by 'a fierce, venomous Dragon-King' with 'psychic powers', the Buddha is undeterred and insists that he will be unharmed. It so comes about that, as the Buddha sits cross-legged in the firehouse, the Dragon-King belches out smoke at him, in response to which the Buddha summons his own psychic powers and, too, belches smoke. Enraged, the dragon now blazes fire, whereupon the Buddha blazes even greater fire, so much so that it seems that the whole place will burn down. Thus, having overcome his hostile roommate through his greater mastery of fire, the Buddha picks up the now diminutive but otherwise

Mucalinda sheltering Gautama Buddha at Wat Phra That Doi Suthep in Chiang Mai, Thailand.

unharmed *nāga* and drops it into his bowl, saying to his astonished hosts, 'his power was overcome by my power', after which he is offered free food and lodgings for as long he should wish.[10]

While *nāgas* in the *Mahavagga* can be either protective or threatening, other *nāgas* with which the Buddha is obliged to deal have the potential to be both. One example of this is when the Buddha seeks to appease the aggrieved divine *nāga* Apalala. This *nāga* took offence when farmers of the Swat Valley (in what is now northern Pakistan) neglected to leave their customary tribute of grain to him for ensuring that their crops were well watered. First sending a powerfully destructive flood, then causing a great drought, Apalala causes it to come about that no crops would grow and that the farmers and their families would duly perish. Hearing of this, the Buddha travels to the Swat River (once known as the Suvastu), where Apalala resides in his palace, and manages not only to persuade the *nāga* to forgive the farmers but to convert him to Buddhism. Thereafter, tribute to Apalala was required just once every twelve years, during which heavy rains would be made to fall, so producing a surfeit of grain but nonetheless causing the river to overflow.[11]

As is apparent in these myths, certain *nāgas* function not only to illustrate the powers of the Buddha but as an explanation for natural phenomena, good and bad. In all likelihood, the idea of the *nāga* as a controller of rain and water emerged as a natural response to the tropical climates of many Asian regions, in which existence can often be hazardous. The fearful propitiation of the *nāgas*, effective or not, would have been – and in some areas still is – a fundamental religious duty.

Particularly relevant to this is that Nature/Culture opposition discussed in the Introduction, which is no better illustrated than in myths of the *nāgas*. In these, some *nāgas* are quite clearly that powerful force that is Nature, and so a threat to all that is life-supporting and -enhancing, while other *nāgas* can be regarded as a personification of Culture and so a guardian of human life. In effect, the *nāga* is as much a projection of human triumphs and failings as it is of monstrous otherness. Unlike other Indo-European dragons, the *nāga* is a creature with which, favourably or not, we can in many ways identify.

## The Chinese *long* dragon

The world is flooded, and Chiyou, the monstrous god of war and weaponry, has rebelled against the divine Yellow Emperor, Huangdi. Unable to overcome Chiyou unaided, Huangdi commands the winged Yinglong, the 'Responding

Dragon', to attack Chiyou on the wilderness of the central plain. Yinglong's opening move is to gather up all the water in his belly with the aim of then releasing it to flood and drown Chiyou and his army. But Chiyou appeals to the wind god, Feng Bo, and the rain god, Yu Shi, to send a gale and a cloud-burst to assist him, in response to which the Yellow Emperor calls upon the goddess Ba to cause a drought. The rain is thus stopped and the way is now open for Yinglong to launch his attack and kill Chiyou.[12] Hereafter, myth merges into historical legend when, in the late third millennium BC, Emperor Yu the Great also enlists Yinglong to aid him in his lifelong task of building canals and water defences.

The myths of the Yinglong dragon and their many variants were set down in the fourth-century BC to first-century AD *Shanhaijing* (Classic of Mountains and Seas). Here, as in Indian mythology, celestial dragons such as Yinglong are invariably perceived as an agency of nature, thus as a power that holds sway over the sea, rivers, lakes and rain. With archaeological finds of dragon mosaics and sculptures dating back over six thousand years, the Chinese *long* is by far the earliest dragon in any mythology. Described during the time of the Han dynasty (206 BC–AD 220) by the philosopher Wang Fu, the appearance of the dragon is said to be composed of a number of actual creatures:

> The people paint the dragon's shape with a horse's head and a snake's tail. Further, there are expressions as 'three joints' and 'nine resemblances' (of

Yinglong as illustrated
in the *Shanhaijing*.

Yin and Yang as
tortoise and dragon,
Chinese wall painting,
8th century.

the dragon), to wit: from head to shoulder, from shoulder to breast, from
breast to tail. These are the joints; as to the nine resemblances, they are
the following: his horns resemble those of a stag, his head that of a camel,
his eyes those of a demon, his neck that of a snake, his belly that of a clam,
his scales those of a carp, his claws those of an eagle, his soles those of a
tiger, his ears those of a cow. Upon his head he has a thing like a broad
eminence (a big lump), called *ch'ihmuh*. If a dragon has no *ch'ihmuh*, he
cannot ascend to the sky.[13]

In addition to this, the *long* is said to have whiskers at the side of its
mouth and, not unlike the *nāga*, a pearl under its throat (though sometimes
in its claws), a feature associating it with wisdom, power and prosperity. The
body of the *long* is covered by 117 scales, 81 of which are positive and 36 negative. The reasoning here is derived from Taoist philosophy, in that 81 is nine
squared, and 36 is six squared. In the numbers nine and six there is a correspondence between the two types of scales and, respectively, the opposing

yet complementary life forces of the positive, active, masculine *yang* ('bright') and the negative, sinister, feminine *yin* ('dark'). One distinction, however, is made between the imperial dragon – those that were embroidered in yellow on an emperor's robes – and all other types, including the Japanese dragon, in that the former have five claws and the latter four or, in some cases, three. Nevertheless, anatomically precise though these dragon features would appear to be, with the exception of the claw count, there are so many other variations in the appearance of dragons that no single one, either in Chinese art or mythology, precisely matches everything given in Wang Fu's description or any other such 'definitive' descriptions.

From the earliest of times, the palace-dwelling dragon was identified with kings and emperors. These rulers would sit on the Dragon Throne, their faces admiringly regarded as a Dragon Face, and, on dying, were said to have ascended to heaven on a dragon's back. Many Chinese rulers saw themselves as descendants of dragons, one example being the third-millennium BC ruler Emperor Yao, who was said to have been sired by a dragon. During

Chinese Imperial dragon embroidered on a ceremonial robe, 19th century.

Illustration from a menu for a dinner in honour of the Chinese diplomat Wu Ting-Fan (1842–1922).

the time of the Song dynasty (AD 960–1279), Emperor Huizong (AD 1082–1135) identified five classes of dragon, which, by implication, suggested imperial dynastic power. Dragons and kings were equated as follows: the Blue Dragon with compassionate and courageous kings; the Red Dragon with kings who bring pleasures and bestow blessings; the Yellow Dragon with kings who spread literacy among the masses and convey their prayers to the gods; the White Dragon with virtuous and pure kings; and the Black Dragon with kings who have mystic powers.[14] Among these, supreme authority was believed to be held by the Yellow Dragon.[15]

Yet this did not mean that emperors could always keep dragons in check, nor did some wise emperors see any advantage in trying to do so. In 523 BC, during the reign of Emperor Zhaogong, the land became flooded and dragons were seen fighting in deep pools. Asked by his subjects to make sacrifices to the dragons and so be rid of both them and the flood, the emperor declined, explaining, 'When I fight, the dragons do not interview me. Why should I be the one to interview the dragons when they fight? If I have nothing to ask of the dragons, they will have nothing to ask of me.'[16] Being indebted to a dragon was clearly something best avoided.

Taking a similarly philosophical view of dragon power was Emperor Yu the Great, who, as previously mentioned, is said to have been aided by the dragon Yinglong in his efforts to control floods. One day, when Yu's boat was carried away by two dragons, all those aboard with him were understandably afraid. But Yu simply laughed and said,

'I received my appointment from heaven, and labour with all my strength to benefit mankind. To be born is the course of things; to die is heaven's decree. Why be troubled by dragons?'

On hearing this dismissal of their authority, the two dragons shamefacedly set down the boat and went quietly away.[17]

The Chinese dragon, then, is as much an expression of political authority as it is one of religious conviction. Reflecting this are ornamental portrayals of the Nine Sons of the Dragon, as listed by the scholar Xie Zhaozhe (1567–1624) in his late sixteenth-century work *Wu za zu* (Five Assorted Offerings).[18] Depicted respectively as dragons that cry, like music, swallow, like heights, kill, enjoy literature, enforce the law, meditate and bear burdens, these ornaments are appropriately placed where their dispositions carry most significance. Thus, for example, the meditative dragon is set at the base of statues of the Buddha; those that like heights, at roof corners; and those that enforce the law, at prison gates.

The most common feature of the Chinese dragon is its association with water. This is apparent in the dragon's physical development, which, in order to achieve its most refined form, can last four thousand years. In the mating process, dragon couples transform themselves into small snakes, whereafter the female lays her eggs on hills or, more often, hides them in pools. It can take over a thousand years for the eggs to hatch, which they do spontaneously. On hatching out as water snakes, the father cries out, causing a fearful wind, which is then calmed by the cry of the mother. Thunder, lightning and torrential rain accompany the hatching. Although legend warns that dragon eggs should not be touched by humans, one story tells how an old woman found five eggs in the grass, which she then undertook to keep safe. In this case, with the parents absent, when they hatched there was no elemental disturbance, so the old woman gathered up the newborn water snakes and put them in a river. For her thoughtfulness, the dragons rewarded her with the gift of prophecy.

Beyond this, after a further five hundred years, the water snake changes into the scaly, serpentine Kiao, which after another thousand years turns into the hornless *long*, a dragon proper. Five hundred years later, the *long* becomes the horned Kiaolong, and finally, after another thousand years, it is transformed into the Yinglong, which is capable of flight. Fully evolved, the horn of the male dragon is strong at the top but thin below, whereas the female is characterized by being straight-nosed with a round mane, thinner scales but a strong tail.[19] The male dragon is said to be particularly lustful.

This can prove advantageous at times of drought, for then, it is said, by exposing a naked woman on a hilltop a male dragon would inevitably be drawn to her. But in expectation of this, magic charms were used to deter the dragon, which would then vent its frustration in the form of heavy rain. Less admirably calculating are accounts of young women being cast to their deaths into lakes and seas in order to mollify a male dragon.

The science of dragons, for it is as much that in Chinese traditions as it is an aspect of a belief system, led to numerous interpretations and reappraisals of their meanings and functions, which includes their extensive medicinal properties. Although the earliest study of the medical uses of dragon body parts, said to be by the Emperor Shennong, who lived 2838–2698 BC, is lost, much of it is quoted in later sources, where it is claimed that dragons would occasionally regenerate by shedding their body parts without suffering any harm. Powdered dragon bones, teeth and horns were believed to be cures for many illnesses, including dysentery, convulsions, ulcers, bowel problems, abscesses, fevers and delusional behaviour, such as the patient being possessed by demons, while dragon fat was used as a preventive medicine and could also be smeared on garments to make them waterproof. In effect, there was no part of a dragon's anatomy that did not have a use, even if this use was sometimes more cosmetic than pharmaceutical. One example of this is dragon saliva, which was usually gathered from the sea after the dragon was believed to have departed, and was considered to be the finest of perfumes.[20]

Generally speaking, the Chinese dragon was regarded as a force that, once appropriately harnessed, could bring both good fortune and good health. This being the case, it is not so surprising that there is rarely any such thing as a heroic dragon-slayer in Chinese myth and legend. Indeed, one tale recounts how a man prepared himself for years to kill a dragon but, despite his eagerness, never had the opportunity to do so. According to the fourth-century BC Taoist philosopher Zhuang Zhou, this man epitomizes the fool and the time-waster.[21] Human respect for dragons was nevertheless attended by a wholly justified fear of them. Some of this *nāga*-like ambivalence can be seen in the following dragon personages.

The Tianlong is a celestial dragon that guards heavenly palaces and pulls divine chariots and as such would appear to pose no threat to mankind. Yet when a certain artist devoted his skill to painting dragons on the walls of his house, it prompted a curious Tianlong to call by and see the paintings for itself. Terrified of the real thing, the painter ran for his life. Controlling the weather is the Shenlong, a creature with a human head, a dragon's body and a drum-like stomach. So terrifyingly large can this creature become that, at its greatest, no one can see it in full. But the Shenlong has a personality flaw, inasmuch as it is slothful. In order to avoid work, it would take the form of a mouse and hide in haystacks, shrubbery or rooftops. Because it hid in such places, however, lightning was likely to strike, a clear sign that the god of thunder was summoning the idle Shenlong back to duty. The underworld guardian of precious metals and jewels is the Fucanglong, which is said to cause volcanic eruptions when it breaks through the earth's surface. One ninth-century BC legend tells how sailors from the Sucheng district in Jiangsu province took care to avoid a certain island, where a brilliant red light was visible by night and the sound of thousands of falling trees could be heard by day. This, believed the sailors, was a Fucanglong building its subterranean palace.[22]

While some dragons incidentally pose threats to human safety, folk-tales are told of dragons that purposefully threaten human life. One such

Dragon medallion, Ming Dynasty (1368–1644), silk and metallic thread tapestry.

The eaves on a traditional palace in Beijing.

concerns the founding of Beijing in the eleventh century BC. When the emperor orders the city to be built on marshy land, the dragons that live there are not pleased. Two of them transform themselves into an elderly couple, enter the city and, bearing two water jars, go before the emperor to seek his permission to fill them and leave. The emperor little suspects that, having granted them permission, it will be into these jars that the dragons will pour all the waters of the region, so rendering the city's land forever arid.

Now realizing that if this couple manage to reach the hills, the water can never be reclaimed, a volunteer is sought to chase after them and smash the jars. This task is taken up by the soldier Gaoliang, who, on catching up with the water thieves, manages to smash one jar before they change back into dragons. Unfortunately for Gaoliang, as he runs back to the city, a great wave of bitter water released from the smashed jar overtakes him and he drowns. The waterway that the wave went on to create is known to this day as the Gaoliang River. As for the jar that did not smash, the uniquely sweet waters it contained can now be found only at Jade Spring Hill, to the west of Beijing's Summer Palace.[23]

While folktales of dragons turning into humans are plentiful, there are also tales of humans turning into dragons. One story in which this happens is set by the river Min in Sichuan province. It is summer, and a great drought has struck the land, so forcing a young boy to search further and further afield for the fresh grass cuttings from which he and his mother make their living. Then one day, miles upriver, he comes across a patch of exceptionally lush grass. Cutting down as much he can carry, he takes it back to his village to sell. Returning to the same spot day after day, he always finds that the grass taken the previous day has regrown. Soon tiring of making this daily trip, he decides to dig deeper into the turf, so that he may take it home and plant it. But when he lifts up the patch of turf, he is staggered when a gleaming pearl drops by his feet.

Once home, he plants the turf patch and gives the pearl to his mother, who immediately recognizes its great value and puts it into an empty rice jar for safe-keeping. Next morning, the boy is disappointed to find his grass patch has withered away, but when he and his mother go to look at the pearl, they now find the jar brim-full of rice. Taking out the pearl, they put it in a jar containing the few coins they have left. Sure enough, when they go to the jar the following day, they find it full of coins. And so it goes on, mother and son getting richer by the day.

But news of their newfound wealth soon spreads, and eventually comes the attention of criminals, who break into their home, set on taking all they can find. Determined that they should not get the pearl, the boy swallows it, at which point his stomach is engulfed in fiery pain. Downing water from the pitcher only causes even greater pain, and the boy desperately casts himself into the river Min. Watched by his horrified mother, the boy swells up and, as thunder roars and the heavens open, his skin turns to scales and on his head horns begin to grow. Now a dragon thrashing its coils by the muddy banks, the one-time boy stares aghast at his mother, then turns and swims away. Forever after, the river Min dragon would ensure that drought would never strike again.

The interesting point about the Gaoliang River folktale and the river Min grass-seller folktale is that they both carry with them those same ambivalences noted in the myths. While some of the water stolen by the aggrieved dragons is recovered, it is nonetheless bitter, and, of course, the hero of the tale is drowned in his efforts to retrieve it. As for the boy and his mother, their immediate problems are solved in the finding of the pearl, but ultimately this brings about their sad separation when the boy is transformed into a dragon by the very same means that brought about their windfall. This, however, has to be seen against the background of the drought, which the boy-cum-dragon brings to an end.

Good fortune and bad fortune go hand in hand in Chinese myths, legends and folktales. Just as in Indian mythology, the dragon and its ways are neither wholly good nor wholly evil; rather they tend to reflect life's uncertainties. And sometimes, as wise emperors clearly understood, no amount of magisterial commands or looking to the skies with ritual offerings will make the slightest difference.

## The Japanese *ryū* dragon

Master of the sea and chief *ryū* is the tutelary 'Dragon-god' Ryūjin (also known as Ōwatatsumi no kami, Great God of the Sea), who lives in his red and white coral palace at the seabed. Able to swallow ships, create whirlpools and control tides with his magical tide jewellery, Ryūjin is for the most part benign, but if disrespected in any way can cause disasters at sea and on land. Ryūjin can also transform himself into a human, often to mate with women. By so doing, Ryūjin becomes the grandfather of the first Japanese emperor, Emperor Jimmu (712–586 BC). Ryūjin's chief servants are turtles, fish and jellyfish. The jellyfish, however, becomes a victim to Ryūjin's rage when he sends if off to bring back a monkey's liver as a cure for an illness he has contracted (or, in some versions, just for the pleasure of its taste). But when a certain wily monkey tells the hapless jellyfish that it must retrieve its liver from a jar hidden deep in the woods and then fails to return, the enraged Ryūjin crushes every bone in the jellyfish's body, so explaining its flaccid form ever since.

Yet Ryūjin could be of great service to Japanese emperors. When set on attacking Japan's hostile neighbours, the Koreans, Ryūjin gives Empress Jingū (AD 169–269) the 'tide-ebbing jewel', the *kanju*, and the 'tide-flowing jewel', the *manju*. When the two navies meet far out at sea, the empress first casts the *kanju* overboard, causing the tide to instantly recede, leaving both fleets stranded on the seabed. While the Japanese sailors are ordered to remain aboard, the Koreans disembark ready to engage in hand-to-hand combat, whereupon the Empress casts overboard the *manju*, so causing the waters to surge back, with the inevitable consequences for the Koreans.

Ryūjin is self-evidently that dragon that is both helpful to its devotees and a threat to them should they cause offence. One Japanese dragon that is nothing but a threat is the eight-headed, eight-tailed, red-eyed Yamata no Orochi, a vast, filthy creature that lives in the foothills of Honshu island. Orochi's favourite dish is human flesh, in particular – not unlike some

Toyohara Chikanobu, *Susanoo Rescues Kushinada Hime from the Dragon*, 1886.

dragons in Greek mythology – that of the virgin girls that he demands be left for him on a yearly basis. One couple has suffered more than most from Orochi's appetite, having already been forced to sacrifice seven of their daughters and now being told that their only remaining daughter must share the fate of her sisters.

155

It is to these distraught parents that the outcast storm god Susanoo comes and asks what it is that troubles them. When told, Susanoo promptly offers to kill Orochi in return for their daughter's hand in marriage. Having been gratefully promised as much, Susanoo casts a spell over the girl, turning her into a fine-toothed comb and then placing her in his hair, a strategy clearly intended for her safe-keeping. Susanoo now tells the parents to build an eight-gated fence around their home with a vat of newly brewed rice wine (sake) just inside each gate. Sure enough, Orochi arrives as expected and, after sniffing the air, each of his heads goes straight for the rice vats and drinks the lot, whereupon Orochi falls down in a drunken stupor. Taking out his great sword, Susanoo steps forward, swipes off the dragon's heads and then slices its body to pieces, where, strangely, he finds another sword even finer than his own.[24] As the nearby river runs red with Orochi's blood, Susanoo returns his bride-to-be to human form.[25]

Set down in the late seventh-century mythico-legendary compendium *Kojiki* (Records of Ancient Matters) and the early eighth-century dynastic histories *Nihongi* (Chronicles of Japan), mythographers have identified the myths recounted above as indigenous. Yet this does not discount the influence of Chinese mythology and, along with it, the Indian *nāga* that came with the introduction of Buddhism to Japan in the mid-sixth century AD. While the Japanese *ryū* can be a worrying omen of disaster, for example, the O-gon-cho, which transforms into a golden bird every fifty years and whose cry heralds famines and earthquakes, others, like Ryūjin, were perceived in a far more positive light. As for the wicked Orochi, whether or not this was wholly Japanese is uncertain, not least because Buddhist imports also tell of multi-headed dragons, some demonic, some deserving of reverence.[26]

One example of a revered and, in its case, revering dragon is told of through its friendship with a temple-dwelling monk whose singing it finds enchanting and spiritually uplifting. The close companionship of the monk and the dragon becomes widely known throughout the kingdom and is honoured by all. But when a drought strikes, the emperor threatens the monk with exile unless he makes his friend do only as dragons can and bring rain. Although this dragon is quite capable of doing as the emperor insists, bringing rain is not something that the higher powers would permit of it. To defy these deities would surely result in its death. While the monk declares that he would rather be exiled than have his closest friend die, the dragon insists on doing the emperor's bidding, come what may, but with one heart-felt request: that the monk preside over its funeral and then build three temples to its memory. Three days later the rain falls, and, as expected, the dragon dies. The monk, true to his word, buries the dragon at what afterwards became known as the Temple of the Dragon Garden, and thereafter builds the Temple of the Dragon Mind, the Temple of the Dragon Heaven and the Temple of the Dragon King.[27]

A similarly helpful dragon resides beneath a body of inland water known as Mano Pond. On summer's days, this dragon would bask at the surface in the form of a water snake. But one day, a predatory *tengu*, a part-human, part-bird, part-dog creature, happens by and seizes the dragon. Surprised when he cannot crush his catch, the *tengu* nonetheless flies back to its mountain nest and forces its water snake into a crack in the rock face. Now dried out, the water snake is unable to resume its dragon form and, so, escape. Then one day, the *tengu* returns with a monk and crams him into the same space. At first surprised when his water snake fellow prisoner starts questioning him, the monk tells how he was seized by the *tengu* as he was collecting the water that he still carries with him. The water snake asks the monk to throw the water over it, and when he does, the restored dragon smashes open the crack and, with the monk aboard, flies off to take him home. But before returning to Mano Pond, the dragon seeks out the *tengu* and takes revenge.

Less helpful dragons, thought to have been directly influenced by Indian and Chinese mythology, are to be found in certain folktales concerning dragon-women. Kiyohime, the 'Purity Princess', is a teahouse waitress who has fallen madly in love with a handsome Buddhist monk from the Dōjōji Temple in Wakayama prefecture. Bound by the rules of his holy order, the monk cannot reciprocate and politely spurns her advances. Devastated by her rejection, Kiyohime devotes her time to studying magic and manages to change herself into a dragon. She then goes in pursuit of the monk at his temple, where, for safe-keeping, his fellow monks have concealed him inside the temple's bell. But Kiyohime spots the unfortunate monk and coils herself around the bell, which heats up to melting point and reduces the monk to ashes.[28]

Unlike Kiyohime, who at least has a motive for killing the poor monk, albeit a deranged one, is the vampiric dragon-woman Nure-onna, the 'Wet Woman', whose practice is to wash her hair by the river. Nure-onna carries with her a bundle that resembles that of a swaddled baby. Should a helpful passer-by offer to hold the bundle as she washes, then it latches firmly on to its holder's hand and grows increasingly heavy, until escape is impossible. The dragon-woman then extends her forked tongue and sucks out all the blood from her victim.[29]

Yoshitoshi Tsukioka, *Kiyohime Turning Into a Serpent*, mid-19th century.

Strongly reminiscent of the Lamia and the Melusine European folk myths (see chapters One and Eight respectively), and doubtless carrying with them the same gender prejudices, another possible origin of these tales lies in an early Japanese myth about Toyotama-hime (Luminous Pearl Princess), the daughter of the dragon sea god, named here as Ōwatatsumi, a by-name for Ryūjin. Reflected in a pool by the gates of her father's palace, the princess sees Hohodemi, a strikingly handsome young man, and asks her father to invite him to visit them. The princess and the young man soon marry, and for three years all is well. But when Toyotama-hime falls pregnant, Hohodemi decides that the child should be born and raised on land. A house is built by the sea, so that the princess can feel as much at home as possible. As childbirth approaches, Toyotama-hime asks her husband to promise not to watch her in labour, to which he agrees.

Yet just as in the Melusine tales, the curious husband breaks his promise and sees his wife giving birth in dragon form. Angered and embarrassed by his treachery, Toyotama-hime deserts both husband and child and returns to her seabed palace, where she makes sure to prevent any further free passage between her father's realm and that of humans. Even so, the princess is still in love with her abandoned husband and sends him both love letters and her young sister to help raise their child. She herself never again returns to land.[30]

A similarly unfortunate encounter, also with the daughter of the dragon sea god Ryūjin, is recounted in a folktale, versions of which date back to the eighth century.[31] Set on the south coast of Japan, the fisherman Urashima Tarō sees some children tormenting a tortoise, which he rescues and sets free. The following day, while out fishing, a large turtle comes to him and tells him that the tortoise was none other than the dragon-princess Otohime, who would now like to thank him in person. Using its magic powers to equip Tarō with gills, the turtle carries him to a splendid sea-bottom palace, where at each of the palace's four walls a different season can be seen. Princess Otohime, now a beautiful woman, fêtes her guest for three days, after which he asks her permission to return to his home to take care of his elderly mother, who is sure to be worrying about him. Sorry that he has to leave, Otohime gives

Nure-onna as depicted in Sawaki Suushi's *Hyakkai-Zukan*, 1737.

Tarō a *tamatebako*, a delicate origami box, telling him that it will keep him from harm but that he must never open it.

On being carried back to land by the turtle, Tarō is startled to find his home vanished and his mother nowhere to be found. He now asks a villager if he knows where the home of Urashima Tarō and his mother is, and is told that there is an old tale of someone by that name who went out fishing one day, never to return. Tarō quickly comes to realize that three hundred years have passed during the three days he spent with Princess Otohime at her father's palace. Mortified, he sits weeping by the sea shore clutching the *tamatebako* in his hand, one side of which falls open, releasing a cloud of white smoke. Suddenly, Tarō finds his skin wrinkled, his hair white and his back bent. About to die, he hears the sad voice of the Princess Otohime drifting across the waves telling him that the box contained his old age.[32]

Not all Japanese dragon-woman tales end unhappily, however. In this final tale, 'Tawara Tōda', or 'My Lord Bag of Rice', as recorded in the early eighteenth-century collection of Japanese folktales *Honchō kwaidan koji*, the hero is rewarded for his bravery by a dragon-woman and, on this occasion, there is no love interest involved.

Back in the early tenth century, a warrior by the name of Fujiwara no Hidesato has set out in search of adventure. Armed with two swords and his bow and arrows, he comes to a bridge over one end of a great lake. Lying across the bridge, with its claws rested on a parapet on one side and its coiled tail across the other side, is a great dragon with smoke and fire streaming

Utagawa Kuniyoshi,
*Urashima Taro
Returning on the Turtle*,
1870–90.

Katsushika Hokusai, *Dragon*, c. 1830.

from its nostrils. But Hidesato refuses to turn back and steps across the drag-on's coils and carries on regardless. As he does so, the dragon disappears into the lake and then returns to the bridge, now as a beautiful woman begging Hidesato to return. This he does, whereupon she tells him that in the two thousand years she has lived under the bridge, she has never encountered anyone as brave as he. She then pleads with him to help her by destroying her most fearsome enemy, a giant centipede that has killed her sons and grandsons.[33] Unhesitatingly, Hidesato agrees.

Stationed by the bridge, Hidesato awaits the centipede's coming and soon he sees two great balls of fire heading towards him, side by side. Realizing that these are the centipede's eyes, Hidesato places an arrow in his bow and takes fire. But now the centipede's vast body, coiling down a mountain, is fully visible, and he sees his arrow glance harmlessly off it. Undeterred, he fires again and again but to no effect, until, with just one arrow left, the

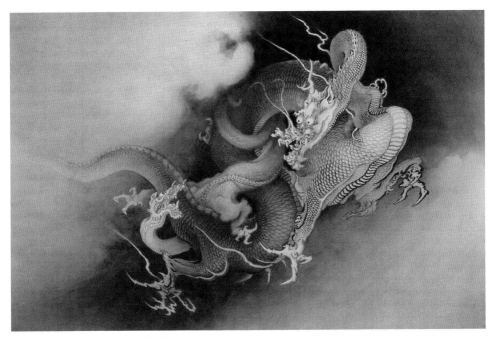

Kano Hogai, *Two Dragons in Clouds*, 1885.

centipede is almost upon him. Then he suddenly remembers an old story telling that human saliva is deadly to centipedes. After wetting the arrow in his mouth, he takes aim and fires, this time hitting the centipede square in the middle of its head, penetrating its brain, extinguishing its fireball eyes and causing it to breathe its last.

The dragon-woman is overjoyed and takes Hidesato to her lake palace, where she feeds him great delicacies and gives him five precious gifts: a never-ending piece of silk; a sword and armour; a temple bell; a pot in which everything cooked will be delicious; and a bag of rice that can never be emptied. Now a man amply provided for and from here on known as Tawara Tōda, 'My Lord Bag of Rice', Hidesato lives out his life in prosperity and good cheer. As for the dragon-woman, he never sees her again. However, legend tells how Hidesato donated the bell to Mii-dera temple at Mount Hiei in Shiga prefecture. When it is stolen by a monk from another temple, the bell speaks to the thief, alarming him so greatly that he casts it into a valley, where it cracks. Later retrieved by its rightful owners, the still grateful dragon-woman, now in the guise of a small snake, comes to the temple and repairs the bell.[34]

THE MOST OBVIOUS DIFFERENCE BETWEEN the myths and legends discussed in this chapter and those discussed in previous chapters is that while the Asian and East Asian dragon can pose a major threat to humanity's survival, it can also be humanity's only hope of survival. This we can see taking place in myths of cosmic significance, as well as in their folktale derivations, where the significance of the dragon is typically terrestrial and localized. Often having godlike status and revered as such, the Asian and East Asian dragon is frequently unpredictable. The issues are invariably those of power and authority, and in these respects, the dragon is simultaneously admired and feared. Yet there is one significant dissimilarity between the East Asian and the Asian dragon, one that also distinguishes the East Asian dragon from all others worldwide. This is that the East Asian dragon is politicized, or, more precisely, imperialized, whereby the dragon's power is often as much an expression of an emperor's or empress's power as it is of its own. While this is not to say that the East Asian dragon has no independence, for at times it quite clearly does, its apparent benevolence can frequently be seen as the face of dynastic authority. In this respect, those Chinese and Japanese dragons that willingly act in service to sovereignty carry with them an extraordinarily effective message about the supernatural nature of those mortals holding the reins of absolute power.

It is perhaps not surprising, then, that what we very rarely see in these myths is the dragon-slaying hero; indeed, the old Chinese saying wishing you well in 'slaying your dragon' simply means good luck in overcoming your

Japanese dragon dance.

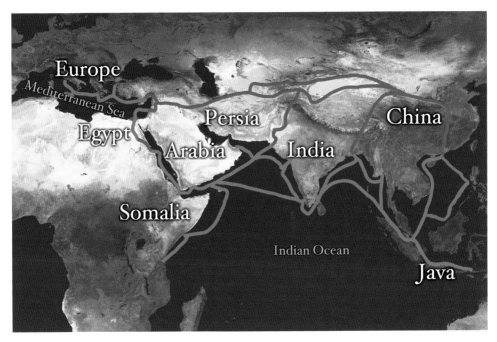

Silk Road routes by land and sea.

current difficulties. Rather, in myths where dragons are slain, it is not by a mere mortal but, more typically, by semi-divine individual, such as Susanoo, or by another being with supernatural powers, such as Garuda. This again is a major distinction from all other the mythologies considered, for what this means is that, despite the East Asian dragon being a mirror image of imperial authority, both the Asian and East Asian dragon can also be a law unto itself. The dragon's autonomy is something that all humans, emperors included, must respect, and, instead of challenging its potential or actual life-threatening behaviour, the only option is to attempt to persuade it to act otherwise, typically in the form of tributes or, as in the interventions of the Buddha, by enlightened argument.

So it is that while the Christian, Germanic, Celtic and classical dragon is commonly either plain evil or something approaching that extreme, it is simply not possible to label the Asian and East Asian dragon in such a way. One reason for this is that, unlike other dragons, many dragons of the East have multifaceted personalities and are as a result subject to complex behaviours. In this sense, they are like humans in that they are capable of acting wisely and foolishly, considerately and vindictively, thoughtfully and rashly. Given these traits, the Asian and East Asian dragon would appear to be hyperboles of humans, our virtues and our vices. As mentioned previously in respect of the *nāga*, just as it is with humans, the dragons of the East are as much an embodiment of Culture as they are of Nature.

The configuration of beliefs about Eastern dragons is due to an entirely different mindset to that which configured the Western dragon. Aside from the 'imperialization' of the East Asian dragon, the key philosophical principles underlying the understanding of dragons are determined by the perspectives of Brahmanism, Hinduism, Confucianism, Taoism, Shinto and Buddhism, wherein absolutist thinking seldom has a propitious outcome. This is particularly true as regards Buddhism. Yet while Buddhist thinking is quite apparent in some dragon myths, legends and folktales, the general view that this led to an amelioration of indigenous dragon lore is extremely hard to prove in every respect, not least because of the complex ancient history of the mythologies.

As for imported influences on the Asian and East Asian dragon, this too is problematic. While some aspects of the Indian dragon were bound to have similarities to other dragons in the Indo-European group, one cannot help but notice the less readily explicable similarities between certain East Asian dragons and those of Western Indo-European mythology. A particularly striking example of this is the Japanese myth of the killing of the eight-headed Orochi by Susanoo, which is reminiscent both of Heracles

Illustration from the *Book of Marvels*, 13th century, written in Old French by Rustichello da Pisa from stories told by Marco Polo.

Folio from the *Shahnameh* of Shah Tahmasp, attributed to Aqa Mirak, *c.* 1525–35.

slaying of the multi-headed Hydra and of the Perseus and Andromeda myth. While some Japanese comparative mythologists have suggested that Greek myths may well have been imported by Central Eurasian Scythian traders, a nomadic people who were most active between the ninth and first centuries BC, there is nonetheless no consensus as regards such cultural contact.[35] Even so, there were bound to have been mythological ideas that migrated from Mediterranean regions to the East Asian, and vice versa, as a result of East–West trade routes, the most trafficked of which was the Silk Road, beginning in the first century BC.[36]

What we can be more certain about is contact between East and West that is well documented, albeit that ideas about the cultures of the East often took the form of that prejudicial belittling known as 'Orientalism'.[37] As discussed in Chapter Three, Alexander the Great and his armies were active in India in the fourth century BC and were troubled by what Alexander believed to be dragons. After Alexander, knowledge of Asia and the beliefs held there would have increased significantly throughout the time of the Roman Empire. Greater understanding of the cultures of Asia and East Asia came about as a result of eastward-bound Christian missionaries from the fourth-century AD, through to Jesuit reports about Chinese philosophy that impacted on Western thinking from the fifteenth century through to the eighteenth. And, of course, where Christianity went, so did Graeco-Roman mythology.

Adding further insights were the likes of Marco Polo, whose travels in the latter half of the thirteenth century took him to the Chinese province of Karazan, where he reported seeing two-legged, glaring-eyed draconic serpents some 9 metres (30 ft) long and 2.5 metres (8 ft) wide with gaping jaws and large teeth.[38] Similarly, John Mandeville's mid-fourteenth-century travels increased both an understanding of, and a curiosity about, the cultures and beliefs of the 'mysterious' East. As the first Westerner to record the 'Melusine' tales that he gathered on his visit to the Mediterranean

Image from the *Shahnameh* showing Barham Gur on horseback killing a dragon.

The djinn Shamhurash as a mounted dragon fighter, 1262.

The Iranian mythical king Faridun in the guise of a dragon testing his three sons in a medieval manuscript.

regions, it is tempting to speculate that there could well have been a Silk Road transmission of them.

While missionaries, explorers, traders and military invaders would most certainly have led to perceptions of cultural difference by both those in the West and the East, albeit not always favourable ones, the influence of Chinese dragon art imports on Persian, Turkish and Mughal artists was profound.[39] This was particularly so during the years of China's Yuan dynasty (1279–1368) and Ming dynasty (1368–1644), when trade links between Iran and China were close and Chinese artists were based in Iran's Rashīd al-Dīn academy at Tabriz. Although pictorial artists across these Islamic regions did not share the Chinese view of the dragon as a creature worthy of reverence, and instead depicted their dragons as a formidable menace to humans, their artworks, if not their values and beliefs, were quite clearly inspired by Chinese traditions.

Yet despite sporadic cultural contacts and, so far as Persia and the Middle East was concerned, partial cultural fusions, Eastern and Western ideas about dragons remained chiefly insular. Firm ground for much more significant cultural understanding and, as a consequence, influence would not be reached until the late nineteenth century, when mass migration to the West from a politically unstable China, mainly to the United States, resulted in far greater knowledge of East Asia than at any previous time. This will be apparent in Chapter Ten, where many modern dragons in fantasy fictions are presented according to the Chinese view of them as life-enhancing.

Reproduction of a painting by Ivan Yakovlevich Bilibin depicting the Zmey Gorynych (Slavic three-headed dragon), 1912.

*seven*

# Dragons in the Anti-establishment Folktale

WHILE THE MEDIEVAL Romance dragons discussed in the following chapter typically reflect the dangers posed to, and the resultant heroics of, the landed gentry, matters were often quite different in folktales. In many of these, the common theme is rags-to-riches, a journey typically involving a relatively low-born or low-ranking male overcoming a dragon and, in so doing, winning the hand of a princess and gaining promotion to the nobility.[1]

A good example of this type of folktale is the Slavic story of the three-headed, fire-spitting dragon Gorynych. This creature's uncle is the sorcerer Chelovek, who could take the form of a giant and whose aim was to make Gorynych the ruler of all Russia. As part of his plan, Chelovek kidnaps the tsar's daughter and imprisons her in a remote tower guarded by Gorynych. Many fail in their attempt to find and free her and so win the great reward promised by her anxious father. Then one day the clever but otherwise untested palace guard Ivan overhears two crows talking about the location of the tower. Ivan advises the tsar as much and, on receiving the magic sword Samosek from his royal master, sets out for the tower. On his arrival, Chelovek and the dragon confront him, whereupon the sword flies from Ivan's hand and impales Chelovek and then proceeds to hack off the heads of Gorynych. In reward for his achievements, Ivan is granted permission to marry the now besotted princess and is raised to the rank of nobleman.[2]

While dragon folktales such as this echo the Perseus and Andromeda type of dragon-slayer myths and are probably indebted to them, others are less conventional. In these, behind the rags-to-riches dramatics there lurk the thinly disguised frustrations that inevitably resulted from the oppression of the peasantry and the lower orders generally, and, as a response to their subjugation, their dreams of a fairer and better life. Hopeless in reality though these dreams would, for the main part, have been, these folktales can nevertheless be regarded as a challenge to the aristocratic elite.

The following tales have been selected as representative of this particular branch of folktale dragon lore, not only for reason of their particular coherence and narrative brilliance but because of the way in which they can be interpreted as signifiers of the ruling classes as, by the very nature of their assumed rights of birth, dragon-like subjugators.

## The Lambton Worm

It is a Sunday in the early decades of the fifteenth century, and on the Lambton Estate near the River Wear in northeast England the young heir to the estate, John Lambton, has gone fishing rather than attend Mass.[3] To the dismay of his father and to the offence of the local peasantry, this fellow has a reputation for dissolute and ungodly behaviour. As he stands in the river loudly cursing his slack line, careless of the solemnity of passing churchgoers, he suddenly gets a bite. But on reeling in his catch, he finds he has caught not the fine fish he was hoping for but a hideous worm with nine holes on either side of its head.[4] Horrified, he hurls the creature into a nearby well, known since as Worm Well. When an old man stops by and asks what sport he is having, John declares that he has caught the Devil himself. Peering into the well, the old man predicts that no good will come of this creature. Not long after, John repents his wickedness and, by way of atonement, journeys to the Holy Land to join the Crusades.

Meanwhile, the worm grows so large that it escapes the well and returns to the River Wear, where it coils itself around a large rock. As it continues to grow, it moves from the river at nightfall to the base of a nearby hill, where over the course of time it becomes large enough to encircle it three times.[5] This monster now takes to terrorizing the countryside, draining the cows of milk and eating alive lambs and even young children, whom it drags from their beds. No one can stop it, not even those knights-at-arms who, on hearing of the worm's ravaging, volunteer themselves to combat it, only to be maimed or to die in the effort. Worse still is the worm's ability to reunite itself with any parts of it that its combatants have hacked off.

Now the worm turns its attention to the estate's manor house, Lambton Hall, and crosses the river bent on destroying it. Only by the daily filling of a large trough with the milk of nine cows and placing it by the hall's entrance is the household able to escape further harm.[6] This sorry state of affairs

The Lambton Worm as depicted on an early 20th-century cigarette card.

CHURCHMAN'S CIGARETTES

THE LAMBTON WORM

continues for seven years, whereupon John Lambton, now a member of the military-religious order of the Knights of Rhodes, returns home.

Shocked by the widespread desolation he encounters, John seeks advice from a local witch. At first, he gets nothing more than her sharp tongue for having brought about this disaster, but on recognizing that his penitence is sincere, the witch relents and tells him that before confronting the worm he must put on his finest armour, having first studded it with dozens of razor-sharp spear heads. But there is one condition: should he succeed in killing the worm, he must then kill the first living thing he encounters. Failure to do this, warns the witch, will mean the next nine generations of Lambton lords will not die in their beds. John prepares himself accordingly and advises his old father that when he hears him sounding his horn, announcing his victory, the estate's fastest dog should be set loose to come to him. In this way, John's first encounter will not be with a fellow human.

Come the hour that the worm is due to cross the river and head for Lambton Hall, John positions himself on a boulder midstream and awaits its arrival. Seeing its one-time captor stationed between it and the Hall, the worm lunges at John and coils itself about him. But, as planned, the spear heads gouge into its flesh, causing large chunks to be severed and washed away until, sliced asunder bit by bit and further injured by John's ever-increasing ability to wield his sword, the worm is utterly mutilated with no prospect of it ever reconstituting itself. Triumphant, John sounds his horn, but on hearing it his father is so overjoyed by his son's victory that he forgets what was agreed and instead sets off running to meet him. Unwilling to kill his own father, whatever the consequences may be, John desperately cries out to him to set the dog loose, but it is too late and killing the dog achieves nothing. Just as predicted, a curse falls on the Lambtons.[7]

There has been some, not wholly improbable, speculation that a dragon-slaying tale was brought back to Lambton Hall by the historical Sir John

George Bewick, *Lambton Worm*, 1890.

Lambton after his time as a Crusader, and that his descendants honoured him with a similar tale recounting that he, too, was a dragon-slayer.[8] Yet as concerns the curse laid on the Lambtons, this must surely have been a retrospective addition to the tale, based on the fact that several subsequent generations of Lambton lords did indeed come to an untimely end.[9] Nevertheless, it is quite possible to read this tale, as it has evolved, not as one in praise of, or commiseration with, the Lambtons but as one critical of their neglect and disregard for the peasantry.

The underlying significance of the Lambton Worm would appear to lie in the ungodliness of the young John Lambton. In this respect, John Lambton's identification of the worm as the Devil can be interpreted as meaning that the worm is a symbolic manifestation of his own sinfulness, a failing that would have been most harshly felt by the local peasantry. Might there then be an element of resentment of aristocratic hauteur, a bitterness which had both a religious and a social class basis? Should this be the case, it could explain why John Lambton's determination to compensate for his wrongdoings, initially by joining the Crusades, is not seen as compensation enough, for it is in his absence that the worm wreaks havoc in the locality. So much is clear in the witch's initial criticism of him on his return. Nor is his killing of the worm sufficient atonement, for John Lambton's victory is, in this sense, pyrrhic. The mayhem unleashed by the Lambton Worm, at first a hardship borne mainly by the peasantry, becomes in the end a curse laid on the Lambtons for the next two hundred years. From the point of view of the peasantry – those who handed down and embellished the tale from generation to generation – its lasting popularity could ultimately be seen to cradle a grim satisfaction.

## The Mordiford Wyvern

In the woods close by the village of Mordiford in Herefordshire, where the River Lugg meets the River Wye, young Maud, the daughter of a local farmer, is picking blackberries. Stooping down, she sees a small, winged, two-legged, flashing-eyed creature, scarcely the size of a cucumber. Dazzled by its beauty, Maud coaxes it towards her and kisses it. Unperturbed by Maud's affection, the creature allows itself to be picked up, and, tucking it in her dress, Maud sets off home to show her family what she now regards as her very own pet. Yet her parents are not so enamoured of Maud's find and immediately identify it as a young dragon, a wyvern, a deadly beast that should be killed there and then. But when Maud pleads with her father to spare it, he relents and, trapping it in a box, takes it to an outhouse for overnight keeping.

Come the morning, before anyone else has woken, Maud goes to the outhouse and, fearful that her parents are still likely to do away with her newfound pet, feeds it some milk and hides it in the woods, where she is sure it will not be discovered. Questioned by her father as to what she has been doing, Maud tells him that the creature has escaped, that it is now nowhere to be found and that maybe the dog has eaten it. Maud then secretly continues caring for her rapidly growing dependant. But so large does it become that very soon milk is not sufficient for its needs and it quits its forest hideaway to seek out a richer diet, one of blood, first from sheep and cattle, then eventually from humans. While to Maud the dragon remains harmless, to the local populace it is a terror from which they desperately need to be freed. Yet such is the dragon's power that all who try to kill it are slain in their efforts, either by its mighty claws or by its poisonous breath.

Time passes and the dragon's ravaging only grows worse. Then one day a prisoner by the name of Garston, a local man sentenced to death for his crimes, declares that he will fight the dragon on condition that should he survive victorious, he is pardoned. It is an offer that cannot be refused. Taking a large barrel and studding its exterior with sharp blades and hooks, Garston places it in the dragon's known path and conceals himself inside, where, armed with a pistol and a large knife, he can keep watch through a peephole. The dragon duly arrives and on smelling human flesh coils itself about the barrel, intending to crush it, at which point it is promptly incapacitated by the lacerations it receives. As planned, Garston fires a pistol shot through the peephole, knocking the dragon to the ground. Emerging quickly from the barrel, Garston now raises his knife and decapitates the beast – but too late, for he inhales its breath and dies. Watching all this is the distraught Maud.

This version, among several others, of the Mordiford Wyvern tale was recounted to J. Dacres Devlin during his stay in Mordiford in 1847.[10] But, as Dacres Devlin recounts, there are at least two other versions, in which the young girl's role is largely irrelevant. In one, deemed to be the oldest, Garston is no criminal but a selfless local nobleman who kills the wyvern and survives. In the other, which follows this earliest known version but precedes the version recounted above, Garston the criminal is victorious and, as promised, reprieved. Notably, as concerns the oldest version, the lords of the manor in Mordiford in the seventeenth and eighteenth centuries were the Garstons, whose family crest depicted a great wyvern, and it seems likely that the Mordiford Wyvern tale was originally told in their honour.[11] What is most interesting here is how Garston the nobleman became Garston the criminal, initially one who is triumphant and gains his freedom but thereafter one who dies in his dragon-slaying efforts.

Given the likely historical sequence of the Mordiford Wyvern tales, what appears to have taken place over time is what has been described as the legend being 'democratized',[12] most likely after either the death or departure of the Garston family. Yet one might also add that the Garston's Wyvern crest is not without relevance. Assuming, as is typically the case, that the Garston crest signified the power and authority of this noble family, one cannot help thinking that in the later versions of the tale, the Mordiford dragon signified the Garstons themselves.

This being so, then the democratized version, in which Garston the criminal triumphs as a dragon-slayer, suggests that the nobility were in a metaphorical sense recompensing for their perceived misdeeds, which may have been no more than them holding sway by dint of birth. But in the tale recounted here, where Garston the criminal is killed, Garston and the dragon simply cancel each other out. In other words, as both the wyvern *and* its ill-fated slayer, the Garstons ceased to have any significance whatsoever, except, that is, as either an old memory or, more likely, a current perception of class injustice, thus not entirely unlike the curse that is said to have fallen upon the Lambtons in those late versions of the Lambton Worm tale.[13]

While Dacres Devlin tries hard to identify the earliest origin of the Mordiford Wyvern, seeing, sometimes rather tenuously, connections with dragon myths of the classical world, Viking tales of dragons and their dragon-prowed longships, and traditional Welsh dragon tales, a more interesting aspect of this particular tale is its local history. Until the early nineteenth century, a painting of a wyvern, most probably a depiction the Garston family crest, was hung on the wall of Mordiford parish church. This, however, was not to the liking of the then parish priest, who saw it as an image of Satan and had it destroyed.

Yet as Dacres Devlin repeatedly notes in respect of his informants, this priest's act of censorship did not prevent this wyvern tale persisting as a reality in the folk imagination. Some decades after Dacres Devlin had departed to his London home, it is said that the Rector of Mordiford came across two old women who, apparently believing that they had found baby dragons, were attempting to drown two newts in the church font. While this is most likely no more than an old joke – one cannot drown a newt, of course – it remains the case that newts were widely regarded as dangerous creatures, for if anyone swallowed their spawn by drinking pond water, it was cautioned, newts would hatch, breed inside the stomach and devour all that is ingested, so bringing about a deeply unpleasant death.[14] Young Maud's foolish refusal to accept that her pet was in any way dangerous may well have originated in such reasonable health warnings.

## The Wawel Dragon

Similar class tensions are also apparent in a fifteenth-century version of a Polish folktale that was first recorded in the thirteenth century by the Bishop of Kraków, Wincenty Kadłubek (1161–1223).[15] This tells how the realm of King Krakus is plagued by a dragon, known fittingly as the 'The Whole-swallower', whose lair is a cave at the foot of Wawel Hill by the Vistula River. Mollified only by the populace feeding it their cattle, the dragon would otherwise have devoured them instead.

Desperate to be rid of this terrible menace, King Krakus orders his two sons, the elder Lech and the younger Krakus II, to kill it. Having at first failed to defeat it in combat, the sons are advised by their father to pack an oxhide with burning sulphur and leave it for the dragon alongside the usual offerings. This they do, and when the dragon swallows it, it is incinerated from the inside out. Yet Krakus II is not content to share the glory and turns

*Wawel Dragon* sculpture by Polish sculptor Bronisław Chromy in Kraków, Poland.

on his elder brother and kills him, thereafter claiming that this was the dragon's work. He thus makes himself successor to the throne of his unwitting father.

Nevertheless, Krakus II's deception is soon discovered, and he is forced into exile for the remainder of his days. Not long after King Krakus dies, and as part of the continuing funeral obsequies, the city of Kraków is founded and the king's virgin daughter, Wanda, is elected to the throne. Some testimony to the once widespread belief in this dragon tale is the fact that since the Middle Ages dinosaur bones, said to be those of the Wawel Dragon, have been hung outside Kraków's Wawel Cathedral. The associated legend claims that the world will end when the bones fall to the floor.

While it is clear that the manner of the killing of the Wawel Dragon is much indebted to the dragon killing in the apocryphal tale of Bel and the Dragon that was once included in the Old Testament Book of Daniel, the conspicuous element of it is, once again, the treachery, and in this case fratricide, by a member of the aristocracy. Although it is perhaps stretching a point to interpret the dragon as a personification of Krakus II, there is nonetheless a symmetry between the dragon's greed and violence and that of the king's youngest son. It may well have been the distrust of some members of the ruling elite by ordinary folk that gave rise to the second, much better-known version of the tale as it was told some two hundred years later.

In this version, the hero is not an aristocrat but a poor cobbler's son named Skuba. Here, the dragon is set on devastating the countryside and any knight who dares confront it is doomed to a fiery death. Nor is the dragon satisfied with mere livestock: once a month it expects a virgin girl to be left at its cave for it to savour. Before long, there are no young girls left to sacrifice – except, that is, just one: the king's daughter, Wanda. Without any option other than to do just as his subjects have done, the king proclaims that any man who can save her will have her hand in marriage. Many accept the challenge, but none succeed. Then the lowly Skuba steps forward. As in the early tale, a farm animal – on this occasion, a sheep – is stuffed with sulphur and left by Skuba for the dragon to feast on; notably, in this version, an idea entirely of the hero's own devising. When the dragon does as Skuba intended, it develops a raging thirst and hurls itself into the River Vistula, half of which it swallows, causing it to swell up and explode. Skuba, as promised, marries Wanda and they live happily ever after, presumably with considerable authority and in great comfort; in other words, in a manner that was the exact opposite to that which Skuba had known in his previous life.[16]

The winning of a virgin bride by overcoming a monster of some variety is an ancient motif and it is highly probable that Skuba's triumph was directly inspired by similar tales in Greek mythology or by later accounts of Christian saints. While there are a number of possible prototypes, ranging from Perseus and Andromeda to St George and the King of Silena's daughter, perhaps the earliest and closest similarity can be found in the myth of Heracles' rescue of Hesione (see Chapter One), who had been staked out as a sacrifice to a sea monster by her father, the king of Troy, as the last remaining virgin girl in his realm.

Other than these likely origins, the most interesting aspect of the two versions of the killing of the Wawel Dragon is that, in the earliest of them, there is no virgin bride to be won but instead a story involving a murderous and deceitful prince, while in the latter version we have a nobody whose intelligence and heroism are rewarded with a rank that would have been beyond the wildest imaginings of his class. While Skuba's achievement is, in any socially realistic sense, pure fantasy, the point surely is that this is what the lower orders substituted for a tradition in which only the upper classes could succeed and where, in the brutally competitive world of these aristocrats, moral values were in deep jeopardy. The implicit comparison with the Krakus II tale that the Skuba tale invites is, then, one loaded with disapproval of the divisiveness of the ruling orders.

## Assipattle and the Stoor Worm

Passed down through the generations for centuries in Orkney, Scotland, and believed to have originated from the settlement of Orkney during the Viking Age, this splendidly fantastical folktale is set in Scandinavia.[17] The drama begins when a vast sea serpent known as the Stoor Worm, which is said to girdle the entire earth, suddenly takes to attacking and despoiling the land and its inhabitants. In desperation, the king seeks the advice of a sorcerer, who tells him that the only way to placate the worm is to feed it seven virgins every Saturday. Just as is commonly the case in such dragon tales, the supply of virgins soon runs out, and, again advised by the sorcerer, the king accepts that he must now sacrifice his own daughter, the princess Gem-de-Lovely, who is adored by all except her wicked stepmother. The only hope for the princess is that, by way of reward for killing the worm, someone will take up her father's offer of herself as a bride, the throne and the great sword Sickersnapper, a weapon once owned by none other than the Norse god Odin.

As news of the king's reward circulates, a farmer's son, Assipattle, declares that he will accept the challenge. Yet Assipattle is known both for his idleness and his fantasizing about himself as some kind of hero, usually out loud as he sprawls by the fire of an evening. His elder brothers and his father are quite used to the work-shy Assipattle's tenuous grip on reality, and they mock him. The only support he has ever received came from his sister, but she has now left home to enter royal service as a maid to Gem-de-Lovely. Nonetheless, determined to prove himself, Assipattle presents himself at the king's court, only to find that his reputation has preceded him and he is rejected, on the grounds that he is a ne'er-do-well. It therefore transpires that, come the Friday before the princess is due to be sacrificed, when there is still no one either willing or capable of confronting the worm, the king resolves to arm himself with Sickersnapper, ready the royal boat and fight the Stoor Worm himself.

Meanwhile, that same day, as the common-folk start to gather by the shore to watch their king take on the worm, Assipattle overhears his parents talking of their horse Teegong, which, he learns, can outrun the wind when its rider blows through the windpipe of a goose. That night, Assipattle goes to the stable, mounts Teegong and rides at full pelt to the coast, where he takes a bucket of burning peat from an old peasant woman and tricks the king's guard into bringing the royal boat ashore, which he then takes for himself.

As the sun rises, Assipattle heads straight for the worm's vast gaping maw and sails into it. After travelling for miles down through its gullet, Assipattle eventually reaches the worm's liver, into which he gouges a hole and empties the burning peat, and, much helped by the now retching and agonized worm, sails back up through its gullet and is vomited out to sea. Gradually consumed from within by fire, the worm stretches its tongue out to the moon's horn, and as its tongue collapses back to earth, a great rift is caused, so creating both the Oresund Strait and the Baltic Sea, while the wrecked teeth from its collapsing head create Orkney, the Shetlands and the Faroe Islands. Now reaching the end of its death throes, the worm's body forms Iceland, and the inferno that is its liver creates Iceland's volcanoes.

Needless to say, the king and the princess are jubilant, and Assipattle is duly rewarded. He and Gem-de-Lovely then ride back to the palace, where they are greeted by Assipattle's sister, who tells them that the sorcerer and the king's wife have been having an affair and that they have now fled. Armed with Sickersnapper, Assipattle rides off in pursuit, hacks down the sorcerer and returns the princess's wicked stepmother to the king, who has her incarcerated in a tower for the rest of her life. The marriage of King Assipattle and Queen Gem-de-Lovely soon takes place; as the earliest collected version of the tale says in the Orcadian dialect, 'An' gin no' deed, dei'r livin' yet' (And if not dead, they are yet alive).[18]

Assipattle and the Stoor Worm is particularly interesting for several reasons. Unlike Skuba, whose triumph, while exceptional, does nothing other than to elevate him from the peasantry to the aristocracy, Assipattle's triumph also leads him to putting paid to treacherous intrigues that threaten the monarchy, for quite clearly the sorcerer and the wicked stepmother were using the problem of the Stoor Worm to further their own ends. In their case, it would seem, the plan was to usurp the throne by getting rid of both the king and his successor, the princess.

Moreover, one outcome of Assipattle's heroics is the creation of new territories. In this sense, Assipattle and the Stoor Worm constitutes a foundation myth, an explanation for the existence of Scandinavian dominated regions, some of which, like Orkney, were far-flung. Assipattle, then, is a creator, more godlike than human. Supporting this is the resemblance of the Stoor Worm to that monster of grotesque proportions in Old Norse mythology the Midgard Serpent, and as regards this doubtless intended similarity, Assipattle acts as a Thor figure, the only one capable of tackling such a threat. The allusion to the patronage of Odin that Assipattle eventually receives in material form as Odin's sword Sickersnapper, as well Assipattle's use of a horse of supernatural speed, which is somewhat reminiscent of Odin's eight-legged steed Sleipnir, further indicates this folktale's associations with Norse mythology.

Besides this and the slightly more complex and ingenious use of the Hesione and Bel and the Dragon motifs, there is the personage of Assipattle himself. We are introduced to the hero as a layabout, a figure who is familiar in early Germanic legend, known in medieval Icelandic sagas as the 'coal-biter' (Old Norse *kolbítr*), that youth who loafs by the fire's ashes, avoiding all work, but in due course goes on to achieve greatness. In Assipattle's case, however, his indolent familiarity with the ashes would appear to have inspired his plan to overcome the Stoor Worm by burning it alive with peat. Some clue to the underlying meaning of all this lies in the name Assipattle.

The presence of the conniving wicked stepmother, and her efforts to do down both her husband and her stepdaughter, immediately calls to mind one of the oldest and most widespread folktales, 'Cinderella', whose derogatory nickname in early German folktales is Aschenputtel or Aschenbrödel, meaning 'Ash-fool', a character who is the embodiment of the unjustly oppressed. Yet while that allusion is self-evidently there in the treatment of Gem-de-Lovely, it is also just as clearly there in the character and actions of Assipattle, whose name can be translated as 'Ash-raker'.[19] As the nineteenth-century philologist and folklorist Jacob Grimm observed, many early Cinderella figures were male. While it is not immediately obvious that there is a sociopolitical message such as those made in the other folktales that have been considered, there is nonetheless a process of dramatic reversal, in which Assipattle represents a new world order and the Stoor Worm the oppression, or at least the limitations and ultimate demise, of the old order. Assipattle is an agent of change for the better for all concerned.

What we have in Assipattle and the Stoor Worm is Old Norse mythology combined with local legend, ancient Greek and early biblical motifs, and traditional North European folktale. One would have to search hard to find a better example of what Jacob Grimm describes as that tale which 'untrammelled in its flight, it can yet settle down in a local home'.[20]

## 'The Dragon of Wantley'

While criticism of the establishment is implicit in the dragon tales considered so far, in the broadside ballad 'The Dragon of Wantley' it is quite explicit.[21] Set at Wharncliffe Crags, on the Wortley estate, a few miles north of Sheffield in Yorkshire, the dragon featured here is clearly not one that was a feared reality; rather, it is a draconic satire targeting the overbearing and ruthless Wortley family, as its local audience would have known.

Throughout the sixteenth century, the Wortleys had gained notoriety for, among other things, forcibly evicting residents from their land in order to extend their hunting grounds, which involved building a lodge at Wharncliffe Crags, enclosing and enlarging their estate, without any consideration for those living there, and raising the estate tithes in order to pay for such developments. The Dragon of Wantley, then, is none other than the Wortleys themselves.[22] As for the ballad's dragon-slaying hero, More of More-hall, this was George Blount, a resident of Moore Hall on the Wortley estate during the 1590s. Blount and his accomplices, who had repeatedly and very publicly criticized the Wortleys for their abuse of power, took them to court in 1603 and won the case, so preventing any further increase of the tithes.[23]

The ballad begins as a parody of traditional dragon-slaying tales, recalling that Hercules clubbed to death 'a dragon at Lerna, / With seven

Bas-relief of the Wantley dragon, Sheffield Town Hall, 1897.

heads, and fourteen eyes' and noting, by comparison, that 'More of More-hall, with nothing at all, / He slew the dragon of Wantley'.[24] Moreover,

> This dragon had two furious wings,
> Each one upon each shoulder;
> With a sting in his tayl, as long as a flayl,
> Which made him bolder and bolder.
> He had long claws, and in his jaws
> Four and forty teeth of iron;
> With a hide as tough as any buff,
> Which did him round environ.
>
> Have you not heard how the Trojan horse
> Held seventy men in his belly?
> This dragon was not quite so big,
> But very near, I'll tell ye.
> Devoured he poor children three,
> That could not with him grapple;

> And at one sup, he eat them up,
> As one would eat an apple.
>
> All sorts of cattle this dragon did eat.
> Some say he ate up trees,
> And that the forests sure he would
> Devour up by degrees;
> For houses and churches were to him geese and turkies;
> He ate all, and left none behind,
> But some stones, dear Jack, that he could not crack,
> Which on the hills you will find.

Enter then the 'furious knight' More of More-hall, famed for his blunt tongue and manly prowess, whom the local children beg to save them from the dragon. Offering More all they possess, he declines any such reward, wanting only 'A fair maid . . . To anoynt me o'er night, ere I go to fight, / And to dress me in the morning.' This much agreed, More, not unlike John Lambton, dons spiked armour, making him appear like 'Some strange, outlandish hedge-hog', a simile which in actuality is an allusion to the legal document put together by George Blount, which included the names and seals of all the plaintiffs.[25] Then, having 'drunk six pots of ale, / And a quart of aqua-vitae', More conceals himself in a well where the dragon is accustomed to drink. And so, when the dragon reaches down into the well only to receive from More a punch in the mouth, the fight begins. What follows in this vulgarly comic encounter is worth giving in full:

> 'Oh,' quoth the dragon, 'pox take thee, come out!
> Thou disturb'st me in my drink.'
> And then he turn'd, and shat at him:
> Good lack! how he did stink:
> 'Beshrew thy soul, thy body's foul,
> Thy dung smells not like balsam;
> Thou son of a whore, thou stink'st so sore,
> Sure thy diet is unwholesome.'
>
> Our politick knight, on the other side,
> Crept out upon the brink,
> And gave the dragon such a douse,
> He knew not what to think:

More of More Hall mortally wounds the Wantley Dragon in an early 19th-century illustration.

'By cock,' quoth he, 'say you so: do you see?'
And then at him he let fly
With hand and with foot, and so they went to 't;
And the word it was, Hey boys, hey!

'Your words,' quoth the dragon, 'I don't understand.'
Then to it they fell at all,

Like two wild boars so fierce, if I may
Compare great things with small.
Two days and a night, with this dragon did fight
Our champion on the ground;
Tho' their strength it was great, their skill it was neat,
They never had one wound.

At length the hard earth began to quake,
The dragon gave him a knock,
Which made him to reel, and straightway he thought,
To lift him as high as a rock,
And thence let him fall. But More of More-hall,
Like a valiant son of Mars,
As he came like a lout, so he turn'd him about,
And hit him a kick on the arse.

'Oh,' quoth the dragon, with a deep sigh,
And turn'd six times together,
Sobbing and tearing, cursing and swearing
Out of his throat of leather;
'More of More-hall! O thou rascal!
Would I had seen thee never;
With the thing at thy foot, thou hast prick'd my arse-gut,
And I'm quite undone for-ever.

'Murder, murder!', the dragon cry'd,
'Alack, alack, for grief;
Had you but mist that place, you could
Have done me no mischief.'
Then his head he shak'd, trembled and quaked,
And down he laid and cry'd;
First on one knee, then on back tumbled he,
So groan'd, kickt, shat, and dy'd.

So it is that beneath the humour of 'The Dragon of Wantley' there
lies a highly charged political message concerning social injustice, one that
still had relevance in the eighteenth century. In 1737, a burlesque Italian-style
opera inspired by the ballad was staged at London's Haymarket Theatre
and later transferred to Covent Garden. With a libretto by Henry Carey

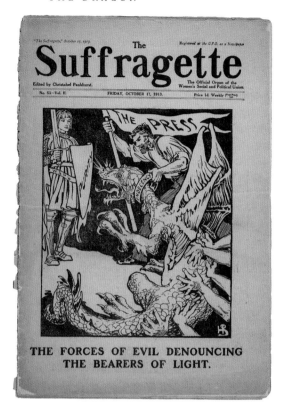

Cover of *The Suffragette*, 1913.

(*c.* 1687–1743) and music by John Frederick Lampe (1703–1751), the opera *The Dragon of Wantley* directed its satire at the then prime minister, Sir Robert Walpole (1676–1745), whose taxation policies had received much criticism. However, the hero of the opera, which initially ran for a record-breaking 69 performances and was still in vogue some fifty years later, stops short of killing the dragon and instead merely wounds it. The Walpole dragon did not warrant the same fate as that of the Wortleys.

THE ANTI-ESTABLISHMENT DRAGON folktale fascinates for a number of reasons. While it would be somewhat anachronistic to suggest that these old tales signified some kind of simmering desire for class revolt, it was nonetheless the case that outbreaks of civil disobedience prompted by social injustices frequently obliged the ruling classes to rethink and revise their practices, however slightly. Nonetheless, although the anti-establishment folktale may not be harbouring any clearly formulated political agenda, its underlying criticism of the social order, often expressed in terms of wishful thinking, does indicate something of the sense of injustice felt by those without a political voice. In these tales, the dragon is not simply, or perhaps not only, an articulation of greed, megalomania, evil or precarious mortality but is an articulation of socially oppressive forces. Eventually, this notion of the dragon as an agent of inequality would go on to become ever more explicitly stated, much as can be seen in the cartoon opposite, for which read the establishment press and men generally, as the enemy of women's suffrage.

Tristan fighting a dragon, fresco, Runkelstein Castle, 14th–15th century.

*eight*

# European Dragons as Fictions and Facts: From Medieval Romance to the Nursery Dragon

THE INFLUENCE OF those Celtic myths and legends discussed in Chapter Five is no better evidenced than in the tragic tale of Tristan (aka Tristram) and Isolde (aka Iseult), much of which is set in Ireland. Tristan is in service to his uncle, King Mark of Cornwall, but as a result of his dutiful killing of the brother of the Irish queen, who had been sent to Cornwall to demand tribute, he has to seek a cure for the battle injuries he has received. The only place he can do this is in Ireland. Disguised as a minstrel and anagrammatically calling himself Tantris, he is healed of injuries by the Irish queen, whose daughter, Isolde, greatly impresses him.

On returning to Cornwall, Tristan tells Mark of Isolde's great beauty and her many accomplishments, and he is again obliged to travel to Ireland, this time to court Isolde as a future bride for Mark. On his arrival, Tristan learns of a terrible dragon that has long been ravaging the land and that the king of Ireland has offered Isolde in marriage to whoever can succeed in killing it. Determined to fulfil his mission, Tristan sets out to confront it, just as many have done in the past, much to their misfortune.

Having tracked the dragon to its lair, Tristan attacks it on horseback, but the horse is consumed by the dragon's fire and then half eaten by it. Even so, Tristan has succeeded in delivering the beast a great wound with his spear, causing it to seek refuge by a cliff. Tristan pursues it and, armed only with his sword and his badly charred shield, manages to bury his sword into the dragon's heart, killing it outright. He now cuts out its tongue and conceals it under his armour by his chest, so that he will have proof that he is the dragon's slayer. So exhausted and fevered is Tristan that he is near death, and in order to cool down he casts himself into a deep rock pool, unaware that the dragon's tongue is continuing to issue noxious fumes.

There now happens by a cowardly steward, who is set on gaining Isolde's hand. Discovering the dead dragon, and with no sign of its slayer, this steward hacks the dragon to pieces and then takes its head in order to convince the king that he is its slayer. He then rides off to Wexford to stake his claim for Isolde. Meanwhile, Isolde and her mother, who had heard the shrieking death throes of the dragon, discover Tristan (whom they recognize only as Tantris), help him out of the rock pool and – once again – set about nursing him back to health. Later, despite their shocked realization that their patient is not the minstrel Tantris but none other than the man who slew the queen's brother, it is they who manage to help Tristan prove that it was he who slew the dragon, not the dishonourable steward. Having thus established his dragon-slaying credentials, Tristan is granted Isolde's hand for King Mark.

This episode of the Tristan story, as set down by the German author Gottfried von Strassburg in the first decade of the thirteenth century,[1] is the prelude to the tragedy of Tristan and Isolde, when they both accidentally drink a love potion while Tristan is journeying to Cornwall to deliver Isolde as Mark's bride-to-be. As is recounted in the sources that Gottfried was drawing on, most notably Thomas of Britain's twelfth-century Old French poem *Tristan*,[2] so great is the agony of their illicitly unbounded love for each other that it proves fatal, and, given that they are both unrepentant, in accordance with the lights of medieval Christianity they are both damned to Hell. Exactly what Gottfried intended in his account of this tragedy continues to be debated, some arguing that he was setting out a critique of the medieval chivalric honour code, others that he sought no more than to point out its limitations.[3] In whichever case, the dragon leaves its legacy as a curse on Tristan and Isolde.

Although unfinished, Gottfried's *Tristan* is arguably the most influential of the many accounts of the legend, it having formed the basis of Richard Wagner's acclaimed opera *Tristan und Isolde* (first performed 1865) as well being an inspiration for numerous modern authors. While the origin of the story is uncertain, it is conjectured that it may date back to tales told of the sixth-century legendary Pictish king Talorc II, which later found their way into Celtic mythology.[4]

Although the dragon episode in *Tristan* is evidently integral to the plot, in other medieval Romances those dragons slain by chivalric knights are often little more than incidental and are there purely to establish the credentials of the hero, rather than adding anything significant to the overarching drama. In, for example, the fourteenth-century poem *Sir Gawain and the*

Tristan combats the dragon in a 13th-century manuscript illustration. The bottom panel shows the steward riding off with the dragon's head.

*Green Knight*, Arthur's court in Camelot is visited by a great green giant, the Green Knight, who demands a duel with Arthur. Gawain, however, will have none of it and steps forward to fight the Green Knight in Arthur's place. Invited to take the first strike, Gawain chops off the Green Knight's

'How Sir Lancelot fought with a friendly dragon', from *The Romance of King Arthur and His Knights of the Round Table* (1920), illustration by Arthur Rackham.

head, only for him to pick it up and tell Gawain that he must now travel to his chapel in the north of the country, where, in a year and a day, he will receive a counter-strike. It is on Gawain's perilous journey round the coast of Wales that he encounters a number of hostile creatures that he must overcome, including 'wormes':

*Sumwhyle wyth wormes he werres, and with wolves als,*
*Sumwhyle wyth wodwos that woned in the knarres,*
*Bothe wyth bulles and beres, and bores otherquyle,*
*And etaynes that hym anelede of the heghe felle.*[5]

Sometimes with dragons he fights, and with wolves also,
Sometimes with trolls who lived in the crags,
Both with bulls and bears, and boars at other times
And giants that pursued him from the high fell.

On arriving at the Green Knight's chapel, having previously been sorely tempted into dishonourable ways by the lady of the house where he stays before completing his journey, Gawain is taught a sharp lesson about the shortcomings of his chivalry. Forever after, as a mark of shame, Gawain wears a green sash that he somewhat uncourageously accepted from the flirtatious lady in order to protect his life, a gesture of humility that all the Knights of the Round Table then adopt. Despite having fended off dragons on his travels, this does not prevent Gawain from being humiliated in the grander scheme of things.

Similarly incidental to the main plot are the dragons in the fourteenth-century English account of the life of Bevis of Hampton. Bevis undergoes many trials against monstrous creatures in his attempt to take revenge on his stepfather, who has colluded with his mother to kill his father.[6] Among them are two dragons that dwell in a dungeon into which he has been cast and, later, the venomous Dragon of Cologne, a king-turned-dragon, which he only survives to overcome after he has repeatedly fallen into a magic pool that heals his wounds.[7] While the tale of Bevis of Hampton primarily concerns his need to redress the crime against his father, it is in another sense the search for his own identity that motivates him.

Tales of the youthful quest knight, then, can often be read as maturation fables; in other words, the knight's quests entail him undergoing tests of his manhood before he can establish his reputation and authority. Much the same could be said of the dragon fights in the fourteenth-century Romances *Sir Degaré* and *Sir Eglamour of Artois*, where both the eponymous heroes are seeking to prove themselves and win the hand of their beloved.[8] In Sir Degaré's case, this also involves him seeking to discover the identity of his real mother. The course of Degaré's search involves the somewhat crude act of his clubbing to death a dragon that is threatening an earl, whereas for Eglamour, his overcoming of a dragon constitutes the one remaining challenge he must meet in order to win the girl. For both these heroes, the dragon episodes are little more than formulaic.

Not unlike these dragon encounters are those of Sir Lancelot, even though, in his case, he is already the most renowned and admired of Arthur's knights. Most of Lancelot's dragon fights are recounted as actual; thus, maidens are saved, imprisoned knights are rescued and villagers are freed from dragon tyrannies. Yet, somewhat more tellingly, there is also the dragon as a symbol of King Arthur himself, whose most trusted ally, Lancelot, is symbolized as a leopard. Nevertheless, the seemingly unbreakable bond between the dragon and the leopard will not last, and in one of Lancelot's prophetic visions the dragon is overcome by the leopard, so foreshadowing the part played by Lancelot and Guinevere's affair in the death of Arthur and the ruination of his kingdom. While this literary symbolism is, in its doom-laden message, revealing, just as it is concerning Gawain, Bevis, Degaré and Eglamour, among others, Lancelot's dragon fights would appear to serve little more purpose than to establish his heroic mettle, as if simply to inform the reader that this is what true knights must do.[9]

## Melusine

While the shift from myth to the literary legends of medieval Romances typically involved a downgrading of both the potency and the wider meanings of dragons, the folktale dragon often carried with it deeper, often troubling messages. This is particularly noticeable in tales of the fairy dragon-woman Melusine, which were most likely derived from Celtic mythology. One example of this is the account of the fairy Lady of the Lake, the lake being Llyn y Fan Fach in South Wales, who is proposed marriage by a local farmer after he happens across her and is immediately love-struck. The Lady accepts on the condition that he promises never to strike her more than three times. But, as is typical of such taboos in folktales, the farmer breaks his promise, albeit that his violence towards her amounts to little more than reproachful taps. Even so, after the third 'blow' the Lady immediately abandons him and returns to the lake, taking with her all the magical livestock she had brought with her as her dowry. Beyond this, the Lady only occasionally reappears in order to train their children as healers, a gift that the Lady's alleged descendants, the historical 'Physicians of Myddfai', were still believed to have inherited as late as the eighteenth century.[10]

Over the centuries, as this tale spread across Europe, the central female character, the 'strong woman', was depicted as increasingly dangerous, until it eventually carried with it similar misogynistic messages to those about the Arthurian sorceress Morgan le Fay, a medieval epitome of menacing female otherness.[11] This gradual demonization of the various Melusines is apparent in *The Travels of Sir John Mandeville*, which was first circulated between 1357 and 1371. Mandeville tells how the daughter of Hippocrates, the ruler of the Greek islands of 'Colcos and Lango', has been cursed by the goddess Diana and changed into a dragon-woman 'a hundred fathom of length'.[12] Living in a cave in an old castle, she emerges two or three times a year but does no harm unless threatened in some way. It is said that should a knight kiss her, then she would become a woman again but that she would not live long afterwards. This, a knight of Rhodes declares he will do; however, when he encounters the dragon-woman he is so horrified that he flees, only to be pursued and caught by her and cast to his death over the sea cliffs.

A short time later, a young man disembarks from his ship and, curious to find out whether the dragon-woman tale is true, goes to the castle cave, where he finds a beautiful woman looking into a mirror and combing her hair. The woman tells him that she will be his lover providing he comes to her the following day and kisses her, even if she is then in the form of a dragon. The young man agrees, but on his return, just like the knight of Rhodes, he takes fright and runs away. At first pursuing him to his ship, the dragon-woman eventually breaks down in tears and returns sorrowfully to her cave. Yet the young man's escape is not without consequence, for he very soon dies, and from this point onward, any man who even so much as sees the dragon-woman also dies. So the tale ends with the dragon-woman forever pining for a knight brave enough to kiss her and cure her of her monstrous affliction.

The earliest literary account of the Melusine tale, in which she is actually named as such, is *Le Roman de Mélusine*, part of *Le Noble hystoire de Lusignan* (The Noble History of the Lusignans) by the French poet Jean d'Arras, published in 1394. This tells how the fairy-woman Pressyne agrees to marry King Elynas of Albany, her one condition being that he never comes to visit her when she is either giving birth or bathing their children, the first-born of whom is Melusine. Predictably, Elynas breaks the taboo, after which Pressyne leaves him and travels with her daughters to the Isle of Avalon. Time passes, until Melusine, now aged fifteen, learns of her father's dishonoured promise, whereupon she and her sisters seek him out and chain him inside a mountain. But as soon as Pressyne hears of this, she is most displeased and punishes her daughters. For Melusine, this entails her mother casting a spell that every Saturday turns her into a dragon from the waist down.

In due course, Melusine takes on the fairy role of guarding a sacred fountain in the province of Poitou in western France, where one day the nobleman Raymondin of Poitiers comes across her. They spend the night in each other's company and Raymondin duly proposes to her. Just like her mother, Melusine accepts the proposal on one condition, which in her case is that Raymondin should never visit her on a Saturday. To all intents and purposes, the marriage is for many years a happy one, and Melusine brings great wealth and fortune to Raymondin's Lusignan dynasty by using her fairy powers to build for him many splendid fortresses and chapels, each taking her just a single night. Together they have ten children, and even though all but two of them are deformed in some way or other, four of them are said to have gone on to achieve great deeds as Crusaders.

Yet Raymondin eventually grows suspicious of what Melusine might be doing on Saturdays and, ignoring his promise, spies on her as she bathes and is shocked to see her serpentine lower body. When he later accuses her publicly of having contaminated their children with her monstrous features, an accusation prompted by one of them having just incinerated his younger brother by burning down his monastery, Melusine is appalled. She then assumes the appearance of a fifteen-foot dragon, gives Raymondin two magic rings, rises into the air, encircles the castle three times and then flies off wailing like a Banshee, that Celtic *Bean Sidhe* or 'Fairy Woman' from which she would also appear to have originated. At night, Melusine would

Melusine's secret discovered, from *Le Roman de Mélusine* by Jean d'Arras, *c.* 1450–1500.

return, always lamenting and always in dragon form, to feed her suckling children, and down through the generations, when an heir to the Lusignan dynasty was about to be born or when the current incumbent or a French monarch was about to die. Needless to say, Raymondin is left distraught for the rest of his days.

While Jean d'Arras' main purpose was to enshrine the rise and eventual fall of the medieval Lusignan dynasty,[13] his and various other representations of Melusine as, on the one hand, a feminine ideal, but on the other a monster, is strongly reminiscent of the Lamia myth. Lamia was that mortal woman from Greek mythology who was raped by Zeus, thence cursed by his wife Hera and as a result doomed to a life of madness, during which she becomes the perpetrator of grotesque infanticides in the form of a dragon-woman. Moreover, this may well be no coincidence, for it is quite possible that during the Middle Ages the Lamia myth and the Celtic folktale had merged together to produce Melusines.[14]

As for whatever patriotic intentions Jean d'Arras might have had, it was what can only be described as the gynophobic message of the Melusine story that assured its widespread popularity as a cautionary tale. So much can be gleaned from numerous European folktales concerning Melusine that were still being collected as late as the nineteenth century. In these, there would appear to have been no debt whatsoever to Jean d'Arras' *Roman*, for there is all but the slightest mention of French politics in them, if indeed any.[15] Quite clearly, Melusine, as an epitomization of the dangerous female, transcended interrogations of time-bound power politics.

## The Faerie Queene

While dragon folktales would continue either to affirm or to question establishment values, dragon tales in medieval and early modern literature eventually culminated, after which the dragon declined as a literary motif. This culmination is marked in Book 1, Cantos i and xi, of Edmund Spenser's epic allegory *The Faerie Queene* (published 1590 and 1596), in which two dragons feature. The first dragon is thought to have been inspired by the ancient Greek primordial dragon-woman Echidna,[16] although it is quite possible that Spenser may also have been drawing on the Melusine/Lamia tradition, and the second dragon is quite explicitly the Book of Revelation's Satan dragon. Both these creatures are, in their differing ways, fundamental to the poem's Protestant view that the Roman Catholic Church was fundamentally evil.[17]

Woodcut illustration
for Book 1 of *The Faerie
Queene* (1590).

The Faerie Queene, Gloriana, is Queen Elizabeth 1, and her emissary
and the hero of Book 1 is the Redcrosse Knight, who over the course of his
adventures becomes identified with the apostle St Peter, St George and,
ultimately, Jesus Christ. Aiding and abetting Redcrosse through his many
perils are King Arthur – from whom, claims Spenser, Queen Elizabeth is
descended – and the maiden Una, signifying the singularity of Protestant
or, more precisely, Anglican 'Truth'. Chief among those seeking to deter,
distract and destroy Redcrosse is Una's female opposite, Duessa, 'Whose
secret filth good manners biddeth not be told' (1.viii.46), and whose duplic-
itousness represents all that was perceived as characterizing the spiritual
dangers inherent in Catholic doctrine and morally questionable practices.

It is at the outset of Redcrosse's journey that he, in company with Una,
comes across a cave deep in the woods. Despite being repeatedly warned
by Una not to enter it, for this, she tells him, is *'Errours den'* (1.i.13), he

somewhat recklessly proceeds, 'full of fire and greedy hardiment' (1.i.14). On entering the cave, Redcrosse immediately encounters a hideous monster, half-serpent and half-woman, and her thousand children 'sucking upon her poisonous dugs' (1.i.15). Daunted by both the light which now shines into the cave and the presence of a knight in full armour, Errour at first retreats into the darkness. But Redcrosse is undeterred and, advancing, he delivers her a sword stroke, only to find himself wrapped in her tail. Urged on by Una to 'Add faith unto your force' (1.i.20), Redcrosse manages to free himself sufficiently to put Errour in a stranglehold, at which point she vomits up a mass of stinking filth that includes 'bookes and papers' (1.i.20), symbols of the Catholic propaganda that Errour personifies. Choking so badly in the foul air that for a while he can no longer fight, Redcrosse eventually rallies himself and, determined not to be shamed, strikes Errour so hard that he decapitates her. Now Errour's brood emerges and begins sucking up her blood with such great appetite that they all swell up and burst.

Redcrosse's victory over Errour is only the start of his spiritual journey, during which the sexually beguiling Duessa succeeds in bringing about Redcrosse's separation from Una and forces him into many mortal dangers, including his imprisonment by a crazed giant, from whom he is freed by Arthur.[18] It is only when Duessa is exposed as a hideous witch that Redcrosse finally learns from Una that his true mission is to free her land and her besieged parents from a vast, fire-breathing, flying dragon. In effect, Redcrosse's mission in confronting this dragon is to ensure the restoration

Henry Ford, illustration for Andrew Lang, *The Red Romance Book* (1921).

of the Reformed Church in England.[19] His fight to achieve as much lasts three days.

On the first day he succeeds in delivering the dragon a wound to the neck, but in return he is almost burned alive by its fiery breath. Fortunately, the dragon hurls him into a fountain, which, it transpires, is the 'Well of Life' that can raise the dead and heal the injured. On the second day, Redcrosse delivers further injuries to the dragon but is again bested and severely wounded. Yet he is once more saved from death when he falls into a healing stream running from the tree of life in the Garden of Eden.[20] On the third day, when the dragon charges with its jaws stretched wide enough to swallow him whole, the reinvigorated Redcrosse manages to stab it deep in the throat, so killing it.

Redcrosse's three-day ordeal can be understood as signifying Christ's crucifixion, his descent into Hell, as represented by the dragon's final, wide-jawed attack, and his ultimate resurrection. As for the healing waters of the well and the sacred stream, these in turn denote baptism and the Eucharist. Moreover, Redcrosse's extraordinary good luck is not really luck at all but due to the will of 'eternal God that chaunce did guide' (1.xi.45). Yet the battle against the dragon-cum-Catholic Church does not end with Redcrosse's killing of the dragon, nor will it until Judgement Day, at which point, infers Spenser, Christ will reveal both Catholic falsehood and Protestant truth.[21]

With the decline of dragons as potent literary motifs after Spenser's *The Faerie Queene*, they very often became little more than verbal metaphors. Shakespeare, for example, refers to dragons eighteen times in his plays, in expressions such as these: 'Come not between a dragon and his wrath' (*King Lear*, 1.1.122); 'For night's swift dragons cut the clouds full fast' (*A Midsummer Night's Dream*, 3.2.379); and 'Did ever a dragon keep so fair a cave?' (*Romeo and Juliet*, 3.2.74). Similarly, in Book 3 of Alexander Pope's *The Dunciad* (1743), his satirical response to the criticism levelled at him by the then Poet Laureate, Colley Cibber, we have the following: 'All sudden, Gorgons hiss, and Dragons glare . . .' (l. 235); 'On grinning dragons thou shalt mount the wind' (l. 268); and 'Reduced at last to hiss in my own dragon' (l. 286).

Continuing with Christian ideas about the personification of ultimate evil, we may look to the more theatrical dragons in Christopher Marlowe's *Dr Faustus* (B-version, 1616) and John Milton's *Paradise Lost* (1674). In *Dr Faustus*, Lucifer and his devils first appear accompanied by a dragon (stage direction, Act 1, Sc. 3), and Faustus, in his search for 'the secrets of astronomy', is drawn across the firmament in 'a chariot burning bright . . . by the strength of yoked dragons' necks' (Act 1, Sc. 7, Chorus 1). In *Paradise Lost*, as in the Book of Revelation, the dragon is, of course, Satan, but unlike in Revelation he is in a curiously forlorn state. As one critic puts it, 'Satan is "confounded though immortal" ... anguished though proud and obdurate ... and though filled with hate and revenge ... he is simultaneously gentle and kind'.[22] While Marlowe's dragons are aspects of the long-standing Christian view of them, Milton's Satan dragon is a far cry from the malevolent Satan dragon in his chief source. Milton's Satan is, one might say, humanized, and is in this sense a precursor of the dragon of modern times.

## Dragons as real-life hazards

While dragons as threats to social stability all but vanished from the literary scene after the Renaissance and, with but a few literary exceptions,[23] would not resume their roles as key figures in the creative arts until the nineteenth century, they nevertheless continued to be seen as actualities. In many cases, the dragon hazard was regarded as one likely to be encountered on the high seas, which, as we all know, has always been a place where piscine and serpentine monstrosities have haunted the imagination of seafarers, sometimes quite justifiably. Testimony to the belief in the sea dragon (*draco maris*) is evidenced by the plethora of dragon images, among other exotic beings, to be found on medieval and early modern maps and manuscripts. Although many of these images are variously referencing Leviathan, the Book of Revelation and bestiaries, many others do not have any clear religious significance and would appear to reflect the mortal fears of the time.[24]

The sea dragons of Greek mythology, such as those dispatched by the vengeful Poseidon and overcome by Heracles and Perseus in their rescues of damsels in distress, had become embedded in European culture by the Middle Ages. Attempts at classifying and identifying such creatures had long been the aim of intellectuals, such as is the case in Pliny the Elder's first-century AD *Natural History*, where he describes a great fish bringing a ship to a standstill.[25] During the Middle Ages, these nautical dragons had become a standard feature of commentaries on natural phenomena. A typical example is Thomas of Cantimpré's thirteenth-century description of nautical monstrosities in his six-volume *De natura rerum* (On the Nature of Things):

> The sea-dragon is an exceedingly cruel monster. It exceeds the terrestrial dragon in length, but lacks wings. It has a coiled tail and a head that is, in relation to the size of the body, small; yet its maw is terrible. Its scales and skin are hard ... Instead of wings it has fins, which it uses for swimming.[26]

Frederick Leighton, *Perseus and Andromeda*, 1891.

Similarly, on the mid-fourteenth-century nautical chart drawn by Domenico and Francesco Pizzigano, a dragon is shown flying above the ocean clutching a man in its jaws while below a ship is being attacked by a giant octopus. And on Andrea Bianco's mid-fifteenth-century *mappa mundi*, two dragons are shown in a watery abyss in the southern ocean.[27]

Probably the best-known warning specifically made against such creatures is the Latin inscription *hic sunt dracones* (or *dragones*), commonly translated as 'here be dragons'. This is noted on two maps, the earliest of which is included in Jean Mansel's universal history *La Fleur des histoires* (The Flower of History, *c.* 1480), where one of the six listed oceans is said to be occupied by a winged dragon; the other is on the Hunt–Lenox Globe of about 1510, where the warning is placed on the southeast coast of Asia, perhaps a reference to the Komodo dragon.

It could not, however, be said that ideas about dragons of the deep led to any consensus concerning their anatomies or behaviours, and it is therefore not surprising that among the host of monstrosities depicted on maps, whales and other sea-dwelling creatures were also depicted. In the case of whales, as time progressed, they were not always seen as a threat but in some

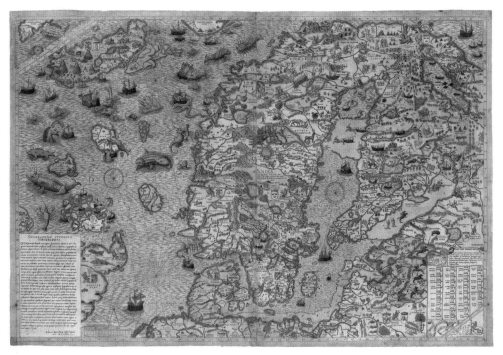

Carta Marina by Antony Lafreri, 1572.

instances – doubtless drawing on the Old Testament's Jonah myth – as a sanctuary. One example of this is Honorius Philoponus' (real name Caspar Plautius) 1621 account of the evangelists accompanying Christopher Columbus on his second voyage to the New World. Depicted in this, stranded on a whale's back, are St Brendan, his fellow travellers and their now abandoned yet still intact ship. Even so, the evangelists appear unthreatened by their cetacean host and are shown to be dutifully kneeling at prayer in front of a communion table.[28]

Beyond the sixteenth century, such cartographic dramatics, favourable or not, became increasingly rare, and instead, more credible sea creatures took their place. Yet this did not mean that dragons, terrestrial or nautical, were yet regarded as fictions. From the Renaissance onwards, we have what might well be called 'the science of dragons'. So it was that, once placed on the dissecting table (theoretically at least), the dragon met with just the same carefully calculated analysis as any other physical being.

Typifying this shift in thinking were the studies of the Swiss scientific polymath Conrad Gesner in his encyclopaedic four-volume *Historia animalium* (History of the Animals; 1551–8), with a fifth, posthumously published volume in 1587 focussing on serpents. This carefully conducted and appropriately sceptical study of all known animals was nonetheless indebted to bestiaries, for it included such mythic creatures as unicorns, basilisks and dragons. Partial English translations of Gesner's first four volumes were made by the English cleric Edward Topsell in his illustrated study *The History of*

From Honorius Philoponus, *Nova typis tranacta navigatio* (1621).

The Lamia dragon-woman from Edward Topsell, *A History of Foure-footed Beastes* (1607).

*Foure-footed Beastes* of 1607, which includes, among several dragon images, the mythic dragon-woman Lamia. The following year, he delivered a full translation of Gesner's serpent volume, wherein Topsell credulously states, 'Among all kindes of Serpents, there is none comparable to the Dragon.'[29]

Bringing further accounts of dragon sightings were those who travelled to lands that were otherwise little known. Richard Hakluyt's *The Principal Navigations, Voyages, Traffiques and Discoveries of the English Nation* of 1589 tells of voyagers seeing elephants in West Africa that 'have continuall warre against Dragons.'[30] Similarly, dragon sightings in South America were included in the work of the Italian naturalist Ulisse Aldrovandi, whose *Serpentum et draconum historiae libra duo* (The History of Serpents and Dragons in Two Volumes) was published in 1640. Testifying to Aldrovandi's belief in dragons as realities is one report he makes of a dragon sighting in which he himself played a part. Here he tells of a peasant running over a small dragon while driving his ox-cart near Bologna. The puzzle, in this case, was that this dragon had only two feet, rather than the expected four, and that it was wingless. Despite being unable to explain the origin of this creature, Aldrovandi had it displayed in the local museum as an example of an invasive dragon.

Also confidently affirming the existence of dragons in his *Mundus subterraneus* (Underground World) of 1664–5 and amassing so much evidence as to make his view irrefutable, or so he believed, was the Jesuit scholar Athanasius Kircher. Kircher's reasoning was not untypical of the time:

> There is a great deal of debate among writers with regards to dragons: do animals of this sort actually exist in nature, or, as is often the case in many other things, can they only be found in fables and fairy tales? And we also were stubbornly undecided for a long time as to whether these animals have ever in fact existed. At last, however, it was necessary for us to set aside our doubts . . . Because monstrous animals of this kind (i.e., dragons) quite often make their nests and rear their young in underground caverns, we assert with a solid basis that they are a verifiable kind of subterranean species, in accordance with the worthy topic of this book.

Support for his conviction of a 'solid basis' for the existence of dragons is Kircher's account of a certain Roman hunter named Lanio, who in 1660 came across a bipedal, web-footed dragon the size of 'a very large vulture' and with a double set of teeth, which he killed by slitting its throat. Yet later that same day, Lanio also died, most likely, thinks Kircher, from either the dragon's toxic breath or its poisonous fumes.[31] Reinforcing Kircher's own identification of the subterranean lairs of dragons in Switzerland was the Swiss prefect of Solothurn Christopher Schorer, who wrote to Kircher telling him of his sighting of a flying, fiery dragon emerging from Mount Pilatus near Lake Lucerne. Given the number of such reports, Switzerland would appear to have been a popular hunting ground for dragons in the seventeenth century.

By the late seventeenth century, more sceptical voices were beginning to be heard. When the renowned botanist, zoologist and taxonomist Carl Linnaeus admired the skill of Hamburg craftsmen who, he perceived, had constructed a seven-headed replica of a Hydra from various animal parts, a specimen for which the owners had just paid a high price in the belief that it was the real thing, he was threatened with prosecution for defaming their property and wisely left town.[32] Although old beliefs die hard, for those who continued to sight, exhibit or document actual dragons, such 'truths' were now being seriously questioned – at least in the increasingly sceptical West. Sealing the fate of dragons as actualities was Charles Darwin.

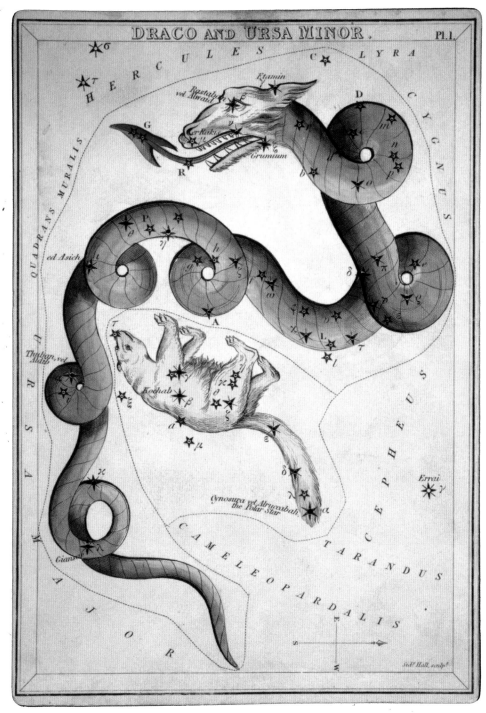

Sidney Hall, astronomical chart of Draco and Ursa Minor, the Dragon and the Little Bear, 1825.

Dragon reconstruction from the Museum of Rudolph II, Prague.

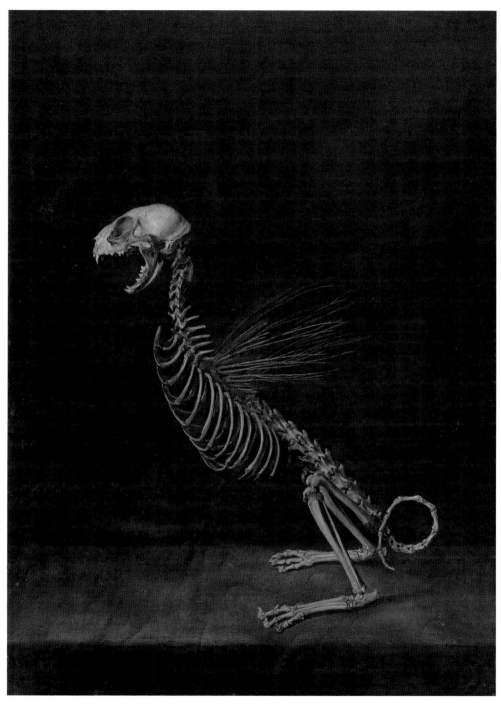

'Dragon' skeleton (actually a cat's skeleton with the wings of a bird) from the
Museum of Rudolph II, Prague, on which the reconstruction is based.

One effect of Darwin's evolutionary theories in his *On the Origin of Species* (1859) was that they divided Christians into two camps: the rationalists, like himself, and the creationists, who refused to accept anything that challenged a literal interpretation of the Old Testament, a religious division that is still present to this day. Darwin's conclusion that dragon-like creatures, such as the pterodactyl, became extinct over 60 million years before recognizably modern humans had evolved did much to put paid to the credibility of dragon sightings.[33] Yet, while scientists now confidently repudiated the continuing existence of dragons, dragon myths began to attract increasing attention. Prompting this, at least in part, was the gradual recovery of the Old North.

From the mid-eighteenth century onwards, educated readers, intellectuals and artists of all kinds in Europe and North America became increasingly enthused about the huge store of myths and legends of pre-Christian Scandinavia that had been preserved in the Icelandic Eddas and sagas. Notable among the artistic creations inspired by Old Northern literature in the latter half of the nineteenth century are Richard Wagner's acclaimed operatic interpretations of the *Saga of the Völsungs* and the *Song of the Nibelungs* in his *Ring Cycle* of 1876, which features the dragon Fáfner and his slayer Siegfried. And in the latter half of the nineteenth century, guided by the Cambridge-based Icelandic scholar Eiríkr Magnússon, there were William Morris's many translations of, and poetic extemporizations on, Icelandic sagas, which drew a wide audience. Indeed, so taken with the *Saga of the Völsungs* was Morris that at Kelmscott Manor, his family retreat in Oxfordshire, he had a garden hedge modelled in the form of Fáfnir, a topiary that has been maintained to this day.

The Old Northern revival did much to encourage a literary challenge to Enlightenment rationalism in the form of the determinedly non-rational fictions of the Gothic novel.[34] Yet among the many monstrous beings that inhabit Gothic fictions, the dragon is rare, quite possibly because their apocalyptic potential would leave little room for any other kind of horror. One exception is Bram Stoker's *The Lair of the White Worm* (1911). Loosely based on the Lambton Worm folktale, Stoker's dragon has not been regarded as his most compelling Gothic creation.[35]

Adding further fuel to the dragon's fire was a partially decayed manuscript dating back almost one thousand years. Containing a text set down in a forgotten language, this unique manuscript had been kept in the library of the English antiquarian Sir Robert Cotton since the seventeenth century. It became known as *Beowulf*. But before turning, in the next chapter, to the massive impact that this Old English poem had on modern literary fantasies in which dragons play a central role, consideration will first be given to the dragon lore of the Romantic Revival and beyond.

## The sexualized dragon of the nineteenth century

Alongside the emergence of the Gothic novel and in many ways complementing it, the Romantic Revival of the late eighteenth century through to the mid-nineteenth century was, like Gothicism, also set on stimulating the emotions. Concerned as much with the medieval as with the classical, awe, dread, the mysterious and nature's formidably sublime northern powers were all major inspirations for Romantic poets. While the politically radical poet and painter William Blake depicted scenes from the Bible, for instance the Great Red Dragon of Hell, the serpent-dragon of Eden and, interestingly, what would appear to be Lilith as Satan, John Keats looked back to the myths of Lamia. Although based primarily on a version of the Lamia myth that he found in Robert Burton's *The Anatomy of Melancholy* (1621),[36] Keats would also have been familiar with Lamia myths from the earliest of times.

The heroine of Keats's 'Lamia' (1820) is more of a deceptive Melusine than a child-killing Lamia. Although tragic, this Lamia is an altogether more sympathetic character than her dragon-woman forebear in Greek mythology, much as Keats's description of her suggests:

> She was a gordian shape of dazzling hue,
> Vermilion-spotted, golden, green, and blue;
> Striped like a zebra, freckled like a pard,
> Eyed like a peacock, and all crimson barr'd;
> And full of silver moons, that, as she breathed,
> Dissolv'd or brighter shone, or interwreathed
> Their lustres with the gloomier tapestries.[37]

Lamia is discovered by the god Hermes during his search for a beautiful nymph, who, it transpires, is invisible to all but Lamia. Desperate to be freed from her serpentine appearance, Lamia tells Hermes that she will make the nymph visible to him if, in return, he will change her into a woman. All is agreed, and as Hermes disappears with the nymph, Lamia undergoes her violent transformation. Now able to interact with humans, she soon falls in love with a handsome young man by the name of Lycius, and they live together in happy solitude for three years. But Lycius then decides they must marry, and despite Lamia's protests, the wedding arrangements go ahead. Yet when Lycius draws up a list of wedding guests, under instruction from Lamia, he deliberately omits to invite his mentor, the philosopher Apollonius, whom Lamia secretly fears might perceive her dragon-woman reality.

Come the wedding day, for which Lamia has magically prepared their home to look like a palace, Apollonius turns up uninvited, and, just as she feared, on seeing Lamia he immediately identifies her as a serpent. Thus

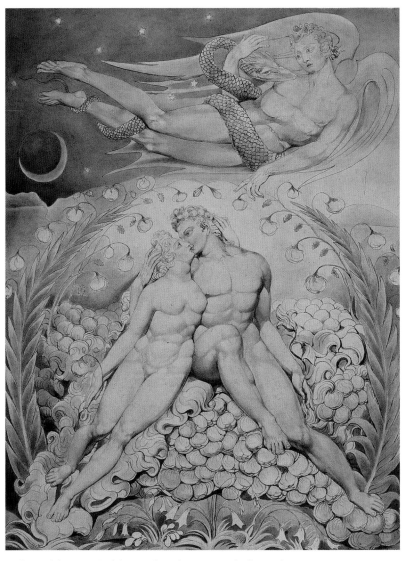

William Blake, *Satan [Lilith] Watching the Caresses of Adam and Eve*, 1808.

exposed, Lamia screams and then vanishes, never to be seen again. Later that night, the grief-stricken Lycius is found dead. Deception and the perils of sensual pleasure are Keats's themes, ones which were close to the young poet's own heart.

The sexualized dragon-woman would go on to be an inspiration for numerous nineteenth-century poets. In 'Christabel' (1797–1801) by Samuel Taylor Coleridge, the mysterious Geraldine is rescued by the poem's misunderstood heroine Christabel but turns out to be an evil serpent, thinly disguised as a forlorn young woman. Anticipating Keats's 'Lamia' was Thomas Love Peacock, whose 'Rhododaphne' (1818), a poem composed under the influence of Percy Bysshe Shelley, tells of the eponymous dragon-woman trying her best to break up two lovers and almost succeeding before the higher powers of 'true love' intervene and destroy her.[38]

Similarly preoccupied with the seductive dragon-woman were Pre-Raphaelite painters. Most likely influencing the Pre-Raphaelites was Johann Wolfgang von Goethe's play *Faust* (1808), where the demonic Lilith makes her literary debut, albeit a brief one, when she is introduced to Faust by Mephistopheles as a woman with 'dangerous hair' (l. 4207).[39] Goethe's influence is most apparent in Dante Gabriel Rossetti's portrait *Lady Lilith* (1868; renamed as *Body's Beauty* in 1873), which depicts a self-absorbed woman combing her hair in her boudoir. Accompanying it is his sonnet of the same name, which ends with mention of Lilith's association with the rose and the poppy, signifying, respectively, sterile love and death, followed, as in *Faust*, by a dire warning about the snake-haired Lilith to all men who might be tempted by her beauty:

> The rose and poppy are her flowers; for where
> Is he not found, O Lilith, whom shed scent
> And soft-shed kisses and soft sleep shall snare?
> Lo! as that youth's eyes burned at thine, so went
> Thy spell through him, and left his straight neck bent
> And round his heart one strangling golden hair.[40]

The following year, Rossetti published his ballad 'Eden Bower' (1869), in which, for the first time in any literary work, Lilith is deemed to be personally responsible for the Fall at Eden. Here, Lilith directs Satan to loan her his serpent body in order for her to take revenge on both God, for not making her Adam's most desired partner, and Adam, for rejecting her in favour of Eve. Highly eroticized and disgustingly monstrous, Lilith is

Dante Gabriel Rossetti, *Lady Lilith*, 1866–8.

presented as the archetypal *femme fatale*. Yet evil as Rossetti's Lilith most
certainly is, the poem sees everything from her point of view as a wronged
woman, the consequence being that the reader has some sympathy with
her. This ambivalence adds complexity to Lilith's motivations, as, on the one
hand, she is a demonic serpent who engineers the greatest crime in biblical
history, while on the other, she has justifications. As one critic notes, the
Lilith of 'Eden Bower', 'allows for feminist interpretation, opening the way
for Lilith's adaptation as a feminist heroine by later writers', although quite
whether this is what Rossetti intended is open to question.[41]

Further visual depictions of the Lamia/Lilith composite include John
Collier's snake-entwined nude *Lilith* (1887); Kenyon Cox's *Lilith* (1892),

which depicts the tempting of Eve in the Garden of Eden; John William Waterhouse's suggestively seductive *Lamia* (1905 and 1909); and James Draper's half-naked *Lamia* (1909) watching a snake crawl up her arm. At one and the same time desirable and dangerous, these Lamia/Lilith paintings reveal a great deal about men's attitudes towards both their own and female sexuality in Victorian times, which while being a distinction that is loaded with hypocrisy, is also one in which the underlying message would seem to carry a fear of nothing less than castration.

Taking what would appear to be a more positive, indeed assertive, attitude towards female sexuality were women painters. Anna Lea Merritt's *Lamia, The Serpent Woman* (1878) shows Lamia, head held high, emerging from the undergrowth, a symbol both of her confinement and her gradual liberation, and in Isobel Lilian Gloag's *The Kiss of the Enchantress* (1890), the dragon-woman quite clearly has command over a besotted knight whose legs are bound in briars. What we have then is male nervousness of female power, on the one hand, and female assertions of their mastery over men, on the other. Summing up this conflict is Evelyn De Morgan's *The Captives* (1888), in which the struggle for women's liberation is expressed in the visual drama

Evelyn de Morgan, *The Captives*, 1888.

of captive women seeking to rise against their vicious, ghostly dragon incarcerators – in other words, men.

Offering, as in 'Eden Bower', a more traditional religious view of Lilith is George MacDonald, whose moribund allegorical fantasy novel *Lilith* (1895) is narrated by the aptly named Mr Vane. Discovering that his late father's library is haunted by its former librarian, Mr Raven, and later encountering this spirit in person, Vane learns that his father had travelled with Raven to an afterlife. Vane soon finds himself making the same journey, but the afterlife he encounters is a deeply troubled one, for the dead cannot rest in peace nor achieve life in death. Understandably fearful and bewildered after his many dispiriting adventures, Vane is eventually aided by Adam – who turns out to be Raven – and Eve. It is from Adam and Eve and his own bitter experience that Vane learns that the root cause of all the problems is the beguiling yet thoroughly wicked, vampiric Lilith, Adam's estranged first wife. Among her many other evil-doings, Lilith retains in her left hand all those waters needed to bring succour to the growth-stifled children, the Little Ones, and allow them to sleep.[42] Once captured, Lilith's hand is cut off by Adam, so releasing the waters and bringing an end to all the miseries. As for Vane, he returns home, older and wiser, to await life in death and salvation.[43]

Steeped in Christian theological allusions, often paradoxically so, the gender values of *Lilith* have been subject to critical examination in more recent times.[44] Nevertheless, as a forerunner of the fantasy fiction genre, MacDonald's *Lilith* would go on to be an influence acknowledged by C. S. Lewis, whose White Witch, Jadis, in *The Lion, The Witch and the Wardrobe* (1950) is said by the character Mr Beaver to be a descendant of Lilith. Also seeming to be a direct influence on Lewis's characterization of the White Witch is Rossetti's 'Eden Bower', for Mr Beaver's assertion that 'there isn't a drop of real human blood in the Witch' is tantamount to a verbatim quote from the poem (see stanza 1, l. 3).[45]

MacDonald's *Lilith*, however, was not the only precedent set for future fantasy fiction writers, for as the century came to a close, the idea of a dragon as a friend to children was also established. And this fun creature, that which might be called the nursery dragon, has gone on to be an inspiration for authors of children's literature ever since.

## The nursery dragon

The earliest interaction between a child and a dragon – one in which, for a change, the child does not get eaten by it – was not a case of the child–dragon friendship; rather, it is one in which the child assumes the role of a dragon-slayer. This parody of the dealings of medieval Romance heroes with dragons occurs in Lewis Carroll's *Through the Looking-Glass, and What Alice Found There* (1871), his sequel to *Alice's Adventures in Wonderland* (1865). In the back-to-front world of the looking-glass, Alice finds a book that she can only read by holding it in front of a mirror. The poem she sees reflected is 'Jabberwocky'.[46]

Written in a nonsense language, replete with archaisms and neologisms, the seven four-line verses of 'Jabberwocky' tell of a young boy setting out with his 'vorpal' sword in search of the Jabberwock, a creature, his father warns him, with 'jaws that bite' and 'claws that catch'. Having rested a while in his search for the creature, 'The Jabberwock, with eyes of flame, / Came whiffling through the tulgey wood, / And burbled as it came', whereupon 'The vorpal sword went snicker-snack', leaving the Jabberwock dead and the young hero to pick up its head and go 'galumphing back' to his proud father, who declares, 'O frabjous day! Callooh! Callay!' 'Jabberwocky' has been translated worldwide, doubtless not without some difficulty.

Once in the nursery, it was probably only a matter of time before the dragon and the child became friends. Initiating this companionship is Kenneth Grahame's short story 'The Reluctant Dragon' (1898; also known as *Dream Days*).[47] Set on England's Berkshire Downs, a young shepherd boy, a keen reader, hears from his father that he has seen a terrifyingly large, scaly, green creature up in a nearby cave. Assured by his son that this is *only* a dragon, the boy then announces that he will pay a call on the dragon to see if it has settled in comfortably. The next day the boy visits the dragon's cave, where the dragon courteously tells him that he is happy where he is and, unlike other dragons, has no interest in 'chasing knights all over the place and devouring damsels' but prefers instead to write poetry. Given their mutual interests, the dragon and the boy quickly become close friends.

But word soon gets out among the locals that there is a dragon living close by, and, fearing the danger it poses, despite the dragon's evident passivity, they summon none other than St George to slay it, who duly arrives and assures the villagers that he will combat the dragon and all will be well.[48] The dragon, however, has no enthusiasm for such an encounter and tells the boy that he is wholly confident that matters can be sorted out peaceably. With

Illustration of the Jabberwock by Sir John Tenniel, 1871.

Maxfield Parrish,
*The Reluctant
Dragon*, 1902.

the help of the boy, an arrangement is made between the dragon and the now sympathetic St George to stage a mock fight. Come the day, the combatants fake the dragon being wounded, though not, of course, fatally, and, having assured the onlookers that the dragon has promised to change his ways and that he is now harmless, St George sends the dragon off to bed.

Grahame's biographer interpreted 'The Reluctant Dragon' as a spoof of the author's own life, in which St George represents the author in his role as a public servant and the dragon his creative and antisocial personal life.[49] While this may well have been Grahame's personal subtext, what is certain is that 'The Reluctant Dragon' provided a model for uncountable dragons intended to stimulate children's imaginations. Yet in any mythico-legendary sense, the amiable and generally empathetic dragon of the nursery is not really a dragon at all, for the nursery dragon plot is one in which that most dangerous creature ever imagined becomes the child's ally and mutual comfort. This may be regarded as something of a paradox, given that the traditional dragon, that fearsome beast that J.R.R. Tolkien called a 'good' dragon,[50] is an expression of everything that threatens our existence. But this paradox is not so difficult to explain, as what all humans want is the power to take charge of their destinies. The nursery dragon is a fantastical conceit for how this fundamental need might be realized, in which the child is as much a dragon as his or her dragon friend. In this respect, the one is the meaning of the other.

THE FATE OF the European dragon, as discussed here, in many ways reflects the broader cultural history of the time in which the dragon was construed. Dragon-slaying in medieval Romance became little more than a compulsory badge of honour that the knight-hero must win for him to have any credibility. With the perhaps inevitable decline of this somewhat clichéd depiction of the dragon, one might have expected any belief in them also to decline. But, on the contrary, the fear of dragons was so deeply ingrained in the human psyche that scholars and scientists continued to study them as genuine threats to human safety. Without doubt underpinning much of this study of the dragon, in all its forms, were religious convictions about the physical presence of evil in the world.

While folktales of the dragon-woman Melusine would go on to achieve high-culture status in the Middle Ages, owing largely to Jean d'Arras' *Le Roman de Mélusine*, belief in dragons as actualities began to fade somewhat after the seventeenth century. Although from this point in time a rather more rational view had begun to emerge, culminating in Charles Darwin's groundbreaking theories of evolution, the Romantic Revival and its offshoots set a challenge to such scientifically detached rationalism. The underlying thinking in this case was that what really governs human thinking is not the intellect but those deeper recesses of the mind that might broadly be articulated as the imagination. As the nineteenth century progressed, emotionally charged expressions of the mysterious and the fearsome came to be represented in literary and artistic creations as part metaphor, part reality, most obviously in ideas about the dragon-woman. But there were tensions, particularly in respect of gender values, for the Victorian patriarchy and its simultaneous yet contradictory fears and desires as regards women were beginning to be seriously questioned by a burgeoning feminist movement.

Despite all this, new forms of literary expression were beginning to emerge, in the form of fantasy fictions. While in some cases, for example

George MacDonald's *Lilith*, the inspiration was, as it had long been, Christian theology, in others, such as William Morris's translations of fantastical Icelandic sagas, most notably the *Saga of the Völsungs*, a wholly different perspective was being expressed, one that had little or nothing to do with Christian theological niceties. Alongside these new departures, we also have the nursery dragon, a precedent that has gone on to deliver us such dragons as Zog and Toothless. Yet as the century turned, it was Old Northern fascinations that would first come to dominate ideas about dragons. Ensuring this was J.R.R. Tolkien's reappraisal of the value of *Beowulf* as art rather than murky history, and his subsequent expression of this art in his Middle-earth fantasies.

The Eustace-dragon with the talking mouse Reepicheep as portrayed in the film *The Voyage of the Dawn Treader* (dir. Michael Apted, 2010).

## nine

# The Old Dragon Revives: J.R.R. Tolkien and C. S. Lewis

IN MAL PEET'S *The Murdstone Trilogy* (first published 2014), the protagonist, Philip Murdstone, is a writer of young adult fiction whose best days are now behind him. Encouraging him to make a departure from sensitive books about troubled adolescents and instead set about writing 'High Fantasy. Sometimes spelled "Phantasy", with a pee-aitch' is his agent, Minerva. When Philip expresses his doubts about whether he could do such a thing, Minerva explains to him the necessary formula.

> 'You've simply got to have a Quest.'
> She wrote QUEST in purple capitals.

Philip protests that his books have always involved quests.

> 'Yes, darling, of course. But in the kind of quest I'm talking about, the hero has to overcome *real* dragons, not gropey games masters or embittered ladies from Social Services.'
>     When Philip had recovered from this stabbing, he said, rather meekly, 'Dragons are compulsory, are they?'
>     Minerva considered this for a moment. 'Well, not necessarily, I suppose. Some other monstery thing might do. Probably best to stick with dragons, though, to be on the safe side.'

Minerva elaborates: there should be a Dark Lord whose 'minions' (a necessary label) oppress dwarves, elves and humans; there should be special swords, a mystical amulet, 'Magick . . . with a *kay*', Good Sorcerers, and so on.[1]

Peet's satire would seem to be primarily directed at the *Eragon* tales written by the teenage Christopher Paolini, for Minerva then goes on to tell the unfortunate author about *The Dragoneer Chronicles*, 'a six-hundred-page fantasy blockbuster written by a seventeen-year-old anorak called Virgil Peroni . . . He got half a mill up front from Armitage Hanks. A full mill for the movie rights,' all of which sounds very like Paolini. But *Eragon* is only one of scores, if not hundreds, of modern fantasy sequences involving dragons, and the source and origin of all of them is not Paolini but J.R.R. Tolkien. As George R. R. Martin, himself the most successful fantasy author of this century, puts it, 'we are all still walking in Bilbo's footsteps.'[2]

But whose footsteps was Bilbo walking in? The answer to this is to be found in Tolkien's life and work. From 1925, as a professor of Anglo-Saxon at Oxford University, Tolkien's duties included the teaching of *Beowulf*, and his hobbies included the reading and study of Old Norse, as well as Old English. In a famous and game-changing lecture delivered to the British Academy in 1936, 'Beowulf: The Monsters and the Critics', Tolkien spoke up for the monsters against the critics, who, he felt, had regarded them as rather beneath the dignity of proper epic. Thus, declared Tolkien:

> A dragon is no idle fancy. Whatever may be his origins, in fact or invention, the dragon in legend is a potent creation of men's imagination, richer in significance than his barrow is in gold. Even to-day (despite the critics) you may find men not ignorant of tragic legend and history, who have heard of heroes and indeed seen them, who yet have been caught by the fascination of the worm.[3]

That fascination, suggested Tolkien, rested on only two 'significant' dragons in northern literature: the dragon Fáfnir, in the story of the Völsungs, and the nameless dragon of *Beowulf*.[4] But in restricting significant dragons to two, Tolkien was, as often, shading the truth, for as he knew very well, there were other dragons in the northern tradition. But those two were certainly significant to him, for already in 1936 they had supplied him with a plot-sequence and a central scene, both of them vital to *The Hobbit*, which would be published the year after his lecture.

It was *Beowulf* that supplied the plot sequence.[5] In the old poem, it will be remembered, a thief stumbles on the sleeping dragon and his hoard, steals a cup and gets away. The dragon awakes and immediately notices the theft, sniffs out the thief's tracks – Tolkien liked that touch – and, in revenge, flies off to 'burn the bright halls' of Beowulf's people. Beowulf then goes to confront and kill the dragon, taking with him eleven companions, plus the thief, who becomes 'the thirteenth man'.

In *The Hobbit*, as Bilbo tells Smaug (pp. 200–202),[6] Bilbo was selected by Gandalf as 'Mr Lucky Number', so as to be with the thirteen dwarves the *fourteenth* man. But the sequence is, with one significant difference, the same. Bilbo steals a cup from the sleeping dragon Smaug, who wakes, notices the theft and flies off to search for the thief.[7] While the dwarves hide inside the entrance to the tunnel, Bilbo then goes back for a second visit. It is after the second visit that Smaug shatters the entrance to the tunnel, trapping Bilbo and the dwarves inside the mountain, and flies off to burn down Laketown (Esgaroth).

The significant difference, then, is Bilbo's second trip down the tunnel, where this time he encounters a dragon who is wide awake and has a conversation with him, a vital scene for dragon-imitators of the future. This scene is based not on *Beowulf* but on another poem, the Old Norse *Fáfnismál* (Lay of Fáfnir) from the *Poetic Edda*. This is potentially a great scene, Tolkien thought, but in the version we have it is one which had not been developed properly. In the *Lay of Fáfnir*, Fáfnir and Sigurd talk while the dragon is dying from Sigurd's sword-thrust. Sigurd refuses to give his name, because, as the poem's copyist explains, 'it was believed in olden times that a dying man's words had great power, if he cursed his enemy by name'.[8] All very wise and sensible. But, even so, Sigurd *does* blurt out his name.

That just did not make sense, thought Tolkien, who rewrote the scene so that Bilbo avoids the temptation to give his name but nevertheless feels, as he later uneasily admits to the dwarves, he has given away more than he realized. Tolkien then grafted the scene into the sequence he got from *Beowulf*, finishing off with an entirely different death scene for Smaug, at the hands of Bard the Bowman. Somewhat reminiscent, doubtless deliberately so, of Sigurd the Völsung learning from nuthatches that it would be unwise to spare the life of the treacherous Regin, Bard learns from a thrush of Smaug's one weak spot and is then able to bring an end to the devastation of Laketown by bringing him down with his Black Arrow.[9] Apart from Tolkien's totally original invention of Hobbits, this combination of *Beowulf* and the Sigurd story is probably Tolkien's most long-term influence on fantasy fiction. This is particularly the case as regards the image of Smaug, that classic early Germanic, treasure-hoarding, fire-spewing beast who is transformed by Tolkien into 'pure intelligent lizard',[10] one with an overwhelming personality – not a likeable one, certainly, but one that is fully realized.

This, then, is how Tolkien's adaptations of his Old Northern sources are played out in Bilbo's two encounters with Smaug. Driving the plot of *The Hobbit* is the determination of Bilbo's employers, the dwarves Thorin Oakenshield and company, to recover their ancestral treasure, a hoard that had drawn Smaug to the dwarves' realm almost two hundred years previously and has been guarded by him ever since as his own. On first entering the mountain tunnel leading to Smaug's lair, Bilbo puts on the Ring of invisibility and finds Smaug sleeping.

> There he lay, a vast red-golden dragon, fast asleep; a thrumming came from his jaws and nostrils, and wisps of smoke, but his fires were low in slumber. Beneath him, under all his limbs and his huge coiled tail, and about him on all sides stretching away across the unseen floors, lay countless piles of precious things, gold wrought and unwrought, gems and jewels, and silver red-stained in the ruddy light. (pp. 193–4)

Having grabbed a 'great two-handled cup' (p. 194), Bilbo flees. But, as the narrator says, 'Dragons may not have much real use for all their wealth, but they know it to an ounce as a rule, especially after long possession; and Smaug was no exception' (p. 195). So it is that, on awaking from his 'uneasy dream' (p. 195) and discovering his loss, the enraged Smaug comes flying, 'licking the mountain-sides with flame, beating his great wings with a noise like a roaring wind' (p. 197), so forcing the dwarves to abandon their ponies to certain death and seek refuge.

Thus far, aside from his 'uneasy dream', Smaug would appear to be little different to the vengeful *Beowulf* dragon. But, as said, Smaug has a personality, and this means that he also has anxieties, on this occasion about the tunnel after discovering his loss.[11]

> There was a breath of strange air in his cave. Could there be a draught from that little hole? He had never felt quite happy about it, though it was small, and now he glared at it in suspicion and wondered why he never blocked it up. Of late he had half fancied he had caught the dim echoes of a knocking sound from far above that came down through it to his lair. (p. 195)

Smaug's criticism of his own poor housekeeping and his consequent worries about his prospective vulnerability effectively humanizes him.

J.R.R. Tolkien,
'Conversation
with Smaug', from
*The Hobbit* (1937).

Bilbo's second journey into Smaug's cave is ignorantly incautious.

'Old Smaug is weary and asleep,' he thought. 'He can't see me and he won't hear me. Cheer up Bilbo!' He had forgotten or had never heard about dragons' sense of smell. It is also an awkward fact that they can keep half an eye open watching while they sleep, if they are suspicious. (p. 199)

This time, he encounters a dragon that is verbally adroit, dripping in ironic mockery and, importantly, so full of himself that he fails to recognize his weak spot, literally so when he proudly rolls over to show Bilbo his gem-studded underbelly. Enquiring of his intruder who this thief might be, Bilbo, while extravagantly kowtowing, responds to Smaug's questions with riddles, for 'This, of course, is the way to talk to dragons, if you don't want to reveal your proper name (which is wise)' (p. 200). Smaug then divisively warns Bilbo about the greed and cunning of dwarves, pointing out the ludicrous impracticalities of their plan to remove so great a store of treasure, let alone the unlikeliness of them being inclined to share it out fairly with Bilbo. Then, when Bilbo ill-advisedly speaks of their plan for revenge and of Smaug's 'bitter enemies', Smaug bellows laughter and says, 'My armour is like tenfold shields, my teeth are swords, my claws spears, the shock of my tail a thunderbolt, my wings a hurricane, and my breath death!' (p. 203). Now realizing that it is time to run for his life, Bilbo is lucky enough to escape unscathed, despite Smaug breathing fire up the tunnel.

Smaug set a fashion for dragons who are, frankly, cleverer than the humans they meet (and in some ways more modern and more civilized). But Tolkien also gave them another dimension, which he had hinted at in 1936 in his lecture. There he had grumbled slightly about the *Beowulf* dragon, for 'not being dragon enough, plain pure fairy-story dragon'. Despite some good touches, like the sniffing out of the thief's tracks, Tolkien thought 'the conception, nonetheless, approaches *draconitas* rather than *draco*; a personification of malice, greed, destruction.'[12] Tolkien put a lot more fairy-story *draco* into Smaug. But he also noted *draconitas*, and in particular what he called in *The Hobbit* 'the dragon-sickness', an infectious and accursed lust for gold that contaminates several characters. He gave dragons, or he brought out in dragons, what had perhaps always been there: a moral element, whereby the dragon is the sin of greed. Not, that is, the modern Wall Street kind, always wanting to grab, but the old miserly kind, that determination to hang on. So, in the case of Smaug: pile up the hoard and lie on it, never sharing (obviously) but also never using, never spending, just gloating. There is less 'otherness' about Smaug than is entirely comfortable.[13]

The main victim of 'dragon-sickness' is the Master of Laketown, who steals the gold given him to relieve the sufferings of his town and flees, only to die at the very end of *The Hobbit*, 'of starvation in the Waste, deserted by his companions' (p. 272). But Thorin the dwarf feels it too. Like a dragon, he will not think of sharing the treasure, even when he needs to. It is Bilbo's greatest achievement that he does not feel the dragon-sickness: he gives away that most precious of objects in the hoard, the Arkenstone, to Gandalf and his allies as a bargaining chip and accepts only a modest reward. That few are immune to dragon-sickness, especially in the modern world, is a thought that preoccupied both Tolkien and C. S. Lewis.

Smaug was, of course, not Tolkien's only dragon, nor the first he thought of. Tolkien's works were so often revised, and so commonly published many years after they were written, that it is hard to know what he did first, or how his thoughts developed, but one can say that dragons throughout his career could be presented morally, triumphantly or bitterly.

Tolkien's most morally oriented dragon tale is the poem 'The Hoard'. When first published in 1923, this had as its title a line from *Beowulf*, 'Iumonna

Gold Galdre Bewunden' (l. 3052), 'The Gold of Men-of-Yore, Wound Round with Spell'. The spell is dragon-sickness, and what 'The Hoard' shows is the sickness being passed on along with the treasure. Tolkien revised the poem repeatedly throughout his life, but only to make that point stronger and stronger.[14]

At the outset, there is what might aptly be called an Elvish 'Golden Age', a time when about 'silver and gold the gods sung', so before 'the pit was dug or Hell yawned, / ere dwarf was bred or dragon spawned'. But 'over Elvenholme the shadow rolled' and brought about their doom, and Greed, at first in the person of a gold-hoarding dwarf, became master. Yet soon the avaricious 'old dwarf in a dark cave' who lusted after kingly power is overcome by a young dragon. In the passing of time, when he has grown old, the dragon is sought out by a young warrior and so too meets a miserable end.

Although not made completely clear in the poem, it would seem that this same warrior does just what the dwarf wanted to do and becomes a king. This, however, brings no comfort, for like the dragon and the dwarf before him, he is so obsessed with the hoard that nothing brings him pleasure, neither food nor drink nor song. Isolated and joyless, this king's nemesis comes to pass when his enemies invade and, having razed his kingdom to the ground, throw his dead body into a pit. Finally, all that remains is the hoard, 'forgotten behind doors none can unlock' and overgrown with grass on which livestock graze.

There are no heroes in 'The Hoard', no one prepared to sacrifice themselves for the betterment of others – no one, except the poet, looking back to those glory days when 'there were Elves of old' who 'sang as they wrought many fair things'. Even the dragon has no personality whatsoever, unless, that is, like all the other characters featured, its descent into sociopathic, paranoid self-obsession is seen as defining its character. On the contrary, the corrupting power of the hoard is all there is. It is not hard to see that Tolkien, a devout Roman Catholic, is delivering a religious message, one in which material possession is exposed as lacking in any spiritual comfort, guidance or understanding. Yet the poem is not without hope, for while Night, here a symbol of spiritual death, shall keep the 'old hoard', the 'earth waits and Elves sleep'. Given time, Tolkien would seem to be saying, redemption is always possible.

Far more genial, and devoted to the triumph of the 'monsters' and the appreciators of fairy tale over critics, sceptics, kings and killjoys, is Tolkien's on the surface of things whimsical short story 'Farmer Giles of Ham' (1949),[15] which features a dragon with many resemblances to Smaug and a hero with certain resemblances to Bilbo. Set in the rural village of Ham in the Middle Ages and in the Middle Kingdom, a blunt-speaking, beer-swilling farmer, Ægidius de Hammo, otherwise known as Farmer Giles, finds himself having to fire his old blunderbuss at a certain stupid giant that has lost his bearings and wandered onto Giles's land, where his clumsiness is causing much crop damage. Despite feeling little more harmed than by 'a few stinging flies' (p. 115), the giant returns home to the 'Wild Hills, and the dubious marches of the mountain-country' (p. 104), where his report of his adventure soon comes to the attention of Chrysophylax Dives, a wealthy dragon 'of ancient and imperial lineage' (p. 116). His curiosity aroused, and somewhat hungry, Chrysophylax flies off to the Middle Kingdom, whose residents believe that dragons are extinct, to see for himself what profit might be had.

Meanwhile, news of Giles's heroics spread far and wide and eventually reach the ears of the king, who rewards him with an old sword, which, unbeknown to the king, turns out to be Caudimordax, 'vulgarly called Tailbiter' (p. 124), an ancient magical weapon that unsheathes itself should a dragon be within five miles and can strike of its own accord. When Chrysophylax arrives not far from Ham and sets about causing ruin and eating all in sight, including a parish priest, the now celebrated but less than enthusiastic Giles is called upon to get rid of him. Emboldened by a few beers, jangling in makeshift chainmail and mounted on his faithful old grey mare, Giles eventually confronts the dragon, who, like Smaug, cunningly greets him with pleasantries, adding, 'let me see, I don't think I know your name?' Unlike Bilbo Baggins, Giles does not resort to riddles but gruffly says, 'Nor I yours . . . and we'll leave it at that' (p. 131). So the conversation continues, with Chrysophylax readying himself to pounce. But Giles is no fool and, fully aware of the dragon's intentions, unleashes Tailbiter, so injuring Chrysophylax badly enough to stop him flying off. Having gained the advantage, Giles and the villagers propose a deal: Chrysophylax must return in eight days with sufficient of his wealth to compensate them for all the damage he has done. Needless to say, time passes and there is no sign of the dragon.

Now the near-bankrupt king gets involved and, mustering his knights, who are more concerned with fashion and etiquette than with dragon-slaying, rides off with Giles to hunt down the dragon and claim the treasure. On hearing their noisy arrival and determined to protect his hoard, Chrysophylax swoops down, kills many and sends the rest packing. Only Giles remains, and, with Tailbiter in hand, the dragon is subdued, forced to bring out his treasure and thereafter to be Giles's lifelong friend and protector. With his wings tied down, Chrysophylax carries the hoard back to

Ham, where he defends Giles from the furious king's soldiers, who are under orders to bring the treasure to the royal coffers. In due course, the generous but politically astute Giles, now known as Lord of the Tame Worm, goes on to become prince, then king, of the newly formed Little Kingdom. Sometime later, having remained true to his master, Chrysophylax is allowed to return to his home, where he evicts (and then eats) a dragon squatter and gives the stupid giant a piece of his mind. As for the king of the Middle Kingdom, all he ever got from Giles was an annual tribute of 'six oxtails and a pint of beer' (p. 161), a laughable concession that ended once Giles had been elevated to the rank of prince.

While obviously delivering a parody of dragon-slayers of old, Tolkien was also having some fun, albeit with a rather pointed scholarly message, in offering up a field day for philologists and toponymists.[16] Yet there are deeper stirrings in 'Farmer Giles of Ham', not unlike those in the anti-establishment folktales discussed in Chapter Seven. The comparison is most evident in the Orcadian tale of Assipattle and the Stoor Worm, which, given its derivation from Old Norse mythology and inclusion of a hero armed with a magic sword riding an exceptionally sturdy horse, may well have been known to Tolkien. But, more than this, as in 'Assipattle', in 'Farmer Giles of Ham' one can readily discern the issue of class conflict.

Representing the common folk is Farmer Giles, who is what might be called a 'reluctant' Beowulf (perhaps a little unfairly), and opposing Giles's interests are, first, the dragon, who is not only very wealthy but of aristocratic descent, and, second, the overbearing king and his foppish knights. While Chrysophylax Dives is ultimately brought to book by Giles and obliged to spend many years in service to him, the king becomes a laughing stock whose authority Giles dismisses out of hand. But the real issue is not the power of dragons or kings but the power of money, here in the form of Chrysophylax's treasure. Once that power is seized by Giles, the whole social order changes. Innocuous though it might otherwise seem, read this way, 'Farmer Giles of Ham' is socially subversive.[17]

Also combining comedy and draconic violence is Tolkien's poem 'The Dragon's Visit' (1937).[18] In this, a green dragon is spotted in the cherry trees of Mister Higgins's garden by a neighbour. When Higgins turns the garden hose on the dragon, he is pleased to be cooled and starts to sing, in the belief that villagers will be enchanted by his voice. But, much to the dragon's disappointment, Higgins sends for the fire brigade, led by the tellingly named Captain George. When the dragon threatens to demolish the church steeple and eat his attackers for supper, Captain George, who is no saint, has the fire hose turned on him, bringing him down from the trees, whereupon his 'underneath / (where he was rather tender)' is poked with poles. Now the dragon does as promised and 'smashes the town to smithereens' and eats all his opponents for supper, whose remains he then dutifully buries.[19] He then sings a sad song reflecting on 'the old order changing' and 'the world getting duller' before flying back 'to a green dragon's meeting.'

While quite possibly satirizing 'The Reluctant Dragon', 'The Dragon's Visit' also has its own message as a lamentation for a heroic age, a theme running throughout Tolkien's work. Accordingly, while dragons, if provoked, will do as they always have, their feeble, foolish, narrow-minded human adversaries have strayed far from the path of the heroes of the myths and legends that Tolkien so admired. His 'mythology *for England*',[20] as his biographer puts it, is in many respects a requiem for a lost past. Tolkien and the *Beowulf* poet were of one mind when it came to regret.

Dragons in Tolkien's masterwork, the trilogy *The Lord of the Rings* (1954–5), are more alluded to as prospective dangers than developed as named characters.[21] Not to be forgotten, though, is his most brutal and wickedly intelligent dragon, the golden Glaurung, the 'Father of Dragons'. Known variously as the Deceiver, the Worm of Greed and the Worm of Morgoth, Glaurung is developed throughout the wider history of Middle-earth in Tolkien's posthumously published mythopoeia *The Silmarillion* (1977).[22] Both a creation and an aspect of the evil genius Morgoth, Glaurung is a combination of the early Germanic dragon, most obviously Fáfnir, and the Book of Revelation's Great Red Dragon of Hell, particularly, so far as Revelation is concerned, in Glaurung's insidiously devious use of false prophecy.[23]

The first of the fire-breathing reptiles known as the Urulóki, Glaurung initially features in Middle-earth's First Age Wars of Beleriand, when he is not yet fully grown. Driven off by the archers of Fingon, Prince of Hithlum, Glaurung's premature disclosing of himself displeases Morgoth. It will be two hundred years before Glaurung, now fully grown, is again unleashed into Beleriand, this time by Morgoth.[24] In the Battle of Sudden Flame, Glaurung leads the Orcs and the sinister Balrogs and succeeds in routing and dispersing the armies of Grey-elves and Men. Following this victory, in the Battle of Unnumbered Tears, Glaurung spearheads a host of dragons and succeeds in killing Azaghâl, Dwarf-lord of Belegost, but not before Azaghâl has plunged his knife into Glaurung's underbelly, so forcing him and Morgoth's armies into retreat. When Glaurung next reappears in Beleriand, he establishes himself as ruler over Nargothrond, where he lies on a vast bed of treasure.

Yet Glaurung's rule does not last long. A few years later the heroic Túrin Turambar, once cursed with a spell of self-loathing by Glaurung, ambushes the Worm as he stretches his body across a deep ravine beneath which flows the River Teiglin. Having driven his magical talking sword Gurthang into the dragon's one weak spot, and believing that he has now put paid to Glaurung's wickedness, Túrin attempts to retrieve his sword, but in so doing is contaminated by the dragon's blood and struck down by his evil glare, so causing Túrin to fall into a deep stupor. But Glaurung leaves a bitter legacy, for when Túrin's beloved Níniel happens across the injured Túrin, the dying Glaurung lifts from her a spell of forgetfulness that he has previously cast over her, the intended result being that she remembers that she is Nienor, Túrin's sister, a fact about which Túrin is equally oblivious. Despairing of her cruel fate, Níniel throws herself into the river gorge. When the now recovered Túrin finally learns of Níniel's death and the reason for it, he loses his mind and bids his sword bring him a swift end. Túrin is buried with all due ceremony, and over his grave commemorative runes are carved: 'TÚRIN TURAMBAR DAGNIR GLAURUNGA' (Túrin Turambar, Slayer of Glaurung). Beneath is written 'NIENOR NÍNIEL', 'But she was not there, nor was it ever known whither the cold waters of Teiglin had taken her.'[25]

Without doubt Tolkien's most horrific dragon creation, Glaurung is as much *draconitas* as he is *draco*. Capable of wickedness by design and simply for the sheer pleasure of it, Glaurung certainly has a personality, even though it is one with no redeeming features whatsoever. Set together, Tolkien's dragons range from the evil and the despotic to the absurd and the comical. Yet while their actions can variously provoke sympathy, amusement, fear and horror, their penchant for destruction is universal. Whatever the setting, Tolkien's 'good' dragons can never be truly tamed, unless, like Chrysophylax Dives, they have no other choice in the matter; not for the time being, that is.[26]

## C. S. Lewis's dragons

In Tolkien's lecture of 1936, just after what he wrote about 'the fascination of the worm', he added, 'More than one poem in recent years . . . has been inspired by the dragon of *Beowulf*.'[27] Apart from his 'The Hoard', Tolkien was most probably referring to two other poems, published by his friend C. S. Lewis, both of which are highly 'Tolkienian' and most likely prompted by what Tolkien had told him about *Beowulf*.[28] By saying as much, the point that Tolkien was set on making is that the fascination with dragons is normal and widespread.

A lapsed Anglican, Lewis recovered his faith, owing in part to Tolkien's influence[29] and in part to the impression made on him by the works of George MacDonald, particularly his novel *Lilith*. Written almost immediately after his conversion is *The Pilgrim's Regress: An Allegorical Apology for Christianity, Reason, and Romanticism* (1933). As the title indicates, allegory is the book's driving force, and it is here that two of the poems Tolkien was thinking of are to be found.[30]

*The Pilgrim's Regress* tells of two dragons: 'The Northern Dragon' and 'The Southern Dragon'. In the former tale, a treasure-hoarding dragon laments his lot in life in song. Regretting having eaten his wife, who 'could have helped me, watch and watch about', he finally appeals to his maker for 'peace', imploring his 'Lord' to kill those men and other dragons that limit his freedom by forcing him to be constantly on his guard. Yet there is one condition: 'But do not say that I should give up the gold.' Although at first sympathetic, the pilgrim soon realizes that the right thing to do is kill the dragon, which he duly does. In the latter tale, the dragon is already dead and it is its slayer who sings of the fiery pain he now endures after brutally killing a dragon and then eating her heart. Seemingly, the dragon slayer has now become dragon-like himself, and as a result, 'Behemoth is my serving man!' and 'Now I know the stake I played for.'[31] The songs of both the dragon and the slayer serve as a warning to the pilgrim about the sins of selfishness and greed.

Similarly functioning as a caution against self-interest is the boy Eustace in Lewis's *The Voyage of the Dawn Treader* (1952).[32] Irritating, work-shy, selfish and so an all-round nuisance to his shipmates, Eustace one day wanders off alone round an island where they have temporarily put ashore. Sure enough, Eustace stumbles across a cave, from which a dragon, a dull-eyed 'old, sad creature', emerges to drink from a pool and then keels over and dies. Taking shelter in the cave for the night, Eustace falls asleep on the dragon's treasure. When he awakes, much to his dismay, he has turned into a dragon, one capable of flight but incapable of speech. Having flown back to his fellow travellers' camp, once the Eustace-dragon manages to convince them that he is their transformed companion, he quickly shows a different, more likeable and cooperative side to himself than had previously been the case when he was a mere boy. Finally, the Christ-like lion Aslan comes to Eustace and leads him to an Edenic garden where, under instruction from Aslan, Eustace scratches off his scales, plunges into a well and re-emerges as his old self, cured, at least for the main part, of his one-time failings.

Eustace's transformation into a dragon is quite clearly indebted to the *Saga of the Völsungs*' Fáfnir and man-turned-dragon tales in such as the *Saga of Gold-Thórir*. But it may also have a source in *Beowulf*, for as critics have noted, the poem has a strange gap in it. It was remarked above that in the poem the thief 'stumbles on the sleeping dragon and his hoard'. But how could it be that one 'stumbles on' a sleeping dragon? Critics have also noted that the dragon itself had somehow stumbled on the hoard, which had been buried for safety by a lone survivor. But after committing the hoard to the ground, with a speech beginning, 'Hold now, you earth' (l. 2247a), the survivor wandered off and left the hoard *'opene standan'* (l. 2271), simply enough, 'standing open', which from any treasure-hoarding practical perspective makes little sense. As anyone who buries a hoard would know, the vital part of the job is not digging the hole: it is filling it in again so as to keep the treasure hidden. Given this curiosity, the thought occurred to several critics, as Tolkien certainly knew, that in some earlier fairy-tale version, the survivor who owned the treasure did not just wander off; instead, he turned into the dragon. To use a phrase found several times in Old Norse, 'he lay down on his gold' and, just as it was with Fáfnir, transmogrified. It is this same transmogrification that we can see in Eustace, whereby the dragon-gold operates on him while he is full of self-obsessed 'dragonish' thoughts.

Yet there the similarities between dragons of the Old North and Lewis's modern fantasy end, for the Eustace-dragon is no ghastly monstrosity. Rather, the boy's dragon appearance functions as a frame for him to reflect on and address his shortcomings; in other words, briefly becoming a dragon is Eustace's penance. Yet as Christian metaphors for moral imperfections, Lewis's dragons, along with the Narnia corpus generally, were not exactly to Tolkien's taste. As he reflected in 1964, '"Narnia" and all that part of C. S. L.'s work should remain outside the range of my sympathy, as much as my work was outside his.'[33] Even so, as fantasies for children, Lewis's Narnia tales were and have remained among the most popular ever written.


THE INFLUENCE of J.R.R. Tolkein's Middle-earth dramas and C. S. Lewis's Narnia tales on modern fantasy fiction would be difficult to overestimate. Selling in their tens of millions – Tolkien's *The Lord of the Rings* trilogy has sold 150 million copies to date – they became a staple of contemporary literature worldwide. This is particularly true as regards Tolkien's *The Hobbit* and *The Lord of the Rings*, which during the 1960s and early 1970s were considered an absolute must-read for those involved in counter-culture protests and the so-called hippy movement generally. That neither Tolkien nor Lewis either supported or approved of such politics is beside the point, for the fact is that no fantasy fiction writer since could claim ignorance of the impact of these founding fathers on their work. It is, then, to that veritable plethora of modern dragons that we now turn.

# ten

# 'A Wilderness of Dragons'

OME THE MID-TWENTIETH century, dragons in literary fictions were represented on three main fronts: the nursery dragon-friend; Tolkien's Old Northern dragons, which are typically no one's friend; and the religious dragon, which could be either satanic or an allegorical vehicle delivering moral warnings and corrections, like C. S. Lewis's dragons.[1] While these would appear to be the major dragon players, one cannot discount the continuing influence of the Graeco-Roman dragon and the growing influence of the East Asian dragon, largely due to numerous studies set on demystifying the East.[2] From here on we have a dragon epidemic, and, as might be expected, the tendency among authors has been to merge the various characteristics of dragons from all those that took hold from the late nineteenth century onwards.

## Sci-fi and fantasy dragons

The following selection of fantasy and sci-fi dragon plots represents but a small few of those in modern literary fictions. The purpose here is to offer some indication, as much as possible in chronological order, of the range and complexity of modern dragons. These plot summaries and their otherworld scenarios are set out to illustrate how dragon traditions have been adapted, and in some cases targeted critically at contemporary society.

Ursula K. Le Guin's Earthsea novels – *A Wizard of Earthsea* (1968), *The Tombs of Atuan* (1971) and *The Farthest Shore* (1972)[3] – are set in a remote archipelago. Pre-industrial but literate, the human inhabitants of Earthsea belong to a number of different races, respectively resembling Native Americans, Middle Eastern and Mediterranean peoples, and North Europeans. Earthsea is also home to a race of dragons. According to Earthsea's creation myths, humans and dragons were once of the same race, but the dragons chose the elemental freedom of fire and air, whereas humans chose service to the masters of water and earth. As a consequence, dragons and humans live apart and are invariably hostile to each other. Dragon predations typically involve their raids into human territories in search of food and treasure, and the only defence that humans can muster comes in the form of their wizard dragonlords, who have gained some mastery of the dragons' ancient tongue, the Language in the Making. A good wizard is one who eschews the necromancy practised by bad wizards and seeks only to maintain life's 'balance', something which only humans are capable of upsetting. So far as the dragons are concerned, humans are an inferior species, undeserving of their respect. Even so, at times of threat to both dragons and humans, cooperation is sometimes the only option.

Le Guin's dragons, then, are projections of what humans might have been had they not chosen earthly comforts – and, as it turns out, discomforts – and had instead, like the dragons, opted for the skies. Doomed to a life after death in the Dry Land, a dull, drab, Hades-like place, human life is typically unexceptional. Yet for those such as Ged, the hero of *A Wizard of Earthsea* and *The Farthest Shore*, who trains to become a mage (a wizard), the mysteries of existence are gradually learned and hard-won wisdom is gained, sometimes thanks to the help of dragons, whether given willingly or not. Ged, indeed, gains mastery over the dragon Yevaud by simply knowing his name, which once uttered obliges Yevaud to do as Ged wishes, so forcing him to swear that neither he nor his dragon-sons will ever again pose a threat to humans.[4]

Openly indebted to Tolkien's fantasy realism, Le Guin's Earthsea novels are also underpinned by the philosophical mysticism and anarchic politics that informed the counter-culture values of the 1960s and '70s.[5] Notably in Le Guin's Earthsea fantasies, female characters, both human and draconic, figure as strongly as male characters, so setting a gender precedent that influenced many subsequent fantasy authors.

In Anne McCaffrey's *Dragonriders of Pern* series, beginning with *Dragonflight* (1968),[6] the variously coloured dragons on the planet Pern are creatures that have been genetically engineered from indigenous fire-lizards, once kept as pets by the early colonists. But all life on Pern is threatened by Thread, a virulent spore that at two-hundred-year intervals travels in clouds from the Red Star, when its orbit is closest to Pern, and devours organic matter. The designed function of Pern's dragons is to exhale fire at Thread before it reaches ground. Capable of both teleporting and of communicating telepathically with their riders, whose intense relationship with their dragon mounts can even involve a form of sexual intercourse, the Pern dragons are devoted servants and friends of humans; indeed, as the only known way to combat Thread, human survival is wholly dependent on them.

Determined to subvert what she perceived as dragon clichés in European myths, legends, folktales and literature, McCaffrey's fire-lizards are obviously influenced by dragons of East Asian mythologies. But in the Pern fantasies, the beneficial and intimate relationship between humans and dragons goes far beyond any mythological prototype and is developed into a symbiosis, one consequence of which is that the dragon is 'de-mythologised'.[7] In effect, McCaffrey's dragons are nursery dragons for grown-ups and are not really dragons in any traditional sense. Yet, while this may well be true, what is particularly striking about the Pern series is that, with the curious exception of the pop song 'Puff the Magic Dragon' (see below), it is the first time in contemporary Western fiction that we have dragons willingly serving as modes of transport for humans.

Offering an entertaining perspective on dragons is Gordon R. Dickson's *The Dragon and the George* (1976).[8] Jim and Angie are a young couple working as college teaching assistants. While Jim works part-time in a history department, Angie's employment is as a lab assistant for the Astral Projection project. But one day a lab device miscalculates and Angie vanishes. Using the same device to try and recover her, Jim finds himself transported to a medieval England of sword and sorcery, where he is shocked to discover that he is now in the body of a dragon known as Gorbash. Assisted by other dragons, to whom he explains that he is really one of the 'georges', in other words, a human, Jim learns from the magician Carolinus that Angie and his namesake's hoard are in the Loathly Tower, guarded over by the dragon Bryagh. After much strife, during which Jim learns to his cost just what a threat the 'georges' can pose to dragons, Jim eventually finds Angie, who has spent her incarceration in Jim's human body, and rescues her. Carolinus now separates Jim from Gorbash, after which, given their newfound friends, Jim and Angie decide not to return to their previous lives.[9]

Not unlike certain dragons of Asia and East Asia, Dickson's dragons are really hyperbolized humans. Similarly, the medieval fantasy world can be seen as a hyperbolization of Jim's and Angie's mundane employment as college teaching assistants. Regulated as it is by auditors and accountants but threatened by the Dark Powers' determination to wreck the essential balance between History and Change, this otherworld is a working-life conceit. To put it another way, *The Dragon and the George* is a satire, one which, were it not for the amusing inversion of the St George myth, could just as easily have had Jim transformed into virtually anything. As a dragon trope, then, Dickson's novel serves as a commentary on our routine powerlessness in the face of bureaucratic controls and change simply for the sake of it. It is in this regard a draconic escape from the banalities of working life that is the stuff of dreams.

Michael Ende's dragon Falkor, who features in *The Neverending Story* (published in German 1979; English translation 1983), is, like McCaffrey's dragons, inspired by those benevolent East Asian dragons that assisted emperors; in Falkor's case, explicitly so. The novel tells of the bookish and lonely young boy Bastian, whose mother has recently died and whose father offers him little comfort. Bastian immerses himself in a book about the world of Fantastica, representing imagination, which is being rapidly consumed by the Nothing, representing apathy and cynicism. Desperate to find a cure for Fantastica's dying Childlike Empress is her young emissary Atreyu. Mounted on the luckdragon Falkor,[10] Atreyu goes in search of an oracle, who tells him that the empress, and so Fantastica, can be saved only if she is given a new name by a child from beyond their borders. Once Bastian realizes that this can only be done by him, he names the empress 'Moon Child' and now physically enters the world of Fantastica. Many adventures follow, during which Bastian's decency of character is severely tested, sometimes to his disgrace. But all is eventually well and Fantastica is restored to its former glory, much thanks to the repentant Bastian and the resolute Atreyu, who are two sides of the same coin.

While Falkor the luckdragon could be seen as little more than an extraordinary mode of transport, he is the only true constant in the novel, one that transcends the debilitations, misfortunes and errors of judgement from which, in one way or another, all the other characters suffer. In effect, Falkor is hope for the future, an optimistic sensibility that Bastian adopts to his benefit when finally seeking a reconciliation with his father.

Another way in which dragons have been used in modern fiction to explore children's problems returns us to Mal Peet's *Murdstone Trilogy*. There, his agent Minerva firmly tells Philip Murdstone that he needs to write about proper fantasy dragons – not, as it were, dragon analogues in the form of 'gropey games masters or embittered ladies from Social Services'. But what if fantasy dragons are analogues of real-world problems? This possibility is taken up very clearly in two young adult novels, *A Game of Dark* (1972) by William Mayne, and Ursula le Guin's *The Beginning Place*, also known as *Threshold* (1980).

As in Ende's *The Neverending Story*, both works centre on young characters trapped in unhappy real-life situations, except in these tales the dragons the children encounter in their fantasy worlds are not in any way their friends. In *A Game of Dark*, Jackson is the child of a crippled father and a mother who is a teacher at his own school and who therefore calls him only by his surname, 'Jackson'. His parents half-consciously bear him an irrational grudge for the accident in which his father was crippled and his sister killed: there is no love in the family. In *The Beginning Place*, similarly, Hugh is the child of a single mother who has reacted to desertion by her husband by keeping her son in a state of permanent dependency. Meanwhile, Irene, also the child of a single mother, is threatened by the unwanted advances of her stepfather, a familiar fairy-tale (and also real-world) situation. How can they escape? The answer, briefly, is that in both books the hero, or the hero–heroine pair, find themselves in another world, where there is a dragon to be slain, one which keeps the fantasy world oppressed by its power of projecting depression and fear. Jackson kills his dragon by the Sigurd method, so by hiding in a pit and stabbing from below. Hugh does likewise, assisted by Irene, who is the wisest of the pair. In the latter case, it is striking, first, that Hugh is injured in the fight, and second, that the dragon turns out to be female.

Hugh has, one can only say, in a subconscious way, killed his analogue-mother; just as Jackson has literally killed the dragon, his 'analogue-father'. Killing one's parents is such an obvious taboo that the event has to be disguised into fantasy, but once the deed has been done in the fantasy world, the teenagers can return to their real world and then, at last, move on. Hugh and Irene leave their stifling or unsafe parental homes, move in together and become adults. Jackson is released from his undeserved burden of guilt and finds a way to love his father. In both books, what has been acted out in the fantasy world is a solution to the 'family drama' of the real world. Rightly did Tolkien say that a dragon is 'richer in significance than his barrow is in gold'; this being the case, authors can continually find new ways to use and exploit this draconic 'treasure'.

More in keeping with well-known European traditions are the typically fierce dragons in J. K. Rowling's Harry Potter series. Making their Hogwarts debut in *The Philosopher's Stone* (1997), Hagrid, Keeper of Keys, wins a dragon's egg, nurtures it until it hatches and names it Norbert, but, despite much effort, his attempts to domesticate it fail. In *The Goblet of Fire* (2000) there is a trainee-wizard tournament in which the contestants have to brave the perils of retrieving a golden egg from one of four dragons. And guarding a vault in *The Deathly Hallows* (2007) is a dragon that is then freed by Harry, Hermione and Ron, who escape on its back. As identified by the Magizoologist Newt Scamander in his *Fantastic Beasts and Where to Find Them* (2001), a compulsory text for all Hogwarts pupils, dragons are from many different places: Norway, Sweden, the Hebrides, Peru, Hungary, Romania, New Zealand, China, Wales and Ukraine. But even though Rowling's dragons all pose dangers, to greater or lesser degrees, very little distinction is made between them in terms of their functions. While dragons can be used to provide challenges for aspiring wizards to overcome, their main value lies in the magical properties of their body parts, not unlike the pharmaceutical and cosmetic uses of 'dragon' body parts in ancient China.

Like Le Guin's Earthsea novels and with a similar political agenda are Michael Swanwick's land of Faerie novels. Also written in homage to Tolkien's Middle-earth fantasies and aimed at challenging those mass-market fantasy derivatives that he saw as enfeebling the genre, Swanwick had this to say: 'the recent slew of interchangeable Fantasy trilogies has hit me in much the same way that discovering that the woods I used to play in as a child have been cut down to make way for shoddy housing developments did.'[11]

Dragons feature prominently in two of Swanwick's novels. In the earliest, *The Iron Dragon's Daughter* (1993), set in the unremittingly exploitative world of Faerie, Jane, the young changeling protagonist, escapes her grim factory job as a builder of iron dragons in company with the manipulative but ill-maintained dragon Melanchthon, a cross between an animal and a war machine. Taken into Jane's care, Melanchthon reveals to her his plan to destroy the universe. Feeling that she has no purpose in life, Jane falls under Melanchthon's spell and, among her many other moral and legal transgressions, becomes a serial killer in order to provide fuel for her dependent dragon mentor. Eventually heading for the Spiral Castle at the spiritual centre of the universe in order to attack it, Jane pilots Melanchthon but is pursued by another dragon-pilot, an ex-lover of Jane's, whom she kills with Melanchthon's rocket-fire. But as they near the castle, Melanchthon's body disintegrates; Jane finds herself inside the castle, where she is confronted by the angry and disappointed Goddess. Having refused to serve the Goddess and wanting only to be punished, Jane is returned to earth to recover herself in a mental institution. Whether Jane will ever achieve the redemption she so badly needs – but hardly deserves – is left unresolved.

In Swanwick's sequel, *The Dragons of Babel* (2008), we are returned to the same cynical universe. Once again, the novel starts with interactions between a dragon and a human, or, rather, near-human, for unlike Jane, the protagonist Will is a fey. This alters the power relationship. While in *The Iron Dragon's Daughter* Melanchthon needed Jane to power him up and pilot him out of the factory, here the dragon, although crashed and damaged as a result of his involvement in the raging wars of Faerie, controls Will mentally from the outset and uses him as his lieutenant in his take-over of a small and all but defenceless village. Yet Will seems to escape from both the village and the dragon into the recognizably modern metropolitan landscape of Babel, a place which in Genesis (11:1–9) is the site of mankind's second fall from God's grace. It is here that Will becomes a politician's lieutenant, or 'ward-heeler'. But nothing is as it seems. A major figure is Will's guide and master, Nat Whilk, a confidence trickster. Tellingly, this character's name is derived from the Old English *nat hwylc*, meaning 'I don't know which', an indication of not only his underlying uncertainties and moral bankruptcy but of those same complexities that addle all of Babel's inhabitants. Perhaps Will has not entirely escaped from dragonish control after all.

Michael Swanwick's psychodrama dragons are central to his critique of contemporary culture and the pursuit of material power. Reminiscent, doubtless deliberately so, of Glaurung's insidious controllery, the dragons of Faerie epitomize the ruthless manipulations of global capitalism. As such, for Jane and Will, happy endings are out of the question. Yet hope is not entirely abandoned, for although unable to better either themselves or their world, Jane and Will have it in them to recognize their failings and, even more so, those of the powers that control them, not least the dragons.

Given the wealth of imaginative possibilities that the fantasy dragon offers, it was inevitable that yet another type of dragon would emerge. There is, then, what might be called a meta-dragon, which in this case is that dragon whose only purpose is to ridicule the serious-minded dragon. The master of this comedic mode is Terry Pratchett. Dragons in the following tales give some idea of Pratchett's ingeniously witty take on them.

In his earliest foray into dragon territory, 'Dragons at Crumbling Castle', a short story for children, the target is the dragon slayer of medieval Romance.[12] In Camelot, all of King Arthur's knights are away on quests, on holiday or off visiting their grandmothers, when dragons invade. It so falls to the young Ralph and his two accomplices, an incompetent knight and a ramshackle old wizard, to deal with the dragon infestation, which, as they discover, is not really of any great threat. In *The Colour of Magic* (1983), the joke is at the expense of Anne McCaffrey's Pern dragons. From Wyrmberg, an upside-down mountain, are dragons that exist only in the imagination.

They can be summoned telepathically by their riders but can suddenly turn up, just because someone is thinking about them.

Pratchett's most extensive treatment of the dragon theme comes in his novel *Guards! Guards!* (1989). This takes the three elements of the traditional iconographic scene familiar from such myths as those of Perseus and Andromeda or St George and inverts or subverts them. They are, of course, a virgin chained to a rock as sacrifice to the dragon; a dragon set on eating the virgin; and a hero to rescue the virgin and slay the dragon. One final element is that in the world of Pratchett's Ankh-Morpork, dragons are thought to be extinct, at least as *Draco nobilis*, the giant dragon of tradition. One dragon, however, is called back magically from the past, or perhaps from some other dimension, by the scheming Wonse, secretary to the Patrician of Ankh-Morpork. His plan is to have the dragon slain by a hero with a shining sword, as would be customary, after which the hero will become King of Ankh-Morpork by popular acclaim and a puppet for Secretary Wonse to manipulate.

The plan works as far as calling up the dragon, but it then incinerates the hero, despite his shining sword, and installs itself as ruler, demanding the traditional tribute of virgins, preferably aristocratic ones, who taste better. This takes us to Lady Sybil Ramkin, who may well be a virgin and is certainly aristocratic. But she is not the young beauty as popularly imagined but middle-aged, stout of build and formidable of character. As the proprietor of the Sunshine Sanctuary for Sick Dragons, Lady Sybil takes care of small swamp dragons, which are often used as cigarette lighters and are liable to be acquired as family pets and then heartlessly discarded, particularly when they show signs of blowing themselves up. She nevertheless ends up as tradition demands: chained to a rock for the dragon to eat.

Time, then, for the hero. While the 'shining sword' hero provided by Wonse proves useless, the next candidate is Captain Vimes of the Guard, a determined republican opposed to any form of kingship, especially dragon kingship. While he at least manages to unchain Lady Sybil from her rock, the job of slaying the dragon falls first to his guard subordinates, one of whom, Sergeant Colon, has a lucky arrow that has never missed its mark. As the dragon swoops in, Colon shoots it, just like Bard the Bowman, aiming for its one vulnerable part. It's a million-to-one chance, which means, by all the old laws of dragon-slaying, a certain hit. Nevertheless, here old laws do not have their way, and the arrow hits a scale and bounces off.

The last and highly suitable hero candidate is Lance-Constable Carrot, a new recruit to the Guard. Carrot is a foundling, brought up by dwarfs and insistent that he is himself a dwarf, despite him being well over six feet tall and with a heroic frame developed by an adolescence spent hauling ore-wagons underground. He is also very likely the rightful king of Ankh-Morpork, possessing a royal birthmark and an ancestral sword, which is not shiny at all and has so many notches it looks more like a saw. Even so, it cuts very well and dates back to the time when kings were real, not for show. But Carrot has no such kingly ambitions, as all he wants to be is a policeman. Once the dragon has been brought down, he does not set about it, like a true dragon slayer, with sword or lance but instead climbs on its wing and declares with satisfaction, 'You're nicked, chummy.'

That which does bring it down in many ways completes the joke. All through the book, one of Lady Sybil's small swamp dragons, Errol, has been eating strange things: coal, a kettle, Carrot's tin of armour polish. Instinct has been stoking the strange chemical factory that is a dragon's insides. At a critical moment, Errol takes off, powered not by wings but by his own white-hot flatulence. This accelerates him to supersonic speed, and it is Errol's final rear-end sonic boom that knocks the great 'noble dragon' out of the sky when it rises to challenge him. It then transpires that the giant dragon, now grounded, has never been King of Ankh-Morpork at all, but Queen, for she is female. She takes Errol's supersonic flatulence as a mating display, flying off with him to happiness, as also occurs with Lady Sybil and Captain Vimes.

A virgin, a threatening dragon, and several human hero candidates, but the real hero of *Guards! Guards!* is *another* dragon. Pratchett's story could not work without his readers' awareness of the way dragon stories are supposed to go. The fun lies in having them go a different way, which after all is more plausible (or at least just as plausible). Nonetheless, this fun can hardly be called satire, for Pratchett clearly loves both traditional dragon stories and the authors he parodies (among them Anne McCaffrey and other fantasy classics, including Tolkien and even *Beowulf*). He shows, in a way, how dragons in the modern world have gone viral.

One further take on dragons that warrants mention, albeit with certain reservations, is Christopher Paolini's *Inheritance Cycle*. Written for the young adult market, Paolini's series of four books, beginning with *Eragon* (2003), have sold in their millions. Critics, however, have been less than impressed by both the author's execution of his plots and his characterizations; for example, as the dragonology expert Thomas Honegger states, 'the great popularity of his books is due more to the fascination with the bond between human protagonist and dragon than to any stylistic mastery on the author's part.'[13]

Clearly indebted, almost to the point of trespass, to Tolkien's Middle-earth fantasies and Anne McCaffrey's Pern dragons, the *Inheritance Cycle* begins with the young Eragon growing up on his uncle's farm in the land of Alagaësia, having been abandoned there at birth by his mother. One day, while out hunting, there mysteriously appears before him what he at first thinks is a blue stone. But, as he soon comes to realize, this is a dragon egg, which unbeknown to him had once been in the possession of a group of elves, who caused it to disappear when they were ambushed by a sorcerer and his brutal accomplices. When the egg hatches, Eragon names the fledgling female dragon Saphira. Shortly after, Eragon's uncle is killed and the farm razed to the ground by two Ra'zac servants of the tyrannical King Galbatorix, and Eragon, along with his infant dragon, sets out to seek vengeance on his uncle's killers. And so his perilous quest begins, forever pitted against dark forces. In due course, Saphira becomes Eragon's closest possible friend and ally and, just as any reader would have expected, his dragon steed.

Whatever one might think about Paolini's often predictable and clichéd plots, there is no denying their remarkable complexity, and in this regard the page-turning thrills of the *Inheritance Cycle* readily account for its huge popularity with young adult readers. Nevertheless, with the exception of the 'good versus evil' diametric, anyone looking for a deeper message is likely to struggle to find one.

Pratchett's meta-dragons apart, two significant trends can be identified among modern dragon depictions. First, dragons, either for good or ill, are often in service to humans, or, alternatively, humans are in service to them. Although in what Swanwick called the recent 'slew' of fantasy fictions plenty of caricatured dragons can be found that are simply agents of random destructiveness, the more sophisticated fantasy and sci-fi narratives give dragons a role that, in one way or another, presents them as conceptual mappings of both human power and powerlessness. Second, unlike dragons of old, the modern dragon can often be seen as the expression of the power and authority of women. Yet, female authority also has its limitations and dangers, the obvious point being that no matter which gender holds the reins of power, the problems of existence remain constant.

## 'Dragons' in crime fiction

While dragons have become endemic in sci-fi and fantasy plots, they also made their way into the crime fiction genre, not as actualities but as aspects of the protagonists' personalities. In Thomas Harris's *Red Dragon* (1981), the first of his four novels featuring the imprisoned forensic psychiatrist and cannibalistic serial killer Hannibal Lecter, the main action centres on another serial killer: one Francis Dolarhyde. This deeply disturbed individual is obsessed with William Blake's painting of the Book of Revelation's Satan-dragon *The Great Red Dragon and the Woman Clothed in Sun* and believes he himself is transforming into a dragon.[14]

Encouraged by secret correspondence from Lecter to complete his draconic transformation, Dolarhyde is also given the home address of Will Graham, the FBI profiler who, at great cost to himself, brought Lecter to justice. Lecter's clear intention is to avenge himself by having Graham and his family murdered. A series of horrific killings ensue, until Dolarhyde is eventually shot dead by Graham's wife after he has entered their Florida home and stabbed her husband in the face. Fear and extreme violence are the key features of Harris's *Red Dragon*, and in this respect both Dolarhyde and Lecter are little different from their sci-fi and fantasy dragon counterparts.

Providing what might be regarded as a somewhat more positive take on a draconic personality, albeit one that is itself damaged, is Stieg Larsson's *Millennium* series: *The Girl with the Dragon Tattoo* (2005), whose original Swedish title, *Män som hatar kvinnor*, tellingly translates as 'men who hate women'; *The Girl Who Played with Fire* (2006); and *The Girl Who Kicked the Hornet's Nest* (2007).[15] The girl in question is Lisbeth Salander, whose traumatic childhood causes her to take brutal vengance on her father, resulting in her being strapped down in a mental institution. But when she is eventually released into care, her carer turns out to be a sadist and a rapist. His crimes against Lisbeth lead her to take revenge by secretly filming his outrages, then Tasering him, tying him to a bed, performing extreme sexual violence on him and tattooing on his abdomen 'I am a sadist pig, a pervert and a rapist'.

Judged variously by other characters to be paranoid, obsessive, schizophrenic and an egomaniacal psychopath, Lisbeth can be seen as a figure modelled upon the ancient Greek Furies, the Erinyes, or on that race of female warriors known as the Amazons, or, given the Scandinavian setting, the Valkyries. Yet whichever mythic prototype we might regard Lisbeth as being modelled upon, she is the ultimate literary depiction of the vengeful female, from whom no man, no matter how physically powerful he might be, is safe.[16] A woman of slight build, weighing a mere 40 kg, Lisbeth is deterred by no one, neither criminals nor those agencies of the state such as the Swedish Secret Service, the Säpo, whose espionage and political scheming are above the law. One telling example of Lisbeth's ruthless ingenuity when it comes to dealing with those who would physically harm or indeed kill her is described in *The Girl Who Kicked the Hornet's Nest*.

Lisbeth is searching through an old industrial building that she has inherited on the death of her father, an eventuality largely of Lisbeth's making, when she comes across two female corpses and then suddenly realizes she has been locked in. This is the work of her brutal half-brother, Niedermann, a man of great size and, what's more, one impervious to pain, a consequence of him having congenital analgesia. Niedermann is set on murdering Lisbeth; her only possible hope lies in her physical agility. Niedermann duly sets about searching the drawers of a cabinet with sliding doors, unaware that Lisbeth has concealed herself beneath it, whereupon Lisbeth, now armed with a large nail gun, pins his feet to the ground with its seven-inch nails. With her attacker now unable to move, despite him feeling no pain, Lisbeth has the upper hand, yet instead of killing him herself, she texts a certain crazed biker gang, who have their own reasons to want Niedermann dead, and then she texts the police. Just as Lisbeth intended, Niedermann is killed and the bikers are arrested, while she makes her escape unharmed and blame-free.

Lisbeth's talents lie not only in her resourcefulness and presence of mind but in her photographic memory and her extraordinary skill as a computer hacker. This latter skill is one she uses most often to investigate crimes against women, as she does in *The Girl with the Dragon Tattoo*, irrespective of the legalities, in her efforts to track down Harriet, who disappeared some forty years ago.

All told, Larsson's *Millennium* series has two main targets. First, there is a feminist critique of the patriarchy's seeming indifference to crimes against women, such as sex trafficking and enforced prostitution. Second, there is the sometimes implicit, sometimes explicit criticism of the modern Swedish state, particularly Säpo, and its failure not only to provide protection for its subjects but, as suits it, to place them in harm's way. As a psychologized dragon-woman, Lisbeth Salander, despite her many failings, is both a force to be reckoned with and a force for good.

## The modern nursery dragon

In 1963 the American trio Peter, Paul and Mary recorded 'Puff the Magic Dragon'. It made it to number one in the U.S. charts and sold massively across the world. Written initially as a poem by Leonard Lipton and later put into song by Peter Yarrow, the lyrics seem innocuous enough. By the sea of a land called Honnahlee, little Jackie Paper is Puff's playmate and his airborne passenger, much to the delight of all who see them. But as Jackie grows older he abandons Puff, who retires tearfully to his cave. And there the song ends. So, a harmless fantasy nursery dragon, set to a memorable tune, about a boy growing up and putting aside his childhood toys.

Or is it? Many have seen less innocent meanings in the song, suggesting that this is not a nursery dragon at all. Perhaps prompted in part by the old Cantonese phrase 'chasing the dragon', a reference to opium smoking, 'Puff the Magic Dragon' has been interpreted as a metaphor for smoking marijuana. According to this view, Puff signifies inhalation and Jackie Paper signifies a joint's cigarette papers, in other words, its paper jacket. Whether or not this interpretation is what was really meant – Lipton fervently denied it – the song nevertheless came to be regarded as a celebration of 1960s drug-sodden hippy identity, although, of course, the eventual abandonment of Puff by Jackie makes little sense in that context.

No such controversies are to be found among the critical appraisals of the wide range of children's fiction in which dragons play the central role. Of these, the two award-winning nursery dragon tales chosen for consideration here have probably been the most influential of recent times: Julia Donaldson's *Zog* (2010), which is written for infants; and Cressida Cowell's twelve-volume *How to Train Your Dragon* series (2003–15), which is written for young adolescents.

Attractively illustrated by Axel Scheffler and narrated by Donaldson in simple rhyming couplets, *Zog* tells of the growing up of the dragon Zog, who, along with his dragon schoolmates under the tuition of Madame Dragon, is expected to master certain, seemingly essential, traditional dragon skills. So, dragons must learn how to fly, roar, breathe fire, capture a princess and, ultimately, fight against a knight. But Zog is a poor student and repeatedly sustains injury in his efforts to gain his teacher's approval. Coming to heal him of his wounds on every occasion is the young Princess Pearl. It so comes about that when Zog has to capture a princess, Pearl volunteers herself, the result being that Zog wins his first 'golden star'. All is well until the mounted knight-at-arms Gadabout the Great arrives on the scene set on battling Zog and rescuing Pearl. But Princess Pearl does not wish to be rescued and return to 'prancing round the palace in a silly frilly dress'; she then stops the fight and declares that she wants to be a doctor, at which point Gadabout the Great announces that he wishes to do likewise. As for Zog, he asks to be their 'ambulance', and off they go as 'Flying Doctors'.

The obvious inspiration for *Zog* is the St George and the Dragon myth, most likely as it was amusingly reinterpreted in Kenneth Grahame's 'The Reluctant Dragon'. Yet here it is not only the dragon that is liberated from his traditional role but the princess and the knight, both of whom reject their stereotypical, gender-defined identities and instead choose to achieve their ambitions in their role as healers. In effect, in its dismissal of that old dragon–girl–slayer 'love triangle', Donaldson's *Zog* carries with it a message to children about independence of mind and social constructiveness. No enlightened parent or carer would take issue with such a message.

Set, for the main part, on the fictional Isle of Berk, Cowell's *How to Train Your Dragon* series begins with the upbringing of the young Hiccup Horrendous III, a member of the Viking Hairy Hooligans tribe. Hiccup, like all the other youngsters, is being trained in the Viking Initiation Programme (later to become the Pirate Training Programme) by the unfailingly loyal but otherwise strict and fearsome warrior Gobber the Belch. The crucial challenge that the trainees must meet is to capture and train a dragon; failure to do so would result in their exile. Although somewhat puny, Hiccup is highly intelligent (not a quality for which he is at first admired) and, as the series progresses, learns to be a highly skilled swordsman, a skill he acquires only when he realizes that he is left-handed.

Having eventually captured a small, green Common-or-Garden dragon, which he names Toothless, Hiccup's new charge soon causes offence to the other dragons and a dragon fight ensues. Regarded as serious

Hiccup and Toothless in the film *How to Train Your Dragon* (2010).

misconduct by Gobber the Belch, exile is imminent for all concerned. But that same night a storm blows up, and three Sea Dragons are washed ashore, so posing a serious danger to the Hairy Hooligans and their tame dragons. It falls to Hiccup, who, quite exceptionally, has mastered Dragonese, the language of dragons, to negotiate with the threatening new arrivals. His cunning plan, aided by the other boys, is to provoke a fight between the two remaining Sea Dragons (the third having been eaten by them). When Hiccup is nearly swallowed by one of them, Toothless comes to his rescue and then succeeds in killing them both. Hiccup and Toothless are thus granted the ultimate Viking accolade. They are heroes. From here on, much of the action centres on Hiccup's gradual retrieval of those agencies of power the King's Lost Things, one of which, it transpires, is Toothless.

Cowell's numerous dragons are not unlike their human masters or adversaries. Some are amiable, some dangerous, some protective, some wholly wicked. Yet, irrespective of Toothless's mischief, the unbreakable bond between Hiccup and Toothless is what is at the heart of the series. In this respect, as is the case with all nursery dragon-friends, Hiccup and Toothless function as guardians and protectors of each other's needs and wants. So it is that when either the boy or the dragon finds itself in mortal danger, their friend is there, in one way or another, to aid them. In effect, Hiccup and Toothless are both aspects of an adolescent's sometimes hazardous journey towards maturity and independence. And that said, one can only add that Cowell's account of this journey is extremely good fun.

## Dragons on film and in RPGS

Given the literary dragon phenomena, film-makers were quick to realize the commercial potential of dragons, the general rule being either the more dangerous or the cuddlier the better. Many of the fictions discussed, both for adults and children, have been made into films, perhaps most notably in recent times Peter Jackson's adaptations of and, for purists somewhat controversial, elaborations on, Tolkien's Middle-earth fantasies (*The Lord of the Rings* trilogy, 2001–3; *The Hobbit* trilogy, 2012–14). Early Germanic sources have provided numerous dragon entertainments; for example, the silent movie *Die Nibelungen: Siegfried* (dir. Fritz Lang, 1924), and in the 1990s and 2000s no less than nine movies based, often very loosely, on the poem *Beowulf*. Besides these, we have dinosaur movies aplenty, such as *The Lost World* (dir. Harry O. Hoyt, 1925) and its successors; *Godzilla* (first version dir. Ishirō Honda, 1954); and the initial *Jurassic Park* trilogy, based on novels by Michael Crichton (dir. Steven Spielberg, 1993 and 1997; dir. Joe Johnston, 2001). As for dragon-slaying heroics, we have the likes of *George and the Dragon* (dir. Tom Reeve, 2004), *The Reign of Fire* (dir. Bob Bowman, 2002) and *Dragon Fighter* (dir. Philip J. Roth, 2003).[17]

Although many dragons of the big screen are little more than hackneyed presentations of dragon horrors, occasionally there is a movie featuring a dragon that has something new and interesting to say. One such is the *Beowulf* movie of 2007. Directed by Robert Zemeckis and scripted by Neil Gaiman and Roger Avary, the main action follows the plotline of its inspiration quite closely. Just as in the poem, the most prominent characters are the Geatish hero Beowulf; the Danish king and queen Hrothgar and Wealhtheow; and the monsters Grendel, Grendel's mother and the dragon. Although Beowulf slays the, in this depiction, pitifully childlike Grendel when he attacks the Danish mead hall, just as he promised Hrothgar he would, what we soon learn is that Grendel is Hrothgar's 'shame', for Grendel is none other than his son, sired by him on Grendel's beguiling yet otherwise monstrous mother.[18] Thereafter, when Grendel's mother has taken vengeance on the Danes and Beowulf then tracks to her watery lair, he too is beguiled, and in return for her promise to grant him great power and immortal fame he agrees to give her a son, as compensation for his killing of Grendel. Their son turns out to be the dragon, whom Beowulf, now king of the Danes and, with Hrothgar having committed suicide, husband to Wealhtheow, eventually kills at the expense of his own life.

As for cursed gold, that is present throughout in the form of a dragon-shaped drinking horn that came into Hrothgar's possession many years previously, after, it is said, he had slain the dragon Fáfnir, that notorious gold-hoarding dragon that is killed by Sigurd in the *Saga of the Völsungs*. It is this that is Beowulf's reward for his killing of Grendel, and it is this that he gives to Grendel's mother as part of the deal they make. Later, this same treasure is found by a certain slave near the lair of Grendel's mother and returned to Beowulf by the slave's master, only for it to fall into the possession of the dragon when Beowulf goes to confront it. Yet there is one more twist, for after Beowulf's Viking-style funeral, Wiglaf, Beowulf's most trusted retainer, finds the dragon-horn half-buried in the sand. Then, as he stares out across the sea, Grendel's mother surfaces and we are left with Wiglaf, too, appearing to be on the brink of succumbing to her seemingly irresistible charms.

Zemeckis's *Beowulf* cleverly exploits the curious gap in the poem, wherein no one witnesses Beowulf's killing of Grendel's mother and the only 'trophy' that he brings back is an ancient sword hilt. However, the most obvious feature of the film is its negative portrayal of male heroics. Although the renown of Hrothgar and Beowulf will forever be celebrated in 'song', something that the likes of Wiglaf are determined to ensure, in actuality Hrothgar is a drunken womanizer and Beowulf is a liar who is prone, as he himself admits, to weakness and folly. Hrothgar and Beowulf may be fearless and powerful, but they are also sexually compromised hypocrites. Were one to look for an uncompromised 'hero' in the film, one need go no further than Grendel's mother, for despite being a threat to all men, she at least is open about her intentions. In short, this *Beowulf* movie raises questions about the authority of men and the subordination of women; if this reading of the film is accepted, then the indiscriminate fury of the dragon unleashed by his mother against Beowulf and his kingdom symbolizes the rage of women who have been betrayed by men.[19]

While movies and novels offer dragon thrills aplenty, nowadays one does not necessarily need either of these for draconic entertainments, for dragons are there on our laptops and tablets in Role Playing Games (RPGs). Beginning with the hugely successful *Dungeons & Dragons* (first published by Tactical Studies Rules, 1974), which continues to this day alongside such games as *The Elder Scrolls V: Skyrim* (Bethesda Softworks, 2011), these RPGs allow us either to command dragons or to develop a strategy for overcoming them.[20] We can all be a Sigurd, a Heracles, a St George, a wizard, a Daenerys Targaryen, a Dragonrider of Pern and so on, depending on how the mood takes us. So far as the psychology of RPGs is concerned, it is not that much different from the suspension of disbelief involved in watching films or reading fictions, except that the player is part of the plot. Either way, the effect is thought to be therapeutic.[21] Or it is as long the player continues to recognize the difference between fantasy and reality, for failure to do so can result in yet another dragon victim.

WERE WE TO look for the key dates in the evolution of the modern dragon there would be three. The first is 1898, with the publication of Kenneth Grahame's 'The Reluctant Dragon'. The taming of the dragon could be regarded as a stripping away of its power, so reducing it to a creature that bears little, if any, resemblance to its mythico-legendary forebears. Although it is tempting to dismiss this development as a trivialization of the dragon, it is nonetheless true that accommodating the dragon in the nursery is a rather more complex matter.

A scene from the film *Dungeons and Dragons* (2000).

The point here is that what is so satisfying and rewarding in befriending the dragon is the very fact that it is a creature of such great power. Thus the nursery dragon's power is neither harnessed nor trivialized but is instead assumed by its nursery friend. Tamed, maybe, but the dragon is not in any way diminished; rather its power acts as a haven in which the child, whether infant or adolescent, can safely explore his or her own potential. As remarked previously, the nursery dragon is an embodiment of our desire or, one might say, need to take control. Although there is no biographical evidence of Grahame having a particular interest in East Asia, his 'reluctant' dragon chimed perfectly with those benevolent 'imperialized' dragons of Chinese mythology. As such, it was never likely to be a passing fad.

The second two dates are inseparable: 1936 and 1937. It was in 1936 that Tolkien gave his seminal lecture on *Beowulf* and in so doing unleashed the dragon in its most fearsome form. Yet the dragon as an allegorized threat to survival was not sufficient for Tolkien, and in 1937 he delivered Smaug, a creature with the same dreadful powers as the *Beowulf* dragon but one with a far more sophisticated identity. Any dragon worthy of note since Smaug has been similarly endowed with a recognizable, if on occasion dangerously unstable, psychology. Tolkien's Smaug set the standard for a credible literary dragon as monster.

Yet, as future dragonologists may conclude, there could well be a fourth key date. This would be 17 April 2011, the premiere of *Game of Thrones*. It is to this phenomenon and the influence of George R. R. Martin that the next chapter is devoted.

Emilia Clarke as Daenerys Targaryen in Season 1 of *Game of Thrones* (2011).

## eleven

# George R. R. Martin's Dragons and the Question of Power

S OME WORKS OF fiction go beyond being influential. They become what scholars call 'hegemonic'; that is to say, no one writing in that area, however much they want to strike out on their own, can avoid either writing like the hegemonic author or otherwise making it clear why they are not and what the differences are. Hegemonic ideas are the ones people have come to expect.

In this way, anyone writing a story with elves and dwarves in it either makes them like Tolkien's (perhaps unconsciously) or has to think up some new angle. 'Orc' is a word Tolkien invented – or, he would say, brought back from forgotten times – but orcs are now familiar in fantasy, as are, if not Hobbits exactly, then halflings or other Hobbit-analogues. Middle-earth has become hegemonic in modern fantasy. It may well be that the hegemonic work for dragons in the future will be George R. R. Martin's *A Song of Ice and Fire* novels and the subsequent *Game of Thrones* television adaptations of his work,[1] especially as there is here no major competition from Tolkien. While elsewhere in Tolkien's fictions we have the likes of Smaug, Chrysophylax Dives and Glaurung, *The Lord of the Rings* is a virtually dragon-free zone, so leaving Martin a relatively clear field.

But were it simply a matter of judging the future of Martin's dragons only in terms of their physical characteristics, one might well conclude that they are unlikely to make that much difference, for they have many traditional features, consolidating our images rather than creating new ones. They fly, they breathe fire, they live, if not forever, then much longer than humans, and as four-limbed creatures (rather than, as is often the case, six-limbed), they are clearly based on the wyvern type of dragon, notable examples of which would be the Roman cavalry's *draco* and the Red Dragon of Wales. But they also have characters which, though not exactly like the highly developed personalities of Tolkien's dragons, for of course they do not speak, mark them out as individuals in their own right, a feature that is most developed as regards Daenerys Targaryen's dragons. And it is in this regard that Martin's dragons, already regarded as key aspects of 'one of the publishing phenomena of this century',[2] may well be hugely influential.

One thing that is clear about Martin's dragons is that, unlike those Old Northern dragons from which Tolkien gained inspiration, they cannot simply be identified as personifications of all that threatens human existence. The obvious point here is that Martin's dragons frequently function as creatures intent on defending human existence, or at least, that is, the existence of those who hold the reins of power and to whom they are in service. In this respect, Martin's dragons are what might be called cultural hybrids, for they can be like those ferocious fire-spewing beasts of North European tradition and, at one and the same time, like those imperialized and thus politicized dragons of Chinese tradition. As is apparent in all the modern dragon fantasies that have been considered thus far, authors have tended to go one way or the other, so making their dragons either untameably hostile or unquestioningly biddable, whereas Martin's dragons are both. Given this hybridity, they are in certain respects unique, and it is for this reason that Martin's dragons could go on to be hegemonic.

## Martin's early dragons

Exactly how Martin came to imagine a dragon that is, on the one hand, the only hope of order and, on the other, sheer chaos is, of course, unknowable. Nevertheless, two early, award-winning fictions by him, in which dragons have key roles, do suggest something about the development of his ideas. These are his sci-fi short story 'The Way of Cross and Dragon' (1978) and his young adult novella *The Ice Dragon* (1980).[3]

Set in a remote future in which travel between populous planets is commonplace, 'The Way of Cross and Dragon' is primarily concerned with what are perceived as Christian heresies. Charged with the responsibility of challenging and eliminating heresies is the story's narrator, Father Damien Har Veris, the Knight Inquisitor of the One True Interstellar Catholic Church of the Earth and the Thousand Worlds. But Father Damien is wracked with doubts about his faith and, after his many years as an Inquisitor, is somewhat cynical about the role he plays. Summoned by the Lord Commander Archbishop to investigate a cult that has canonized Judas Iscariot, Father Damien sets out as a passenger aboard his space-ship, named *Truth of Christ*, to the planet Arion, where the cult has taken hold. On his journey, he reads the 'bible' of the heretics, *The Way of Cross and Dragon*, in which Judas is a low-born man who early in life masters dark arts and learns how to tame dragons.

Impressed from the outset by the coherence, pictorial artistry and inventiveness of the heretical bible, Father Damien reads how Judas, 'astride the greatest of his dragons', soon becomes the Dragon-King ruler over a great empire stretching from Spain to India, with his luxurious court at Babylon. Functioning as the power behind Judas's throne are the dragons, 'the most fearsome of God's creatures'. Judas tolerates no dissent in his realm, and when a troublemaking prophet, one Jesus of Nazareth, comes to his attention, he has him bound and beaten and, before turning him back out on the street, his legs amputated.

But now Judas repents, sends his dragons away and, for a year, becomes the Legs of Jesus, carrying him wheresoever he wishes to preach. When Jesus finally heals himself, the dragons are recalled and sanctified, and, dragon-mounted, Judas becomes a disciple, whose allotted task is to spread the word of Christ overseas. But on his return, arriving in Jerusalem, he finds that Jesus has been crucified that very day. His faith faltering, Judas' response is to have his dragons lay waste to the seats of power, to personally strangle to death Simon-called-Peter and feed his body to the dragons for betraying Jesus three times, and finally, as 'funeral pyres', to have the dragons start fires across the world.

Only on the third day, when Jesus is resurrected, does Judas come to understand the error of his ways. The dragons are recalled, the fires extinguished, Peter made whole again, so to become the first Pope, and all dragons, everywhere on Earth, are made to die, 'for they were the living sigil of the power and wisdom of Judas Iscariot, who had sinned greatly'. Judas' penance is to be blinded, his powers taken from him, and thereafter to be known only as the Betrayer, left to wander the earth for a thousand years, during which, despite his many charitable works, he is persecuted by the 'bloated and corrupt' Church that Peter had founded. In the end, Jesus comforts the reformed Judas and, before allowing him to die in peace, tells him that in time there will be those who recognize 'Peter's Lie' and remember the truth about the life of St Judas. This, then, is the basis of the heresy.

On his arrival in Arion, Father Damien readies himself for a combative theological debate, but when he confronts the psychically gifted leaders of the Judas cult, they openly admit to being both atheists and Liars, for whom the Truth is no more than entropy and despair. Perceiving from the outset Father Damien's personal lack of conviction, the Liars invite him to join them, but he declines, for he still believes that Truth, however unpalatable it might be, is undeniable. Allowed to leave unharmed and unhindered, Father Damien duly sets about planning the demise of the Judas cult. Even so, he has been unsettled by the experience and is forced to recognize that all faiths, no matter how noble their intentions, are in the embrace of fabrications. On his return journey, Father Damien renames his spaceship *Dragon*, an ironic expression both of his own power as an Inquisitor and his personal doubts about the faith he will continue to defend.

In many respects a much simpler tale is Martin's compelling variant of the nursery dragon, *The Ice Dragon*. Set, for the main part, in the frozen landscapes of winter, the winged ice dragon is thought to be the cause of the severe arctic conditions and, as such, a creature beyond human reach or control. But the young girl Adara, a 'winter-child', whose mother died giving birth to her during the coldest winter anyone can remember and whose father, despite knowing that he is being unreasonable, resents her, is locked into an emotionally expressionless – a frozen – state of mind. Adara not only identifies with the ice dragon but gradually befriends it. Although it is a creature much smaller than those cold-shy 'ugly' dragons ridden by the king's warriors, such as her uncle Hal, battling the fire dragons in the far north, it is nevertheless one feared and loathed by all – except Adara.

It is during the winter of Adara's fifth birthday that the ice dragon first lets her ride on its back. Their friendship deepens, and for the next two winters they are inseparable. Adara confides her friendship in no one, least of all her father, whose inclination, were it possible, would be to have the ice dragon driven away or, better still, killed. Then, with Adara now aged seven, disaster falls, for that summer the king's armies are forced into retreat by the invading armies of the north aboard their fire dragons. With injured and dying soldiers packing the roads heading south, the locals are advised to do likewise, but Adara's father will have none of it, much to Adara's relief. It so comes about that when Hal brings news of the imminent arrival of the fire dragons and agrees to take Adara south with him, Adara flees.

Hiding herself far out in the country, Adara witnesses the arrival of the mounted fire dragons and the incineration of Hal aboard his own, now exhausted and half-maimed, dragon steed. Concealing herself for the night in a cave, Adara senses a strange cold coming from outside, though it is still summer. Sure enough, the ice dragon has returned and has been busy freezing the land with its icy breath. They soar together into the sky and head for colder climes, but on passing over her family's farm, Adara hears her father crying out. Despite being vulnerable to anything warm, let alone fire, the ice dragon nonetheless accepts Adara's pleas for it to turn back.

A fierce battle ensues, but the ice dragon, with Adara still aboard, quickly gains the upper hand and freezes to death its fire dragon foes and their riders. But it comes at a cost, for the ice dragon is seriously wounded by dragonfire and, with one wing burned off, crashes to the ground. Herself unhurt, Adara runs to her home, where she finds all her family, including her father, wounded but alive. As for the ice dragon, all that remains of it is a cold pond. Adara, however, is freed from her frozen self and from then on 'smiled and laughed and even wept like other little girls'; in other words, what the ice dragon has given to Adara is that which she most needed: normality.

What we have then in both these tales are dragons as weaponry and, as such, agents of human political power, irrespective of right or wrong. And in *The Ice Dragon*, we have a dragon whose own power is invested in a young girl. Set together, there is what we might call the germ of an idea in which female authority is derived from a mastery over dragons; in effect, a prototype for what would become, some fifteen years later, Daenerys Targaryen, the Mother of Dragons. But before turning to Daenerys and her dragons, account should be taken of the dragon 'back story', which is set during that fractious period when dragons were believed to have become extinct.

## Westeros dragons of old

Where did the dragons come from, and what caused their disappearance (and, indeed, their re-emergence)? Something of an answer to this is to be found in the collaborative illustrated volume *The World of Ice and Fire: The Untold History of Westeros and the Game of Thrones*, and in Martin's eighty-page novella *The Princess and the Queen; or, The Blacks and the Greens*.[4]

To take the matter of origin first, while there is no authoritative account,[5] the Valyrians (who were the first dragonlords) believed that dragons were hatched, as one might expect for creatures of fire, in the volcanic mountains known as the Fourteen Flames. It was the eruption of these that brought about the Doom of Valyria, and of Valyrians and dragons together; apart, that is, from the few of both who were preserved by Aegon Targaryen: his family, followers and some dragons who had fled to Dragonstone in the far west, on the eastern shores of Westeros. Aegon was the many-greats grandfather of Daenerys, who was born some three hundred years later. For half that period, dragons dominated warfare in the lands of the west, until the last of them died during the reign of Aegon III 'Dragonbane' in the year

153 AC (After the Conquest); Daenerys's father, Aerys II, was born in 244 and died in 283.

What made them die out? Seemingly, it was their use and value as weapons of mass destruction. So much is made clear in *The Princess and the Queen*. In reading this, it helps to think of the dragons as the 'capital ships' of warfare in the Martin universe. In our twentieth century, capital ships were the big-gun battleships that decided the battles of Tsushima and Jutland early in the century and remained a threat into the Second World War. To many admirals' consternation, however, for most of the Second World War the new capital ships turned out to be not battleships but aircraft carriers, like HMS *Ark Royal*, USS *Enterprise* and the Japanese carriers that attacked Pearl Harbor and were sunk at Midway. In the wars of the twentieth century, other ships played their part, scouting, distracting, escorting and sinking merchant vessels, but in tests of strength, capital ships were what counted, for they decided the outcomes of campaigns. As do Martin's dragons.

This, then, is what happens in *The Princess and the Queen*, which tells the story of the civil war fought between rival branches of the Targaryens over 150 years before the *Song of Ice and Fire* series opens. The war, known as 'the Dance of the Dragons', is in essence a 'stepmother' war. The princess is Rhaenyra, daughter of King Viserys I by his first wife. The queen is his second wife, Alicent, acting on behalf of her son (by Viserys), later King Aegon II. So who is the rightful heir: Rhaenyra, who is the elder and whom Viserys designated as his successor, or Aegon, who is Viserys's son? The legal point could be disputed, but in the event it comes down to force. At the start, Aegon has 'Every visible symbol of legitimacy':[6] the Iron Throne, King's Landing, the crown and sword of Aegon I the Conqueror, anointed by the septons and crowned by the Kingsguard. Rhaenyra, by contrast, is a refugee. But she has taken refuge at Dragonstone, from where Aegon the Conqueror launched his conquest of Westeros with his three dragons. And with Dragonstone, she has dragons.

The odds at the start of the war are eight dragons for Rhaenyra against four for Alicent and Aegon. Dragons win battle after battle. Vermax, ridden by Rhaenyra's son Jacaerys and backed up by the four new dragons, destroys the fleet of the Free Cities. Tessarion, ridden by King Aegon's brother Daeron, brings victory at the Battle of Honeywine. The lords of Westeros are kept loyal by the threat of Vhagar, who destroys the castles of several rebellious or wavering lords, including Harrenhal, and the threat means that Rhaenyra, who has taken King's Landing with a force of six dragons, has to keep several as 'air-cover', while others search out Vhagar and Tessarion, operating in pairs against the threat of King Aegon's two most formidable dragons.

The next decisive factor is caused by the general and well-merited fear of dragons as a whole. In King's Landing, captured and held by Rhaenyra, Aegon's surviving dragons (apart from Tessarion, still at liberty and still a menace) are kept chained in the Dragonpit: Helaena's Dreamfyre, and two young ones not of fighting age, Shrykos and Morghul. Along with them is Joffrey's Tyraxes, while Rhaenyra also has her own Syrax, whom she keeps by her, not in the Dragonpit. By this time the distinction between 'our' dragons and 'their' dragons no longer means much to their victims, and the King's Landing mob is stirred up by a preacher who tells them that dragons will come to burn them all unless they purge their sins in dragon's blood.

Can a mere mob deal with dragons, even chained ones? At a cost, yes. When the mob breaks into the Dragonpit, the two young ones are killed by axe or lance, and Tyraxes gets caught up in his own chains, so he too can be killed. Dreamfyre, however, has already broken two of her chains, doing so at the moment that her rider Helaena, across the city and well away from the Dragonpit, died by suicide. When the mob arrives Dreamfyre breaks free and incinerates hundreds, until a crossbow bolt puts out one of her eyes and she flies into the dome above the pit, breaking it and being crushed under the rubble. Meanwhile, Prince Joffrey, desperate to reach and rescue his dragon Tyraxes, makes the fatal mistake of trying to borrow his mother's dragon, Syrax. But dragons do not accept new riders, even familiar ones. She throws Joffrey to his death and then descends in rage on the mob, only to be killed herself.

The only dragons to survive 'the Dance of Dragons', then, are Silverwing, her rider dead, who flies off to live in the wild; the young Nettles's Sheepstealer, both dragon and rider never seen again; Cannibal, too wild ever to be ridden, who vanishes; and a young dragon called Morning. Seventeen others are killed, most of them by other dragons.

What does one learn about dragons from this account? One fact is that, like Anne McCaffrey's Pern dragons, they have some kind of telepathic bond with their riders, as shown by Dreamfyre's sensing of the death of her rider Helaena. Riders affect dragons, but one may well wonder, first, whether dragons also affect riders, especially Targaryens, and second, whether this is not just physical but mental: for when Rhaenyra gives birth to another child, it is a monster, stillborn, heartless, with a 'stubby, scaled tail'.[7] Dragons are also vulnerable to attack from humans, especially by arrow or scorpion bolt, but not very vulnerable. Even crippled and grounded they are extremely dangerous. As war weapons, they are much more effective when ridden, as shown by Tessarion's misguided attack on Vermithor. They are angry creatures who do not need to be goaded to fight, whether humans or each other, but they need to have targets indicated. Finally, their loyalty to their riders is extreme, somewhat in contrast to much of the human population of Westeros.

While, for the main part, dragons in the civil wars play out their roles effectively and often admirably, the circumstances are not ones in which political power is in any way conditioned by moral considerations; rather, it is nothing less than a fight to the death, in which moral considerations have little or no place. But in the fraught career of Daenerys Targaryen, matters are somewhat different, for however flawed her judgements might be, she nevertheless has a strong sense of right and wrong. The actions of her dragons, then, are inevitably viewed according to how her ideals are undermined and to what extent this is the fault of her 'children' or more a consequence of her own pursuit of political power – or both. Whatever one might conclude, Daenerys's dragons cannot be removed from the moral complexities of the political equation, and as such they are cast into the limelight.

## Daenerys Targaryen and her dragons

By the time of Daenerys, then, dragons are extinct as far as anyone knows. 'Dragons are gone', say the Dothraki, 'It is known' (vol. 1, pp. 227–8).[8] The start of the new era comes with the gift of three dragon eggs to Daenerys by Magister Illyrio, the merchant-prince who brokers her wedding to Khal Drogo. Illyrio says they come 'from the Shadow Lands . . . The eons have turned them to stone' (vol. 1, p. 99).[9] In other words, they are thought to be little more than fossils, treasured only for their rarity and beauty.

What brings them to life is, of course, the fire of Khal Drogo's funeral pyre, but there seem to be non-physical causes as well, connected with the Targaryen blood. As Daenerys's brother Viserys says every time he is thwarted in any way, 'you do not want to wake the dragon', meaning the dragon in himself. In this he resembles Shakespeare's King Lear, who said, very similarly, 'Come not between the dragon and his wrath' (Act 1, Sc. 1). Lear is an old man who has some of the symptoms of early dementia, while Viserys is a foolish young one with delusions of grandeur – fatal delusions, as becomes apparent when he provokes Khal Drogo once too often and too openly. But do the Targaryens really have something of the dragon in them?

In *Game of Thrones*, one indicator comes when Daenerys experimentally puts an egg in a glowing brazier, presumably to see if it will hatch.[10] When her maid touches the egg, it burns her, but Daenerys is unhurt and unmarked: she is fireproof. Dragons seem to come to her assistance after her marriage. She is finding life among the Dothraki painful and exhausting: saddle sores, blisters, and a husband who uses her roughly and inconsiderately. She even contemplates suicide. But then she has a dream of a dragon, in which she embraces dragonfire. The next day she is stronger and able to stand up to her bullying brother. She has been tempered in the fire.

Daenerys's career as a master of dragons begins with a tragedy. She is not long from giving birth to a child, who is repeatedly predicted to be 'the stallion who mounts the world', when Khal Drogo receives a severe wound in a duel that comes about from him supporting his wife when she intervenes to protect female captives who are being repeatedly raped. While all predict that Drogo's death is imminent, Daenerys refuses to accept the verdict, perhaps due her feeling in some way responsible. Determined to have him cured, Daenerys commands an enslaved witch, the *maegi* Mirri Maz Duur, to use whatever power she has to save him in return for her freedom. Despite being told by Mirri that 'only death may pay for life' (vol. 1, p. 686), Daenerys insists.

But the taboo 'bloodmagic' that Mirri employs fails, and Drogo is left in a vegetative state. Worse still, Daenerys now gives birth but is told that the child has been stillborn and that, much like Rhaenyra's child before her, its corpse is 'Monstrous . . . scaled like a lizard, blind, with a stub of a tail and small leather wings like the wings of a bat' – and, rather oddly, that 'He had been dead for years' (vol. 1, p. 731). Whether or not the child has been murdered, so leaving the way open for a Dothraki warrior to succeed Drogo, or whether the vengeful Mirri's magic has caused the death is not made clear, for Daenerys herself never sees the corpse. Nevertheless, given what follows, it seems she suspects the latter.

Daenerys now smothers her irretrievably comatose husband in a mercy killing. It seems then that, if she could get away from the Dothraki with the assistance of Ser Jorah, the exiled lord who has sworn loyalty to her, she could sell her dragon eggs and live the rest of her life in Westeros as a rich woman. Instead, she ties the now openly resentful Mirri to the pyre, sets the eggs down by Drogo's body, lights the pyre and walks into it herself.

Is this *sati*, or suttee, the self-sacrifice of a widow? Or does she at some level know what she is doing and what will happen to her? Whichever it is, the act is the first unmistakable sign of Daenerys's supernatural abilities.

When the fire burns out, she is sitting in the ashes, her clothes and hair burned off[11] but herself unhurt and with the three dragons, who have hatched out in the heat of the pyre, twined round her, 'and the night came alive with the music of dragons' (vol. I, p. 780). It is from here on that the Mother of Dragons becomes queen over the remaining Dothraki. As for the dragons, Daenerys names them in dedication to her late husband and her two dead brothers, so the black-and-scarlet Drogon, by far the largest of three, the green-and-bronze Rhaegal, and the cream-and-gold Viserion.

One could also say that from here on there is a contrast between Daenerys's human nature and her dragon nature; and the theme that Martin introduces is the major theme of allegorical fantasy in the modern era, that of power and control. Daenerys thus has 'a gentle heart', or so some say. She tries to protect women from rape by the Dothraki; she looks at the face of every child crucified by the slavers of Yunkai; everywhere she goes, she frees the slaves; she pays compensation; she closes the fighting pits of Meereen; and she tries to introduce the principle of a fair trial, even for her enemies. All liberal, modern, even democratic, insofar as an absolute monarch can be democratic. And this, of course, is the question.

On the other hand, she herself is capable of shocking acts of revenge. With absolute power ready to hand in the shape of her dragons, the command she can give them – '*dracarys!*' – unleashes the devastating dragonfire on her enemies. The temptation for Daenerys, in a word, is not simply to be draconic but to be 'draconian', a word that derives from a classical Greek judge of legendary severity called Draco. But 'draco', as we know, also means 'dragon', and 'draconian' could well be translated as 'dragonish'. Daenerys's temptation, then, is to use her power and so to dissolve every opposition by the word *dracarys*, blowing her enemies away in a waft of dragonfire. It raises the modern question (analogous to the one posed by Tolkien's Ring): does absolute power corrupt absolutely or will Daenerys's human benevolence win out over her dragon wrath?

This issue is what provides the tension for much of the Daenerys-oriented story and, as such, also for the dragon-oriented story. To deal with Daenerys first. After her emergence from Drogo's funeral pyre, she faces endless crises, many of them connected with the slaver-cities.

At Qarth, believing that she has found a financial backer for her invasion of Westeros, she is double-crossed and chained in a dungeon, foolishly, with her dragons, which though still only babies, can already breathe fire. For the first time, Daenerys uses the *dracarys!* command to incinerate her captor, whereafter she has his two accomplices, one of whom is her maidservant, locked in a vault and left there to die of starvation. At Astapor, it is Daenerys who executes a double-cross. Having agreed to swap Drogon for an army of Unsullied, those formidable castrated warriors who obey whoever holds 'the golden whip', she then commands them to wipe out their former masters and become free, which they duly do without any intervention from Drogon, just as might be expected.

In both these cases, brutal though her actions are, Daenerys could be forgiven, for she has right on her side. However, at Meereen, where she avenges the Masters' crucifixion of 163 children by executing the same number of Masters, her sense of justice is highly questionable, for among them are men not personally guilty. So it is that when she then tries to establish freedom, good governance and the principle of a fair trial for all, she is, to say the least, being hypocritical, inasmuch as this is a principle she has not herself followed. Moreover, some slaves do not want to be free, for they would be exchanging an established position for nothing. And when she orders the gladiatorial 'fighting pits' closed, she faces what we now call an 'insurgency', with the Sons of the Harpy murdering her men by night.[12] Her attempt to establish equality before the law, by executing without trial one of her own supporters for murdering an insurgent Son of the Harpy, backfires spectacularly, with even the freed slaves throwing rocks at her for executing one whom they regard as one of their own.

Meanwhile, in the interests of humanity, Daenerys has forfeited her easy solution, the dragons. She pays compensation for the goats they kill, but then Drogon kills a child (TV season 4, episode 10). While Drogon remains wild, Daenerys has the other two dragons, Viserion and Rhaegal, chained in a dungeon. It seems you can have one or the other: dragons or democracy.

It is, then, something of a bleak irony that the vexed situation in Meereen is resolved by dragonfire. Attacked by insurgents in the gladiatorial arena, which she has been forced to reopen, Daenerys is saved by the sudden reappearance of Drogon. He incinerates the Sons of the Harpy and allows Daenerys to mount him and fly off, as the first dragonrider for 150 years. For all the good intentions that Daenerys might have had, it is quite apparent that she cannot govern effectively without the overpowering force of the dragons.

Turning to the dragon-oriented story: if the story centred on Daenerys is an account of what Tolkien called *draconitas*, thus dragonishness and draconianism, as is seen in the problem of power and the restraints on power, then the story centred on the dragons is about *dracones*, dragons as creatures in themselves. Drogon, Viserion and Rhaegal are sometimes likeable, in a dangerous dog kind of way, and they quite clearly love their mother. There are several scenes in which they nuzzle up to her, even when they have grown huge and frightening, to have their great crocodile-heads stroked. In one scene, though (TV season 4, episode 1), Drogon snaps at her when she tries to stop them tussling over a dead goat. And Drogon, of course, is a child-eater, and all three would certainly be man-eaters if left to themselves.

Two scenes in the TV versions show matters from the dragons' point of view. One has already been mentioned: after a father shows Daenerys the charred bones of his child, killed by Drogon, Daenerys decides to imprison and chain her other two dragons. After she has herself locked their iron collars, she leaves, with Viserion and Rhaegal calling out pitifully after her. It is, here again, an ironic scene, as Daenerys has been so passionate about freeing often ungrateful slaves and now chains her own 'children'.

The sequel to that scene is in episode 2 of season 6. Daenerys has flown off on Drogon, leaving her advisers unsure what to do. When it is pointed out that Viserion and Rhaegal are not thriving in captivity, Daenerys's most intelligent and trusted adviser, Tyrion Lannister, says that is always true of dragons, and he decides to free them. This is a dangerous business, for the dragons are understandably hostile and suspicious when it comes to their dealings with humans. But Tyrion and the handmaiden and translator Missandei, who has been trying to feed them, insist that dragons 'have affection for their friends' as well as 'fury for their enemies'. They may not be able to talk, but they are intelligent and perhaps can understand speech or can at least discern attitude.

Tyrion then goes down the tunnel to the dungeon where they are kept. This is a very Bilbo-esque scene, it must be said. Tyrion is not a Hobbit but he is a 'halfling'; one of his nicknames is 'the Halfman'. In *The Hobbit*, Tolkien explained that going down the tunnel to investigate Smaug was 'the bravest thing Bilbo ever did'. But while what Bilbo hears in front of him is only the sound of Smaug snoring, what Tyrion hears are wide-awake dragons screeching, growling and rattling their chains. Nevertheless he goes on, enters the dungeon, and starts talking to the dragons, very gently, as he tries to get close enough to undo the bolts on their iron collars. What he tells them is how much he has always loved dragons. When he was a child, he says, he asked his father, Tywin, for a dragon: 'It wouldn't even have to be a big dragon ... It could be little, like me ... My father told me the last dragon had died a century ago. I cried myself to sleep that night.' The dragons listen and once again we are shown a frightful dragons' head looking interested, receptive and perhaps even sympathetic. Tyrion gets one bolt off, and the other dragon comes over, realizing what is happening, and offers its neck so it too can be released. By this stage, one is all for the dragons and for Tyrion. In a way they are more human, more open to negotiation, than most of the people Daenerys and Tyrion have to deal with.

HOW, THEN, so far as Martin's dragons generally are concerned, and, in the *Game of Thrones* context, so far as their dragonish 'mother' is concerned, can we judge what his message is set on conveying?

It is clear that for Tolkien, as in the whole ancient northern tradition behind him, dragons represented above all the sin of greed, and greed, as noted in the discussion of *The Hobbit*, is the 'dragon-sickness'. This has not quite vanished from Martin's dragons. In a brief scene in season 3 episode 7, Daenerys refuses the bribe of a chest of gold, and the disappointed negotiator orders his slaves forward to take the chest away, its gold plainly visible, whereupon one of the dragons immediately hisses and lunges forward to protect it. 'Come not between a dragon and his gold', one might say, for as we know, dragons collect and protect their hoards, from *Beowulf* to Terry Pratchett.

But for Martin, the dragon-sin, or the dragon-temptation, is not greed but wrath. Daenerys can at any point say 'dracarys!' and solve her political problems by force. But could such a solution ever work long-term? What Varys the arch-plotter says is that Westeros needs on the Iron Throne of the Seven Kingdoms 'someone who is stronger than Tommen, but gentler than Stannis. A monarch who could intimidate the High Lords and inspire the people. A ruler loved by millions, with a powerful army and the right family name' (season 5, episode 1).

But love is not gained nor gentleness demonstrated by incinerating people on impulse. And as the modern world has learned to its cost, it is very hard for the exercise of force, even with the best of intentions, not to become a habit, an easy way out that is, in the end, self-defeating and self-destructive. Western powers have the analogue of dragonfire at their command, with airstrikes, smart bombs, cruise missiles and nuclear weapons. While they are at least reluctant to deploy them, when they do, it is invariably with troublingly mixed results.

In the heroic world of *Beowulf* and Sigurd the Völsung, the characteristic bad ruler was the one who hoarded his gold like a miser or buried it in the ground. This is what happens to the dragon's gold at the end of *Beowulf*, buried 'as useless to men as it ever was', says the poet scornfully (l. 3168). Modern governments feel no such urge to hoard. If we have a sin of greed, it is not the miserly kind – getting wealth just to keep it – but the more active kind, doing anything just to get it, and then, as likely as not, spending it in conspicuous consumption in the form of yachts, private jets or other such extravagances.

Our characteristic modern sin is the urge to use power in the service, often, of some ideology: fascism, communism, their variants and their antagonists. That is why *The Lord of the Rings* is essentially about rejecting power, in the shape of the Ring. Martin's story offers a whole series of alternative images of government, good and bad. In this, the dragons are there to tell us something about the temptations, and the requirements, of power. In effect, inseparable as they are, Daenerys and her dragons are nothing less than an analogue for, and as such a critique of, Western democracies, their good intentions and their conspicuous failings. Political power, no matter how fair-minded the intent, will always be compromised by expediency.

One question remains, and this concerns the extent to which the portrayal of Daenerys Targaryen and her dragons can be viewed in any way as supportive of feminist ideals. The Martin universe is most certainly a brutal one, in which women bereft of power are often treated appallingly. The Dothraki, for instance, view the gang rape of their female captives not only as an expression of their authority but as something that is deserved; for them, rape is nothing other than the spoils of war. And when Daenerys tries to intervene to stop such barbarities, the consequences are the deaths of both her husband and her unborn child. Yet, on the other hand, both in the civil wars and in Daenerys's chequered career, we have many women who exercise great power and authority over men. How can this be reconciled, or, in fact, does it need to be?

In an interview with the *Telegraph* reporter Jessica Salter, in which she notes that 'more than half his fans are women', Martin asserted that he is 'a feminist at heart'. Nevertheless, he recognizes that, as some feminists have pointed out, any man claiming to be an actual feminist is being 'hypocritical'. When then questioned about his depictions of women, he had this to say: 'Male or female, I believe in painting in shades of grey . . . All of the characters should be flawed; they should all have good and bad, because that's what I see. Yes, it's fantasy, but the characters still need to be real.'[13]

Throughout this book, particular attention has been paid to those dragon-women, such as Lilith, Lamia and Melusine, who are quite clearly the product of male fears about female power. But no matter how we might view Martin's female characters as challenges to male authority, one could not say that they are in any way male constructs. Rather, they are, as Salter puts it, 'the strength of the series', or, as the *New Yorker* television critic Emily Nussbaum says, '[they provide] insight into what it means to be excluded from power: to be a woman, or a bastard, or a "half man".'[14] Whether or not Martin can be seen as a feminist, what is apparent is that he is an egalitarian, one for whom social realism, not social idealism, is the issue. As Daenerys, herself, perceives, when reflecting on her dragon-power:

> Mother of dragons . . . Mother of monsters. What have I unleashed upon the world? A queen I am, but my throne is made of burned bones, and it rests on quicksand . . . I am the blood of the dragon . . . If they are monsters, so am I.[15]

What Martin would seem to be saying is that, with rare exceptions, irrespective of the consequences, when our backs are against the wall, all humans will choose whatever power they can grasp, rather than be seen to be weak and vulnerable. Martin's dragons are metaphors for this amoral pragmatism.

Dragon tattoo illustration.

*conclusion*
# The Dragon and Fear

T HE DRAGON IS an imaginary being. It does not exist; nor has
it ever existed. So much is obvious. Or is it? As psychologists
have observed in respect of dreams and delusions, there is
often a very thin line between reality and imagination; indeed, it is sometimes so thin that it is simply not possible to make a distinction between
the two. It is in this liminal space that the dragon exists. The question as
to why this should be raises those philosophical and metaphysical questions that have troubled our species since consciousness dawned. In order
to understand, to some degree at least, why the dragon has its place among
our deepest fears, we need first to look at the way in which the human mind
functions.

As we have seen in myths, legends and, more recently, fantasy fictions
worldwide, the dragon can variously be interpreted as nature's formidable
powers, the socially ruinous consequences of greed, unchecked violence and,
ultimately, death itself. In all these fears for our survival, the unstable
common ground is chaos, that most dreaded of circumstances when our
powers are at their lowest ebb. In order to avoid the ultimate consequences
of chaos, that is to say, mass extinction, the only imperative for our survival
strategy is to devise as many means as possible for prolonging life. This,
however, by the very nature of mortality, can never quite be sufficient.

As discussed in the Introduction, an anthropological perspective on
this is the Nature/Culture opposition. But, as noted, our efforts to limit
the impact of Nature, that which cannot be controlled, by establishing the
defensive mechanisms of Culture are profoundly undermined by the fact
that we are composed of both Culture and Nature. In short, despite all our
best efforts to control Nature, death remains an inevitability. Moreover, our
need to impose order can in itself be our undoing when individual survival

is given priority over collective survival. Given this perspective, the dragon can be seen as an embodiment of Nature, of all, including ourselves, that determines the precariousness of existence. Yet there is another way of looking at things, in this case from a psychoanalytical point of view, where we are provided with a useful language for analysing the complexities of the human mind.

## The dragon as id

Freudians have explained human behaviour as governed by two opposing forces: the id and the superego. The id is essentially deeply antisocial and is governed entirely by individual urges, or, more precisely, instincts set on personal gratification without any consideration for the effects that this might have on others. Freud saw these as fundamental drives, among which, he argues, are 'cannibalism, incest and lust for killing'.[1] Simply enough, the id drive is contrary to everything required for collective survival.

The superego, by contrast, is not a natural instinct but something learned. Taught by parents and other social authorities, the superego can best be equated with conscience, a regulatory moral framework by which the self is subordinated to a higher, collective good. Yet superego directives cannot, in all cases, be regarded as voluntary, for as Freud says, 'a majority of people obey the cultural prohibitions . . . only under pressure of external coercion.' Given that these externally coercive forces most commonly take the form of the law or religious moral absolutism, when humans by necessity function in accordance with superego dictates, they are frequently motivated more by fear than selflessness. Moreover, while few would question the need to staunch bloodlusts and the damaging consequences of incest (let alone cannibalism), doing so would not necessarily prevent aggression, sexual lust, lies, fraud and calumny, just 'so long as they can remain unpunished for it.'[2]

Rarely, however, can anyone be said to be entirely governed by either of these opposing forces, except, so far as the id is concerned, where we have psychopaths, and so far as the superego is concerned, where we have saints or an equivalent selfless ideal. For the overwhelming majority of us, our psychologies are in a constant state of flux between unconscious id drives and the conscious recognition that our own survival is best ensured by the demands of the superego. Indeed, the very fact that superego demands are, in one way or another, legislated is in itself testimony to the ineradicable powers of the id. This, then, is the vexed condition of that intermediary mentality known as the ego, a principle that is in permanent negotiation between the id and the superego. Accordingly, that which we consider to be our conscious self is deeply unstable, governed as we are by both the dark individualism of the id and the enlightened collectivism of the superego. Nor it is the case that superego collectivism is always, if ever, applied to our species as a whole, for there always have been and always will be wars.

It is as a consequence of the interminable battle between the id and the superego that certain primitive desires and fears are constantly at the boundary of our consciousness. These desires and fears are both a result of our own id drives and of our certain knowledge that the same drives are at work in all other humans. The manifestations of this conflict between that which might simply be called right and wrong are expressed in our mythologies, our attempts to explain life in terms of the hyperbolization of good and bad powers. Among those mythological forces that seek to militate against the success of powers for the collective good is that catch-all figure of destructiveness we call the dragon.

It is, moreover, irrelevant whether the dragon is placated or confronted and overmastered. Although some dragons in some cultures may sometimes be supportive, for example the 'imperialized' Chinese and Japanese dragon, the primary concern of all dragons, those that are unconstrained by the superimposition of human authority, is themselves. The dragon, in effect, is the id, that embodiment of chaos which, except when it is not otherwise expedient, simply does not recognize any interests other than its own. The logic of this argument is that, if the dragon is id chaos, then the heroic dragon slayer and, to an extent, the revered dragon emperor are superego order. As previously said, encounters with dragons take place on the threshold of identity, so in a space and time outside any conventional understanding of these dimensions. The explanation for this, simply enough, is that dragon power exists both in the fraught recesses of the mind and in the awareness of our helplessness in the face of nature's ultimately uncontrollable forces.

## The dragon and the patriarchy

One other consideration about the dragon remains, and this stems from the recognition that collective survival requires all possible security, traditionally as directed by the patriarchy. As has been remarked upon throughout, often seen as a threat to this security is the dragon-woman, a male construct intended as a warning about the perceived dangers of unchecked female sexuality. This figure is variously given form as the unbiddable Lilith, the cursed 'anti-mother' Lamia and the deceptive Melusine. Much the same could be said of the virgin girl who is left exposed as a sacrifice to an insatiable dragon. In these tales, it is the dragon-slaying hero who wins the girl and, typically, by prior agreement with her father, is then presented with her as his bride. The female in these myths has no autonomy whatsoever; rather, she is simply moved from one male authority to another. As has been argued in respect of such tales, the dragon in these cases is the unwanted suitor, and its serpentine appearance is quite clearly a signifier of unregulated phallic power. A dragon with a taste for young virgins might well be interpreted as signifying a sexual predator, and therefore a threat to social order and gene pool stability.

While the modern dragon-woman of fantasy fictions has in many ways overturned and repudiated misogyny and gynophobia, and while feminists have sought to 'reclaim' the likes of Lilith, the challenge to gender prejudice still has some distance to travel before the old dragon-woman myths can be seen for exactly what they are: male fears. The id, in this case, is a combination of megalomania and paranoia. As many dragon experts have said, the dragon is unlikely ever to go away. While this is most certainly true, there are still ways open to free its depredations from the divisive colorations of gender.

FINALLY, THEN, IS the Jorge Luis Borges quote given at the outset of this book correct in saying that the meaning of the dragon is as obscure to us as the meaning of the universe? Certainly, it is perfectly possible to analyse what dragons might mean to different cultures at different times, but that is another matter altogether. We can, for example, be confident in interpreting the early Germanic dragon as an epitomization of all that threatens tribal security: greed, feud and everything opposed to societal bonds. Similarly, we can readily regard that imperialized, so-called benevolent dragon of Chinese mythology as an expression of absolute political power, just as we can see the Celtic dragon as a configuration of those limitations placed on mortals seeking access to higher powers. But this does not mean that we have grasped, in some definitive way, the meaning of dragons.

The analyses that this book has attempted to provide of those various, clearly essential cultural values and the projection of the threat to them in the form of a dragon may well be open to debate, but, whatever one might think, this does not, nor could it ever, amount to a precise meaning of the idea of the dragon phenomenon. To provide that would require not only an understanding of ourselves but an understanding of the meaning of life.

While various religions have given us dragons in an attempt to provide an answer to that greatest of mysteries, mortality, it could hardly be said that any consensus has been reached. In the final analysis, the dragon is an enigma, one in which the ultimate significance of its formidable power will forever elude us. And this being the case, it is not so surprising that contemporary novelists and scriptwriters have been able to adapt the dragon to fit whatever message they are set on delivering. In the end, the nearest we can get to defining the meaning of the dragon is simply to say that it is nothing more or less than our fear of the unknown, and as such our only possible responses are either confrontation or, in one way or another, accommodation. Or, to put it in a draconic context, slay it (the hero), harness its power as your own (the Chinese emperor, the dragon rider, the nursery dragon) or, an often regretted response, somehow seek to appease it. Whichever way, it is a matter of life and death.

# REFERENCES

## Introduction

1 Jorge Luis Borges with Margarita Guerrero, trans. Norman Thomas di Giovanni, *The Book of Imaginary Beings* [*Manual de zoología fantástica*, 1957] (Harmondsworth, 1974), p. 12.

2 Carl Sagan, *The Dragons of Eden: Speculations on the Evolution of Human Intelligence* (New York, 1977). Sagan's science-based argument is very reminiscent of that of the psychologist Carl Jung, whose notion of the 'collective unconscious' was first put forward in his 1916 essay 'The Structure of the Unconscious'.

3 David E. Jones, *An Instinct for Dragons* (New York and London, 2002), p. 36.

4 For fuller discussion of this with a focus on the Norse god Thor, see Martin Arnold, *Thor: Myth to Marvel* (London, 2011), pp. 38–48.

5 See Georges Dumézil, *The Destiny of the Warrior*, trans. Alf Hiltebeitel [*Heur et malheur du guerrier: Aspects mythiques de la fonction guerrière chez les Indo-Européens*, 1969] (Chicago, IL, 1973), and Georges Dumézil, *Gods of the Ancient Norsemen*, ed. Einar Haugen, trans. Francis Charat [*Les Dieux des Germains*, 1959] (Berkeley, CA, 1973).

6 E.O.G. Turville-Petre, *Myth and Religion of the North: The Religion of Ancient Scandinavia* (London, 1964), p. 104.

7 The idea of the Rainbow Serpent, Snake or Monster is to be found in many cultures; for example, in Africa, in the Congo regions and Nigeria, as well as in Haiti, Melanesia, Polynesia and Papua New Guinea. It is not in all cases, including in some Aboriginal Australian myths, benevolent.

8 Claude Lévi-Strauss, *The Raw and the Cooked*, trans. John and Doreen Weightman [*Le Cru et le cuit*, 1964] (London, 1970).

## 1 Dragons in Greek and Roman Mythology

1 See Daniel Ogden, *Dragons, Serpents, and Slayers in the Classical and Early Christian Worlds: A Sourcebook* (Oxford and New York, 2013), pp. 141–5. Dragons as dangerous actualities continued to be written about as serious threats to the Romans, such as the first-century AD account of dragons by Pliny the Elder in his *Natural history*.

2 For Alexander the Great's fourth-century BC 'factual' account of a dragon attack on his army, see the discussion of his letter to Aristotle in Chapter Three.

3 A description of the Roman legion's *draco* was made in the late fourth century by the Roman historian Vegetius. See Pat Southern and Karen R. Dixon, *The Late Roman Army* (New Haven, CT, and London, 1996), p. 98. The *draco* standard was also borne by the Frankish cavalries of the Carolingian Empire in the ninth century.

4 See *The Republic by Plato*, p. 30, at www.idph.net/conteudos/ebooks, accessed 10 June 2016.

5 The Trojan War, a historical event that is judged to have taken place in the mid-thirteenth century BC, is chiefly recorded in Homer's *Odyssey* and *Iliad*, which are believed to have been composed *c.* 750–650 BC.

6 For Hesiod, see Hesiod, '*Theogony*' *and* '*Works and Days*', trans. M. L. West (Oxford and New York, 2008). For Apollodorus, see Apollodorus, *The Library of Greek Mythology*, trans. Robin Hard (Oxford and New York, 2008). As Hard notes in his introduction (pp. vii–xxxiv), scholars had once credited this particular account of the myths to Apollodorus of Athens (*c.* 180–125 BC), but anachronisms in the text suggest a much later composition.

7 A fully sourced and comprehensive study of Greek mythology is Robert Graves, *The Greek Myths: Complete Edition* (London and New York, 1992). For a scholarly study of dragons in early sources, see Ogden, *Dragons, Serpents, and Slayers*, and Daniel Ogden, *Drakōn: Dragon Myth and Serpent Cult in the Greek and Roman Worlds* (Oxford and New York, 2013).

8 Campe is most probably Echidna (discussed in following sections): see Joseph Fontenrose, *Python: A Study of Delphic Myth and its Origins* (Berkeley and Los Angeles, CA, 1980), p. 243.

9 The rule of Cronus is categorized by Hesiod as first of Five Ages, the Golden Age, a time when those humans that were first created lived long and vigorous lives of great plenty. With the exception of the fourth age, the Heroic Age, when mankind's lot temporarily improves, the second, third and fifth ages – Silver, Bronze and Iron, respectively – mark an ever-increasing decline in human comfort and longevity, until human existence consists of no more than toil, misery and wrongdoing. See Hesiod, '*Theogony*' *and* '*Works and Days*', pp. 40–42.

10 Hesiod, '*Theogony*' *and* '*Works and Days*', p. 20.

11 For this and the previous two quotes, Hesiod, '*Theogony*' *and* '*Works and Days*', p. 39.

12 Hesiod, in his *Works and Days*, does not explain why Hope is left inside the jar, and later versions of this myth say that Hope, too, is set free, so preventing mankind from committing mass suicide. Homer tells how there are two jars held by Zeus, one containing evils, the other blessings. Zeus allots to mankind a mixture of both jars, depending on his whim. See Homer, *The Iliad*, trans. Martin Hammond (London and New York, 1987), Ch. 24, p. 401.

13 Hesiod, '*Theogony*' *and* '*Works and Days*', p. 12.

14 Apollodorus, *The Library*, p. 35. According to the sixth-century BC *Homeric Hymn to Apollo*, Typhon is the asexually born child of Hera: see 'Homeric Hymn to Apollo', https://msu.edu/~tyrrell, accessed 14 June 2016. More

commonly, however, Typhon is said to be a son of Gaia; see for example Hesiod, *Theogony*, p. 27.

15  Delphyne may be either another name for, or a confusion with, the snake-dragon Python, who according to some accounts was the original oracle at Delphi. According to the Roman author Hyginus (*Fabulae*, 140), Python was killed by the Olympian sun god Apollo, whose mother, the goddess Leto, had been pursued by Python under instruction from Hera for having had sexual relations with Zeus and so giving birth to Apollo. Known thereafter as the Temple of Apollo, the Oracle was presided over by the High Priestess Pythia. This, however, is one of the most confused and complex of myths. For the numerous literary sources, see Ogden, *Dragons, Serpents, and Slayers*, pp. 39–44.

16  Apollodorus simply refers to these as 'ephemeral fruits', *The Library*, p. 36.

17  Epitomizing the dragon-woman in her most ferocious form is Echidna's daughter Chimaera, a fire-breathing monster who, according to Hesiod, is eventually slain by the hero Bellerophon mounted on his winged stallion Pegasus: see Hesiod, *Theogony*, p. 12.

18  Other versions of this myth say Danae was imprisoned in a brass tower with a skylight.

19  This account of the battle is derived from Ovid's *Metamorphoses* (first published AD 8). See Mary M. Innes, trans., *The Metamorphoses of Ovid* (Harmondsworth, 1955), p. 113.

20  According to Ovid, it was Athene (Lat. Minerva) who had transformed the once beautiful Medusa into a grotesque creature for coupling with Poseidon (Lat. Neptune) in her temple, thus defiling it. See *Metamorphoses of Ovid*, p. 115.

21  Hera is said to be an offspring of Cronus and Rhea, and is thus Zeus' sister.

22  In some variants, this role is given to Eileithyia, the goddess of childbirth; in others Hera prevents Eileithyia from entering Alcmene's chamber.

23  Such births, known as heteropaternal superfecundation, are common among animals but rare among humans. According to Diodorus Siculus writing between 60 and 30 BC, Heracles is first given the name Alcaeus.

24  Athene is therefore a half-sister to Heracles.

25  In other, later sources, the killing of the lion, said in these sources to be the Nemean Lion, is Heracles' first labour.

26  Some sources say that he also murdered Megara, while others say that his shame resulted in his not being able to bear the sight of her any longer and so giving her to his nephew Iolaus.

27  The number of the Hydra's heads varies according to sources, ranging from just one to several hundred. Only according to Apollodorus is one of the nine heads immortal. The association of this myth with the slaying of the seven-headed Lotan by Baal in Canaanite mythology is noted in Peter Hogarth and Val Clery, *Dragons* (London, 1979), p. 29.

28  Eurystheus also discounted Heracles' fifth labour, the cleaning of the Augean Stables, on the grounds that Heracles was paid, albeit reluctantly, by King Augeas for his services.

29  According to the third- or second-century BC *Kyklos historikos* by Dionysius of Samos, Heracles kills the female dragon Scylla for snatching up some of

Geryon's cattle, after which Scylla's father, Phorcys, brings her back to life with fire. For a rationalization of this myth in ancient Greek sources and for further references to Scylla in her better-known role in Homer's *Odyssey*, see Ogden, *Dragons, Serpents, and Slayers*, pp. 179–84.

30 Apollodorus, *The Library*, p. 81.

31 See Hesiod, *Theogony*, p. 18. It is at the outset of this labour that Heracles encounters the bound and tortured Prometheus and, having killed the eagle, sets him free.

32 Decorated vases from the sixth century BC depict the sea god in this labour as the half-man, half-fish deity Triton.

33 According to Ovid, Atlas was turned to stone when Perseus showed him the head of Medusa: *Metamorphoses of Ovid*, p. 111. This, of course, cannot be reconciled with the account of Heracles' eleventh labour.

34 In some versions of this labour, Atlas plays no part at all and Heracles picks the apples himself, having slain Ladon. This would be consistent with Eurystheus' insistence that Heracles must always act alone.

35 For an elaborate fifth-century gloss (*scholia*) on Homer's reference to this episode, which includes mention of Hesione, see Ogden, *Dragons, Serpents, and Slayers*, p. 154.

36 For a discussion of this 'reborn' theory, see Chapter Four, concluding paragraphs.

37 The only other living figures able to enter Hades were all, like Heracles, heroes, typically ones that were divinely ordained. These were Odysseus, Aeneas (with the Sibyl), Orpheus, Theseus (with Pirithous) and, in Ovid's *Metamorphoses*, Psyche.

38 For an analysis of the poetical formulaics used in a number of sources to describe the shameful killings of innocents by Heracles, see Calvert Watkins, *How to Kill a Dragon: Aspects of Indo-European Poetics* (Oxford, 1995), Ch. 38, pp. 374–82, esp. pp. 379–82.

39 See Ogden, *Drakōn*, pp. 166–8.

40 As in this tale and in Heracles' fight with the Hydra, a spring-guarding monster is also told of in the tale of a young woman with a baby who shows warriors a spring but sets down her child, who is then eaten by the Dragon of Nemea. For sources, see Ogden, *Dragons, Serpents, and Slayers*, pp. 119–22.

41 According to Apollonius of Rhodes' influential *Argonautica* (*c.* AD 270–45), which tells of Jason's pre-Trojan War quest to win the Golden Fleece, half the teeth extracted by Cadmus came into the possession of Aeëtes, King of Colchis, who gives them to Jason as part of the test he sets him. When Jason sows them in the ground and the warriors spring up, his task is to kill them all. Having passed this test, thanks to the help given him by Aeëtes' daughter, the love-struck Princess Medea, Jason goes on to overcome the dragon of Colchis that guards the Golden Fleece and regains his father's usurped throne. For the various Greek sources for this legend, see Ogden, *Dragons, Serpents, and Slayers*, pp. 125–33.

42 The similarities between the Lamia myth and that of Medea, who kills her children by Jason in revenge for his taking a new wife, are discussed in Sarah Iles Johnston, 'Corinthian Medea and the Cult of Hera Akraia', in *Medea: Essays on Medea in Myth, Literature, Philosophy, and Art*, ed. James J. Clauss

and Sarah Iles Johnston (Princeton, NJ, 1977), pp. 44–70. It is said by
Apollodorus (*The Library*, p. 57) that after her infanticides, Medea flees in
a sun chariot drawn by winged dragons.

43 For all sources concerning Lamia, including tales where a dragon-like monster
named Lamia is slain, see Ogden, *Dragons, Serpents, and Slayers*, pp. 97–108.
See also the following: Chapter Two for the myths and legends of Lilith,
with whom Lamia is associated; and Chapter Eight for the Melusine folktale
tradition and nineteenth-century depictions of Lamia/Lilith in art and
literature.

44 See Sigmund Freud, 'The Sexual Aberrations', in *Three Contributions to the
Theory of Sex*, trans. A. A. Brill (New York and Washington, DC, 1920), at
www.gutenberg.org, accessed 15 June 2016. For critical assessment of Freud's
analysis of female sexuality, see Juliet Mitchell, *Psychoanalysis and Feminism:
A Radical Reassessment of Freudian Psychoanalysis* (Harmondsworth, 1975),
esp. pp. 95–131.

45 Exceptions to the malevolent monstrosity rule are two dragons noted in
*De natura animalium*, a study by the Roman author Aelian (Claudius
Aelianus, *c*. AD 175–235). Intent on showing 'universal reason' and 'rational
behaviour in the animal kingdom', Aelian tells of one dragon coming to the
aid of a young man under attack by bandits, and another guarding the body
of a prince slain by his brothers until he can be given a dignified burial. See
Jonathan Evans, 'The Dragon', in *Mythical and Fabulous Creatures: A Source
Book and Research Guide*, ed. Malcolm South (New York, 1987), pp. 27–58,
p. 37.

46 For Virgil's account of Laocoön's warning, see Virgil, *The Aeneid*, trans.
W. F. Jackson Knight (Harmondsworth, 1958), Book II, ll. 26–57, p. 52. For
the various accounts of Laocoön's death and a discussion of their complexities,
see Ogden, *Dragons, Serpents and Slayers*, pp. 134–40.

47 G. S. Kirk, *Myth: Its Meaning and Functions in Ancient and Other Cultures*
(Berkeley and Los Angeles, CA, 1970), p. 198.


## 2 Dragons in the Bible and Saints' Lives

1 Unless otherwise stated, all Bible quotes are from the King James Version
(KJV).

2 The Eden serpent is one of only two talking animals in the first five books
of the Bible, the other being Balaam's divinely inspired donkey (Numbers 22).

3 For a translation, see Siegmund Hurwitz, *Lilith, The First Eve: Historical
and Psychological Aspects of the Dark Feminine*, trans. Gela Jacobson, 3rd edn
(Einsiedeln, 2009). Hurwitz notes that the name used for Lilith in the epic
of Gilgamesh is Ki-sikil-lil-la-ke ('the maiden of Lilith'), p. 49.

4 This tale has been reconstructed from the eleventh of twelve tablets that
are dated from the thirteenth to the tenth centuries BC. For a translation
of this episode, see Stephen Mitchell, trans., *Gilgamesh: A New English Version*
(London, 2004), Book XI, pp. 191–9.

5 The name Lilith, sometimes accompanied by an image of her as a night
hag, appears on a number of bowls and amulets from the sixth century BC
onwards. Lilith is also included in a list of monsters in a Dead Sea Scrolls

Hebrew-language text known as the 'Songs of the Sage' that is believed to date from the first century BC.

6  The rabbinical mystical commentary the Zohar, which became known in Christian Europe from the thirteenth century AD but dates back to the second century BC, contains a number of elaborations on Lilith's significance, identifying her as the malevolently sexualized female aspect of Satan, his so-called 'left emanation'. Lilith has also been identified with the Greek myths concerning Lamia and the Lamiai. For other studies of Lilith, besides that of Hurwitz, see the following: Barbara Black Koltuv, *The Book of Lilith* (Lake Worth, FL, 1986), and Raphael Patai, *The Hebrew Goddess*, 3rd edn (Detroit, MI, 1990), pp. 221–54.

7  While there is no scholarly agreement as to when the canon of the Tanakh was fixed, the second century BC seems likely. As to when its development began, this could be from the eighth to the sixth century BC. Its narrative origins, however, are likely to be far older.

8  The KJV of the Old Testament depended greatly on William Tyndale's Bible of 1534, which was translated directly from the Hebrew Bible.

9  The primeval Sumerian serpent-dragon Kur is said to be an accomplice or possibly an offspring of Tiamat.

10  As the Hebrew God was at one time referred to as Baal, and since Yam is also known as Lotan, it has been suggested that this myth corresponds to God's challenge to Leviathan. For such suggestions and for accounts of the Baal Cycle, see for example Daniel Ogden, *Dragons, Serpents, and Slayers in the Classical and Early Christian Worlds: A Sourcebook* (Oxford, 2013), p. 259, and Jonathan Evans, *Dragons: Myth and Legend* (London, 2008), pp. 49–57.

11  Evans, *Dragons: Myth and Legend*, p. 49.

12  See Erik Hornung, *The Secret Lore of Egypt: Its Impact on the West* (Ithaca, NY, and London, 2002).

13  Mehen is represented as encircling the world in the form of two snakes, so indicating the union of Ra and Osiris, this latter being the god of the underworld and of the dead. Another world encircling serpent in Egyptian mythology is Sito, who also symbolizes the cosmic order: see Pat Remler, *Egyptian Mythology A to Z*, 3rd edn (New York, 2010), 'Serpent Gods', pp. 173–4.

14  In the Torah, when Aaron throws the rod down it becomes a *tanniyn* (dragon), but when Moses throws it down it becomes a *nachash* (serpent).

15  Echoes of this story are also to be found in Acts of the Apostles (28:3–6), when Paul's saintliness prevents him from being harmed after he is bitten by a viper, and in the apocryphal Gospel of Thomas, where the child Jesus miraculously cures another child who has been similarly bitten. Both these tales are noted in Ogden, *Dragons, Serpents, and Slayers*, entry 127, p. 194.

16  Whether or not the 'great fish', translated as 'whale' by William Tyndale in 1534, that swallowed Jonah as part of God's corrective of his initially unwilling messenger (Jonah 1:17; 2:1; 2:10) could also be considered draconic is questionable. Apart from Jesus' comparison of his impending suffering to Jonah's piscatorial incarceration (Matthew 12:40), the Jonah 'fish' played no future role in Bible-inspired dragon tales, such as those told of in saints' lives.

17  Literally, the term 'neesings' means sneezes, but here it most likely indicates the water spouting from Leviathan's mouth.

18  This does not include references to Rahab, which is sometimes identified as meaning Egypt (Psalm 87:4, Psalm 89:8–10, Isaiah 51:9) and sometimes as meaning 'fierceness', 'insolence' or 'pride' (Isaiah 30:7, Job 9:13, Job 26:12). According to medieval Jewish folklore, Rahab is a sea dragon, possibly identifiable with Leviathan. This is not to be confused with Rahab the prostitute in Joshua 2.

19  Emil G. Hirsch, Kaufmann Kohler, Solomon Schechter, Isaac Broydé, 'Leviathan and Behemoth', *Jewish Encyclopedia*, www.jewishencyclopedia.com, accessed 4 April 2014.

20  Luther Link, *The Devil: A Mask Without a Face* (London, 2004), pp. 75–6.

21  The Septuagint was translated from the Hebrew Bible between the third and the first century BC. The removal of the apocryphal books from the KJV happened in 1885.

22  The name Bel is most likely derived from the Canaanite god Baal and from the byname Bel as applied to the Babylonian god Marduk: see Peter Hogarth and Val Clery, *Dragons* (London, 1979), p. 27.

23  For an English translation of the Bel and the Dragon tale, see David Norton, ed., *The Bible: King James Version with the Apocrypha* (London and New York, 2006), pp. 1471–2.

24  For a discussion of the historical interpretations of the Book of Revelation, see Stephen T. Asma, *On Monsters: An Unnatural History of Our Worst Fears* (Oxford and New York, 2009), pp. 67–71.

25  Exactly who this visionary was continues to be debated. Traditionally, it was thought to be John the Apostle, but more recently it has been argued that it was John of Patmos, about whom little is known.

26  Each section has seven subsections, the number seven being of symbolic significance in scriptural tradition.

27  In Revelation 17, the bearer of the Mother of Harlots, otherwise known as the Great Whore of Babylon, is similarly described. The inspiration behind this creature and the others envisioned in Revelation are most likely to be those told of in Daniel's vision in the Book of Daniel 7. For an analysis of the relation between Daniel and Revelation, see James D. G. Dunn, 'The Danilic Son of Man in the New Testament', in *The Book of Daniel: Composition and Reception*, ed. J. J. Collins, P. W. Flint and C. VanEpps (Leiden, 2002), pp. 528–49.

28  This text, in five chapters, was initially written in Greek in the fifth century AD and also survives in later Latin and Slavonic translations. For a full translation see M. R. James, 'The Gospel of Bartholomew' (1924), at www.gnosis.org, accessed 3 April 2014.

29  A cubit is typically 44 cm or 18 in.

30  See Samantha Riches, *St George: A Saint for All* (London, 2015), esp. pp. 7–21 and pp. 92–3.

31  For an extensive Coptic account of George's persecution by Diocletian, see ibid., pp. 9–11.

32  See 'The Passion of St George (BHO 310)', trans. E.A.W. Budge (1888), pp. 203–35, at www.ucc.ie/archive/milmart/BHO310.html, accessed 2 August 2016.

33 For a discussion of the various Greek sources that would seem to have inspired the account of George's dragon-slaying, see Ogden, *Dragons, Serpents, and Slayers*, pp. 251–2. For an assessment of the St George legend and its Greek mythological influences, which includes an analysis of George's persecution by the Dadianus dragon, see Joseph Fontenrose, *Python: A Study of Delphic Myth and Its Origins* (Berkeley and Los Angeles, CA, 1959), Appendix 4, 'Saint George and the Dragon', pp. 515–20.

34 For this account, see Ogden, *Dragons, Serpents, and Slayers*, pp. 249–50.

35 Jacobus de Voragine, *The Golden Legend: Readings on the Saints*, trans. William Granger Ryan, 2 vols (Princeton, NJ, 1993), vol. I, pp. 238–42, esp. pp. 238–40.

36 For an assessment of the St George myth in more contemporary English culture, see Riches, *St George*, Ch. 6: 'St George and England: A Re-emerging Relevance?', pp. 120–34.

37 For the full ballad as preserved in the National Library of Scotland – Crawford 1349, see 'New Ballad of St George and the Dragon', http://ebba.english.ucsb.edu, accessed 2 December 2016.

38 For further discussion of the Brinsop and Ulffington dragons, see Jacqueline Simpson, *British Dragons* [1980] (Ware, 2001), pp. 53–4.

39 For discussions of 'The Reluctant Dragon' and the nursery dragon phenomenon, see chapters Eight and Ten, respectively.

40 For a discussion of rabbinical biblical commentaries on the Bible that had absorbed aspects of Egyptian mythology, including the idea that Leviathan is an evil serpent that encircles the world, see Marc Michael Epstein, 'Harnessing the Dragon: A Mythos Transformed in Medieval Jewish Literature', in *Myth and Method*, ed. Laurie L. Patton and Wendy Doniger (Charlottesville, VA, 1996), pp. 352–89, p. 363.

41 For the original early accounts of the *Shepherd of Hermas*, the *Passion of St Perpetua* and the *Acts of Thomas* dragon tales, see, respectively, Ogden, *Dragons, Serpents, and Slayers*, pp. 196–9, p. 199 and pp. 202–4.

42 The following tales are preserved in the *Acts of Philip*, the *Martyrion of Philip* and, credited to Abdias, the *Historia Apostolica*. For the relevant extracts from these sources, see Ogden, *Dragons, Serpents, and Slayers*, pp. 207–20.

43 Echidna is most surely a reference to the ancient Greek Titan monster, many of whose dragon offspring are slain by Heracles. See Chapter One.

44 For the *Acts of Sylvester* dragon tale and related sources, see Ogden, *Dragons, Serpents, and Slayers*, pp. 221–7.

45 For the various sources for the following tales, see Ogden, *Dragons, Serpents, and Slayers*, pp. 228–38 and pp. 244–6.

46 For the curious legend of St Margaret being a maiden in distress who is rescued from a dragon by St George, see Simpson, *British Dragons*, pp. 106–7.

47 Bede, *A History of the English Church and People*, trans. Leo Sherley-Price, revd R. E. Latham (Harmondsworth, 1968), I.I, pp. 39–40.

48 For the myth that Conan, the son of the Fenian Cycle hero Fionn mac Cumhaill, killed Caoranach centuries before Patrick's arrival, see Máire MacNeill, *The Festival of Lughnasa, Parts I and II* (Dublin, 1982), p. 503. For a further discussion of Patrick and the expulsion of snakes from Ireland, see Chapter Five.

49  Jacobus de Voragine, *The Golden Legend*, vol. i, pp. 193–6, p. 192. For other cited sources regarding Patrick's miracle, see Ogden, *Dragons, Serpents, and Slayers*, pp. 247–8.

## 3 The Germanic Dragon, Part i: Old Norse Mythology and Old English Literature

 1  Author's translation of ll. 26–7. For a full translation of this poem, see Richard Hamer, trans., *A Choice of Anglo-Saxon Verse* (London and Boston, MA, 1970), pp. 109–15. This poem is also known as 'Maxims ii'.
 2  Translation adapted from Britannia History, *Anglo-Saxon Chronicle* (London, 1912), at www.britannia.com, accessed 12 December 2016. For a full translation of the *Chronicles*, see Michael Swanton, ed. and trans., *The Anglo-Saxon Chronicles* (London, 2000).
 3  For highly scholarly studies of dragons in Germanic sources, see Joyce Tally Lionarons, *The Medieval Dragon: The Nature of the Beast in Germanic Literature* (Enfield Lock, Middlesex, 1998); Christine Rauer, *Beowulf and the Dragon: Parallels and Analogues* (Cambridge, 2000); and Jonathan Evans, '"As Rare as They Are Dire": Old Norse Dragons, *Beowulf* and the *Deutsche Mythologie*', in *The Shadow Walkers: Jacob Grimm's Mythology of the Monstrous*, ed. Tom Shippey (Turnhout, 2005), pp. 207–69.
 4  Iceland was first settled in the late ninth century AD and converted to Christianity in the year 1000.
 5  Snorri Sturluson, *Edda*, trans. Anthony Faulkes (London, 1995), 'Háttatal' (list of verse forms), Section 6, p. 170.
 6  For full translations of these Eddic sources, see respectively: Carolyne Larrington, trans., *The Poetic Edda* (Oxford, 1996); and Snorri, *Edda*. All author's translations of the *Poetic Edda* that follow are made from Finnur Jónsson, *Sæmundar-Edda: Eddukvæði* (Reykjavik, 1926).
 7  As noted by the Old Norse expert Rudolf Simek, over time, Níðhögg becomes associated 'like the dragon in Christian visionary literature, with elements of hell-like places of punishment'. See Rudolf Simek, *Dictionary of Northern Mythology*, trans. Angela Hall (Cambridge, 1993), 'Niðhöggr' entry, p. 231.
 8  Neither the *Poetic Edda* nor the *Prose Edda* provide any more information about the serpents listed here, except that the *Prose Edda* states that certain of their names are either epithets for gold or sword names. See Snorri, *Edda*, p. 19 and p. 137.
 9  'The Sayings of Grímnir', verses 34 and 35, author's translation. The *Prose Edda* adds that it is at Hvergelmir, the source of all rivers, that Níðhögg does most damage to Yggdrasill. See Snorri, *Edda*, p. 57.
10  *Völuspá*, verses 37 and 38, author's translation.
11  Ibid., verse 66.
12  The tale of Thor and Útgard-Loki is found exclusively in the *Prose Edda*. See Snorri, *Edda*, pp. 37–46.
13  The account given here is taken from Snorri, *Edda*, pp. 46–7. See also Larrington, trans., *The Poetic Edda*, for 'Hymir's Poem' (*Hymiskviða*), pp. 78–83.

14 For discussion of the Eddic tradition in which Thor attacks and, in some accounts, appears to kill the Midgard Serpent, prior to his encounter with it at Ragnarök, see Martin Arnold, *Thor: Myth to Marvel* (London, 2011), pp. 24–7.

15 Thor's 'nine steps' probably refer to the nine worlds of the Norse cosmos.

16 *Völuspá*, verse 56 (otherwise given as verses 54–5/56), author's translation.

17 The Middle High German poem *Ortnit* also features the killing of a hero by a dragon: see Joyce Tally Lionarons, '"Sometimes the Dragon Wins": Unsuccessful Dragon Fighters in Medieval Literature', in *Essays on Old, Middle, Modern English and Old Icelandic: In Honour of Raymond P. Tripp, Jr*, ed. Loren C. Gruber (Lampeter, 2000), pp. 301–13.

18 Apart from a number of genealogical references in *The Anglo-Saxon Chronicles*, Woden is mentioned in only two other surviving Old English sources, both heavily Christianized. In *Maxims 1*, 'Woden made idols, but the Almighty made heaven': see T. A. Shippey, ed. and trans., *Poems of Wisdom and Learning in Old English* (Cambridge, 1976), pp. 64–75, p. 71. In 'The Nine Herbs Charm', 'Woden then took nine glory twigs, Smote the serpent so that it flew into nine parts': see R. K. Gordon, trans., *Anglo-Saxon Poetry* (London, 1967), pp. 92–4, p. 93.

19 In this digression, as also in the one discussed below, the name Sigemund is identifiable with that of Sigmund, the father of the hero Sigurd, who is the slayer of the dragon Fáfnir in the Icelandic *Saga of the Völsungs* (see Chapter Four). It is unlikely that the *Beowulf* poet was misinformed in this regard, especially given that his audience would have been well versed in the old tales. It therefore seems that there was an older legend in which Sigmund/ Sigemund was the dragon-slayer and that, in later expansions of it, his son was given that role. No proof either way is forthcoming.

20 See Jane Chance, 'Grendel's Mother as Epic Anti-type of the Virgin and Queen (1986)', in *Interpretations of Beowulf: A Critical Anthology*, ed. R. D. Fulk (Bloomington, IN, 1991), pp. 251–63.

21 *Beowulf*, ll. 1709–22, author's translation. For a full translation of the poem, see *Beowulf*, ed. and trans Michael Swanton (Manchester, 1978).

22 For a discussion of irony in *Beowulf*, see T. A. Shippey, 'The Ironic Background (1972)', in *Interpretations of Beowulf*, ed. Fulk, pp. 194–205.

23 *Beowulf*, ll. 913–15, author's translation.

24 J.R.R. Tolkien, '*Beowulf*: The Monsters and the Critics', in *The Monsters and the Critics and Other Essays*, ed. Christopher Tolkien (London, 1997), pp. 5–48, p. 30.

25 For all the following modern English translation extracts from these sources, see Andy Orchard, *Pride and Prodigies: Studies in the Monsters of the 'Beowulf'-Manuscript* (Toronto, 1995): *The Wonders of the East*, pp. 185–203; *The Letter from Alexander to Aristotle*, pp. 225–53; *Liber monstrorum*, pp. 255–317. For a consideration of later medieval bestiaries, see Chapter Five.

26 For an exploration of the relationship between the *Liber monstrorum*, *Beowulf* and the writings of the seventh-century scholar and poet Aldhelm, the Abbot of Malmesbury (later the founding Bishop of Sherborne Abbey), who wrote about dragons as personifications of evil and temptation, see Michael Lapidge, '*Beowulf*, Aldhelm, the *Liber Monstrorum* and Wessex', *Studi Medievali*, 3rd ser., 23 (1982), pp. 151–92.

27  The *Liber monstrorum* is clearly based on the second- to fifth-century AD Greek bestiary *Physiologus*. See Chapter Five for further discussion.

28  Exactly who this last creature was is unclear but it may be Geryon (see Chapter One).

29  Alexander is one of the pagan heroes, along with Hector and Julius Caesar. The Jews are Joshua, David and Judas Maccabeus, and the Christians are King Arthur, Emperor Charlemagne and the eleventh-century Frankish Crusader Godfrey of Bouillon.

30  Cited in Daniel Ogden, *Drakōn: The Dragon Myth and Serpent Cult in the Greek and Roman Worlds* (Oxford and New York, 2013), p. 334.

31  A further association of Alexander with a dragon is recorded in an embellished seventh-century AD Syriac translation of the *Alexander Romance*. Probably inspired by the Book of Daniel's Bel and the Dragon (see Chapter Two), Alexander is said to have killed the dragon by tricking it into swallowing a concoction of gypsum, pitch, lead and sulphur. For a translation of this account, see Daniel Ogden, *Dragons, Serpents, and Slayers in the Classical and Early Christian Worlds: A Sourcebook* (Oxford and New York, 2013), pp. 272–3. For an account of the life of and legends about Alexander in the travel writings of Sir John Mandeville, published in the mid-fourteenth century, see Asa Simon Mittman and Susan M. Kim, 'Monsters and the Exotic in Medieval England', in *The Oxford Handbook of Medieval Literature in English*, ed. Elaine Treharne and Greg Walker (Oxford and New York, 2010), pp. 677–706, esp. pp. 697–9.

32  It has been suggested by some scholars that the *Beowulf* dragon's name is Stearcheort, meaning 'Strong-heart'. See *Beowulf*, ll. 2288b and 2552a.

33  For the alternative view that Beowulf is himself a monster, one that from a Christian perspective on the pagan past signifies the vice of pride, see Orchard, *Pride and Prodigies*, esp. Ch. 2. For a review of Orchard's study that is critical of his conclusions, see John M. Hill, *Modern Philology*, xcvi/1 (1998), pp. 58–61.

## 4 The Germanic Dragon, Part 2: Sagas of Ancient Times

1  Dragons are also prominent in the late Icelandic chivalric sagas known as the *riddarasögur*, which were clearly inspired by medieval Romance cycles. In *Erex saga*, for example, a knight is rescued from the mouth of a dragon by the saga's hero, who then refuses his reward, in this case the knight's entire kingdom. For a discussion of this episode, see Jonathan Evans, 'Semiotics and Traditional Lore: The Medieval Dragon Tradition', *Journal of Folklore Research*, xii/2–3 (1985), pp. 85–112, pp. 92–5.

2  For a translation and discussion of the *Saga of the Völsungs*, see Jesse L. Byock, trans., *The Saga of the Volsungs: The Norse Epic of Sigurd the Dragon Slayer* (Harmondsworth, 2000).

3  See Árni Björnsson, *Wagner and the Volsungs: Icelandic Sources of 'Der Ring des Nibelungen'* (London, 2003). For a discussion of the influence of Wagner's *Ring* cycle on the Nazis, see Martin Arnold, *Thor: Myth to Marvel* (London, 2011), pp. 126–32.

4  For a useful set of classifications of dragon types and the sources for them, see Inger M. Boberg, *Motif Index of Early Icelandic Literature* (Copenhagen, 1966), pp. 38–9 (B10–B11.11.6); and p. 56 (D190– D199.4).

5   See 'The Lay of Fafnir', in *The Poetic Edda*, trans. Carolyne Larrington (Oxford, 1996), pp. 157–65.

6   For an analysis of the helm of terror's significance and the inference that Sigurd and Fáfnir's relationship can be interpreted as that between son and father, see Ármann Jakobsson, 'Enter the Dragon: Legendary Courage and the Birth of the Hero', in *Making History: Essays on the 'Fornaldarsögur'*, ed. Martin Arnold and Alison Finlay (London, 2010), pp. 33–52.

7   Snorri Sturluson, *Edda*, trans. Anthony Faulkes (London, 1995), p. 99.

8   For a comprehensive list of Scandinavian and German analogues to the *Saga of the Völsungs*, see R. G. Finch, ed. and trans., *The Saga of the Volsungs* (Edinburgh, 1965), pp. ix–xiii.

9   For a translation of the *Song of the Nibelungs*, see A. T. Hatto, trans., *The Nibelungenlied* (Harmondsworth, 1969). For a comprehensive reference source, see Francis G. Gentry et al., eds, *The Nibelungen Tradition: An Encyclopedia* (London and New York, 2011).

10  The *Song of the Nibelungs* (*Nibelungenlied*) is widely considered to be a deliberate modernization of traditional legends in order to reflect late twelfth-century tastes.

11  For the first mention of Siegfried and the dragon, see Hatto, trans., *The Nibelungenlied*, Ch. 3, p. 28; for Siegfried's betrayal and subsequent murder, see Chs 15 and 16.

12  For a translation of *Thidrek's Saga*, see Edward R. Haymes, trans., *The Saga of Thidrek of Bern* (New York, 1988).

13  As is noted by Jessie Byock, 'The absence of evidence that the Icelandic saga audience understood or gave any thought to the ethnic difference between the Huns and the Germanic tribesmen is noteworthy. The oriental origin of Attila is forgotten, and he is treated as one of several competing leaders in the migration period.' See 'Introduction', in *The Saga of the Volsungs*, trans. Byock, p. 12.

14  The possible historical origins for the legend are discussed in Byock, trans., *The Saga of the Volsungs*, pp. 11–26.

15  Ibid., p. 79. After Brynhild's death, Gudrun's disastrous life is the chief focus of the saga.

16  In the *Saga of the Völsungs*, Odin's determination of the death of Sigmund suggests that he is taking him to Valhalla, just as he has taken Sigmund's incestuously born son Sinfjötli earlier in the saga. In the mid-tenth-century Old Norse poem *Eiríksmál*, Sigmund and Sinfjötli greet the arrival in Valhalla of the Viking king Erik Bloodaxe. For a discussion and translation of *Eiríksmál*, see Nora Kershaw (Chadwick), ed. and trans., *Anglo-Saxon and Old Norse Poems* (Cambridge, 1922), pp. 93–9. For a description of Valhalla and its inhabitants, see Snorri, *Edda*, pp. 31–3.

17  For these Eddic lays, see 'Brynhild's Ride to Hel', in *The Poetic Edda*, trans. Larrington, pp. 192–204, and 'The Whetting of Gudrun', ibid., pp. 234–7. J.R.R. Tolkien's rather free poetic rendering of Sigurd's life, loves and tragedy infers that Sigurd did get to Valhalla. This, however, is poetic licence: see J.R.R. Tolkien, *The Legend of Sigurd and Gudrún* (Boston, MA, 2009).

18  Brynhild's murderous, dragon-like rage when she sees the wounds on Sigurd's dead body is described in 'Guðrúnarkviða in fyrsta' (The First Lay of Gudrún),

where it is said that 'fire burned in her eyes, venom she breathed':
verse 27, author's translation. For a discussion of this, see Thomas D. Hill,
'Guðrúnarkviða in fyrsta: Guðrún's Healing Tears', in *Revisiting the Poetic Edda:*
*Essays on Old Norse Heroic Legend*, ed. Paul Acker and Carolyne Larrington
(London and New York, 2013), pp. 107–16, esp. pp. 109–10.

19   *Beowulf*, l. 455, author's translation.

20   An example of this is to be found in the dragon-infested *Yngvars saga víðförla*
(Yngvar's Saga). See 'Yngvar's Saga', in *Vikings in Russia: 'Yngvar's Saga' and*
*'Eymund's Saga'*, trans. Hermann Pálsson and Paul Edwards (Edinburgh,
1989), pp. 44–68. For a discussion of the dragon episodes, see Galina
Glazyrina, 'Dragon Motifs in *Yngvars saga víðförla*', in *The Fantastic in Old*
*Norse/Icelandic Literature: Sagas and the British Isles*, ed. John McKinnell,
David Ashurst and Donata Kick (Durham, 2006), pp. 288–93.

21   For a discussion of dragon depictions in medieval art across the Viking world,
see Paul Acker, 'Dragons in the Eddas and in Early Nordic Art', in *Revisiting*
*the Poetic Edda*, ed. Acker and Larrington, pp. 53–75.

22   See Philip Westbury Cardew, trans., *A Translation of 'Þorskfirðinga (Gull-*
*Þóris) saga'* (Lampeter, 2000). For a list of other sources which contain this
particular motif, see Jonathan Evans, '"As Rare As They Are Dire": Old Norse
Dragons, *Beowulf* and the *Deutsche Mythologie*', in *The Shadow Walkers: Jacob*
*Grimm's Mythology of the Monstrous*, ed. Tom Shippey (Turnhout, 2005),
pp. 207–69, p. 250.

23   Cardew, trans., *A Translation of 'Þorskfirðinga'*, p. 136. As Cardew notes, pp.
117–19, further detail concerning how Valr and his two sons became dragons
are told of in the *Saga of Halfdan Eysteinsson* (*Hálfdanar saga Eysteinssonar*).
See 'Halfdan Eysteinsson', in *Seven Viking Romances*, trans. Hermann Pálsson
and Paul Edwards (London, 1985), pp. 171–98, Ch. 26, pp. 196–8.

24   A similar tale is told of the Viking warrior Bui the Stout, who during a
great sea battle jumped overboard with two chests of gold and is said to
have later transformed into a dragon (*ormr*). See N. F. Blake, trans.,
*The Saga of the Jomsvikings* (London, 1962), pp. 37–8 and p. 43. Available
at http://vsnrweb-publications.org.uk, accessed 1 August 2016.

25   In all likelihood, Thórir was an historical character, for the settlement of
his family in Iceland and Thórir's gaining of much gold in Norway are briefly
told of in the twelfth-century *Landnámabók* (*Book of the Settlements*). For
this entry, see Cardew, trans., *A Translation of 'Þorskfirðinga'*, pp. 114–15.

26   Ibid., p. 133.

27   Ibid., p. 138.

28   For a discussion of this and the saga's other analogues, see 'Intertextualities',
in Cardew, *A Translation of 'Þorskfirðinga'*, trans, pp. 109–20. For a detailed
analysis of the Bear's Son structure as regards Thor's battles with various
monstrous beings, see John McKinnell, 'Þórr and the Bear's Son', in *Meeting*
*the Other in Norse Myth and Legend* (Cambridge, 2005), pp. 126–46.

29   This is discussed in G. V. Smithers, *The Making of Beowulf* (Durham, 1961),
p. 11.

30   Cardew, trans., *A Translation of 'Þorskfirðinga'*, p. 166.

31   While humans who turn into dragons are not uncommon in Old Norse
sources, one curious instance, in *Morkinskinna*, of the reverse, is the dragon

that appears in golden-skin human form and seduces the wife of a friend of
Harald Hardrada. It may well be, as Harald concludes, that the dragon-man
had once been a sorcerer who, previously, had transformed into a dragon. For
a discussion of this, see Evans, '"As Rare As They Are Dire"', pp. 247–8.

32  See Ben Waggoner, trans., *The Sagas of Ragnar Lodbrok* (New Haven, CT,
2009), pp. 1–41.

33  'Krákumál', stanza 1, author's translation from Guðni Jónsson and Bjarni
Vilhjálmsson, '*Krákumál (Fornaldarsögur Norðurlanda)*', at www.heimskringla.
no, accessed 23 June 2017. For a full translation of the poem, see Waggoner,
trans., *The Sagas of Ragnar Lodbrok*, pp. 76–83.

34  More serpentine dragon associations can be seen in the names of two
of Ragnar's sons: Sigurd Snake-in-the-Eye and Ivar the Boneless.

35  One possibility is that the Viking chieftain known as Reginheri, who led
the siege of Paris in 845, was Ragnar Lodbrók. For an examination of the
historicity of Ragnar, see Elizabeth Ashman Rowe, *Vikings in the West:
The Legend of Ragnarr Loðbrók and His Sons* (Vienna, 2012).

36  Saxo Grammaticus, *The History of the Danes*, ed. Hilda Ellis Davidson, trans.
Peter Fisher, Books I–IX (Cambridge, 1998), Book 9, pp. 210–11.

37  Lathgertha is also named as Ragnar's first wife in the *Saga of Ragnar Lodbrók*,
although it involves no courtship heroics on Ragnar's part.

38  Saxo, *History*, Book 9, pp. 280–82.

39  See Jacqueline Simpson, ed. and trans., *Scandinavian Folktales*
(Harmondsworth, 1988), pp. 42–3.

40  Saxo, *History*, Book 2, p. 40. For the strikingly similar story of the dragon-
slayer Fridlef (Fridlevus), see Saxo, *History*, Book 6, pp. 168–9.

41  For a translation of this episode in *Hrólfs saga kraka*, see Christine Rauer,
*Beowulf and the Dragon: Parallels and Analogues* (Cambridge, 2000), pp. 169–70.

42  'The Sayings of the High One' ('Hávamál'), *Poetic Edda*, verse 76, ll. 3–4,
author's translation.

43  Walter J. Ong, *Orality and Literacy: The Technologizing of the Word* (London
and New York, 1988), pp. 54–5.

44  *Beowulf*, ll. 2890b–2891, author's translation.

45  Hilda R. Ellis, 'The Hoard of the Nibelungs', *Modern Language Review*,
XXXVII/4 (1942), pp. 466–79, p. 476. For a further discussion of *draugr* and
dragons, see Evans, '"As Rare As They Are Dire"', pp. 259–60.

46  Joyce Tally Lionarons, *The Medieval Dragon: The Nature of the Beast in
Germanic Literature* (Enfield Lock, Middlesex, 1998), p. 63; see also pp. 59
and 65.

47  Ibid., p. 68.

## 5 Dragons in Bestiaries and Celtic Mythology

1  For a discussion of the Anglo-Saxon bestiary *Liber monstrorum*, see
Chapter Three.

2  T. H. White, trans., *The Book of Beasts: Being a Bestiary from a Latin
Translation of the Twelfth Century* [1954] (Mineola, NY, 2009).

3  For a discussion of inscriptions and carvings influenced by bestiaries, see
J. Romilly Allen, 'Lecture VI: The Medieval Bestiaries', in *Early Christian*

*Symbolism in Great Britain and Ireland before the Thirteenth Century* (London, 1887), at http://bestiary.ca, accessed 22 September 2015.

4 White, trans., *The Book of Beasts*, pp. 14–15. The belief that dragons also fear the trees in which doves live, named here as the Indian 'Perindeus' fruit tree, is explained as the tree itself being God the Father and its shade God the Son, see pp. 159–60.

5 Ibid., pp. 165–7.

6 Ibid., pp. 170–73. For a discussion of Lilith, see Chapter Two.

7 For an examination of Viking influence on Celtic art and design, see Aidan Meehan, *Celtic Design: The Dragon and the Griffin, The Viking Impact* (London, 1995). For a history of the Viking presence in Ireland, see Martin Arnold, *The Vikings: Culture and Conquest* (London, 2006), Chs 4 and 5.

8 One name given to this fairy otherworld is Tír na nÓg (Land of Youth).

9 Fionn mac Cumhaill is named Fingal in James Macpherson's highly influential eighteenth-century fabrication of Scottish/Celtic mythology (1761–5).

10 Traditions that refer to heroes as having dragon qualities would suggest a pre-Christian view, whereas dragons that are seen as the most dangerous of beings suggests a post-conversion view of them.

11 A tale with a similar triumphant conclusion is told of Fionn's son, Conan, fighting his way out of the belly of the dragon Caoránach, which came to life in Lough Derg when the shin bones of Fionn's mother were cast into it. For the 'reborn' hero theory as applied to such encounters, see Chapter Four, concluding paragraphs. For the account of St Patrick's supposed combat with Caoránach, see Chapter Two.

12 See Eoin MacNeill, trans., *Duanaire Finn: The Book of the Lays of Fionn*, Part 1 (London, 1908), pp. 191–3.

13 See Standish Hayes O'Grady, trans., *The Colloquy with the Ancients* [1175–1200] (Whitefish, MT, n.d.), p. 65. The *Colloquy* was first set down in the twelfth century. In order to avoid confusion, personal names in the various sources have been standardized; thus Mesgedhra is given as Mesgegra and Conchobar as Conachar.

14 For the full account, see Whitley Stokes, trans., 'The Siege of Howth', *Revue Celtique*, VIII (Paris, 1887), pp. 47–64.

15 For the full account, see Eleanor Hull, trans., *The Cuchullin Saga in Irish Literature* (London, 1898), pp. 267–72.

16 The author also suggests that Conachar's rage might otherwise have been caused by the same news as delivered to him by 'Altus, the [Roman] Consul, who came from Octavius to demand tribute from the Gaels'. Ibid., pp. 271–2.

17 The earliest of a number of accounts of Fergus mac Léti's life is found in the *Senchas Már*, dating from the late seventh or early eighth century. The legend as told here draws on this and later versions: see Dáithi Ó hÓgáin, 'Fearghus mac Léide', in *The Lore of Ireland: An Encyclopedia of Myth, Legend and Romance* (Woodbridge, Suffolk, 2006), pp. 215–17, and D. A. Binchy, trans., 'The Saga of Fergus mac Léti', *Ériu*, XVI (1952), pp. 33–48.

18 The issue here is 'the law of distraint', in other words, the extent to which a landlord is entitled to seize property from those living on his land, just as Fergus does at the outset of the myth. See Neil McLeod, 'Fergus mac Léti and the Law', *Ériu*, LXI (2011), pp. 1–28. For the Indo-European analogues to this

myth, see Calvert Watkins, *How to Kill a Dragon: Aspects of Indo-European Poetics* (Oxford, 1995), Ch. 45, pp. 441–7.

19 For this account, see A. H. Leahy, ed. and trans., 'Tain Bo Fraich', in *Heroic Romances of Ireland*, vol. II (London, 1906), at www.sacred-texts.com, accessed 5 December 2015.

20 See J. F. Campbell, 'The Death of Fraoch', in *The Celtic Dragon Myth with the Geste of Fraoch* [1911], trans. and intro. George Henderson (Sioux Falls, SD, 2009), pp. 49–54.

21 In George Henderson's introduction to *The Celtic Dragon Myth*, p. 32, he notes the similarity of this to Greek myths, most evidently, he suggests, those versions of the myth of dragon-guarded golden apples of the Garden of the Hesperides in which Heracles himself picks the apples.

22 In Celtic mythology, the rowan tree was believed to be a tree of life, a *crann bethadh*, that was guarded by a green dragon and which signified a gateway between earth and the realm of the gods. By uprooting one, Fraoch could be regarded as having committed a sacrilege punishable by death. For a summary of the Gaelic teaching implied in the tree of life legend, see Henderson, *The Celtic Dragon Myth*, p. 49 n. 54.

23 Ibid., trans. of v. 24, p. 53.

24 There are, however, several Latin sources for a dragon tale involving the perhaps historical late fifth- or early sixth-century Welsh saint Samson of Dol, one of which is set in Cornwall. In this, Samson is said to have dragged an evil dragon from its cave and hurled it from a great height, so killing it. For the various sources, see Daniel Ogden, *Dragons, Serpents, and Slayers in the Classical and Early Christian Worlds: A Sourcebook* (Oxford, 2013), pp. 154–5.

25 Geoffrey's chief sources are believed to be Gildas, *De excidio et conquestu britanniae* (On the Ruin and Conquest of Britain), from the sixth century, and ascribed to Nennius, *Historia Brittonum*, from the ninth century. Among other possible sources are the poetry of the sixth-century Welsh bard Taliesin, Bede's eighth-century ecclesiastical history, and tenth-century Welsh annals and hagiographies. For an examination of Geoffrey's life and work, see John Jay Parry and Robert Caldwell, 'Geoffrey of Monmouth', in *Arthurian Literature in the Middle Ages: A Collaborative History*, ed. Roger Sherman Loomis (Oxford, 1959), pp. 72–93.

26 Merlin is clearly modelled on Myrddin, the wizard and prophet 'Wild Man of the Woods' figure who is alluded to in a number of early Welsh sources. For a discussion of the Myrddin legend, see A.O.H. Jarman, 'The Merlin Legend and the Welsh Tradition of Prophecy', in *The Arthur of the Welsh: The Arthurian Legend in Medieval Welsh Literature*, ed. Rachel Bromwich, A.O.H. Jarman and Brynley F. Roberts (Cardiff, 1991), pp. 117–45.

27 The following abridged account of Merlin's prophecy is drawn from Lewis Thorpe, trans., 'The Prophecies of Merlin', in *Geoffrey of Monmouth: The History of the Kings of Britain* (Harmondsworth, 1966), pp. 171–85.

28 A similar account concerning a fight between what are regarded as the same red and white dragons is told in the tale of the Welsh brothers Lludd and Llefelys in the *Mabinogion*. This is preserved in manuscripts from the twelfth and thirteenth centuries but rooted in much older oral traditions. See Gwyn Jones and Thomas Jones, trans., *The Mabinogion* (London, 1949), pp. 90–94.

29   Having triumphed in battle, Uther has two golden dragons made, one of
     which he carries into future battles. See Thorpe, trans., *Geoffrey of Monmouth*,
     pp. 200–202.
30   One curious and, indeed, unique case of a literary dragon being viewed in a
     positive light in the European Middle Ages can be found in one of Marie de
     France's late twelfth-century fables. In this tale, the actual villain of the piece is
     a man whom a dragon trusts to guard its egg-bound treasure, only to discover
     that he intended to crack open the egg, steal the treasure and kill it. See
     Mary Lou Martin, 'De dracone et homine', in *The Fables of Marie de France*
     (Birmingham, AL, 1984), pp. 146–9.

## 6 Asian and East Asian Dragons

 1   The generic distinctions of Chinese dragon tales are helpfully observed in
     Qiguang Zhao, *Asian Culture and Thought*, vol. XI: *A Study of Dragons, East
     and West* (New York, 1992), see esp. Ch. 1, 'Our Approaches to Dragonology',
     pp. 1–11.
 2   Ralph T. H. Griffith, trans., *Rig-Veda*, hymn XXXII (1896), at
     www.sacred-texts.com, accessed 8 July 2016.
 3   Tales about *nāgas* are present in mythologies throughout Southeast Asia.
 4   Kisara Mohan Ganguli, trans., *The Mahabharata*, Book 1, Section 20
     (1883–96), at www.sacred-texts.com, accessed 8 July 2016. Hereafter referred
     to as the *Mahabharata*.
 5   Cited in Marinus Willem de Visser, *The Dragon in China and Japan* [1913]
     (Miami, FL, 2007), p. 12.
 6   *Mahabharata*, Adi Parva, Sections 23–4, at www.sacred-texts.com.
 7   For this myth and further accounts of *nāga* myths from across Asia, see Doug
     Niles, *Dragons: The Myths, Legends, and Lore* (Avon, MA, 2013), pp. 87–111.
     See also Peter Hogarth and Val Clery, *Dragons* (London, 1979), pp. 42ff.
 8   Mani Vettam, *Puranic Encyclopaedia: A Comprehensive Dictionary with
     Special Reference to the Epic and Puranic Literature* (Delhi, 1975), pp. 97 and
     332. Ulupi's seduction of Arjuna is recounted in Book 1, Section 216, of the
     *Mahabharata*, at www.sacred-texts.com. Arjuna is instructed in the ways
     of selflessness by Krishna in the *Bhagavad Gita* section of the *Mahabharata*
     (Book 6, Sections 25–42).
 9   The Bodhi tree is referred to in the Mahavagga as the 'Royal tree' and the
     'Mucalinda tree'. Ānandajoti Bhikkhu, trans., 'The Great Chapter: Vin. Mv.
     1', www.ancient-buddhist-texts.net, accessed 22 July 2016. For the Mucalinda
     myth, see '1. The First Teachings', pp. 25–7, '3: The Story about the Mucalinda
     (Tree)'.
10   'III: The Miracles at Uruvelā', pp. 95–100, '21: The First Miracle (The Dragon-
     King – Prose)', and '22: The First Miracle (The Dragon-King – Verse)', ibid.
11   For a version of this myth, see J. P. Vogel, *Indian Serpent-lore: Or, The Nāgas
     in Hindu Legend and Art* [1927] (Whitefish, MT, 1972), pp. 121–2.
12   See Lihui Yang and Deming An, *Handbook of Chinese Mythology* (Oxford,
     2005), 'Yinglong', pp. 234–5. For other figures mentioned in this myth, see
     further entries in the *Handbook*.
13   Cited in de Visser, *The Dragon in China and Japan*, p. 70.

14 See Carol Rose, 'The Oriental Dragon', in *Giants, Monsters and Dragons: An Encyclopedia of Folklore, Legend, and Myth* (New York and London, 2000), pp. 279–80, p. 280.

15 For the legendary history of the dealings between Chinese emperors and dragons, see Yuan Ke, *Dragons and Dynasties: An Introduction to Chinese Mythology*, trans. Kim Echlin and Nie Zhixiong (London, 1993).

16 Cited in Roy Bates, *Chinese Dragons* (Oxford and New York, 2002), p. 20.

17 Cited in Richard Barber and Ann Riches, *A Dictionary of Fabulous Beasts* (London, 1971), p. 52.

18 Cited in de Visser, *The Dragon in China and Japan*, pp. 101–2.

19 Ibid., pp. 71–7.

20 For these and other uses of a dragon's anatomy, see Hogarth and Clery, *Dragons*, pp. 59–63. Hogarth and Clery suggest that 'dragon saliva' was most likely to have been the ambergris secretion of sperm whales, p. 63.

21 Cited in Jorge Luis Borges with Margarita Guerrero, *The Book of Imaginary Beings*, trans. Norman Thomas di Giovanni [*Manual de zoología fantástica*, 1957] (Harmondsworth, 1974), p. 43.

22 Other dragon types are the Dilong, the controller of rivers, lakes and seas; the Panlong, the lake dragon that has not ascended to heaven; the Huanglong, the yellow, hornless dragon symbolizing the emperor; the Feilong, the winged dragon that rides on clouds and mist; the Zhulong, the giant red solar deity that created day and night by opening and closing its eyes and created seasonal winds by breathing; and the Chilong, the hornless dragon or mountain demon. For a study of the names of dragons and their various functions, see Michael Carr, 'Chinese Dragon Names', in *Linguistics of the Tibeto-Burman Area*, XIII/2 (1990), pp. 87–189.

23 For further accounts of this tale and that of the boy and the pearl, below, see the following: Ash DeKirk, *Dragonlore: From the Archives of the Grey School of Wizardry* (Wayne, NJ, 2006), pp. 83–5, and Niles, *Dragons: The Myths, Legends, and Lore*, pp. 67–9 and pp. 71–2.

24 This sword, the Kusanagi, has the same legendary importance as King Arthur's sword Excalibur and is one of the Three Sacred Treasures of imperial Japan. For legends about the Kusanagi, see Donald A. MacKenzie, *Myths of China and Japan* (London, 1923), pp. 101–5.

25 Basil Hall Chamberlain, trans., *The Kojiki or 'Records of Ancient Matters'*, vol. 1, Section 18, 'The Eight-Forked Serpent', pp. 71–5 (1919), at www.sacred-texts.com, accessed 20 July 2016.

26 *Nihongi*, at www.hudsoncress.net/html/library.html, accessed 2 July 2017.

27 For this tale and the Mano Pond tale, below, see Niles, *Dragons: The Myths, Legends, and Lore*, pp. 82–5. These tales are online at http://dragonsaroundtheworld.weebly.com, accessed 20 July 2016, and at www.blackdrago.com, accessed 20 July 2016.

28 An early version of this folktale is given in Ueda Akinari, *Ugetsu Monogatari; or, Tales of Moonlight and Rain* [woodblock, 1776], trans. and ed. Leon M. Zolbrod (London, 1972), n. 490, p. 252.

29 This tale belongs to that type of Japanese evil spirit tales known as *yōkai*. For this account of Nure-onna, see the online database entry at http://yokai.com, accessed 26 July 2016.

30 See Norman Havens and Nobutaka Inoue, ed. and trans., *An Encyclopedia of Shinto (Shinto Jiten)* (Tokyo, 2006), p. 66.

31 The following version is based on the account of it given in the fifteenth-century folktale collection known as *Otogizōshi*. Numerous versions can be found online, for example, Yei Theodora Ozaki, *Japanese Fairy Tales* (New York, 1908), at www.surlalunefairytales.com/ebooksindex.html, accessed 2 July 2017. For an alternative published account, see Jonathan Evans, *Dragons: Myth and Legend* (London, 2008), pp. 28–35.

32 Dragon associations excepted, striking similarities between this tale and Celtic tale of the human hero Oisin (aka Ossian) travelling with the fairy queen Niamh to the supernatural realm of Tír na nÓg are noted in Idries Shah, *World Tales: The Extraordinary Coincidence of Stories Told in All Times, in All Places* (London, 1991), p. 359.

33 The centipede is known to be the creature that Asian and East Asian dragons fear most.

34 In the version of 'My Lord Bag of Rice', as recorded in the fourteenth-century collection *Taiheiki*, the hero's encounter is with a dragon king in the form of a small man. The account given here combines some of the descriptive elements of this version with the briefer dragon-woman version recounted by de Visser, *The Dragon in China and Japan*, pp. 191–2. For the dragon king version and many other such tales, see Ozaki, *Japanese Fairy Tales*.

35 For one of many Western critics who see such cultural contacts as a given, see Ernest Ingersoll, *Dragons and Dragon Lore: A Worldwide Study of Dragons in History, Art and Legend* [1928] (London, 2007), pp. 67–8. In personal correspondence with the Japanese historian Professor Kikuo Morita (Shukutoku University, Tokyo), he points out that Japanese experts, notably Professor Atsuhiko Yoshida (Gakushuin University, Tokyo), have remarked upon these similarities, albeit that firm conclusions are unlikely ever to be reached.

36 In fact, remnants of Chinese silk have been found in Egypt dating back to 1070 BC. Exactly how this came about is unknown but it may well suggest that East–West trading contact long pre-dated the Silk Road.

37 For an analysis of the impact of East Asian beliefs and philosophy on the West, see, for example, Shu Zeng, 'Love, Power and Resistance: Representations of Chinese–Caucasian Romance in Twentieth-century Anglophone Literature', PhD thesis, University of Hull (2016), Ch. 1, pp. 23–68. For an analysis of the reception history of Chinese culture in the West during the long eighteenth century, see Ros Ballaster, *Fabulous Orients: Fictions of the East in England, 1662–1785* (Oxford and New York, 2005), Ch. 4, pp. 193–53.

38 See Benjamin Colbert, ed., *The Travels of Marco Polo*, trans. William Marsden (Hertfordshire, 1997), Book 2, Ch. 40, pp. 151–2. That Samuel Taylor Coleridge's poem 'Kubla Khan; or, A Vision in a Dream: A Fragment' (1797) was inspired by the continuing popularity of Polo's travel writing indicates the measure of its cultural longevity and, one might add, accepted credibility. Coleridge read of Polo's description of Kublai Khan's palace in Samuel Purchas, *Purchas, His Pilgrimage; or, Relations of the World and the Religions, Observed in all Ages and Places Discovered, from the Creation unto This Present* (1613).

39 For a study of this phenomenon, see Norah M. Tilley, *Dragons in Persian, Mughal and Turkish Art* (London, 1981).

## 7 Dragons in the Anti-establishment Folktale

1 It goes without saying that there is a vast number of folktales involving dragons. In mainland Britain alone, almost two hundred such tales – or in many cases vestiges of tales – have been identified. See, for example, Ralph Whitlock, *Here Be Dragons* (London, 1983).

2 For a fuller account of this and other Slavic dragon tales, see Doug Niles, *Dragons: The Myths, Legends, and Lore* (Avon, MA, 2013), pp. 146–53.

3 There are many versions of this tale. The following account of it is based on those given by D. L. Ashliman: 'Dragon Slayers: An Index Page', at 'Folklore and Mythology: Electronic Texts', www.pitt.edu/~dash/folktexts.html, accessed 4 May 2015, and on an anonymous pamphlet of some antiquity, for which see Jacqueline Simpson, *British Dragons* [1980] (Ware, Herts, 2001), pp. 137–40. Ibid., pp. 141–2, for a regional dialect folksong recounting the legend, dating from the nineteenth century.

4 The term 'worm' is derived from the Old English noun *wyrm*, meaning 'reptile', 'serpent', 'snake' and 'dragon'.

5 Worm Hill, as it became known, is on the outskirts of the village of Fatfield near Sunderland, Tyne and Wear.

6 For the curious significance of milk in respect of tales concerning dragons/serpents, see Simpson, *British Dragons*, p. 39.

7 Two folktales with a number of similarities to that of the Lambton Worm are those of the Linton Worm, set in the Scottish Borders, and the Worm of Cnoc-na-Cnoimh, set in Sutherland. In these cases, the heroes slay the dragons using the 'Bel and Dragon' method (see below, 'The Wawel Dragon' and 'Assipattle and the Stoor Worm') and no curse ensues. For accounts of these folktales, see Daniel Ogden, *Dragons, Serpents, and Slayers in the Classical and Early Christian Worlds: A Sourcebook* (Oxford and New York, 2013), pp. 278–9.

8 For another tale of a dragon slaying that came back to Western Europe during the Crusades, see that of 'The Dragon of Rhodes' and its slayer Dieudonné de Gozon of Languedoc, as recounted in Niles, *Dragons: The Myths, Legends, and Lore*, pp. 144–5.

9 Simpson, *British Dragons*, pp. 65 and 123.

10 J. Dacres Devlin, *The Mordiford Dragon and Other Subjects* (London, 1848).

11 The wyvern was and still is the commonest dragon type to be found on heraldry and as mascots generally.

12 Simpson, *British Dragons*, p. 66.

13 A similar tale to that of the Mordiforn Wyvern, in which a dragon is dispatched by a man of low birth, one John Smith, is set in the ancient village of Deerhurst, near Tewksbury, Gloucestershire. However, in this tale the dragon slayer is rewarded with much land and there is no suggestion that the nobility is in any way culpable. See Simpson, *British Dragons*, pp. 66 and 78. A full account of this, which attempts to see a connection with Deerhurst's remarkable medieval history, can be found at www.information-britain.co.uk/loredetail.php?id=47, accessed 5 March 2016.

14  Simpson, *British Dragons*, p. 45.

15  Wincenty Kadłubek's account is recorded in his *Chronica seu originale regum et principum Poloniae* (Chronicle or Origin of the Kings and Princes of Poland). For a translation of this, see Ogden, *Dragons, Serpents, and Slayers*, pp. 275–6.

16  In some versions of the tale, Skuba eventually succeeds to the throne.

17  The following account combines those given in Walter Traill Dennison, 'Orkney Folklore: Sea Myths 3', *Scottish Antiquary*, v (1891), pp. 130–33, and Ernest Marwick, *The Folklore of Orkney and Shetland* (Edinburgh, 1974), pp. 139–44.

18  Dennison, 'Orkney Folklore', p. 133.

19  Tom Muir, 'Tales and Legends', in *The Orkney Book*, ed. Donald Omand (Edinburgh, 2003), pp. 240–47, p. 245.

20  James S. Stallybrass, trans., *Teutonic Mythology* [1883; from Jacob Grimm, *Deutsche Mythologie*, 1835], vol. III, 4th edn (Mineola, NY, 2004), p. xv. For Grimm's remarks on traditional Cinderella tales, see vol. IV, p. 388.

21  This anonymous ballad was first recorded in 1685 and was included in Thomas Percy's highly influential eighteenth-century collection *Reliques of Ancient English Poetry* (1765), available at www.exclassics.com, accessed 12 May 2015. For 'The Dragon of Wantley', see Book 4, Section 8. The poem is also reproduced in Simpson, *British Dragons*, pp. 146–50.

22  The ballad metaphorically describes the damage done to the locals by the Wortleys, wherein the obscure reference to 'Matthew's house' (verse 5, not cited here), an informant of Thomas Percy suggested, was 'a keeper to Mr Wortley' at Wharncliffe Lodge.

23  David Hey, *Yorkshire from AD 1000* (London and New York, 1986), pp. 123–4. Hey also notes the extravagant and, it seems, criminal lengths gone to by one Gilbert Dickenson, a steward of the nearby Lord of Hallamshire, in order to draw attention to the unprincipled Wortleys. Dickenson would appear to have been jailed for his actions but received a free pardon in 1605.

24  Percy suggests that 'If any one piece, more than other, is more particularly levelled at, it seems to be the old rhiming legend of Sir Bevis', or perhaps, Percy further suggests, that same Romance tale as mediated through Edmund Spencer's *Faerie Queen* (Book 1, Canto XI).

25  Simpson, *British Dragons*, p. 130.

## 8 European Dragons as Fictions and Facts: From Medieval Romance to the Nursery Dragon

1  The dragon episode and its context is recounted in chapters 11–14 of Gottfried's uncompleted *Tristan*. See Gottfried von Strassburg, *Tristan*, trans. A. T. Hatto (Harmondsworth, 1960), pp. 150–90.

2  Thomas of Britain's *Tristan* survives in eight fragments, most of which concern the latter part of the Tristan and Isolde tragedy.

3  For a discussion of this controversy, see Martin H. Jones, 'The Depiction of Military Conflict in Gottfried's *Tristan*', in *Gottfried von Strassburg and the Medieval Tristan Legend: Papers from an Anglo-North American Symposium*, ed. Adrian Stevens and Roy Wisbey (Woodbridge, Suffolk, 1990), pp. 45–66.

4  For a consideration of the possible origins of the Tristan legend, see Ronan
   Coghlan, *The Encyclopaedia of Arthurian Legends* (Shaftesbury, Dorset, 1991),
   pp. 206–9.

5  J. J. Anderson, ed., *Sir Gawain and the Green Knight, Pearl, Cleanness, Patience*
   (London, 1996), p. 197.

6  For a synopsis of 'Bevis of Hampton' followed by the complete Middle
   English poem, see Ronald B. Herzman, Graham Drake and Eve Salisbury,
   eds, *Four Romances of England* (Kalamazoo, MI, 1999), pp. 187–340.

7  'Bevis of Hampton', ll. 2658–92, ibid., pp. 271–7. Bevis is believed to have been
   a real historical figure. In his case, there is no association with King Arthur. For
   a discussion of medieval literature concerning medieval knights and dragons,
   see the following: Thomas Honegger, 'A Good Dragon is Hard to Find:
   From *Draconitas* to *Draco*', in *Good Dragons are Rare: An Inquiry into Literary
   Dragons East and West*, ed. Fanfan Chen and Thomas Honegger (Frankfurt,
   2009), pp. 27–59, esp. pp. 31–3, and Thomas Honegger, '*Draco litterarius*: Some
   Thoughts on an Imaginary Beast', in *Tiere und Fabelwesen im Mittelalter*, ed.
   Sabine Obermaier (Berlin and New York, 2009), pp. 133–45, esp. pp. 135–41.

8  For 'Sir Eglamour of Artois', see Harriet Hudson, ed., *Four Middle English
   Romances* (Kalamazoo, MI, 1996), at http://d.lib.rochester.edu/teams,
   accessed 12 April 2016. For *Sir Degaré*, see Walter Hoyt French and Charles
   Brockway Hale, eds, *The Middle English Metrical Romances*, 2 vols [1930]
   (New York, 1964), vol. I, pp. 287–320. A similarly much-travelled knight-hero
   is told of in the Romance of Guy of Warwick, who during one his journeys
   intervenes to rescue a lion from a dragon that is attacking it. The tale is
   recounted in French and English versions dating from the thirteenth to the
   seventeenth century; see, for example, William B.D.D. Turnbull, ed., *The
   Romances of Sir Guy of Warwick, and Rembrun his Son* (Edinburgh, 1840).

9  Lancelot's dragon fights and the dragon/leopard symbolism are chiefly
   recorded in the thirteenth-century *Prose Lancelot* section of the Vulgate Cycle
   and in Thomas Malory's *Le Morte d'Arthur*, which was composed in the mid-
   fifteenth century. For a helpful collection of essays examining the complexities
   of the sources for tales of King Arthur and the Knights of the Round Table,
   see Roger Sherman Loomis, *Arthurian Literature in the Middle Ages:
   A Collaborative History* (Oxford, 1959).

10 For this tale and an analysis of its subsequent variants and possible origins by
   the nineteenth-century English folklorist Sabine Baring-Gould in his *Curious
   Myths of the Middle Ages* (1866), see John Matthews, ed., *Myths of the Middle
   Ages: Sabine Baring-Gould* (London, 1996), Ch. 8, 'Melusine', pp. 76–95.
   A full version of this tale is available online at www.sacred-texts.com,
   accessed 20 April 2016.

11 For an analysis of Melusine in respect of female otherness, see Amy A.
   O. Lambert, 'Morgan le Fay and Other Women: A Study of the Female
   Phantasm in Medieval Literature', PhD thesis, University of Hull (2016),
   Ch. 4, pp. 156–90, esp. pp. 162–9.

12 John Mandeville, *The Travels of Sir John Mandeville* [1357–71], Ch, 4, at
   www.gutenberg.org, accessed 21 April 2016.

13 Based, at least in part, on Jean d'Arras' *Roman* is the poem by Couldrette, who
   in the early fifteenth century retold the Melusine story as part of his ladies'

'spinning yarns': see Matthew W. Morris, 'Introduction' to *A Bilingual Edition of Couldrette's 'Melusine', or, 'Le Roman de Parthenay', Mediaeval Studies*, xx (Lewiston, NY, 2003). For a discussion of Jean d'Arras' historical motivations, see Daisy Delogu, 'Jean d'Arras Makes History: Political Legitimacy and the *Roman de Mélusine', Dalhousie French Studies*, LXXX (2007), pp. 15–28.

14  The English folktales of the 'Nursery bogy' child-killing dragon-woman, such as Jenny Greenteeth, whose lair lies beneath ponds or pools covered in green slime in Lancashire, and Peg Powler, who inhabits the River Tees in the northeast of the country, may also be derived from the Lamia/Melusine legends. For accounts of these folktales, see the relevant entries in Carol Rose, *Giants, Monsters and Dragons: An Encyclopedia of Folklore, Legend, and Myth* (New York and London, 2000), pp. 194 and 288, respectively. For the entry on worldwide 'Nursery Bogies', see p. 271.

15  For ten folktale versions translated by the folklorist D. L. Ashliman, visit 'Melusina (Mélusine, Melusine)', at 'Folklore and Mythology: Electronic Texts', www.pitt.edu/~dash/folktexts.html, accessed 2 July 2017. For Jean d'Aras' full tale, see Donald Maddox and Sara Sturm-Maddox, trans. and eds, *Melusine; or, The Noble History of Lusignan* (University Park, PA, 2012).

16  For a discussion of Spenser's likely classical sources for the dragon-woman, see Douglas Brookes-Davies, *Spenser's 'Faerie Queene': A Critical Commentary on Books I and II* (Manchester, 1977), p. 19.

17  See A. C. Hamilton, ed., *Spenser: The Faerie Queene* (London and New York, 1977).

18  This seven-headed 'Gyant', known as Orgoglio (Pride), which features in Book I, Cantos vii and viii, has a number of draconic features and is clearly referencing both the Satan dragon of Revelation and Heracles' battle against the Lernaean Hydra. For a discussion of Orgoglio, the two dragons discussed here that are named as such and the dragon-like Geryoneo of Book 5, Canto x, which is said to be the of son Geryon, who also was slain by Heracles, see Maik Goth, 'Spenser's Dragons', in *Good Dragons are Rare*, ed. Chen and Honegger, pp. 97–117.

19  Elizabeth Heale, *The Faerie Queene: A Reader's Guide*, 2nd edn (Cambridge, 1999), p. 42.

20  The similarity here to the healing waters that cured Bevis of Hampton during his dragon fight is no coincidence.

21  A precedent for and likely influence on Spenser's dragons is *The Example of Virtue*, an early sixteenth-century poem by Stephen Hawes. In this, the dragon has three heads, signifying the World, the Flesh and the Devil. For a discussion of this poem, see C. S. Lewis, *The Allegory of Love: A Study in Medieval Tradition* [1936] (Oxford and New York, 1958), pp. 285–7.

22  Elizabeth Ely Fuller, *Milton's Kinesthetic Vision in Paradise Lost* (Lewisburg, PA, 1983), p. 51.

23  One such would be Marie Catherine d'Aulnoy's 'love conquers all' parable *Serpentin Vert (The Green Serpent)* of 1698, the inspiration for which was the Greek myth of Eros and Psyche. Translation available at 'Green Serpent', www.surlalunefairytales.com/authors/daulnoy.html, accessed 2 July 2017.

24  See the following: Alixe Bovey, *Monsters and the Grotesques in Medieval Manuscripts* (London, 2002), Chet Van Duzer, *Sea Monsters on Medieval*

*and Renaissance Maps* (London, 2013), and Damien Kempf and Maria L. Gilbert, *Medieval Monsters* (London, 2015). For a detailed discussion of representations and ideas about sea dragons, see Thomas Honegger, 'The Sea-dragon: In Search of an Elusive Creature', in *Symbolik des Wassers in der Mittelalterlichen Kultur*, ed. Gerlinde Huber-Rebenich et al. (Berlin, 2017), pp. 521–31.

25  Van Duzer, *Sea Monsters on Medieval and Renaissance Maps*, p. 90.
26  Honegger, 'The Sea-dragon', p. 525.
27  For an image of this map scene, see Van Duzer, *Sea Monsters on Medieval and Renaissance Maps*, fig. 30, p. 52.
28  Ibid., p. 116.
29  Cited in Peter Hogarth and Val Clery, *Dragons* (London, 1979), p. 169. For Hogarth and Cleary's detailed consideration of the science of dragons from the Renaissance to the late eighteenth century, to which much of this section is indebted, see pp. 164–87.
30  Ibid., p. 177.
31  For the above extracts and others from Kircher's *Mundus subterraneus*, see Anne E. G. Nydam's helpful online blog: 'Kircher's Dragons', http://nydamprintsblackandwhite.blogspot.co.uk, accessed 24 July 2012.
32  Although Linnaeus lists Draco is his classificatory scheme *Regnum animale* (1735) under the catch-all heading 'Paradoxa', his intention would appear to have been to debunk the dragon myth. The *Regnum animale* can be viewed at https://commons.wikimedia.org, accessed 2 August 2016. In his two-volume *Systema naturae* (1758 and 1759), Draco is listed as signifying nothing more than 'gliding lizard'.
33  An amusingly straight-faced, 'scientific' study of contemporary dragon sightings, focussing on the conclusions reached by 'verminologists' about their origins, habits, anatomy and dangers, is Pamela Wharton Blanpied, *Dragons: The Modern Infestation* (Woodbridge, Suffolk, 1980).
34  For a discussion of this, see Martin Arnold, 'On the Origins of the Gothic Novel: From Old Norse to Otranto', in *Bram Stoker and the Gothic: Formations and Transformations*, ed. Catherine Wynne (Basingstoke, 2016), pp. 14–29.
35  Thomas Pynchon's postmodern novel *Mason and Dixon* (1997) also recounts the Lambton Worm tale (Episode 60).
36  For Keats's 'Lamia' with Burton's Lamia anecdote appended, see, for example, John Keats, *Keats's Poetry and Prose*, ed. Jeffrey N. Cox (New York and London, 2009), pp. 412–29.
37  Keats, 'Lamia', Part 1, ll. 47–53, in Keats, *Keats's Poetry and Prose*, p. 414. For an analysis of Keats 'Lamia', see 'John Keats's "Lamia" (1819)', at Feminism and Women's Studies, www.feminism.eserver.org, accessed 1 August 2016.
38  In 1869 Elizabeth Barrett Browning, in her nine-book epic *Aurora Leigh* (1856), mentions Lamia several times in a metaphorical sense as a negative portrayal of women. A more positive view of Lilith is delivered by Robert Browning in his poem 'Adam, Lilith and Eve' (1883), where Lilith is less demonic and more an emotionally fraught lover of Adam.
39  For an analysis of this scene, see '"Walpurgis Night" Scene of Goethe's "Faust, Part 1" (1808)', at Feminism and Women's Studies, www.feminism.eserver.org, accessed 1 August 2016.

40 For the full 'Body's Beauty', visit www.poeticous.com, accessed 1 August 2016.

41 For the full 'Eden Bower', visit www.poemhunter.com, accessed 1 August 2016.

42 The water-retaining dragon has no precedent in Western mythologies. Coincidental although it may well be, one cannot help noticing that it is strongly reminiscent of certain dragons in Asian and East Asian mythologies (see Chapter Six).

43 For a discussion of the repeated trafficking of Vane through the portal between this world and the otherworld, see Tom Shippey, 'Liminality and the Everyday in *Lilith*', in *Lilith in a New Light*, ed. Lucas D. Harriman (Jefferson, NC, and London, 2008), pp. 15–20.

44 See, for example, William Gray, 'The Angel in the House of Death: Gender and Subjectivity in George MacDonald's *Lilith*', in *Death and Fantasy: Essays on Philip Pullman, C. S. Lewis, George MacDonald and R. L. Stevenson* (Newcastle upon Tyne, 2008), pp. 25–42.

45 C. S. Lewis, *The Lion, The Witch and the Wardrobe* [1950] (London, 2009), Ch. 8, pp. 90–91.

46 Lewis Carroll, *Alice Through the Looking-glass, and What She Found There* (London and Boston, MA, 2009), 'Jabberwocky', Ch. 1, p. 29.

47 Kenneth Grahame, *The Reluctant Dragon* [1898] (London, 2008).

48 Local legend tells that St George fought a dragon on the Berkshire Downs (now reclassified as in Oxfordshire) near Uffington: see Jaqueline Simpson, *British Dragons* [1980] (Ware, Herts, 2001), p. 54. For a discussion of the St George myth in English folklore, see Chapter Two of this volume, the section on 'Saints' lives'.

49 Peter Green, *Kenneth Grahame: A Biography* (London, 1959), pp. 182–3.

50 J.R.R. Tolkien, *The Monsters and the Critics and Other Essays*, ed. Christopher Tolkien (London, 1997), p. 17.

## 9 The Old Dragon Revives: J.R.R. Tolkien and C. S. Lewis

1 For all quotations, see Mal Peet, *The Murdstone Trilogy* [2014] (Oxford, 2015), pp. 13–21.

2 George R. R. Martin, 'Introduction' to *Meditations on Middle-earth*, ed. Karen Haber (New York, 2001), pp. 1–5, p. 5.

3 Tolkien's lecture has been reprinted several times and is cited here from the collection J.R.R. Tolkien, *The Monsters and the Critics and Other Essays*, ed. Christopher Tolkien (London, 1997), pp. 5–48, p. 16. By the 'men not ignorant of tragic legend' Tolkien meant men like himself and C. S. Lewis; and the 'heroes' they had seen were their comrades of the First World War, both Lewis and Tolkien being infantry combat veterans of that war.

4 Ibid., p. 12. For accounts of the plots and significances of the dragons in *Beowulf* and the *Saga of the Völsungs*, see chapters Three and Four, respectively. See Chapter Three, note 32, for the possibility that the *Beowulf* dragon did indeed have a name.

5 Tolkien said this was 'not [done] consciously': see Douglas Anderson, *The Annotated Hobbit* (London, 1988), Ch. 12, note 2, p. 228.

6 All page numbers for quotations from *The Hobbit* are from J.R.R. Tolkien, *The Hobbit, or There and Back Again* (London, 1995).

7 The name Smaug is taken from the past tense of the old Germanic verb *smugan*, 'to squeeze through a hole'. In Old English and Old Norse variants of *smugan*, it also carries meanings associated with magic and craftiness. See Tom Shippey, *The Road to Middle-earth*, 4th revd edn (London, 2005), p. 102.

8 'The Lay of Fáfnir', prose interjection between verses 1 and 2: author's own translation from Finnur Jónsson, *Sæmundar-Edda: Eddukvæði* (Reykjavík, 1926), *Fáfnismál*, pp. 294–306, p. 294. For a full translation of this poem, see Carolyne Larrington, trans., *The Poetic Edda* (Oxford, 1999), pp. 157–65.

9 See Jesse L. Byock, trans., *The Saga of the Volsungs: The Norse Epic of Sigurd the Dragon Slayer* (Harmondsworth, 2000), p. 66; Tolkien's biographer notes that Tolkien had initially intended that Bilbo would kill Smaug but later thought it too unlikely an act for this character: see Humphrey Carpenter, *J.R.R. Tolkien: A Biography* [1977] (London, 2002), Part 5, Ch. 1, p. 239. Understanding the language of birds is also part of the Sigurd and Fáfnir scene.

10 This was said by Tolkien in a radio interview of 1965. Cited in Thomas Honegger, 'A Good Dragon is Hard to Find: From *Draconitas* to *Draco*', in *Good Dragons are Rare: An Inquiry into Literary Dragons East and West*, ed. Fanfan Chen and Thomas Honegger (Frankfurt, 2009), pp. 27–59, p. 30.

11 Honegger, 'A Good Dragon is Hard to Find', p. 48.

12 For this and the previous quotation, see Tolkien, '*Beowulf*: The Monsters and the Critics' in Tolkien, *The Monsters and the Critics*, ed. C. Tolkien, p. 17.

13 See Honegger, 'A Good Dragon is Hard to Find', and Shippey, *The Road to Middle-earth*, p. 104.

14 The poem's publishing history is given in T. A. Shippey, 'The Versions of "The Hoard"', *Lembas*, 100 (2001), pp. 3–7. For the poem, see J.R.R. Tolkien, 'The Adventures of Tom Bombadil', in *Tales from the Perilous Realm* (London, 2008), pp. 228–31.

15 All page numbers in the text are taken from 'Farmer Giles of Ham', in Tolkien, *Tales from the Perilous Realm*, pp. 99–165.

16 For a discussion of the plot significances of Tolkien's witty philological pedantry, see Shippey, *The Road to Middle-earth* (2005), pp. 111–14.

17 For a consideration of hagiographic motifs in the tale, see Honegger, 'A Good Dragon is Hard to Find', pp. 49–53.

18 'The Dragon's Visit' was first published in *The Oxford Magazine*, LV/11 (1937), available at 'Feature: "The Dragon's Visit" by J.R.R. Tolkien', www. twilightswarden.wordpress.com, accessed 13 November 2016.

19 As noted by Honegger, 'A Good Dragon is Hard to Find', p. 38, in the 1961 version, the green dragon is slain by the sole survivor, Miss Biggins.

20 Carpenter, *J.R.R. Tolkien: A Biography*, Part 3, Ch. 1, p. 125.

21 The exception is Scatha the Worm, who is mentioned in passing towards the end of *The Lord of the Rings* and is noted as having been slain by the Rohan warrior Fram in Appendix A: see J.R.R. Tolkien, *The Lord of the Rings* (Boston, MA, and New York, 2004), pp. 978 and 1064–5.

22 J.R.R. Tolkien, *The Silmarillion*, ed. Christopher Tolkien (London, 2008). In Tolkien's children's tale *Roverandom* (written 1927; published posthumously

in 1998), the canine hero, initially known as Rover, is pursued around the moon by the Great White Dragon. Critics have noted light-hearted similarities in *Roverandom* to aspects of *The Silmarillion*: see Wayne G. Hammond and Christina Scull, eds, *The Lord of the Rings: A Reader's Companion* (London, 2005), p. lxxii. For *Roverandom*, see Tolkien, *Tales from the Perilous Realm* (London, 2008), pp. 1–97.

23 Mentioned only briefly is the largest of Tolkien's dragons, the winged monster Ancalagon the Black, who along with 'well-nigh all the dragons' is slain by Eärendil: Tolkien, *The Silmarillion*, Ch. 24, 'On the Voyage of Eärendil and The War of Wrath', pp. 295–306, pp. 302–3.

24 For the following two battles, see Tolkien, *The Silmarillion*', Ch. 18, 'Of the Ruin of Beleriand and the Fall of Fingolfin', pp. 174–88, and Ch. 20, 'Of the Fifth Battle: Nirnaeth Arnoediad', pp. 222–34.

25 Tolkien, *The Silmarillion*, Ch. 21, 'Of Túrin Turambar', pp. 235–71, p. 271.

26 For a discussion of Tolkien's Middle-earth dragons, see Jonathan Evans, 'The Dragon-lore of Middle-earth: Tolkien and Old English and Old Norse Tradition', in *J.R.R. Tolkien and His Literary Resonances: Views of Middle-earth*, ed. George Clark and Daniel Timmons (Westport, CT, and London, 2000), pp. 21–38.

27 Tolkien, '*Beowulf*: The Monsters and the Critics', p. 16.

28 We can be sure of this because Tolkien actually quoted his own poem and Lewis's 'The Northern Dragon' in his draft for the lecture, see Michael D. C. Drout, *Beowulf and the Critics by J.R.R. Tolkien* (Tempe, AZ, 2002), pp. 56–8. They are not referenced in the published version of the lecture.

29 Tolkien, however, was deeply disappointed that Lewis did not convert to Catholicism.

30 C. S. Lewis, *The Pilgrim's Regress: An Allegorical Apology for Christianity, Reason, and Romanticism* (London, 1933), available at 'The Pilgrim's Regress', www.fadedpage.com, accessed 1 August 2016.

31 For both these poems, later known respectively as 'The Dragon Speaks' and 'The Dragon Slayer', see ibid., Book 10, Chs 8 and 9.

32 C. S. Lewis, *The Voyage of the Dawn Treader* [1952] (London, 1970). For the Eustace-dragon episode, see Chs 6 and 7, pp. 90–121.

33 Carpenter, *J.R.R. Tolkien: A Biography*, Part 5, Ch. 2, p. 268.


## 10 'A Wilderness of Dragons'

1 The phrase 'wilderness of dragons' was used critically of *Beowulf* by R. W. Chambers in his *Widsith: A Study in Old English Heroic Legend*, which is cited deprecatingly by Tolkien: see J.R.R. Tolkien, *The Monsters and the Critics and Other Essays*, ed. Christopher Tolkien (London, 1997), pp. 11–12. Here, it simply means a great many of them.

2 Among many such early studies are Marinus Willem de Visser's *The Dragon in China and Japan* (1913), Donald A. MacKenzie's *Myths of China and Japan* (1923) and Ernest Ingersoll's *Dragons and Dragon Lore* (1928).

3 Later Earthsea novels include *Tehanu* (1990) and *The Other Wind* (2001).

4 Ursula Le Guin, *A Wizard of Earthsea*, Ch. 4: 'The Loosing of the Shadow', in *Earthsea* (London, 1977), pp. 62–102, esp. pp. 98–102.

5  For a *Guardian* newspaper interview with Le Guin in which she discusses the counter-culture politics and values in her work, see 'Chronicles of Earthsea' (Ursula Le Guin Q&A), www.theguardian.com, 9 February 2004.

6  The series actually began with McCaffrey's novelette *Weyr Search*, which was published in the sci-fi magazine *Analog* (October 1967), pp. 8–60, then the following year incorporated into *Dragonflight*. Anne McCaffrey wrote all the Pern novels until 2003, after which she co-authored them with her son Todd, who continued the series after Anne's death in 2011.

7  This demythologizing of the Pern dragon is noted by Thomas Honegger, 'A Good Dragon is Hard to Find: From *Draconitas* to *Draco*', in *Good Dragons are Rare: An Inquiry into Literary Dragons East and West*, ed. Fanfan Chen and Thomas Honegger (Frankfurt, 2009), pp. 27–59, p. 54.

8  *The Dragon and the George* is based on Dickson's novelette of the same name published in 1957.

9  Further accounts of Jim and Angie's adventures are given in numerous sequels, beginning with *The Dragon Knight* (1990).

10  In the German original, Falkor is named 'Fuchur', a derivation of the Japanese 'Fukuryū' meaning 'lucky dragon'. Whether meant or not, the irony here is that 'Fukuryū' is best known in the West as the name of the Japanese fishing boat whose crew suffered radioactive contamination from the thermonuclear detonation on Bikini Atoll in 1954.

11  Nick Gevers, 'The Literary Alchemist: An Interview with Michael Swanwick' (1999), www.infinityplus.co.uk/nonfiction/intms.htm, accessed 14 August 2016.

12  This tale, written by Pratchett when he was still quite young, is included in the collection of the same name, which was not published until 2014.

13  Honegger, 'A Good Dragon is Hard to Find', p. 41. Honegger goes on to compare Paolini's fantasies with Barbara Hambly's 'more successful creation of dragon-characters' in her Winterlands novels: *Dragonsbane* (1985), *Dragonshadow* (1999), *Knight of the Demon Queen* (2000) and *Dragonstar* (2002).

14  As has been noted by critics, Harris mistakenly cites Blake's painting as *The Great Red Dragon and the Woman Clothed with the Sun* (c. 1805–10, Brooklyn Museum, New York) while actually describing the version titled above (c. 1803, National Gallery of Art, Washington, DC).

15  A fourth book in the series, *The Girl in the Spider's Web* (2015), was written by David Lagercrantz.

16  For an online lecture by Tom Shippey in which he analyses Lisbeth Salander's character and behaviour and to which this section is much indebted, see 'Lisbeth Salander: Avenging Female Fury', www.thegreatcoursesplus.com, accessed 12 February 2017.

17  For an analysis of cinematic dragons, Thomas Honegger, 'From Bestiary onto Screen: Dragons in Film', in *Fact and Fiction: From the Middle Ages to Modern Times. Essays Presented to Hans Sauer on the Occasion of his 65th Birthday*, ed. Renate Bauer and Ulrike Krischke, Texte und Untersuchungen zur Englischen Philologie 37 (Frankfurt, 2011), pp. 197–215. For Honegger's online lecture 'From Fafner to Smaug: Dragons on the Silver Screen', visit www.lecture2go.uni-hamburg.de, 10 July 2015.

18  Grendel was also portrayed as the son of Hrothgar and Grendel's mother in
    the movie *Beowulf* directed by Graham Baker in 1999. No dragon features in
    this retelling.

19  For a review of the film suggesting that it is 'satirical', see Roger Ebert, '*Beowulf*,
    www.rogerebert.com, 14 November 2007.

20  For a description of RPGs, particularly *Dungeons & Dragons*, see Doug Niles,
    *Dragons: The Myths, Legends, and Lore* (Avon, MA, 2013), pp. 193–216.

21  For a relatively early argument about RPGs as therapy, see John Hughes,
    *Therapy is Fantasy: Roleplaying, Healing and the Construction of Symbolic Order*
    (1988), at www.rpgstudies.net, accessed 23 August 2016.

## 11 George R. R. Martin's Dragons and the Question of Power

1   Despite certain discrepancies in plots and characterizations, the term 'Martin's
    dragons' is used throughout this chapter to apply to the dragons in both the
    books and television adaptations of them. The obvious point here is that there
    would be no *Game of Thrones* without Martin's books, let alone the fact that
    he has acted as consultant throughout the TV series and as the scriptwriter for
    several episodes. The chief scriptwriters for the TV seasons are David Benioff
    and Dan Weiss; the other scriptwriters include Bryan Cogman, Dave Hill,
    Jane Espenson and Vanessa Taylor.

2   Alison Flood, 'George R. R. Martin Revolutionised How People Think about
    Fantasy', *The Guardian*, 10 April 2015, www.theguardian.com.

3   George R. R. Martin, 'The Way of the Cross and Dragon (1978)', in *The
    Oxford Book of Science Fiction Stories*, ed. Tom Shippey (Oxford and New
    York, 1993), pp. 454–71; and George R. R. Martin, *The Ice Dragon*, with
    illustrations by Luis Royd [1980] (New York, 2014).

4   George R. R. Martin, Elio M. García Jr and Linda Antonsson, and various
    artists, *The World of Ice and Fire: The Untold History of Westeros and the
    Game of Thrones* (London, 2014), and George R. R. Martin, 'The Princess
    and the Queen, or, The Blacks and the Greens', in *Dangerous Women*,
    ed. George R. R. Martin and Gardner Dozois (New York, 2013),
    pp. 703–84.

5   For what follows here, see Martin, García and Antonsson, *The World of Ice
    and Fire*, pp. 13 and pp. 26–7.

6   Martin, 'The Princess and the Queen', p. 712.

7   Ibid., p. 711. In this she resembles Daenerys; see below. Targaryen children
    carry dragon eggs around with them, presumably in the hope of achieving
    pre-hatch bonding. As said above, maybe this works both ways. Dragons
    and dragon eggs should be kept at a distance, then, during pregnancy – a
    precaution Daenerys does not observe.

8   References to the texts of the *A Song of Ice and Fire* series are by volume
    number and page. The reference given here as vol. 1 is to George R. R. Martin,
    *A Game of Thrones* [1996] (London, 2011).

9   In season 1, episode 1 of the TV series it has become 'the ages have turned them
    to stone'. This is mentioned only to indicate that the book and TV versions
    do not always agree; in fact they increasingly differ, and over more important
    issues than this one.

10 Before that she had similarly stepped into a bath which was much too hot, according to the cry of warning from her maid, but Daenerys does not feel the heat.

11 In the TV version (season 1, episode 1) her hair is unaffected by the fire, presumably in order to make for a more glamorous Daenerys.

12 The harpy is the presiding icon of Meereen, a female figure with four limbs again: two legs, two wings.

13 Jessica Salter, 'Game of Thrones's George R. R. Martin: "I'm a Feminist at Heart"' ( interview with Martin), The Telegraph, 1 April 2013, www.telegraph.co.uk.

14 Ibid.; Nussbaum cited ibid.

15 George R. R. Martin, A Dance with Dragons (London, 2012), p. 185.


## Conclusion: The Dragon and Fear

1 Sigmund Freud, The Future of an Illusion, in Civilisation, Society and Religion (Penguin Freud Library, vol. XII), ed. Albert Dickson, trans. James Strachey (London and New York, 1991), pp. 181–241, p. 189.

2 For this and the previous quote, see ibid., p. 191.

# BIBLIOGRAPHY

Primary sources

Anderson, J. J., ed., *Sir Gawain and the Green Knight, Pearl, Cleanness, Patience* (London, 1996)

Ashliman, D. L., 'Folklore and Mythology: Electronic Texts', www.pitt.edu/~dash/folktexts.html, accessed 3 June 2017

d'Aulnoy, Marie Catherine, *Serpentin Vert/The Green Serpent* (1698), at www.surlalunefairytales.com/authors/daulnoy.html, accessed 3 June 2017

Bede, *A History of the English Church and People*, trans. Leo Sherley-Price, revd R. E. Latham (Harmondsworth, 1968)

Bhikkhu, Ānandajoti, trans., *The Mahavagga*, at 'The Great Chapter', www.ancient-buddhist-texts.net, accessed 3 June 2017

Binchy, D. A., trans., 'The Saga of Fergus mac Léti', *Ériu*, XVI (1952), pp. 33–48

Blake, N. F., trans., *The Saga of the Jomsvikings* (London, 1962), at http://vsnr-web-publications.org.uk, accessed 3 June 2017

Byock, Jesse L., trans., *The Saga of the Volsungs: The Norse Epic of Sigurd the Dragon Slayer* (Harmondsworth, 2000)

Campbell, J. F., trans. and intro. George Henderson, *The Celtic Dragon Myth with the Geste of Fraoch* [1911] (Sioux Falls, SD, 2009), pp. 49–54

Cardew, Philip Westbury, *A Translation of 'Þorskfirðinga (Gull-Þóris) saga'* (Lampeter, 2000)

Carroll, Lewis, *Alice Through the Looking-glass, and What She Found There* (London and Boston, MA, 2009)

Chamberlain, Basil Hall, trans., *The Kojiki* (1919), at www.sacred-texts.com, accessed 3 June 2017

Cowell, Cressida, *How to Train Your Dragon* (London, 2003)

Davidson, Avram, *Rogue Dragon* (New York, 1965)

Davidson, Hilda Ellis, ed., and Peter Fisher, trans., *Saxo Grammaticus: The History of the Danes*, Books I–IX (Cambridge, 1998)

Dickson, Gordon R., *The Dragon and the George* (New York, 1976)

Donaldson, Julia, *Zog* (London, 2010)

Ende, Michael, *The Neverending Story* [1979], trans. Ralph Manheim (New York, 1983)

Finch, R. G., ed. and trans., *The Saga of the Volsungs* (Edinburgh, 1965)

Flood, Alison, 'George R. R. Martin Revolutionised How People Think about Fantasy', *The Guardian*, 10 April 2015, www.theguardian.com

French, Walter Hoyt, and Charles Brockway Hale, eds, *The Middle English Metrical Romances*, 2 vols [1930] (New York, 1964)

Ganguli, Kisara Mohan, trans., *The Mahabharata* (1883–96), at www.sacred-texts.com, accessed 3 June 2017

Gevers, Nick, 'The Literary Alchemist: An Interview with Michael Swanwick' (1999), at www.infinityplus.co.uk/nonfiction/features.htm, accessed 3 June 2017

Gordon, R. K., trans., *Anglo-Saxon Poetry* (London, 1967)

Gottfried von Strassburg, *Tristan*, trans. A. T. Hatto (Harmondsworth, 1960)

Grahame, Kenneth, *The Reluctant Dragon* [1898] (London, 2008)

Griffith, Ralph T. H., trans., *Rig-Veda* (1896), at www.sacred-texts.com, accessed 3 June 2017

Hamer, Richard, trans., *A Choice of Anglo-Saxon Verse* (London and Boston, MA, 1970)

Hamilton, A. C., ed., *Spenser: The Faerie Queene* (London and New York, 1977)

Hard, Robin, trans., *Apollodorus: The Library of Greek Mythology* (Oxford and New York, 2008)

Harris, Thomas, *Red Dragon* (New York, 1981)

Hatto, A. T., trans., *The Nibelungenlied* (Harmondsworth, 1969)

Haymes, Edward R., trans., *The Saga of Thidrek of Bern* (New York, 1988)

Herzman, Ronald B., Graham Drake and Eve Salisbury, eds, *Four Romances of England* (Kalamazoo, MI, 1999)

Hesiod, *'Theogony' and 'Works and Days'*, trans. M. L. West (Oxford and New York, 2008)

Homer, *The Iliad*, trans. Martin Hammond (London and New York, 1987)

—, *The Odyssey*, trans. Martin Hammond (London, 2013)

Hudson, Harriet, *Four Middle English Romances* (Kalamazoo, MI, 1996), at http://d.lib.rochester.edu/teams, accessed 3 June 2017

Hull, Eleanor, trans., *The Cuchullin Saga in Irish Literature* (London, 1898)

Jacobus de Voragine, *The Golden Legend: Readings on the Saints*, trans. William Granger Ryan, 2 vols (Princeton, NJ, 1993)

James, M. R., trans., 'The Gospel of Bartholomew' (1924), at http://www.gnosis.org/library.html, accessed 3 June 2017

Jones, Gwyn, and Thomas Jones, *The Mabinogion* (London, 1949)

Jónsson, Finnur, *Sæmundar-Edda: Eddukvæði* (Reykjavík, 1926)

Jónsson, Guðni, and Bjarni Vilhjálmsson, *Fornaldarsögur Norðurlanda*, *Krákumál*, at www.heimskringla.no, accessed 3 June 2017

Keats, John, *Keats's Poetry and Prose*, ed. Jeffrey N. Cox (New York and London, 2009)

Larrington, Carolyne, trans., *The Poetic Edda* (Oxford, 1996)

Larsson, Stieg, *The Girl Who Kicked the Hornet's Nest*, trans. Steven T. Murray (Stockholm, 2007)

—, *The Girl Who Played with Fire*, trans. Steven T. Murray (Stockholm, 2006)

—, *The Girl with the Dragon Tattoo*, trans. Steven T. Murray (Stockholm, 2005)

Le Guin, Ursula K., *The Beginning Place* [aka *Threshold*] (New York, 1980)

—, *Earthsea* [containing *A Wizard of Earthsea*, *The Tombs of Atuan* and *The Farthest Shore*] (London, 1977)

Leahy, A. H., ed. and trans., 'Tain Bo Fraich', in *Heroic Romances of Ireland*, vol. ii (London, 1906), at www.sacred-texts.com, accessed 3 June 2017

Lewis, C. S., *The Lion, The Witch and the Wardrobe* [1950] (London, 2009)

—, *The Pilgrim's Regress: An Allegorical Apology for Christianity, Reason, and Romanticism* (London, 1933), at www.fadedpage.com, accessed 3 June 2017

—, *The Voyage of the Dawn Treader* [1952] (London, 1970)

McCaffrey, Anne, *Dragonflight* (New York, 1968)

MacDonald, George, *Lilith* (London, 1895)

MacNeill, Eoin, trans., *Duanaire Finn: The Book of the Lays of Fionn*, Part i (London, 1908)

Maddox, Donald, and Sara Sturm-Maddox, trans. and eds, *Melusine; or, The Noble History of Lusignan* (University Park, pa, 2012)

Mandeville, John, *The Travels of Sir John Mandeville* (London, 1900), at www.gutenberg.org, accessed 3 June 2017

Martin, George R. R., *A Dance with Dragons* (London, 2012)

—, *A Game of Thrones* (New York, 1996)

—, *The Ice Dragon* [1980] (New York, 2014)

—, and Gardner Dozois, eds, *Dangerous Women* (New York, 2013)

—, Elio M. García Jr and Linda Antonsson, *The World of Ice and Fire: The Untold History of Westeros and the Game of Thrones* (London, 2014)

Martin, Mary Lou, *The Fables of Marie de France* (Birmingham, al, 1984), pp. 146–9

Mayne, William, *A Game of Dark* (Boston, ma, 1971)

Mitchell, Stephen, trans., *Gilgamesh: A New English Version* (London, 2004)

*The Nihongi*, at www.hudsoncress.net/html/library.html, accessed 3 June 2017

Norton, David, ed., *The Bible: King James Version with the Apocrypha* (London and New York, 2006)

O'Grady, Standish Hayes, trans., *The Colloquy with the Ancients* (Whitefish, mt, n.d.)

Ovid, *The Metamorphoses of Ovid*, trans. Mary M. Innes (Harmondsworth, 1955)

Ozaki, Yei Theodora, *Japanese Fairy Tales* (New York, 1908), at www.surlalunefairytales.com/ebooksindex.html, accessed 3 June 2017

Pálsson, Hermann, and Paul Edwards, trans., *Seven Viking Romances* (London, 1985)

—, trans., *Vikings in Russia: 'Yngvar's Saga' and 'Eymund's Saga'* (Edinburgh, 1989)

Paolini, Christopher, *Eragon* (New York, 2003)

Peet, Mal, *The Murdstone Trilogy* [2014] (Oxford, 2015)

Percy, Thomas, *Reliques of Ancient English Poetry* (1765), at www.exclassics.com, accessed 3 June 2017

Plato, *The Republic*, at www.idph.net/conteudos/ebooks, accessed 3 June 2017

Pratchett, Terry, *The Colour of Magic* (Buckinghamshire, uk, 1983)

—, *Dragons at Crumbling Castle, and Other Stories* (London, 2014)

—, *Guards! Guards!* (London, 1989)

Rossetti, Dante Gabriel, 'Body's Beauty', at www.poeticious.com; 'Eden Bower', at www.poemhunter.com; both accessed 1 August 2016

Rowling, J. K., *Fantastic Beasts and Where to Find Them* (London, 2001)

—, *Harry Potter and the Deathly Hallows* (London, 2007)

—, *Harry Potter and the Goblet of Fire* (London, 2000)

—, *Harry Potter and the Philosopher's Stone* (London, 1997)

Salter, Jessica, 'Game of Thrones's George R. R. Martin: "I'm a Feminist at Heart"', *The Telegraph*, 1 April 2013, www.telegraph.co.uk

Shippey, Tom, ed., *The Oxford Book of Science Fiction Stories* (Oxford and New York, 1993)

Snorri Sturluson, *Edda*, trans. Anthony Faulkes (London, 1995)

Stokes, Whitley, trans., 'The Siege of Howth', *Revue Celtique*, VIII (Paris, 1887), pp. 47–64

Swanton, Michael, ed. and trans., *The Anglo-Saxon Chronicles* (London, 2000)

—, ed. and trans., *Beowulf* (Manchester, UK, 1978)

Swanwick, Michael, *The Dragons of Babel* (New York, 2008)

—, *The Iron Dragon's Daughter* (London, 1993)

Thorpe, Lewis, trans., *Geoffrey of Monmouth: The History of the Kings of Britain*, (Harmondsworth, 1966)

Tolkien, J.R.R., 'The Dragon's Visit', *The Oxford Magazine*, LV/11 (1937), available at www.twilightswarden.wordpress.com, 13 November 2010

—, *The Hobbit, or There and Back Again* (London, 1995)

—, *The Legend of Sigurd and Gudrún* (Boston, MA, 2009)

—, *The Lord of the Rings* (Boston, MA, and New York, 2004)

—, *The Silmarillion*, ed. Christopher Tolkien (London, 2008)

—, *Tales from the Perilous Realm* (London, 2008)

Turnbull, William B.D.D., ed., *The Romances of Sir Guy of Warwick, and Rembrun his Son* (Edinburgh, 1840)

Ueda Akinari, *Ugetsu Monogatari, or Tales of Moonlight and Rain*, trans. and ed. Leon M. Zolbrod (London, 1972; first published in woodblock in 1776)

Vance, Jack, *The Dragon Masters* (New York, 1962)

Waggoner, Ben, trans., *The Sagas of Ragnar Lodbrok* (New Haven, CT, 2009)

White, T. H., trans., *The Book of Beasts: Being a Bestiary from a Latin Translation of the Twelfth Century* [1954] (Mineola, NY, 2009)

## Music

Peter, Paul and Mary, 'Puff the Magic Dragon', lyrics by Leonard Lipton, music by Peter Yarrow (1963)

## Film and television

Benioff, David, and D. B. Weiss, et al., scriptwriters, *Game of Thrones* (Time Warner, HBO: 2011–)

Bowman, Bob, dir., *The Reign of Fire* (2002)

Honda, Ishirō, dir., *Godzilla* (1954)

Hoyt, Harry O., dir., *The Lost World* (1925)

Jackson, Peter, dir., *The Hobbit* trilogy (2012–14)

—, *The Lord of the Rings* trilogy (2001–3)

Lang, Fritz, dir., *Die Nibelungen: Siegfried* (1924)

Reeve, Tom, dir., *George and the Dragon* (2004)

Roth, Philip J., dir., *Dragon Fighter* (2003)

Spielberg, Steven, dir., (1993 and 1997); Joe Johnston, dir., (2001), *Jurassic Park* trilogy

Zemeckis, Robert, dir., *Beowulf* (2007)

RPGS

*Dungeons & Dragons* (first published by Tactical Studies Rules, 1974)
*The Elder Scrolls v: Skyrim* (Bethesda Softworks, 2011)


Secondary sources

Acker, Paul, 'Dragons in the Eddas and in Early Nordic Art', in *Revisiting the Poetic Edda: Essays on Old Norse Heroic Legend*, ed. Paul Acker and Carolyne Larrington (London and New York, 2013), pp. 53–75
Allen, J. Romilly, 'Lecture vi: The Medieval Bestiaries', in *Early Christian Symbolism in Great Britain and Ireland before the Thirteenth Century* (London, 1887), at www.bestiary.ca, accessed 3 June 2017
Anderson, Douglas, *The Annotated Hobbit* (London, 1988)
Arnold, Martin, 'On the Origins of the Gothic Novel: From Old Norse to Otranto', in *Bram Stoker and the Gothic: Formations and Transformations*, ed. Catherine Wynne (Basingstoke, 2016), pp. 14–29
—, *Thor: Myth to Marvel* (London, 2011)
—, *The Vikings: Culture and Conquest* (London, 2006)
Asma, Stephen T., *On Monsters: An Unnatural History of Our Worst Fears* (Oxford and New York, 2009)
Ballaster, Ros, *Fabulous Orients: Fictions of the East in England, 1662–1785* (Oxford and New York, 2005)
Barber, Richard, and Ann Riches, *A Dictionary of Fabulous Beasts* (London, 1971)
Bates, Roy, *Chinese Dragons* (Oxford and New York, 2002)
Björnsson, Árni, *Wagner and the Volsungs: Icelandic Sources of 'Der Ring des Nibelungen'* (London, 2003)
Bland, Lucy, *Banishing the Beast: English Feminism and Sexual Morality, 1885–1914* (Harmondsworth, 1995)
Blanpied, Pamela Wharton, *Dragons: The Modern Infestation* (Woodbridge, Suffolk, 1980)
Boberg, Inger M., *Motif Index of Early Icelandic Literature* (Copenhagen, 1966)
Borges, Jorge Luis, and Margarita Guerrero, *The Book of Imaginary Beings* [*Manual de zoología fantástica*, 1957], trans. Norman Thomas di Giovanni (Harmondsworth, 1974)
Bovey, Alixe, *Monsters and the Grotesques in Medieval Manuscripts* (London, 2002)
Brookes-Davies, Douglas, *Spenser's 'Faerie Queene': A Critical Commentary on Books i and ii* (Manchester, 1977)
Budge, E.A.W., trans., 'The Passion of St George (BHO 310)' (1888), at www.ucc.ie/archive/milmart/George.html, accessed 3 June 2017
Carpenter, Humphrey, *J.R.R. Tolkien: A Biography* [1977] (London, 2002)
Carr, Michael, 'Chinese Dragon Names', *Linguistics of the Tibeto-Burman Area*, xiii/2 (1990), pp. 87–189
Chance, Jane, 'Grendel's Mother as Epic Anti-type of the Virgin and Queen (1986)', in *Interpretations of Beowulf: A Critical Anthology*, ed. R. D. Fulk (Bloomington, in, 1991), pp. 251–63
Coghlan, Ronan, *The Encyclopaedia of Arthurian Legends* (Shaftesbury, Dorset, 1991)
Colbert, Benjamin, ed., *The Travels of Marco Polo*, trans. William Marsdon (Ware, Hertfordshire, 1997)

Dacres Devlin, J., *The Mordiford Dragon and Other Subjects* (London, 1848)

DeKirk, Ash, *Dragonlore: From the Archives of the Grey School of Wizardry* (Wayne, NJ, 2006)

Delogu, Daisy, 'Jean d'Arras Makes History: Political Legitimacy and the *Roman de Mélusine*', *Dalhousie French Studies*, LXXX (2007), pp. 15–28

Dennison, Walter Traill, 'Orkney Folklore: Sea Myths 3', *Scottish Antiquary*, V (1891)

Drout, Michael D. C., *Beowulf and the Critics by J.R.R. Tolkien* (Tempe, AZ, 2002)

Dumézil, Georges, *The Destiny of the Warrior* [*Heur et malheur du guerrier: Aspects mythiques de la fonction guerrière chez les Indo-Européens*, 1969], trans. Alf Hiltebeitel (Chicago, IL, 1973)

—, *Gods of the Ancient Norsemen* [*Les Dieux des Germains*, 1939], ed. Einar Haugen, trans. Francis Charat (Berkeley, CA, 1973)

Dunn, James D. G., 'The Danilic Son of Man in the New Testament', in *The Book of Daniel: Composition and Reception*, ed. J. J. Collins, P. W. Flint and C. VanEpps (Leiden, 2002), pp. 528–49

Ellis, Hilda R., 'The Hoard of the Nibelungs', *Modern Language Review*, XXXVII (1942), pp. 466–79

Epstein, Marc Michael, 'Harnessing the Dragon: A Mythos Transformed in Medieval Jewish Literature', in *Myth and Method*, ed. Laurie L. Patton and Wendy Doniger (Charlottesville, VA, 1996), pp. 352–89

Evans, Jonathan, '"As Rare as They are Dire": Old Norse Dragons, *Beowulf* and the *Deutsche Mythologie*', in *The Shadow Walkers: Jacob Grimm's Mythology of the Monstrous*, ed. Tom Shippey (Turnhout, 2005), pp. 207–69

—, *Dragons: Myth and Legend* (London, 2008)

—, 'The Dragon', in *Mythical and Fabulous Creatures: A Source Book and Research Guide*, ed. Malcolm South (New York, 1987), pp. 27–58

—, 'The Dragon-lore of Middle-earth: Tolkien and Old English and Old Norse Tradition', in *J.R.R. Tolkien and His Literary Resonances: Views of Middle-earth*, ed. George Clark and Daniel Timmons (Westport, CT, and London, 2000), pp. 21–38

—, 'Semiotics and Traditional Lore: The Medieval Dragon Tradition', *Journal of Folklore Research*, XXII/2–3 (1985), pp. 85–112

Feminism and Women's Studies, www.feminism.eserver.org, accessed 3 July 2017

Fontenrose, Joseph, *Python: A Study of Delphic Myth and Its Origins* (Berkeley and Los Angeles, CA, 1980)

Freud, Sigmund, *Three Contributions to the Theory of Sex*, trans. A. A. Brill (New York and Washington, DC, 1920), at www.gutenberg.org, accessed 3 July 2017

Fuller, Elizabeth Ely, *Milton's Kinesthetic Vision in Paradise Lost* (Lewisburg, PA, 1983)

Gentry, Francis, G., et al., eds, *The Nibelungen Tradition: An Encyclopedia* (London and New York, 2011)

Glazyrina, Galina, 'Dragon Motifs in *Yngvars saga víðförla*', in *The Fantastic in Old Norse/Icelandic Literature: Sagas and the British Isles*, ed. John McKinnell, David Ashurst and Donata Kick, preprints of the 13th International Saga Conference, Durham and York, 6–12 August 2006 (2006), pp. 288–93

Goth, Maik, 'Spenser's Dragons', in *Good Dragons are Rare: An Inquiry into Literary Dragons East and West*, ed. Fanfan Chen and Thomas Honegger (Frankfurt, 2009), pp. 97–117

Graves, Robert, *The Greek Myths: Complete Edition* (London and New York, 1992)

Gray, William, *Death and Fantasy: Essays on Philip Pullman, C. S. Lewis, George MacDonald and R. L. Stevenson* (Newcastle upon Tyne, 2008), pp. 25–42

Green, Peter, *Kenneth Grahame: A Biography* (London, 1959)

Hammond, Wayne G., and Christina Scull, eds, *The Lord of the Rings: A Reader's Companion* (London, 2005)

Havens, Norman, and Nobutaka Inoue, ed. and trans., *An Encyclopedia of Shinto (Shinto Jiten)* (Tokyo, 2006)

Heale, Elizabeth, *The Faerie Queene: A Reader's Guide*, 2nd edn (Cambridge, 1999)

Hey, David, *Yorkshire from AD 1000* (London and New York, 1986)

Hill, John M., *Modern Philology*, xcvi/1 (1998), pp. 58–61

Hill, Thomas D., 'Guðrúnarkviða in fyrsta: Guðrún's Healing Tears', in *Revisiting the Poetic Edda: Essays on Old Norse Heroic Legend*, ed. Paul Acker and Carolyne Larrington (London and New York, 2013), pp. 107–16

Hirsch, Emil G., et al., *Jewish Encyclopedia*, www.jewishencyclopedia.com

hÓgáin, Dáithi Ó., *The Lore of Ireland: An Encyclopedia of Myth, Legend and Romance* (Woodbridge, Suffolk, 2006)

Hogarth, Peter, and Val Clery, *Dragons* (London, 1979)

Honegger, Thomas, 'A Good Dragon is Hard to Find: From *Draconitas* to *Draco*', in *Good Dragons are Rare: An Inquiry into Literary Dragons East and West*, ed. Fanfan Chen and Thomas Honegger (Frankfurt, 2009), pp. 27–59

—, '*Draco litterarius*: Some Thoughts on an Imaginary Beast', in *Tiere und Fabelwesen im Mittelalter*, ed. Sabine Obermaier (Berlin and New York, 2009), pp. 133–45

—, 'From Bestiary onto Screen: Dragons in Film', in *Fact and Fiction: From the Middle Ages to Modern Times. Essays Presented to Hans Sauer on the Occasion of his 65th Birthday*, ed. Renate Bauer and Ulrike Krischke, Texte und Untersuchungen zur Englischen Philologie 37 (Frankfurt, 2011), pp. 197–215

—, 'The Sea-dragon – in Search of an Elusive Creature', in *Symbolik des Wassers in der Mittelalterlichen Kultur*, ed. Gerlinde Huber-Rebenich et al. (Berlin, 2017), pp. 521–31

Hornung, Erik, *The Secret Lore of Egypt: Its Impact on the West* (Ithaca, NY, and London, 2002)

Hughes, John, *Therapy is Fantasy: Roleplaying, Healing and the Construction of Symbolic Order* (1988), at www.rpgstudies.net, accessed 3 July 2017

Hurwitz, Siegmund, *Lilith, The First Eve: Historical and Psychological Aspects of the Dark Feminine*, 3rd edn, trans. Gela Jacobson (Einsiedeln, 2009)

Ingersoll, Ernest, *Dragons and Dragon Lore: A Worldwide Study of Dragons in History, Art and Legend* [1928] (London, 2007)

Jakobsson, Ármann, 'Enter the Dragon: Legendary Courage and the Birth of the Hero', in *Making History: Essays on the 'Fornaldarsögur'*, ed. Martin Arnold and Alison Finlay (London, 2010), pp. 33–52

Jarman, A.O.H., 'The Merlin Legend and the Welsh Tradition of Prophecy', in *The Arthur of the Welsh: The Arthurian Legend in Medieval Welsh Literature*, ed. Rachel Bromwich, A.O.H. Jarman and Brynley F. Roberts (Cardiff, 1991), pp. 117–45

Johnston, Sarah Iles, 'Corinthian Medea and the Cult of Hera Akraia', in *Medea: Essays on Medea in Myth, Literature, Philosophy, and Art*, ed. James J. Clauss and Sarah Iles Johnston (Princeton, NJ, 1977), pp. 44–70

Jones, David E., *An Instinct for Dragons* (New York and London, 2002)

Jones, Martin H., 'The Depiction of Military Conflict in Gottfried's *Tristan*', in *Gottfried von Strassburg and the Medieval Tristan Legend: Papers from an Anglo-North American Symposium*, ed. Adrian Stevens and Roy Wisbey (Woodbridge, Suffolk, 1990), pp. 45–66

Kempf, Damien, and Maria L. Gilbert, *Medieval Monsters* (London, 2015)

Kershaw (Chadwick), Nora, ed. and trans., *Anglo-Saxon and Old Norse Poems* (Cambridge, 1922)

Kircher, Athanasius, *Mundus Subterraneus* (1664–5), see Anne E. G. Nydam at http://nydamprintsblackandwhite.blogspot.co.uk/2012/07/kirchers-dragons.html, accessed 24 July 2012

Kirk, G. S., *Myth: Its Meaning and Functions in Ancient and Other Cultures* (Berkeley and Los Angeles, CA, 1970)

Koltuv, Barbara Black, *The Book of Lilith* (Lake Worth, FL, 1986)

Lambert, Amy A. O., 'Morgan le Fay and Other Women: A Study of the Female Phantasm in Medieval Literature', PhD thesis, University of Hull (2016)

Lapidge, Michael, '*Beowulf*, Aldhelm, the *Liber Monstrorum* and Wessex', *Studi Medievali*, 3rd ser., XXIII (1982), pp. 151–92

Larrington, Carolyne, *Winter is Coming: The Medieval World of Game of Thrones* (London and New York, 2016)

Lévi-Strauss, Claude, *The Raw and the Cooked* [*Le Cru et le cuit*, 1964], trans. John and Doreen Weightman (London, 1970)

Lewis, C. S., *The Allegory of Love: A Study in Medieval Tradition* [1936] (Oxford and New York, 1958)

Link, Luther, *The Devil: A Mask Without a Face* (London, 2004)

Linnaeus, Carl, 'Regnum animale' (1735), at www.commons.wikimedia.org, accessed 3 July 2017

Lionarons, Joyce Tally, *The Medieval Dragon: The Nature of the Beast in Germanic Literature* (Enfield Lock, Middlesex, 1998)

—, '"Sometimes the Dragon Wins": Unsuccessful Dragon Fighters in Medieval Literature', in *Essays on Old, Middle, Modern English and Old Icelandic: In Honour of Raymond P. Tripp, Jr.*, ed. Loren C. Gruber (Lampeter, 2000), pp. 301–13

Loomis, Roger Sherman, *Arthurian Literature in the Middle Ages: A Collaborative History* (Oxford, 1959)

MacKenzie, Donald A., *Myths of China and Japan* (London, 1923)

McKinnell, John, *Meeting the Other in Norse Myth and Legend* (Cambridge, 2005)

McLeod, Neil, 'Fergus mac Léti and the Law', *Ériu*, LXI (2011), pp. 1–28

MacNeill, Máire, *The Festival of Lughnasa, Parts I and II* (Dublin, 1982)

Martin, George R. R., 'Introduction', in *Meditations on Middle-earth*, ed. Karen Haber (New York, 2001)

Marwick, Ernest, *The Folklore of Orkney and Shetland* (Edinburgh, 1974)

Matthews, John, ed., *Myths of the Middle Ages: Sabine Baring-Gould* (London, 1996)

Meehan, Aidan, *Celtic Design: The Dragon and the Griffin, The Viking Impact* (London, 1995)

Mitchell, Juliet, *Psychoanalysis and Feminism: A Radical Reassessment of Freudian Psychoanalysis* (Harmondsworth, 1975)

Mittman, Asa Simon, and Susan M. Kim, 'Monsters and the Exotic in Medieval England', in *The Oxford Handbook of Medieval Literature in English*, ed. Elaine Treharne and Greg Walker (Oxford and New York, 2010), pp. 677–706

Morris, Matthew W., 'Introduction', in *A Bilingual Edition of Couldrette's 'Melusine', or, 'Le Roman de Parthenay'*, Mediaeval Studies, xx (Lewiston, NY, 2003)

Muir, Tom, 'Tales and Legends', in *The Orkney Book*, ed. Donald Omand (Edinburgh, 2003), pp. 240–47

Niles, Doug, *Dragons: The Myths, Legends, and Lore* (Avon, MA, 2013)

Ogden, Daniel, *Dragons, Serpents, and Slayers in the Classical and Early Christian Worlds: A Sourcebook* (Oxford and New York, 2013)

—, *Drakōn: Dragon Myth and Serpent Cult in the Greek and Roman Worlds* (Oxford and New York, 2013)

Ong, Walter J., *Orality and Literacy: The Technologizing of the Word* (London and New York, 1988)

Orchard, Andy, *Pride and Prodigies: Studies in the Monsters of the 'Beowulf'-Manuscript* (Toronto, 1995)

Parry, John Jay, and Robert Caldwell, 'Geoffrey of Monmouth', in *Arthurian Literature in the Middle Ages: A Collaborative History*, ed. Roger Sherman Loomis (Oxford, 1959), pp. 72–93

Patai, Raphael, *The Hebrew Goddess*, 3rd edn (Detroit, MI, 1990)

Rauer, Christine, *Beowulf and the Dragon: Parallels and Analogues* (Cambridge, 2000)

Remler, Pat, *Egyptian Mythology A to Z*, 3rd edn (New York, 2010)

Riches, Samantha, *St George: A Saint for All* (London, 2015)

Rose, Carol, *Giants, Monsters and Dragons: An Encyclopedia of Folklore, Legend, and Myth* (New York and London, 2000)

Rowe, Elizabeth Ashman, *Vikings in the West: The Legend of Ragnarr Loðbrók and His Sons* (Vienna, 2012)

Sagan, Carl, *The Dragons of Eden: Speculations on the Evolution of Human Intelligence* (New York, 1977)

Shah, Idries, *World Tales: The Extraordinary Coincidence of Stories Told in All Times, in All Places* (London, 1991)

Shippey, T. A., 'The Ironic Background (1972)', in *Interpretations of Beowulf: A Critical Anthology*, ed. R. D. Fulk (Bloomington, IN, 1991), pp. 194–205

—, 'Liminality and the Everyday in *Lilith*', in *Lilith in a New Light*, ed. Lucas D. Harriman (Jefferson, NC, and London, 2008), pp. 15–20

—, *Poems of Wisdom and Learning in Old English* (Cambridge, 1976)

—, *The Road to Middle-earth*, 4th revd edn (London, 2005)

—, 'The Versions of "The Hoard"', *Lembas*, 100 (2001), pp. 3–7

Simek, Rudolf, *Dictionary of Northern Mythology*, trans. Angela Hall (Cambridge, 1993)

Simpson, Jacqueline, *British Dragons* [1980] (Ware, Herts, 2001)

—, ed. and trans., *Scandinavian Folktales* (Harmondsworth, 1988)

Smithers, G. V., *The Making of Beowulf* (Durham, 1961)

Southern, Pat, and Karen R. Dixon, *The Late Roman Army* (New Haven, CT, and London, 1996)

Stallybrass, James S., trans., *Teutonic Mythology* [1883] [from Jacob Grimm, *Deutsche Mythologie*, 1835], 4 vols, 4th edn (Mineola, NY, 2004)

Tilley, Norah M., *Dragons in Persian, Mughal and Turkish Art* (London, 1981)

Tolkien, J.R.R., *The Monsters and the Critics and Other Essays*, ed. Christopher
    Tolkien (London, 1997)
Turville-Petre, E.O.G., *Myth and Religion of the North: The Religion of Ancient
    Scandinavia* (London, 1964)
Van Duzer, Chet, *Sea Monsters on Medieval and Renaissance Maps* (London, 2013)
Vettam, Mani, *Puranic Encyclopaedia: A Comprehensive Dictionary with Special
    Reference to the Epic and Puranic Literature* (Delhi, 1975)
Virgil, *The Aeneid*, trans. W. F. Jackson Knight (Harmondsworth, 1958)
Visser, Marinus Willem de, *The Dragon in China and Japan* [1913] (Miami, FL, 2007)
Vogel, J. P., *Indian Serpent-Lore: Or, the Nāgas in Hindu Legend and Art* (Whitefish,
    MT, 1972; first published 1927)
Wagner, Richard, trans. Margaret Amour, *Siegfried and the Twilight of the Gods*
    (London and New York, 1911)
Watkins, Calvert, *How to Kill a Dragon: Aspects of Indo-European Poetics*
    (Oxford, 1995)
Whitlock, Ralph, *Here Be Dragons* (London, 1983)
Yang, Lihui, and Deming An, *Handbook of Chinese Mythology* (Oxford, 2005)
Yuan Ke, *Dragons and Dynasties: An Introduction to Chinese Mythology*, trans. Kim
    Echlin and Nie Zhixiong (London, 1993)
Zeng, Shu, 'Love, Power and Resistance: Representations of Chinese–Caucasian
    Romance in Twentieth-century Anglophone Literature', PhD thesis,
    University of Hull (2016)
Zhao, Qiguang, *Asian Culture and Thought*, vol. XI: *A Study of Dragons, East and
    West* (New York, 1992)

# ACKNOWLEDGEMENTS

My primary thanks for their invaluable advice are to Professor Tom Shippey (Emeritus, St Louis University), Professor Katharine Cockin (University of Exeter), and Professor Dr Thomas Honegger (Friedrich-Schiller Universität Jena). I am also grateful to the following people: Professor Philip Cardew (Leeds Beckett University); Tim Spillane, MA; Kit Lawrence; Scott Connell; Tomoko Miyairi (University of Hull); Peter Norton; Fiona Norton, MA; and Ernest and Sebastian Brenchley. Many thanks, too, for the encouragement of Ben Hayes (Commissioning Editor, Reaktion Books) and the help and patience of Martha Jay (Managing Editor, Reaktion Books). Finally, I am deeply grateful to my wife, Maria, for accompanying me on dragon hunts and for tolerating my incessant commentaries on dragon finds.

Any errors of fact or judgement are entirely of my own making.

# PHOTO ACKNOWLEDGEMENTS

The author and the publishers wish to express their thanks to the below sources of
illustrative material and /or permission to reproduce it.

Alamy: pp. 31, 139 (Heritage Image Partnership Ltd), 75, 82, 166 (Art Collection 3),
112, 140, 145 (Paul Fearn), 134 (IMAGEMORE Co., Ltd), 142 (Richard Maschmeyer),
155 (Art Collection 2), 170, 173 (Chronicle), 178 (Vova Pomortzeff), 224 (Photo 12),
252 (Atlaspix), Entertainment Pictures), 258 (AF Archive); AKG Images: pp. 146
(Roland and Sabrina Michaud), 159 (Pictures from History); Bridgeman Images:
pp. 44 (Alinari), 118 (Lambeth  Palace Library, London, UK), Bodleian Library:
p. 229; © The British Library: p. 94; © The Trustees of the British Museum: p. 46;
Chemical Engineer: p. 184; Getty Images: pp. 190, 193 (De Agostini Picture Library);
Arnar Bergur Gudjonsson: p. 6; The Jewish Museum, New York: pp. 51, 53; Library
of Congress, Washington, DC: pp. 68, 160, 163, 209; LSE Library, London: p. 188; NASA:
p. 164 (Goddard Space Flight Center); National Library of France: p. 198; New York
Public Library: p. 148; The Metropolitan Museum of Art, New York: p. 151; Carole
Raddato: p. 14; Shutterstock: pp. 106 (Amy Johansson), 129 (Khumthong), 138
(Amornpant Kookaki), 152 (hxdyl), 274 (Mirro); Takewaway: p. 143; Victoria
and Albert Museum, London: p. 136; Wellcome Collection: p. 167.

# INDEX

Page numbers in *italics* refer to illustrations